THE VULNERABLE AMERICANS

BOOKS BY CURT GENTRY

The Vulnerable Americans

John M. Browning: American Gunmaker (Co-author)

The Madams of San Francisco

*The Dolphin Guide to San Francisco and
the Bay Area—Present and Past*

THE
VULNERABLE
AMERICANS

CURT GENTRY

DOUBLEDAY & COMPANY, INC.
GARDEN CITY, NEW YORK
1966

TO MY MOTHER AND FATHER

ACKNOWLEDGMENTS

Many people concerned with reducing the vulnerability of American consumers and businessmen contributed to the making of this book. I should like to acknowledge each but am unable to do so for two reasons: many of those who provided much of the basic information, people in various city, state, and federal agencies, are unknown to me by name, although their efforts are most thankfully remembered; others shared their information and impressions with me on the understanding that their names not be used. To both groups I can only express my collective thanks.

Those whose invaluable assistance I am able gratefully to acknowledge include:

Chief Inspector H. B. Montague, Post Office Department, Washington, D.C.; Mr. Edward J. Chapin, Chief Editorial Services Branch, Food and Drug Administration, Washington, D.C.; Mr. Gordon R. Wood, Los Angeles District Director, Food and Drug Administration, Los Angeles, California; and Mr. Allan Bille, of the same office.

Mr. Howard Jewel, former Chief Consumer Frauds Division, and Mrs. Nancy Jewel, Executive Secretary to the Attorney General of the State of California, San Francisco, California; Mr. Louis J. Lefkowitz, Attorney General of the State of New York, and Mr. Barnett Levy, Assistant Attorney General in Charge of Consumer Frauds and Protection Bureau, New York City, New York; and Mrs. Helen Nelson, Consumer Counsel to Edmund G. Brown, Governor of the State of California, Sacramento, California.

Mr. Vernon A. Libby, Executive Vice-President and General Manager, San Francisco Better Business Bureau, San Francisco, California; and Mr. Philip L. Ennis, Secretary-Manager, Retail Merchants Association, Inc., Oakland, California.

Mr. W. P. Mullane, Jr., Public Information Supervisor, American Telephone and Telegraph Company, New York City, New York;

and Mr. Larry Coffin, News Manager, Pacific Telephone and Telegraph Company, San Francisco, California.

Mr. N. Morgan Woods, Manager, Claims Bureau, American Insurance Association, New York City, New York; Mr. Charles C. Clarke, Assistant General Manager, Insurance Information Institute, New York City, New York; and Mr. Richard S. Jacobson, Director of Public Affairs and Education, American Trial Lawyers Association, Boston, Massachusetts.

Whenever possible in the text I have attempted to cite my indebtedness to other writers whose work I have consulted, but extra-special thanks, for frequent borrowings, are due Mr. Hillel Black, author of *Buy Now, Pay Later* and co-author of *The Thief in the White Collar;* Mr. Ralph Lee Smith, author of *The Bargain Hucksters* and *The Health Hucksters;* and Mr. Frank Gibney, author of *The Operators.*

To those I may have inadvertently omitted I can only add the consolation that you won't be blamed for the author's errors or personal opinions.

Curt Gentry

CONTENTS

PREFACE

THE FRAUDULENT CLIMATE

For better or worse, the climate affects our thinking, our moods, and our acts. The climate of fraud which overcasts America today so touches every part of our lives that, except in extreme circumstances and election years, we are inclined to take it for granted.

The condition is not new: what *is* new is its extent.

During the nineteenth century, when immigration was high, education low, and opportunity waiting just around each corner, sociologists estimate that probably one out of every ten adult Americans fell victim to a swindle or fraud during his lifetime.

Times have changed. Americans have grown wiser, more sophisticated, less gullible, and, alas, perhaps even less imaginative. Today, ten out of ten adult Americans are the victims of swindles and frauds, not once or twice during their lifetimes but almost every time they make a purchase, cast their votes, pay their taxes, invest in the future, seek happiness, entertainment, or love.

Never before in the history of the United States have so many been swindled so often in so many different ways out of so much—with so few protesting voices.

We might well envy our gullible ancestors who bought the Brooklyn Bridge, the Information Booth in Grand Central Station, or a money-making machine. They were had, they soon knew it, and that was that. The cost most often was their savings, their trust, and a little of their pride. Yet they had the dubious advantage of knowing they had been swindled, for whatever experience is worth. We are often cheated and never learn of it. And, thanks to the most comprehensive system of credit selling yet devised, we may for years go on paying for frauds succumbed to in the past.

Age does not automatically confer wisdom. Every year, with predictable sureness, hundreds will fall for one of the three *big cons:* the wire, the payoff, the big store. While thousands more will lose their savings to *short con* variations: the pigeon drop, the Spanish prisoner, the sick engineer, coin matching, stock schemes, the gypsy fondle, the diamond switch. At hand is a book entitled *Swindles and Bunco Games in City and Country.* Published in 1904, it lists over 200 then-current gyps. This author has found all but 13 in use today. Most of the oldtime con games not only survive but remain unbelievably effective. Their total take is miniscule, however, compared to the tariff exacted by their more updated counterparts, their decline less a tribute to increased common sense than to the ease with which most of the modern cons can be effected and, in many instances, to their borderline—or total—legality.

Illegitimate operators annually reap $50 million from the new advance-fee swindle, $500 million from home-repair rackets, $500 million from self-improvement and work-at-home gyps, and another $500 million from fraudulent land sales, according to the Association of Better Business Bureaus.

Millions more are lost to phony charities, or to fraud connected with regular approved charities.

Last year fraudulent cancer cures took some $100 million and thousands of lives. Five million suffering Americans put out $252 million for gadgets and products which falsely claimed to relieve the pains of arthritis (far exceeding private funds available for scientific research into the cause and cure of this disease). Nutritional quackery took twice as many for nearly twice as much, accounting for $500 million of the more than $1 billion the Food and Drug Administration estimates that Americans spent on falsely promoted, worthless, and dangerous drug products. Of this, much came from the little of those who could least afford it, the aged.

These are only a few of the major swindles. The estimates in each case are "conservative"; in each case, too, they represent an "all-time high," which, in all probability, will give way to another peak this year, and another next, far out of proportion to population growth. Add to these mail frauds, gyps in automobile and home sales, the huge amount lost daily in consumer trickery (involving the manufacture and sale of nationally known products by seemingly respectable businessmen), the cost of monopoly and price-fixing and bid-rigging and market-allocation and tax-evasion. Add, too, the cost of battered dreams, whether for a business of one's own or a desert

Camelot. Plus the high cost of happiness, hopefully poured into dance studios, social clubs, reducing salons.

Hypothetically, with extreme caution and a near-hermetic existence, the wary American could possibly (but not probably) avoid every one of these and the numerous other swindles and frauds directed at separating him and his money. Assuming he did, he would remain no less vulnerable, for fraud today wears a double face. Heads, you're swindled directly; tails, you're swindled more circuitously. There is only one thing wrong with this analogy—it implies chance or choice. Ordinarily we are given neither. We lose both ways. If there is any consolation in knowing that one's misery is not singular but commonly shared, the duped consumer may draw momentary ease from the fact that he is not the only mark. He may even, if he is so inclined, look toward the future and see hopeful portents—a rapidly approaching day when he will no longer be the biggest mark. For the fastest-growing branch of swindlery today has as its primary target not the individual, but business itself.

According to the U.S. Department of Commerce, last year American businesses lost well in excess of $1 billion to highly varied, sometimes simple, often extremely specialized forms of fraud. These were "known" losses; as-yet-undiscovered losses may tally this much or more.

Some sample cases from the past several years: In Lincoln, Nebraska, a country banker "hypothecated" $1.5 million. In New Jersey a roly-poly ex-hog butcher took some of America's most astute corporations for between $150 million and $200 million, in the largest swindle in the history of American finance. In a retail store you patronized, a clerk took one amount from a customer, then rang up another on the cash register. A gang of forgers used their own plane to fly over the country, scattering bad checks. A desperate man sent up a whole batch of fraudulent checks as "kites"; when they came down, a bank and a business fell with them. A thirty-one-year-old aircraft worker from Huntington Park, California, conspired to defraud an insurance company by having his arms, legs, fingers, and ribs smashed with a brick. A nineteen-year-old shipping clerk from Queens, New York, was given the modern equivalent of a magic wand, a credit card, which he used unwisely if well. In Florida a man designed an electronic device to cheat the telephone company; in Connecticut a young executive and his wife accomplished the same thing with no device whatever. Another executive discovered that he need no longer pad his expense account; there was a much easier way. The vice-president of a corporation robbed it—not of cash or negotiable securities but of a single tiny piece of plastic more redeemable than gold.

One man made over $2 million promising to sell businesses. Another made almost as much buying businesses and using their good credit ratings to defraud wholesalers and manufacturers. On the West Coast an attractive ex-model ran up $86,249 in unpaid bills on 511 charge accounts. On the East Coast a housewife discovered an amazing thing—in the better stores you don't need a charge account to charge and take something.

If this provides some solace, here it also ends. For each year we, the vulnerable Americans, pick up the tab for these losses also—in higher purchase prices, costlier insurance rates, larger service charges, increased taxes, and a multitude of hidden costs.

Who pays? We do. And often we not only pay but pay again and again. Take as an illustration one of the more common forms of concealed fraud—the kickback. Say the purchasing agent for a restaurant you patronize is receiving kickbacks from his suppliers. He may be doing this on many items, but we'll consider just one—an item that ordinarily costs the restaurant 33⅓¢. Instead of charging the restaurant this amount, however, the supplier charges 35⅓¢, 2¢ of which makes its way back into the purchasing agent's pocket.

Who pays? You do, of course. A mere 2¢? You should be so lucky. In the restaurant business, food costs usually account for about one-third of the sale dollar. In other words, the food cost is tripled to make up the menu price. 33⅓¢ × 3 = $1.00. But 35⅓¢ × 3 = $1.06. You, the customer, pay 6¢ for that 2¢ of graft. This is on a single item on a single dinner.

In department and retail stores, operating on a 40–50 percent markup, you pay about two times the kickback.

In a bar, where liquor costs are about 25 percent of the selling price, you pay four times the amount of the fraud, whether you buy Old Rot Gut or the most delicate of aged brandies.

In many areas of business, fraud adds as much as 15 percent to consumer prices. The climate of fraud is near omnipresent. No American is totally invulnerable to it, regardless of his economic station.

There is no way to put a price tag on fraud. Much of it goes unreported, much undetected. The FBI in its annual Uniform Crime Reports estimates that losses from fraud are at least three times as great as the combined losses from all the robberies, burglaries, ca thefts, and bank holdups in the United States. "It is probable that if all cases of fraud could be recorded," observed criminologist Edwin H. Sutherland, "fraud would rank close to drunkenness and disorderly conduct in frequency."[1] Sutherland voiced this opinion in the 1940s; were he alive today, he would undoubtedly find fraud the unquestioned loss leader. But even if exact figures were available, it would still be impossible to measure the cost of fraud, for it is not and never has been a simple dollars-and-cents proposition. The deceptive TV commercial, the rigged quiz show, the slack-fill package, the kited check, the petty chiseling, and the grandiose scheming—each reflects something about the condition of our society, just as our attitudes toward them reveal something even more fundamental about the health of the body public.

In the pages that follow you will meet a gallery of rogues, rascals, swindlers, gypsters, pro and con men. Some—Joseph "Yellow Kid" Weil, Count Victor Lustig, Jefferson Randolph "Soapy" Smith, and Albert "The Mad Doctor of Market Street" Abrams, among others —are from the past. The majority, however, are from the immediate present and represent a new breed of con men.

More than time divides these two generations of defrauders.

The old-fashioned swindler had a personal touch. Though he used accomplices when pulling off one of the big cons, he worked alone within the swindle, establishing individual rapport. To him each mark was different, and he had a special knack—what was known as the *grift sense*—for sizing up the mark's weaknesses and points of greatest vulnerability. His strongest weapon was his victim's latent dishonesty, his desire to make an easy buck whatever the means, and he prided himself on cheating only those with larceny in their hearts. He had charm, effrontery, a sense of dramatic timing, and a talent for playing many parts, and his relationship with his pigeon was multifaceted. The Yellow Kid, in one of his more philosophic moments, once said, "I was a psychologist. My domain was the human mind. A Chinese scholar with whom I once studied told me, 'People always see themselves in you.' With this understanding I entered the lives of my dupes . . . It was very simple. My purpose was invisible. When they looked at me they saw themselves. I only showed them their own purpose."[2] The oldtime swindler aimed for big solitary scores—plucking a banker from Kansas City for a hundred grand on a rigged horse race (Weil), selling the Eiffel Tower to a scrap-metal dealer for a quarter million (Lustig). To each transaction he devoted time and consideration; and, whatever the con, his machinations followed a series of clearly defined stages. His was a special trade, with its own techniques, rules, and vocabulary. A traditionalist, he took old and well-established tricks and specially modified them to fit the occasion. He has been called "the aristocrat of the criminal professions," and even though this romanticizes his role somewhat, in two particulars it is true: he was a criminal, he didn't think of himself as anything else; and he was a professional.

By contrast, his modern counterpart is almost wholly impersonal. He may be charming, suave, debonair—but none of these qualities is essential, for often he neither sees nor is seen by his victims. While Weil's purpose may have been invisible, sometimes this is the only thing one can see about his neo-version. He may be impersonal to the point of being an *it* rather than a *he*, as the most successful swindlers today are incorporated. He rarely works alone. He devotes little time to studying his victims; others are hired to do this for him. He may never personally engage in swindlery; others can do this for him too. (Often, in the chronicle that follows, you'll have trouble even identifying the villain.) The modern swindler isn't concerned with the avarice of his victims; his most potent weapon is their indifference. Nor does he refer to them as "suckers," "pigeons," and "marks." This doesn't mean he doesn't have a special vocabulary. He does, but it has its roots in Wall Street and Madison Avenue, in the realms of advertising and business. To him they are simply "customers," "clients," and "consumers." He too has the grift sense, and it is exceptionally well developed, but it is geared not to the one but to the many. He usually scorns the single large score, finding a low-unit, high-volume operation easier, safer, and far more profitable. He, too, has a remarkable sense of timing; indeed, time is his greatest ally, and the *time gap*, a derivation of Einstein's theory of relativity and the space-time continuum, is his most important safeguard: he operates in the present, using the newest techniques, while those charged with his apprehension, working with antiquated laws, operate ineffectually in the past. He doesn't think of himself as a criminal, and he doesn't resemble our preconceptions of one. Suited in respectability, he considers himself a businessman, and for the most part the law thinks of him in the same way. He is certainly not a "professional criminal" in the sense in which the law defines that term, i.e. "a person who makes his living at lawless pursuits"; whenever possible and practical, he is law-abiding to the letter. He seldom has a criminal record, for though he is sometimes caught and sometimes tried, he is rarely convicted, and the chances are that, even should this unusual event occur, his punishment will consist of a reprimand, a cease-and-desist order, or, at the most severe, a nominal fine which his company will pay and which may even be tax-deductible. He doesn't consider his methods fraudulent: they are necessary expedients to keep up with the competition. He doesn't even consider them unethical: everybody's doing it.

Yet while he may lack the romantic aura with which time has softened the image of his progenitors, he is not without considerable fascination, for, utilizing the most up-to-date techniques of advertising and merchandising, his tricks are often wondrously ingenious, the extent of his depredations are unprecedented, and his horizons are not limited to defrauding the basically dishonest. His victims are you, and I, and all the other vulnerable Americans.

"It was never like that in my time," Joseph "Yellow Kid" Weil, surviving dean of the oldtime American con men, told a Senate subcommittee recently, with mixed anger and nostalgia. "Our victims were mostly industrialists and bankers."[3]

Times have changed, and with them one of the oldest maxims of fraud:

Today you *can* cheat an honest man, *not only easily but often.*

I

CAVEAT EMPTOR AND THE
VULNERABLE AMERICANS

If confidence men operate outside
the law, it must be remembered
that they are not much further
outside than many of our pillars of
society who go under names less
sinister. They only carry to an ultimate and very logical conclusion
certain trends which are often inherent in various forms of legitimate business.

David W. Maurer
The Big Con

CHAPTER 1

WORDSMITHING:

THE ART OF ARTIFICE

FTC ORDER HITS HOLLYWOOD BREAD

Washington—AP—Feb 13 1963.
The Federal Trade Commission today ordered National Bakers Services of Chicago to stop advertising
that its "Hollywood Bread" contains fewer calories than other
commercial bread.

FTC Chairman Paul Rand Dixon
said the only reason a slice of
Hollywood bread has fewer calories than a slice of standard white
bread is that it is sliced thinner.

ONCE upon a decade a new game fad sweeps across the United
States, captivating its inhabitants. In the nineteen twenties it was
Mahjong; during the Depression thirties, Americans from every
economic strata owned hotels and real estate via Monopoly; the
forties brought Canasta; the fifties, Scrabble.

The most popular game of the nineteen sixties is called *Wordsmithing.* It isn't a new game, but many of its variations are new,
as is the extent of its acceptance. The players on one side are advertising men, manufacturers, wholesalers, and retailers; opposite
them is the American public, its members quite often unaware that
they're even playing.

The rules are simple. The game can be played anywhere and by any number. One side needs only a product, ingenuity, and a medium of communication; the other, only money and trust. The object of the first team is to capture the trust of the second and, in so doing, make them spend their money. This is done through *wordsmithing* —arranging words and phrases in such a way that they (1) make a true statement and (2) at the same time convey, or, better still, *suggest* a meaning which they don't actually possess. For example, take this TV commercial of a few seasons ago:

ARRID IS ONE-AND-ONE-HALF TIMES AS EFFECTIVE AS ANY OTHER LEADING DEODORANT TESTED.

We can assume this statement is true, and that Arrid's makers and advertising agency undoubtedly have evidence to support it if challenged. Nor are they to be blamed if the public chooses to misinterpret it. Yet, unless one were listening carefully—and who listens carefully to commercials?—he just might come away with the impression that Arrid is one-and-one-half times more effective than any other leading deodorant. The catcher here, of course, is that word "tested." Giving it some thought, one might come up with a number of questions: How many other leading deodorants were tested? One? All? Who conducted the test or tests? How representative were they? Were they conducted scientifically, in a manner free from bias? The real catch is that few of us would give it that much thought.

Another:

THREE OUT OF FOUR DOCTORS RECOMMEND THE MAJOR INGREDIENT IN ANACIN FOR THE RELIEF OF SIMPLE HEADACHE PAIN.

Once in a critical mood, this seems easy. How many doctors were interviewed? Were four doctors picked whose opinions were already known? Or were a number of doctors questioned, in sets of four, until three in one set so recommended? If your reasoning has followed this pattern you've been misled, for this part of the statement means exactly what it implies—if all the doctors in this country were questioned, at least 75 percent would make this representation. The catcher here is "major ingredient." Three out of four doctors *would* and *do* recommend the major ingredient in Anacin—but by the generic name by which that ingredient is best known: *aspirin*.

THE GREATER STAINLESS STEEL BLADE WAS PRE-
FERRED OVER EACH OF THE COMPETITIVE BLADES BY
A WIDE MARGIN.

Were the competitive blades also stainless steel?

These are examples of wordsmithing in its most common form,
what in one leading New York advertising agency is called—though
not in the presence of clients—the "half-Webb," derived from TV's
Dragnet and Jack Webb's fondness for the expression, "Just the facts,
Ma'm." Like many another label created by the promise factories,
this is somewhat deceptive, since often the public isn't given even
half the facts necessary to full understanding.

Who could fail to be impressed with the Flavoramic Coffeemaker
on learning, via TV, that it was endorsed and recommended by not
one but three testing firms: the Product Testing Company, the
Product Testing Bureau, and the Consumer Research Bureau? Yet
even the most impressionable might be quickly unsold if the announcer also mentioned—he didn't, of course, as the Federal Trade
Commission noted—that all three "testing firms" were owned and
operated by Damar Products, Inc., Elizabeth, New Jersey, which also
manufactured the coffeemaker.

Another common wordsmithing variation involves the use of words
with double meanings, as two young secretaries (one from Denver,
the other from Detroit) unhappily discovered.

The Denver miss had been saving for months to buy a cashmere
coat, priced in a leading store at $110. She was still short of the neces-
sary amount when, walking along 15th Street, she saw a similar coat
in the window of a smaller, less prestigious store. The price tag said
$69.95! Entering the store and trying on the coat, she found she
looked absolutely enchanting. Still, even though the coat *seemed*
perfect, the price disparity had created a slight doubt. "Are you *sure*
this is cashmere?" she asked the clerk. "Miss, you have my personal
guarantee that coat is made of cashmere," she heard him answer.
No doubts left, she happily made her bargain purchase. On arriving
home and unwrapping the package, she discovered the label
inside the coat gave its composition as 60 percent Cotton, 40 percent
Re-used Wool. Had the clerk lied to her? Certainly not. The brand
name was MAID OF CASHMERE.

Her Detroit counterpart also bought a coat, in this case a fur
jacket, but she was careful to examine the label first, finding the
legend "NORTHERN SEAL jkt." For a time the term "Northern

Seal" was used widely, if not altogether legally, as a trade-synonym for "rabbit." When even her best friends *did* tell her, she sought a refund, and, failing in this, took the matter to court. Challenged, the furrier argued that he had complied with the law to the letter— he had correctly identified the product on the label as required. The court thought not, finding that most customers would assume, as had the girl, that "jkt." was an abbreviation for "jacket" rather than "jackrabbit."

Among the double-meaning forms of wordsmithing, brand names rate a category all their own. SIX MONTHS FLOOR WAX, LIFE-TIME SEAT COVERS, PERMANENT ANTI-FREEZE, FIRST QUALITY NYLONS—simple trade names or unsupported allegations regarding the performance of the product? In each case the FTC ruled the name was also a claim, and, since the claims were bogus, we see these names no more.

It should be noted that wordsmithing, like any other game, has its referees—among them the Federal Trade Commission, the Better Business Bureaus, the Food and Drug Administration, the Post Office Department, certain law-enforcement agencies, and various consumer groups. The differences, however, are that many of the rules have to be improvised to fit the occasion, often they are set aside on technicalities, and the referees are not so omnipresent as one side would like the other to believe. Moreover, the referees are notoriously poor sports: they refuse to view wordsmithing as a game.

Characteristically unsportsmanlike, the FTC recently invaded, without invitation, still another previously unchaperoned playing field, that of company names. Acting in the public interest (which, in these cases, ranged from bargain-hunting shoppers to couples contemplating uncomplicated sexual intercourse), the FTC found wordsmithing in a number of firm names. A chain of thirty-four East Coast discount department stores, ATLANTIC MILLS THRIFT CENTER (which usually referred to itself in advertising simply as ATLANTIC MILLS, and which often made price comparisons between "the retail price" and "our mill price"), was ordered to drop the word MILLS from its name and stop pretending that it was anything more than a retailer. STANDARD MILLS, INC., a New York City textile jobber, was allowed to keep its name, so long as an appropriate disclaimer was used in ads. HERITAGE FURS VANCOUVER FUR FACTORY, a Portland, Oregon, retail furrier, was given a consent order requiring it to stop implying that it was a manufacturer. THE JUVENILE FURNITURE MANUFACTUR-

ING COMPANY, "America's Largest Juvenile Chain—Stores from Coast to Coast," whose slogan was "Get Down to Earth Prices from the Factory," was given a consent order barring use of the name, the earthy slogan, various pricing deceptions, the implication that the firm had a factory, and the claim that it operated nationwide— its "Coast to Coast" stores being one retail outlet in Ohio and another in Kentucky. INSTITUTE was ordered dropped from several other firm names. THE NATIONAL RESEARCH CORP., Lafayette, Louisiana, was ordered to drop the word RESEARCH from its trade name, along with false therapeutic claims for its Enurol liquid and capsulettes. NRC's "research department," the FTC noted, consisted of one man, whose formal education had ended with high school, who had never taken any courses in chemistry, nutrition, biology, or any other scientific field, and who, prior to developing Enurol, had been in the cattle business. And C.D.I. LABORATORIES, a New York City distributor of a calendar-slide birth-control device, was given a consent order enjoining it from using the word LABORATORIES, thereby implying that the respondents owned and operated a testing laboratory in connection with their business when they did not. The company was also ordered to stop advertising its birth-control device as "foolproof."

Our preferences and prejudices add variety to the game. We Americans hold certain presumptions self-evident: the best watches are made in Switzerland, the choicest cigars in Cuba, Britain excels in woolens, France in designs, real straw hats are made in Italy, Germany makes the best cameras and binoculars, the finest diamonds must pass through Belgium or Holland, Ireland is second to none in linens, and Japan is best at imitations. These and other international prejudices are reflected in and preserved by the "country of origin" requirements in the various fiber, textile, and product-labeling acts.

During 1964 the FTC obtained these consent orders: The Lucien Piccard Watch Corporation, New York City, was ordered to stop claiming that the company had been established in Switzerland in 1837, that it had a Swiss factory, and that its watches were designed and manufactured in Switzerland—the company actually having been founded in New York City in 1926 as A. Blumstein, Inc., the watch movements having been imported from Switzerland and assembled here in domestic cases, and the founding year 1837 belonging to a separate company from which Piccard ordered a few of its watch parts. Timely Clothes, Inc., Rochester, New York, was ordered to stop implying that its POUND STERLING suits were other than American-made. An East Coast furrier, who advertised and labeled his furs DESIGNED BY ANDRE FATH PARIS (both ads and labels lacked a comma), thereby implying that the furs were designed by a French designer or were manufactured, styled, or created in France, when both the designing and manufacturing had occurred in the United States, was ordered to "cease and desist" said claims, the fictitious Mr. Andre Fath Paris notwithstanding. A Fall River, Massachusetts, firm was prohibited from advertising "Genuine Imported Milan Hats," since the hats were not made in Italy of wheat straw in the Milan weave, but rather were manufactured in this country from braid manufactured in Japan from hemp imported from the Philippines. A Chicago firm had to stop using Germanized brand names for its locally manufactured optical products. A Manhattan diamond merchant had to cease calling his firm "the New York branch of Antwerp Distributors of Belgium," a nonexistent outfit. Four affiliated New York companies were prohibited from advertising "Irish" tablecloths and napkins unless they also mentioned that they were made in Japan. And a half-dozen cigar makers were told to stop pretending they had circumvented the Cuban trade blockade through the use of names such as HAVANA BLUNTS, HAVANA PALMAS, CLEAR HAVANAS, WINTERS HAVANA SPECIALS, and HABANA.

In addition to the half and double variations, there is the adjective form of wordsmithing, which consists of slipping in an extra word—an unhidden persuader. The scene is a large supermarket in the Los Angeles area. A woman shopper stands before the canned-orange-drink display, carefully considering the merits of the different brands. A discreet distance away, peeking from behind the breakfast foods, a marketing analyst watches as she finally selects a can and drops it into her shopping cart. Rushing out, the surveyor presents his credentials and asks the woman what motivated her choice. "Economy," she answers proudly, pointing to the lettering on the can: JUMBO QUART. In the realm of wordsmithing, where what counts is not the thought but the act it triggers, this is twice as good as GIANT PINT, though only one-fourth as effective as BIG GALLON.

Even those unappreciative of the ludicrousness of TV's armpit commercials must have had some sympathy for that helpful meddler Kathy Winters, when, after spending several seasons convincing her every acquaintance she needed the deodorant "ice-blue Secret,"

Kathy suddenly found she had to unsell them in order to resell them on her sponsor's "improved" product, "*new* ice-blue Secret." Thanks in part to Kathy, in part to exposés such as Vance Packard's *The Wastemakers*, Americans have grown a bit more skeptical of that word *new*. As well they might, for, like *free, limited time, limited quantity, once only, last chance, nationally known,* and *fully guaranteed*, it is now of uncertain meaning.

When Westinghouse put its Glas-gard TV picture tubes on the market in the fall of 1962, they advertised them as NEW WESTING-HOUSE GOLD STAR PICTURE TUBES, "new and fresh from the factory." Misrepresentation, cried the FTC, pointing out that the "new" tubes utilized "used" glass envelopes. Westinghouse, in reply, argued that no misrepresentation had occurred, that there was a statement to the effect that the glass envelopes were "re-used" on the side of each tube, on the cartons in which they were shipped, and on each service warranty. Though the FTC Hearing Examiner first ruled against Westinghouse, the full Commission, on appeal, sided with the firm and set aside the complaint.

Sometimes the absence of the word *new* is even more significant than its presence. In August 1964, the FTC cited two golf-ball manufacturers who, though neither had used the word *new*, hadn't used the word *old* either, both having failed to disclose in advertising and packaging that they were selling old balls which had been washed, rebuilt, or reconstructed.

Often, through wordsmithing, a liability can be made to seem an asset. It is doubtful whether many motorists would be inclined to buy a motor oil if the wording on its container stated, "This is old oil, reclaimed from motor crankcases, reprocessed and repackaged." It's a different story—and quite legal—when the label reads "re-refined." But it remained for a Chinese herbalist in California to use reverse-English wordsmithing, turning contempt to praise with a sign which read: THESE HERBS CITED BY THE FOOD AND DRUG ADMINISTRATION.

There is imitative wordsmithing—#5 CHANEL PERFUME; concealed wordsmithing—in compliance with the law, the watch was imprinted with its place of origin, MADE IN HONG KONG, only the lettering was inside the case; microscopic wordsmithing—"This guarantee good only if warranty card and sales receipt are received by the manufacturer within five days after purchase"; invisible wordsmithing—the manufacturer's name and address weren't given; superlative wordsmithing—the "first line" or best-grade tires of one manufacturer were designed STANDARD, HIGH STANDARD, and DELUXE HIGH STANDARD, while his lesser-quality tires (which he was pushing) bore the names SUPER STANDARD, SUPREME HIGH STANDARD, SUPER DELUXE HIGH STANDARD, and PREMIUM.

And there is wordsmithing by magnification: WILLIAM FAULK-NER reads the bold lettering on the front cover of one paperback, ERNEST HEMINGWAY dwarfs the title on another. Both are mediocre short-story collections with a single story by the name author. Backgrounded by the royal grin, DUKE ELLINGTON is the only wording on the jacket of one phonograph record album. Inside, the Duke is represented on a single band with a single selection to which he no longer holds a single right. The sign hanging above a table of electric skillets and fryers reads GENERAL ELEC-TRIC, not mentioning that only minor parts in the lesser-known brands are made by the better-known firm.

Thus far all the forms of the game have rated this designation by omission (failing to reveal material facts) or addition (the insertion of immaterial facts, unredeemable promissory notes). Even when *all* the facts are given, the whole truth told, it may still be word-smithing. The undisputed classic here dates from the late 1950s, when a Chicago television firm offered its 21-inch TV sets at what seemed an exceptionally low price, unless, that is, the newspaper reader happened to follow the asterisk down to the whisper in small print which noted that the size of the picture tube had been reached by measuring it diagonally. A close contender for honors is the more recent ad of a Washington, D.C., car dealer, headlined: IMAGINE— $1,000 FOR YOUR 1960 CAR! When prospects drove in, they learned this wasn't a promise, only a suggestion that they use their imaginations.

For years several huge industries played a similar form of the game. Most manufacturers of sleeping bags and linens labeled their products by "cut size" rather than "finished size." The cut sizes of tablecloths, doilies, dresser scarves, place mats, and napkins are usually larger than their finished sizes, because the finishing process involves sewing a hem to secure the edges; the difference in sleeping bags is more pronounced, because it also includes stuffing. Too, the next time a yachtsman or salesman brags about the measurements of a boat, it might be well to ask if he's talking about "straight length," the distance of a straight line from stem to stern, or "gunwale length," which includes the curved areas.

You've lost the wordsmithing game when you sign a sales contract full of beguiling guarantees, only later to learn that two little words you've overlooked are even more important—*as is*, meaning you've agreed to accept the merchandise in the condition in which you received it. You're a loser, too, when you buy the high-octane gasoline you believe necessary for your car's needs—be it high-quality regular, premium, super-premium, ethyl, super-ethyl—when, as is sometimes the case, the same gas is in all the pumps, for wordsmithing requires no awareness on the part of the purchaser, and is, of course, best played without it.

Some forms of wordsmithing have been with us so long and are so familiar that we take them for granted. GOING OUT OF BUSINESS (someday). SELLING OUT (we sell it, you carry it out). LAST DAY OF SPRING SALE (the pre-summer sale starts tomorrow). BARGAIN DAY (hurry, only 365 this year). FIRE SALE (get the wastepaper basket ready; I'll get the matches). If usage hasn't made them acceptable, it has at least made them unavoidable. Equally ancient and equally omnipresent are the techniques of dual pricing. But given a new name, some interesting variations, and placed in a special milieu, they become another new "fun" game—*pricemanship*.

Pricemanship is wordsmithing with figures. The rules and the teams remain the same, as does the game's object. Trust is still required, but is more easily relinquished here, as pricemanship is best played in a magic realm, a consumer's Disneyland—the world of *bargain, discount, wholesale, factory,* and *below-cost* prices.

There was a time when, to make a bargain believable, some stated or implied justification for price cutting was essential. The store was overstocked, or the item was overpriced, or buying in huge quantities had made possible a lower per-item cost, or the item was a "loss leader" (underpriced in order to attract customers who, once inside, would presumably buy enough regularly priced, and sometimes overpriced, items to make up the difference). This ended with World War II. During those fat lean years, almost any product could be sold under the counter at a high price by virtue of its supposed scarcity. With the war's end and the flood of government-surplus stocks, the pattern was again reversed. Taking advantage of the cut-rate atmosphere, fast-buck operators set their first prices fictitiously high, marking them up in order to knock them down. "Wholesale" catalogue houses sprang up in the hundreds, some legitimate, many not, the latter often adding mystery, excitement, and the thrill of vicarious lawbreaking to the game by offering unnamable FAMOUS NAME-BRAND MERCHANDISE ("the manufacturers, such as WEST---HOUSE, won't allow us to mention their names") at coded costs ("fair-trade regulations prohibit us from openly advertising these phenomenally low prices").* Added to this were the legitimate discount houses, specializing in foreign goods or buying and selling in quantity. Many long-established businesses soon found they had to cut prices in order to compete. The result, particularly evident in the last decade, has been a pricing revolution in many fields. In the sale of phonograph records, for example, in many areas the regular retail price has become the exception, the discount price the rule. The advent of wide-scale retail discounting has made the marketplace a bargain paradise in which competition is often justification enough for the most drastic price cuts, and into which walks the potential consumer, his suspicions lessened, his gullibility increased, more than ever before vulnerable to a game he doesn't even know he's playing.

If usage indicates popularity, the most popular form of the game of pricemanship is *false comparatives*.

The following story is fictionalized. The names given the manufacturer, the retailer, and the product are not actual names, nor are they intended to suggest the names of real people or any existent product. The incidents herein related were compiled from a variety of case histories and assembled in a nonidentifiable way for illustrative purposes only. One would like to add that any similarity to past and present practices is purely coincidental. Alas . . .

Manufacturer Cheap makes a variety of notions, one of which is a perfume called Xotique. Xotique is not an expensive perfume—as a matter of fact, chemically it's not a perfume at all but a cologne; the bottle (a perfume bottle, needless to say) and the label are the most expensive things about it. The label is particularly attractive, with a French scene as background. However, in accordance with federal laws, the country of origin, U.S.A., is printed there too, albeit as

---

* There was method in this mystery. The WESTERNHOUSE refrigerators did eventually become famous, for their mechanical defects, while the coded-price gimmick seemed an easy way to beat legal liability for fictitious pricing. If a customer saw a carving set code-priced at X2995Y999, he interpreted this to mean the "list price" was $29.95, the "sale price" $9.99. The important thing, so far as the catalogue houses were concerned, wasn't that the item had never sold for $29.95, nor that it could be purchased in most stores for $3.98, but that they themselves hadn't actually made any false claims.

inconspicuously as possible. Mr. Cheap sells Xotique to wholesalers and retailers throughout the United States at 50¢ per one-ounce bottle.

Among his customers is Mr. Gyp, who operates a small store where he sells second-rate watches, cameras, jewelry, and similar items. Mr. Gyp has just received a gross of one-ounce bottles of Xotique. He wants to sell them at a "bargain" price which will at the same time assure him a good profit. How can he do this? Easily, by using one of the multitudinous forms of pricemanship, at which he is something of an expert. He chooses one of the oldest, most common, and safest. He prices a bottle at $18 and puts it on the shelf; for some reason it doesn't sell; the next day he reduces the price to $4.95 and puts a sign in his window:

JUST ARRIVED
LARGE SHIPMENT
Xotique Perfume
WAS: $18 AN OUNCE
OUR SPECIAL SALE PRICE: $4.95

Simple as the sign may seem, its creator considers it a minor masterpiece. Mr. Gyp has never read a book on psychology, but he has learned from experience certain psychological oddities. JUST ARRIVED makes the item sound imported; LARGE SHIPMENT indicates he's overstocked and anxious to sell, even if at a loss; the use of both as an announcement indicates that the item may ordinarily be hard to get. Much of the credit, of course, belongs to the brand name, which sounds French, and which, together with public awareness that French perfumes are often very expensive, gives him a wide latitude in setting his own first price. AN OUNCE is added to emphasize the outlandish cost. By contrast, the sale price, $4.95, seems both reasonable and a bargain. (Mr. Gyp may look down on the intelligence of his customers, but he does not make the mistake of believing them stupid. He's well aware that few, if any, would actually believe they were saving $13.05, the difference between the two prices. Most would consider the first price unreasonable; this is exactly what he wants, the overpricing thereby providing another justification for the sale, as well as causing the customer to relax his guard, believing he has seen through the artifice.) In terms of profits, the most important symbol in the sign is the figure $4.95, which means a markup of 990 percent; in the matter of legality, the most important word is WAS, for in choosing it Mr. Gyp has avoided a number of legal pitfalls.

REGULARLY PRICED or USUALLY or RETAIL VALUE or SOLD AT are dangerous words, since he can't substantiate them. VALUE is open to legal debate. FORMERLY would be acceptable, but there is a finality to it, and Mr. Gyp wants to give the impression that this is a bargain which won't be repeated. PRICED ELSE-WHERE would be all right, if he still had a working arrangement with the merchant down the street, but that ended some time ago, in an argument over who was to be low man on some of the fastest-moving items. WAS is quite satisfactory. Before long he places another order for the perfume, this time for two gross.

The routine arrival of a letter from the local Better Business Bureau disturbs Mr. Gyp not at all. It may concern his sale of Xotique, those $10 watches tagged REDUCED TO $9.99, the doubled-price items on his 50% OFF table, or the 51-gauge, 15-denier nylons he's selling at "factory" prices, neglecting to mention that the comparison price is for first-quality nylons, while his are imperfects or irregulars or seconds. He'll never know, for he files the letter in the wastepaper basket unopened. As Mr. Gyp is well aware, the BBB is primarily a fact-finding organization; it has no enforcement powers. It does have several weapons it can use in combating deception and fraud, but Mr. Gyp is immune to each. Mr. Gyp is the weakest link in the effectiveness of the BBB; he knows it and makes the most of it.

Since its beginnings in 1912, the Association of Better Business Bureaus has had two stated goals: to protect the public from fraudulent business practices, and to help business establish and maintain high standards of advertising and selling. It is, however, a business organization. Formed as a nonprofit membership corporation, the BBB is an integral part of business and is supported by business, its membership represents all the various lines of business (today more than 150,000 member business firms participate), and its officers and board of directors are representative businessmen elected by the members. Business-oriented, it places major emphasis on self-regulation, business regulated by business rather than by an outside agency.* To achieve this it relies heavily on voluntary compliance. The trouble is, this doesn't work with the Mr. Gyps.

* Acting in behalf of both business and the consumer, the BBB has helped prove that the interests of these two groups are not necessarily incompatible. The attempt to please both, however, occasionally leads to some interesting

Each time the local BBB receives what appears to be a legitimate complaint concerning Mr. Gyp's business practices, he is sent a copy and given an opportunity to present his side of the story. With a firm concerned with that intangible called "reputation," this may prove effective in clearing up misunderstandings, bring to the attention of management abuses or practices previously overlooked, and often lead to some settlement or redress. But Mr. Gyp isn't concerned with his reputation, nor is he concerned that, by his not replying, the letter will go into his BBB file as an "unadjusted complaint." The BBB does not rate or recommend businesses; it will, upon request, give a "reliability report" on a specific business, noting the number of unadjusted complaints on record, leaving conclusions to the caller. Mr. Gyp is aware that few people bother to check with the BBB before patronizing a place of business.

Voluntary compliance has other forms.

The BBB's member businesses subscribe to a code of business ethics, a set of periodically revised standards set forth in the BBB's *Guide for Retail Advertising and Selling.* Mr. Gyp, perhaps needless to say, doesn't belong to the BBB.

When abuses appear to be widespread in an industry or field, the BBB often calls a trade-practice conference to discuss the problems with industry leaders and, if possible, to formulate solutions. (The FTC and FDA do this also.) In this it works closely with existing business organizations. Mr. Gyp doesn't belong to the Retail Merchants Association in his community, or to any other trade group. He is a loner and accountable only to the law, when applicable and if enforced.

When voluntary compliance fails, the BBB presents its investigative findings to the appropriate law-enforcement agency for possible action. Here again Mr. Gyp is immune. It isn't that Mr. Gyp hasn't broken any laws—he's broken a number of them, but has carefully chosen which laws to break. His fictitious pricing of Xotique could, technically, be considered fraud, but it isn't likely; fraud statutes are usually enforced only for outright swindles. In his city, as in most, and in his state, as in nearly all, there are so-called "printer's ink" statutes covering deceptive advertising. Often these are laxly enforced or applied only to major abuses. Pricesmither Gyp has made a token effort to obey the letter of the law. If—improbably—he were

---

moments, not all of them lacking humor. The BBB Fact Booklet *Schemes,* for example, which catalogues dozens of common business frauds, opens with the line, "Business is honest and fair to the public—almost 100% so."

charged, tried, and convicted, it would be for a misdemeanor, with—quite probably—a light fine. Mr. Gyp can afford to ignore the BBB's letters. He's a gambler playing probabilities, and, in the matter of false comparatives, he's at present a winner, as are many like him.

As for the federal laws, which are more stringently enforced, there are statutes such as 18 USC 287, covering false claims, and 18 USC 1001, covering false statements. There are postal-fraud statutes 18 USC 1341 and 39 USC 4005. Even more explicit to the offense is a Federal Trade Commission ruling which states that, for a bargain to be *bona fide,* the former price must be one at which the article was offered to the public "on a regular basis for a reasonably substantial period of time . . ." Since Mr. Gyp does no business by mail, the postal laws don't apply. Since all his business is conducted in his own state, he neither is breaking the federal laws nor do his activities come under the interstate-commerce jurisdiction of the FTC.

Manufacturer Cheap's activities do, and at the moment he's preparing to flout that authority in several interesting ways, secure in the knowledge that he will never see the inside of a courtroom, since he, too, is a specialist in the games of wordsmithing and pricemanship.

Xotique has proven to be one of Mr. Cheap's best-selling products. Unfortunately, from Mr. Cheap's point of view, in several large states there are not only specific laws covering deceptive pricing and false comparatives, but these laws are strictly enforced. California's Comparative Price Law, 17501, for example, reads in part: "No price shall be advertised as a former price of any advertised thing, unless the alleged former price was the prevailing market price as above defined within three months next immediately preceding the publication of the advertisement or unless the date when the alleged former price did prevail is clearly, exactly and conspicuously stated in the advertisement." Laws in several other states are similarly worded. But don't worry—Mr. Cheap will out.

As a temporary measure, Mr. Cheap's salesmen reach a private understanding with the company's wholesale and retail customers in these areas. Each is sent a shipment of Xotique with a suggested selling price of $16 per ounce (Mr. Cheap estimates the worth of the perfume at a little less than Mr. Gyp, but then he knows what goes into it). The shipments are on consignment; the discount is standard, allowing for only an average profit. No one pays his bill, no one is dunned for it, and no one sells much Xotique, for a while.

Ninety-one days later, each dealer receives a letter from Mr. Cheap announcing a price cut, retroactive, to 50¢ per ounce; an amended bill is attached. The dealer, who has offered the product for at least ninety days at full price, can now sell it as a *bona fide* bargain.

Mr. Cheap hasn't been inactive in the meantime. He has taken a small ad in a national magazine. The ad, headed AS ADVERTISED IN . . . ,* is blown up to full-page size and copies are sent to all his customers. The ad offers Xotique at $16 an ounce "in better stores." In one of those "better stores," Mr. Gyp takes down his own sign, marks and puts up the ad instead. He can now show tangible proof that he is selling the perfume at a bargain price and, as far as the law is concerned, he's untouchable. Mr. Gyp still buys Xotique at 50¢ and still sells it at $4.95; Mr. Cheap more than makes up for the cost of the ad in increased sales.

Mr. Cheap continues these activities for the better part of a year before the understaffed FTC, after a thorough investigation, issues a Complaint.

It isn't that Mr. Cheap's activities have gone unobserved during this period, rather that he has had to wait his turn—his violations, for example, being (1) less damaging than a merger which would force a dozen small companies out of business, (2) less dangerous than the unchecked sale of silk illusion, used for communion and wedding veils, guaranteed to make either occasion unusually memorable if the veil comes in close proximity to a cigarette or candle flame. "Few Federal agencies have thrust themselves so conspicuously into so many corners of American business life as the Federal Trade Commission," noted the New York *Times* in July 1964. "Whether the issue is growth by merger in the dairy products industry, suspected price collusion on tires or on anti-biotics, or the use of mock-ups in television commercials, the FTC is ready to brandish the requisite law suit, court order, advisory opinion or trade regulation, all in the name of maintaining free and fair competi-

---

* Many magazines, *Life* and *Good Housekeeping* among them, have strict advertising standards designed to forestall this and similar practices. *Good Housekeeping* has gone to court repeatedly to challenge misuse of its Seal of Approval, as has the Consumers Union, which never permits any advertising or commercial use of its *Consumer Reports* findings. But violations are near-continuous. The ad agency's moral dilemma when a sponsor's product receives a high *Consumer Reports* rating is obvious: against the strong temptation to exploit the unbiased finding is the fear of making the Consumers Union and its activities too well known.

tion."[1] In recent months the FTC has investigated the TV broadcast-rating systems, accused Topps of attempting to set up a monopoly in baseball trading cards in bubblegum packages (later dismissing the charge as unwarranted), charged the Surprise Brassiere Company with favoring some of its customers over others in promotional allowances, made the manufacturer of a wax polish agree to stop advertising that use of his product would make speedboats travel 3 to 5 knots faster, and ruled that a blood bank and hospital were engaged in an illegal conspiracy to hamper and restrain the exchange, sale, and distribution of human blood.

Often a single cease-and-desist order will cover a catalogue of abuses. One against a Minneapolis, Minnesota, jewelry and souvenir distributor noted that, contrary to representations in the firm's advertisements: the likeness of the Pope on their Pope John jewelry was not etched in gold and did not contain gold; the Ten Commandments on their candy dish were not imprinted in gold and did not contain gold; their Cross necklaces did not contain natural stones but imitations; their Sweater Guard was not composed of genuine Mother-of-Pearl but an imitation; their Turquoise rings did not contain genuine turquoise but an imitation; their boxed Colored Pearl sets did not contain genuine pearls but imitations; and their Mink-Trim dolls and Peewee Twins were not made by Indians.

Like Mr. Gyp, Mr. Cheap is a gambler, betting that he can persist in his activities for a profitable interval without reprimand. The odds are heavily in his favor. During fiscal year 1963, the FTC received 5871 public complaints deemed serious enough for investigation—a great many from businessmen complaining about the practices of their competitors. Many times that number of possible violations were referred to the FTC by Congress or government agencies or were discovered by the FTC's own investigative staff. Most of these complaints involved deception and fraud against consumers, particularly through false advertising. That same year the nation's advertising expenditure amounted to $12 billion; the portion of the FTC's budget devoted to being watchdog over advertising was about $4 million. That year, too, to cite just one unenviable task, FTC investigators reviewed the scripts of, or monitored live, 516,352 radio and TV commercials and read 302,572 pages of printed advertising matter, with 61,300 separate advertisements being forwarded to the FTC's legal department for examination and possible corrective action. The total FTC staff, including clerks and stenographers, was 1178.

Though often criticized for all manner of sins, the FTC can't be accused of failing to give due process. Upon receiving the Complaint, Mr. Cheap has thirty days in which to file an Answer. If this is deemed unsatisfactory, this much time or longer may elapse before a date is set for an Initial Hearing before an FTC Hearing Examiner. If the evidence goes against Mr. Cheap, the examiner will issue an Initial Decision ordering him to "cease and desist" his false advertising and billing practices. This is still not a final decision; it may be reviewed and set aside, or it may be appealed. If appealed, the case may eventually be heard by a board made up of all five FTC Commissioners.* If the evidence still goes against Mr. Cheap, a Final Order will be issued. But even then no action will be taken against Mr. Cheap unless, after a ninety-day grace period, he persists in his violation. Being a regulatory agency, the FTC has no enforcement powers. Brought to court by the Justice Department for disobeying the FTC order, Mr. Cheap, if convicted, could be fined $5000 a day for every day he disobeyed the FTC's Final Order. This rarely happens. Some charged companies will continue the practice up to the Final Order, then drop it while appealing the decision through the FTC and the courts (anyone receiving an FTC order may petition a U.S. Court of Appeals to review and set aside the order). Others stop with the original complaint, since the Commission frequently takes this into consideration and drops the charge. The majority, however, find another solution preferable. This is the one Mr. Cheap chooses. He agrees to a Consent Order.

A Consent Order is in itself a remarkable bit of wordsmithing, a kind of face-saving semantics. After the investigation and complaint, but before the first formal hearing, Mr. Cheap is offered the privilege of accepting an order to cease and desist from the practices without litigation and without a finding of law violation. Mr. Cheap agrees. The last paragraph of the Consent Order is generally worded as follows: "The agreement is for settlement purposes only and does not constitute an admission by respondents that they have violated

* The five Commissioners are appointed by the President for seven-year terms; no more than three may be of the same political party. The President also designates one as Chairman. The FTC's current Chairman, Paul Rand Dixon, a former top staff man on Senator Estes Kefauver's Senate Antitrust Subcommittee, was appointed by President Kennedy in February 1961, and is generally credited with revitalizing the not always overconscientious agency. Observed the New York *Times* in typical understatement, "Dixon brings a Kefauver kind of crusading zeal to his job and has annoyed advertising agencies and businessmen with the vigor of his activities."

the law." In short, Mr. Cheap and his company agree not to commit these illegal acts in the future, while at the same time not admitting that they have ever done so in the past.

About 75 percent of all FTC cases end in Consent Orders. Other regulatory agencies have similar agreements, as does the Post Office Department in its Affidavit of Discontinuance. It can be argued, without much debate, that such agreements are to the benefit of nearly everyone concerned. The alleged practice is halted, without litigation costly to the accused, the Government, and the taxpayer. The public is served. That the unscrupulous sometimes take advantage of the provision, or the provisions of full process, engaging in illegal practices on a short-term basis for low-unit, high-volume profits, is one of the risks inherent in the system. It is also one of the breaks of the game of pricemanship.

Perhaps the expression "short-term" is used inadvisably. A deceptive ad on TV, for example, may run six months to a year before being stopped, or as long as it might ordinarily run. A mail-order entrepreneur may mail out 500,000 circulars advertising nonexistent merchandise at bargain prices, receive replies (with cash) from maybe 1 percent of them, pocket the proceeds and skip, with three or more months passing before the Post Office Department receives its first complaint. A real-estate bunco artist in the Far West was able to bank a sizable fortune offering arid desert "homesites" as "retirement havens" for the elderly, before—after seven years of litigation—he was eventually forced to retire himself (he was never convicted—he simply went out of business). It took the FDA ten years of legal action and three trips to the U.S. Supreme Court to halt the sale of the notorious Hoxley cure for cancer (and this worthless mixture of cooking herbs and weeds is still being sold surreptitiously).

This is one phase of the *time gap* (the length of time between the commission of an act and the halting of it), and there is no more important weapon in the arsenal of the modern swindler. Testifying before a Congressional committee, FTC Chairman Paul Rand Dixon observed: "any half-qualified lawyer can block the FTC from forcing a change in misleading advertisements for four or more years without even half-trying."

Just because Mr. Cheap agrees to a Consent Order doesn't mean he need drop out of the game. If he feels it worth the trouble, he can go out of business, reopen under another name, and emerge as a new player, taking advantage of the time gap all over again. But why bother, when all he need do is switch to some other variation of the game, such as *preticketing?*

As originally played, in the last half of the 1940s, preticketing was comparatively simple. Manufacturer X made a pen-and-pencil set which ordinarily sold for $2.98 retail. To save the retailer the trouble of making up his own fictitious first price, to lend authenticity to the "bargain," and, of course, to boost his own sales, he had printed on the box, or on an affixed label or ticket, MANUFACTURER'S SUGGESTED RETAIL PRICE: $7.50. Thus are bargains made.

By the late fifties the game had grown more varied and blatant. In 1958, a watch wholesaler ran a two-page ad in a trade magazine; the wholesale prices of the watches shown ranged from $9.50 to $14.90. For the convenience of the retail merchant, there was a special order blank at the bottom of the page. It read: "I want these free resale tags with my order: ☐ $16.95 ☐ $24.95 ☐ $29.95 ☐ $39.95 ☐ $49.95." Realizing that the degree of gullibility may differ regionally, the wholesaler offered a variety of first prices, saying in effect: You know how stupid your particular customers are—choose your own "list" price.

An intensive crackdown on preticketing by the FTC, BBB, and various consumer groups in 1958–59 resulted in some changes in the game. Coro, Inc., is a New York City manufacturer and distributor of watches and costume jewelry, whose annual sales of approximately $30 million are made primarily to retailers such as department and variety stores. In the mid-fifties—prior to the crackdown— Coro, deciding to compete in supplying the newly thriving, highly profitable catalogue-house business, brought out a special line of items which it sold to the houses through full-color dummy catalogue pages and one of the subtler forms of preticketing, a simple mathematical code known as the "three-time formula." For illustration, one of the pages sent potential customers in 1956, showing Coro's "Nancy" necklace and earring set, had at the bottom of the page:

Jobber Cost	Dealer Cost	Suggested Line	Your corresponding price line as it is to print:
$5.50	$8.25	$16.50	

As later explained by the FTC, the Jobber Cost was Coro's price to the catalogue houses; the Dealer Cost was the suggested resale price, the price at which the cataloguers should sell the set to their customers; the Suggested Line was the suggested fictitious first price, arrived at by multiplying the cost by three, or $5.50 x 3 = $16.50; and the blank space was for the dealer to fill in this or any other fictitious first price he preferred. The three-times price, or 200 percent markup, was standard in most catalogue houses.

Came the crackdown, Coro, according to FTC Chairman Dixon, "apparently aware of the illegality of supplying its customers with these blatantly fictitious prices, made a rather transparent attempt to transfer 'responsibility' to its catalogue house customers." In 1960, Coro's price entry for its "Riviera" jewelry set was the simplified:

Your Cost   *Your corresponding price*
                 line as it is to print:

$7.00   _____

Innocent enough, except that it was accompanied by a separate letter explaining the three-times formula, a copy of which the FTC, by some manner or means, managed to obtain. When cited in 1963, Coro argued that it was merely following the instructions of the catalogue houses in preticketing the items, that it was no more responsible than "the printer who set the type for the price line." The FTC credited Coro with a bit more importance. Coro then contended that, since the practices had been abandoned, the matter should be dismissed or, at the very least, "a very narrow cease and desist order" issued. In reply, the FTC was less than sympathetic: Coro, the opinion stated, "stopped violating the law when it was learned that the law's hand was already on its shoulder, and it stopped then because it wished to avoid the embarrassment of having its violations exposed to the public view, and the inconvenience of having to comply with the law's requirements in the future." As for the scope of the order, which covered various other deceptive pricing and guarantee claims, Chairman Dixon said: "To enter an order that prohibits only one of several means of engaging in a particular unlawful practice is to invite ingenious attempts to circumvent it. If this respondent is honestly resolved to eschew fictitious pricing of all kinds in the future, then it should be wholly unconcerned with whether our order prohibits all or only one of the methods of doing it." The FTC issued its Final Order in November 1963.

It can't be said that the FTC's decision in the Coro case and others like it has lessened the popularity of preticketing and the other modes of pricemanship. The record number of fictitious pricing complaints received by the FTC during the last half of the fifties has been more than topped by new records in the first half of the sixties, accounting for more than a third of all complaints received. Many of these involved well-known firms. During the past two years the FTC has obtained cease-and-desist orders involving preticketing against Benrus, Helbros, and Gruen, plus some dozen only slightly lesser-known watch companies, plus some two-dozen large catalogue houses, to mention only a few of the players.*

Numbers, like prices, are often misleading. As New York's veteran bunco detective Daniel J. Campion once observed, "A long record doesn't necessarily mean an important criminal. Often it may mean just the reverse, that he's a poor thief or he wouldn't have been caught so many times."[2] The increasing number of cases doesn't necessarily mean either a new crime wave or unusually stringent regulation. (Control, the FTC frankly admits, has of necessity largely been a matter of "scattered fire.") When the feeling "Everybody's doing it" prevails, offenses become more blatant.

The word "offenses" may in itself offend some, since in our climate of fraud we rarely call anything unpleasant by its correct name. Not only do words serve as protective coloration for the act, it is not uncommon for their users to come to believe that they are one and the same. False claims become "permissible puffery," artifice "the art of selling"; exaggerated merits are defensible as "sales stimulation," rigged quiz shows excusable as "entertainment"; embezzlement is "hypothecating"; a price-fixing bill, which once bore the misnomer "Fair Trade," is now known as "Quality Stabilization"; a kickback is a "cooperative allowance"; and deceit has become a many-faceted "game." A good label will do wonders for a very bad product, though, as Shakespeare observed, the odor remains.

The examples in this chapter have a number of things in common: None is a *swindle*, as that word is traditionally defined. No one

---

* Complaints are rarely for a single offense. Benrus, for example, was cited (and later given a cease-and-desist order) for preticketing, making false guarantee claims, misrepresenting the metallic composition of some of its watch parts, advertising some of its watches as "shock proof" when they were not, issuing often unredeemable "allowance certificates," and making false trade-in allowances (a $20 trade-in, for example, being allowed on any make or model watch, regardless of age or condition, when purchasing a new $59.50 Benrus—which regularly sold for $39.50).

was promised something for nothing and given the opposite instead. There was no appeal to the mark's larceny, avarice, or greed.

Each is a *fraud,* by dictionary definition—i.e. "deceit, trickery, sharp practice, or breach of confidence, by which it is sought to gain some unfair or dishonest advantage; any deception, artifice, or trick" —and by legal definition—"an intentional perversion of truth for the purpose of inducing another in reliance upon it to part with some valuable thing belonging to him . . . ; a false representation of a matter of fact (whether by words or conduct, by false or misleading allegations, or by concealment of that which should have been disclosed) which deceives and is intended to deceive another so that he shall act upon it to his legal injury." But in most of our states few law-enforcement agencies would so consider it, and, if they did, few judges would so find it. Each of the examples lies on the borderline of *enforceable* legality. But there are some signs of change. Judge Irving Kaufman, U.S. Court of Appeals, recently observed, "The courts are no longer content to insist simply upon the most literal truthfulness . . . for we have increasingly come to recognize that advertisements as a whole may be completely misleading though every sentence separately considered is literally true."

Dishonest? It depends upon who answers the question, and to whom it applies. In the fall of 1963 the *American Salesman* magazine reported the results of a survey it had conducted. The question: Do you consider modern advertising honest and ethical? Of those salesmen responding, 77 percent said they believed it was, although 50 percent said the ads of their competitors sometimes took an unethical approach.

Deceitful? It depends upon who's reading the non-gold-inscribed Eighth and Ninth Commandments on that candy dish. Our era of fuzzy morality may well be remembered for its facility in combining relativity and semantics.

It could be argued that the need to substitute synonyms for proper names indicates a sense of guilt, born of a strong—if unusually well-concealed—sense of morality. It could also be argued that it is nothing more than a good business practice. *Wordsmithing* and *pricemanship* are polite words befitting a polite society engaged in impolite practices. Perhaps it's time to be impolite and call the game by its real name, *Deception,* and to note that deception is the smog in our climate of fraud.

In the following chapter we'll see how the game is played visually, or how Seeing is Deceiving.

CHAPTER 2

THINGS ARE SELDOM WHAT

THEY SEEM

> Things are seldom what they seem,
> Skim milk masquerades as cream.
>
> W. S. Gilbert
> *H.M.S. Pinafore*

W. S. GILBERT penned these lyrics well before the advent of television. Things are still seldom what they seem, only more so, only today it is cream which masquerades as cream.

When former Federal Communications Commission Chairman Newton N. Minow made his much quoted, little heeded 1961 speech before the National Association of Broadcasters, comparing television broadcasting to a "vast wasteland," he neglected to mention that the desert was complete with mirages. Early in the development of the medium, technicians discovered that the television camera was capable of playing pranks, creating special optical illusions.

No matter how strong the detergent, white shirts photographed tattletale gray.

An actress dressed in a certain shade of red reduced the off-camera crew to uproarious laughter, because on-camera she appeared quite nude.

Allowances had to be made for these and many more unusual effects. Some concerned the commercials. The announcer who sipped a famous brand of tea, between sips extolling its refreshing flavor, had to have a fine memory for taste, since on-camera real tea looks like colored water, colored water like real tea. Cream, by contrast, improves with viewing, appearing richer and thicker than it actually is. This posed an interesting philosophical problem. Which, then, was more deceptive—the imitation that looked as good as the real, or the real that looked even better? Who, then, if anyone, was to be blamed (or cited)—Mr. Lipton, for using a substitute, or Miss Borden, for using her own product?

This was, throughout the late 1940s and all but the last two months of the 1950s, not only unanswered but mostly unasked, for it was presumed that any deceptions in television advertising came under the jurisdiction of the Federal Communications Commission, an assumption shared by everyone except the FCC.

In the interim, broadcasters, advertising agencies, and commercial sponsors were not long in discovering that wordsmithing could be played visually as well as verbally, that what at first had seemed liabilities can be turned into assets. Dressed in a blue coat, which appeared white, an actor who now looked like a doctor could discourse authoritatively on the digestibility of his sponsor's product, while a housewife, invited to the testing laboratories of a soap company, could—after having spent several hours in a makeup chair, and after having signed a TV release contract which guaranteed a "session fee" of $108 and which might, with enough repeat showings, go up to $1808, and without having ever studied at Actors Studio —looked surprised (1) on learning the soap she had been using was said company's, and (2) on discovering she was on TV.*

Nearly every form of wordsmithing was adaptable to this new medium, but the half-truth form retained its popularity. For as the shockproof, waterproof watch was shot from a cannon (courtesy U.S. Army), dropped from an airplane (courtesy U.S. Air Force), sunk with a submarine (courtesy U.S. Navy), dragged behind a PT boat (courtesy U.S. Coast Guard)—each time surviving intact and still ticking—who, after this exciting "visual proof," would be so cynical as to wonder how many times each experiment had been conducted, with the loss of how many watches, before one watch came through photographically unscathed?

The thin line between exaggeration and deception was crossed over inevitably and with record haste. A few examples will indicate just how far.

During 1957 and 1958, General Motors and the Libby-Owens-Ford Glass Company aired some twenty-three commercials purport-

---

* In the early days of TV advertising, one of the toothpaste companies for a time eliminated the error factor by putting their own brand in both tubes tested.

ing to be scientific experiments demonstrating the superiority of glass used in the windows of GM automobiles. Though the commercials differed, their message, conveyed by both audio and visual effects, could be summarized as follows: all automobiles used *safety plate glass* in their windshields, but only GM cars used it in all their windows, front, sides, and rear, and of equal grade and quality; non-GM cars used *safety sheet glass* in their side and rear windows, and this safety sheet glass was the same as ordinary home window glass, which, as everyone knew, was notorious for its distortion. (No one said that it also shattered easily, but wordsmithing is the art of the unstated implication.)

Beginning with a false premise, or rather a near-complete set, since the safety plate glass GM used in the side and rear windows of its vehicles was not the same quality as that used in windshields, but lower, while the safety sheet glass used in the side and rear windows of competitors' vehicles was not the same grade and quality as the glass used in home windows, but higher—the proving of these claims necessarily required a wee bit of deception:

In one commercial the television audience was given the opportunity to compare the view as seen through the side windows of two automobiles, the first safety plate glass (GM), the second safety sheet glass (non-GM). The first scene was exceptionally sharp and clear, the second far less so. The first was exceptionally sharp and clear because there was no glass in the window.

In another commercial the sheet-glass distortion was achieved by using unusual camera angles and special lenses.

In still another, the view through the side window of a GM vehicle was contrasted to the view through ordinary home window glass—by inference, the glass supposedly used in non-GM cars. The latter view was wavy, badly blurred, distorted. Which was understandable, considering that the window had first been smeared with Vaseline.

Borrowing from the magician's repertory, the Winston Sales Company, Inc., of Chicago, demonstrated on TV the qualities of its kitchen table knife by using it to saw through a nail. A closeup of the knife blade then showed an edge so sharp one couldn't believe it had ever been used. It hadn't; the nail had been sawed most of the way through prior to the demonstration, and a second knife was used for the on-camera cutting.

There was something deceptive for everyone in the family. What young girl wouldn't want a famous-name doll after she'd seen it move its arms, roll over, and perform various other beguiling tricks on TV? What boy wouldn't want a set of more than 200 Revolutionary War soldiers, each 4 inches long, three-dimensional, multicolored, with rifles and cannons that emitted real smoke and blasts of fire; or, if he were really a progressive youth, a Robot Commando that would Turn Left, Move Forward, Turn Right, and Fire a Missile on voice command? How to explain, when the actual doll, once purchased, proved quite stationary, that only the cameraman could make her so perform? Or that the "three-dimensional" soldiers were cardboard and the only possible way to get smoke and fire out of the cannons would be to burn them with a match? Or that to make the "voice-operated" Robot Commando move, one also needed to move a lever?

In those instances when no explanations will prove satisfactory, one might as well tell the truth: "It's this way, children. Since 60 percent of the toy industry's sales occur in the months of November and December, a number of the toy companies have found 'one-shot' or 'hit-and-run' deception both safe and effective." (So explains Daddy, still swearing under his breath because the little log-cabin set he purchased for Junior did not contain enough logs in a single set to construct the little log cabin depicted on the box.) "This, children, is the real 'educational TV,' designed to help prepare you for adult reality in our climate of fraud."

Only Grandmother is blissfully unconcerned. As she was telling the ladies at the W.C.T.U. meeting just the other day, what she likes about TV is its honesty. For example, that nice man on TV told her that if she took liquid Geritol she'd feel better, and she did and she does! Of course, the nice man didn't mention that the alcoholic content of liquid Geritol is 12 percent.

It was not until after the payola and rigged quiz-show "scandals" of 1958 and 1959 that the responsibility for policing TV commercials settled more or less firmly on the FTC rather than on the industry-dominated FCC.* When, on November 1, 1959, FTC Chairman Earl W. Kintner announced a crackdown on "illegal huckstering" and "advertising excesses that dance on the edges of the law," the FTC had only three paid employees monitoring live TV broadcasts for possible advertising deceptions. These three men monitored daily

---

* For the story of how the FCC came to be known as "our timid watchdog" and "America's least-regulatory agency," see Meyer Weinberg's *TV in America: The Morality of Hard Cash*, Ballantine Books, 1962, and Newton N. Minow's *Equal Time: The Private Broadcaster and the Public Interest*, Atheneum, 1964.

programs in the Washington, D.C., area from 8:30 A.M. to 4:30 P.M. Three FTC attorneys monitored the evening programs, from the time they arrived home up to about 1 A.M., without pay. Staff members in the FTC's nine field offices similarly volunteered their time. When a suspected false claim was observed, the monitor had to write the sponsoring company for a sample of its product for testing, as the FTC's annual testing budget allowance of $23,000 wasn't sufficient to cover product purchases also.

Although the FTC had earlier obtained cease-and-desist orders for scattered false claims on TV, it was not until January 8, 1960, that the agency took on the problem of visual deception and sham or faked demonstrations, with its complaint against the Colgate-Palmolive Company and its advertising agency, Ted Bates, Inc., New York City.

Compared to all the fuss it occasioned, the demonstration was itself quite simple. To "prove" the moisturizing qualities of Colgate's Rapid Shave, a gob of the shaving cream was spread on a piece of sandpaper; a razor was then drawn down the center of the sheet, shaving a clean swath.

Or so it seemed. Those who chose to repeat the experiment in their own homes got rather different results, as did the FTC in its tests. Several dozen razor blades later, agency testers succeeded in shaving one piece of sandpaper, after soaking it in a dish of the shaving cream for eighty minutes.

The differing results weren't entirely due to a difference in climate, the FTC finally discovered. The piece of "sandpaper" used in the commercial was actually a sheet of Plexiglas, on which someone had sprinkled loose sand.

"Appearances to the mind are of four kinds," observed the Greek stoic philosopher Epictetus. "Things either are what they appear to be; or they neither are, nor appear to be; or they are, and do not appear to be; or they are not, and yet appear to be. Rightly to aim in all these cases is the wise man's task." It is perhaps not too surprising that in their rush to exploit the exciting possibilities of the new medium, some confused stoicism with sophistry.

Few FTC complaints have been so hotly contested, for the Colgate action went beyond the question of the alleged merits of one brand of shaving cream, threatening to set a precedent regarding the permissibility of using mock-ups and substitute materials in all TV demonstrations. Too, the also cited advertising agency, Ted Bates, Inc., was attempting to settle the matter of ad agency involvement in such complaints with the defense that it "neither knew nor had reason to know a mock-up or prop was used, and that the qualities of the shaving cream were misrepresented."

This was a remarkable defense in any case, but even more so here, considering that just three weeks earlier Rossiter Reeves, board chairman of the Bates firm, had been quoted in an *Advertising Age* interview (later reprinted in pamphlet form by the Bates firm) as saying: "We maintain a big, costly Science Department to check the validity of our claims. I do not believe that any agency in the business goes to such lengths—in testing, in clinical research, in evaluation—to make sure that we are not misrepresenting a product's performance."[1]

On January 25th, Bates took full-page ads in the New York *Times*, New York *Herald Tribune*, Washington *Post*, Washington *Star* and Chicago *Tribune*, defending "imaginative advertising" against the FTC's "mere subjective opinion that minor props and artifices have resulted in horrendous deceits." This was a bold new move, seeking public support against an FTC decision, but it apparently had little real effect, as, when the FTC issued its final cease-and-desist order (on December 29, 1961, nearly two years after the initial complaint), the order fully justified the advertisers' worst fears, ruling against both Bates and Colgate on the charge of misrepresenting the qualities of the shaving cream and prohibiting both from engaging in any spurious television demonstrations, any use of deceptive mock-ups, and any use of any substitute material in any commercial. This decision was appealed in court. The First Circuit Court of Appeals handed down its decision on November 20, 1962, upholding the FTC in all particulars but also ruling that, as worded, the FTC order was too broad, in effect prohibiting the use of mock-ups and substitute materials in every hypothetical situation. The court sent the order back to the FTC for rewording.

The new order, written by Commissioner Philip Elman, drew a fine and still much debated line, one enclosing an area far broader than anticipated. It also settled, for the moment, the tea-cream issue. "It is not enough for sellers to refrain from misrepresenting the merits of their wares," Elman noted; "the law prohibits them from making any material misrepresentations designed to influence the public in choosing what, and what not, to buy. What is essentially involved in this phase of the case is the question of whether an advertiser may lie to prospective buyers to convince them that certain real qualities of a product actually exist . . ." The FTC's answer was No. "To say that selling is an art does not mean that artifice must be tolerated," Elman said; "it would be a cynical subversion of the policy of the law to allow technical limitations of a particular medium to become lawful justification for resort to falsehoods and deception of the public."

One part of the hypothetical tea-cream question was settled in the order. "There is nothing objectionable in showing a person drinking what appears to be iced tea, but for technical photographic reasons is actually colored water [since] the appearance of the liquid is merely an incidental aspect of the commercial, is not presented as proof of the fine color or appearance of the tea, and thus in no practical sense would have a material effect in inducing sales of the product."

As for the cream, the judge had considered this in the appeal decision. Should the advertiser, asked the court, "be allowed to use his own cream if he knows that by the normal photographic process its color would be changed so as to appear substantially better on the screen than it was?" Answered the court for the FTC, "We suspect the Commission would think it clear he could not."

Thus the false may be fair and the real may be fraudulent. And thus deception, like morality ever relative, has become even more so.

While these arguments were going on, the FTC cited General Motors and the others whose cases have already been mentioned. Two other shaving-cream commercials were also found deceptive. Interestingly enough, one "proved" that its shaving cream was superior because it was thicker, while the other "proved" that its cream was superior because it wasn't. The Mennen Company, in a commercial for its Sof' Stroke aerosol shaving cream, showed a skin diver attempting to shave underwater. When he tried to use the "other brands" they dissipated in the water like soapsuds; when he applied Sof' Stroke, however, it went on thick and smooth and stayed on until he shaved. Proof of its richness, said the announcer. Proof that Sof' Stroke mixed with toothpaste was thicker, said the FTC. Mennen signed a consent order. In the opposite case, Carter Products and its advertising agency (Sullivan, Stauffer, Colwell & Bayles) were cited for a Rise shaving-cream commercial. In this demonstration, which took place abovewater, an actor applied "ordinary" shaving cream to his face; it dried out while he was still shaving, making him wince with pain as he attempted to cut through it. When he put on Rise, however, the razor moved smoothly down his cheeks for a gentle, close shave. Proof that Rise was creamier, said the announcer. Proof that the actor was clean shaven before the second demonstration, the FTC said, also observing that the first goop wasn't "ordinary" shaving cream but a special quick-drying substance especially concocted for the tests. Carter and its agency fought back, and while the court agreed with the Commission's decision on the merits, it set aside the order, suggesting clarification in its language.

The Rapid Shave "sandpaper test" first appeared on TV screens in the latter half of the 1950s. In December 1964, Colgate and Bates carried their appeal to the U.S. Supreme Court, conceding, in effect, that the commercial was false and misleading, but challenging the FTC on grounds that its order would render impossible the use of substitute materials in proving real claims. Representing the FTC, Philip B. Heymann of the Justice Department explained that the agency had no objection to the use of mock-ups or props so long as the audience wasn't told or given the impression that it was seeing genuine proof. "This case is not about mock-ups," he said. "It's about misrepresentations."

"What about those ads I've seen on television," Justice Arthur J. Goldberg asked, "of an aspirin going down and around and around . . . ?"

"Your Honor," Heymann replied, "I don't think anyone in the country believes that's a real stomach."[2]

On April 6, 1965, the Supreme Court, by a seven to two vote, upheld the FTC order. Attempting to interpret the complex decision as to what was and was not acceptable, CBS commentator Eric Sevareid concluded it meant "a fake is a fake, but a genuine fake isn't."

Meanwhile, back at the studio, something of a *non sequitur* was supplied in the otherwise undeceptive Alka-Seltzer commercials which appeared in the fall of 1964 and ended with the line: "We couldn't say that on television if it weren't true."

The television screen is at best a flat microcosm. For a wide-screen, cinemascopic view of three-dimensional wordsmithing in practice, let's switch to the marketplaces of America. But first, for just a moment, let's visit briefly with one of our earliest native American wordsmithers.

Jefferson Randolph "Soapy" Smith has been called "the grand-daddy of American con men," and while this isn't strictly true—he had a number of remarkable predecessors—he did provide some of the more memorable moments in the history of American swindlery.

There was the time, in '98, when Soapy, together with his Denver criminal brethren and sistren, joined the rush to the Klondike. On reaching Skagway, Soapy arrived at the same decision which provided the basis for some of America's greatest family fortunes: it was far easier to take the gold from the miners than from the ground. With this in mind, he rented a makeshift store and hired a painter to make up a large sign. The moment the sign was hung, the second rush was on, for Soapy, aware of the loneliness of the miners, had chosen his words carefully. The sign simply read TELEGRAPH OFFICE.

For $5 Soapy would accept a telegram to anyplace in the world. If the miner would return in two or three hours, and he invariably did, for another $5 he would hand him a collect reply. Soapy didn't actually say he would send the telegrams, nor that he had actually received the answers—he just supervised the operation while his assistants collected the money and composed reassuring replies.

When word finally got around that there was no telegraph line out of Skagway, Soapy had a new sign made. This one read INFORMA-TION OFFICE. For a fee Soapy would, among other things, give directions, help the miners write out their claims, and give advice on the safest place to store gold. At its worst, it was half-truth word-smithing. Soapy in turn sold this information to a gang of robbers, burglars, and claims jumpers.

But it is with Soapy's earlier history that we are concerned here, and the derivation of his nickname. He came by this, and his first fortune, on the streets of Denver, working his own modification of the shell game. Instead of using three nutshells and a pea, he used several bars of soap and a U.S. greenback. While his audience watched, the distinguished Mr. Smith would take a $5 bill and wrap it around a bar of soap, which he would then rewrap identically with the other bars stacked up before him. He would then shuffle the bars, carefully, so as not to confuse his prospective marks, who would wager $3 that they could pick the right bar. And they often did—at first. (Of course they were *shills*, in Smith's employ, who later had to return what they'd won.) Increasing the size of the bills and the bets, he would then trim his real marks. It is said that even his fellow con men could never determine at just which point Soapy palmed the bill. It may well be that, in time, Soapy Smith's real claim to fame will be that he was the granddaddy of one of America's most popular games—*deceptive packaging*.

If you entered a grocery store in the early years of this century,

the shelves that confronted you offered such an abundance of choice
—perhaps as many as 300 separate items, only a small number of
which were packaged and labeled—that to be sure of obtaining the
best quality, quantity, and cost, you had to rely heavily on the
knowledgeability and suggestions of your grocer.

Today there are some 7000 separate items on the shelves of the
average neighborhood supermarket. Most are prepackaged, and
most of the packages have labels. Yet the contents are now often a
mystery to both buyer and seller.

Once the grocer did the selling. Today the package is the salesman, and while one hesitates to accuse anyone of lying, a very great
number of packages are doing just that.*

Item: A box of macaroni and cheese. On the front of the box the
label reads "Serves 4 to 6." On the side of the box the label says "A
complete meal for 3 or 4 persons." Contents: an adequate side dish
for 2.

Item: Two packages of beef steaks, same company, same brand.
First label: "8 oz. Serves 3." Second label: "7 oz. Serves 4."

Little fibs or little people?

Item: When the public discovered that its hot dogs were tasting
different lately, and learned that this was due to the excessive use
of "extenders" (such as nonfat dry milk, cereal, and starch), many
meat packers brought out ALL-MEAT FRANKFURTERS. Department of Agriculture inspectors have since found numerous instances
where only the label was changed.

Many packages don't exactly lie; they just don't tell the whole
truth.

Item: A 1-lb. package of bacon, the cellophane peek-a-boo
window showing lean slices, but not the fatty pieces at the side or
under the first layer.

Item: Meat or poultry, prepackaged in a cardboard tray, sealed

---

* We not only pay for believing the lie, we also pay for the ink with which it
was printed and the paper it was printed on. While the benefits of modern
packaging are obvious—greater purity, safety, attractiveness, and convenience
—most of us are unaware of what we pay for these benefits. By one conservative
estimate, that of Senator Philip A. Hart (Michigan), $10 million per year is
the direct cost to the consumer of the packaging of household items. This figures
out to about $190 per year for the average family, or, as California Consumer
Counsel Mrs. Helen Nelson has put it, "about $16 a month for containers—
which can't be eaten, can't be drunk, can't be used to clean with or wash with,
can't be used for anything except to stuff the garbage can. And then we have
to pay again to have them hauled away."

in cellophane, the cardboard conveniently hiding from view chunks of bone or fat. In reply to customer complaints, supermarket operators usually say the cardboard is essential to "absorb the juices." In several metropolitan areas, however, you can find meat and poultry prepackaged in cardboardless transparent plastic trays.

Some packages tell the truth, only they double it.

Item: A TV dinner with two thick and savory slices of roast beef depicted on the label, but only one inside the package.

Some tell the truth, only they reverse it.

Item: Feature credits. In Hollywood there are special mediation boards to determine who gets what billing in screen credits, printed advertisements, and on theater marquees. Unlike movie stars, however, packaged items have no such spokesmen. Consider the plight of the poor underrated bean, which for years has had to be content with the designation "Pork and Beans" when "Beans with a blob of pork fat" would be more fitting and accurate.

With a minimum of effort, you can find every form of wordsmithing, visual and verbal:

The simple substitute form. Item: Whether advertised on restaurant menus as Salisbury steak, ground tenderloin steak, ground sirloin steak, chuckburger, beefburger, or steakburger, or whether the meat-counter label identifies it as ground beef, ground chuck, ground round, chipped-beef steak, steak paddies, beef paddies, cube steak, sandwich steak, minute steaks, steakettes, or chopettes, it's still wordsmithed hamburger.

The simple superlative form. Item: The vanishing pint. Many soft drinks once bottled at 16 oz. are now bottled at 12, 14, and 15 oz. Others, like Coke, though remaining a full 16 oz., are advertised as "half-quarts."

The adjective superlative form. Item: When Pall Mall first introduced the term "King Size," it was illustrative of a difference— King-Size Pall Malls were longer than regular-size cigarettes. Today a scanning of the powdered-soap boxes in an average supermarket reveals the following sizes: King, Monarch, Regular, Thrift, Economy, Super Economy, Large Economy, Extra Large, Extra Large Economy, Giant, Family, and Jumbo. The Jumbo in one brand may be the Family in another, the Giant simply the Large. In one brand of toothpaste, the Giant size is larger than the Family size. In another brand, the Family size dwarfs the Giant. In still another, Large is the smallest size. If it is any consolation to puzzled consumers, manufacturers are sometimes confused too, or would appear to be.

In mid-1962 the FDA seized 5400 jars of Giant Economy-size Maxwell House coffee when it was found that they were priced at more per ounce than the smaller, regular-size jar.

There is a magic phrase now widely used in manufacturing and packaging circles but rarely heard by the consumer: *packaging to price at the retail level.* Unwordsmithed, this means increasing the price without increasing the price. This may sound impossible but it isn't. How is it done? By reducing the net contents without changing the price. And, often, without changing the size of the container.

Item: A well-known brand of soap powder, recently given the *New*-ballyhoo. The change: two ounces less powder and a sturdier cardboard box.

Item: The shrinking candy bar.

Item: For years many housewives preferred to buy canned fruits and vegetables—corn, green and waxed beans, beets, peas, apricots, peaches, pears, apple sauce—in the No. 2 can, which contained about 20 oz. Today there is a new No. 2 can, used by many of the major brands, which looks about the same, and feels about the same, but holds only 16 oz. To further complicate things, two other once-uncommon sizes have now become exceedingly common—the No. 303, which holds about 17 oz., and the No. 300, which holds about 14½ oz. It's hard to tell them apart unless you look for the numbers—which aren't always given.

Item: Razor blades. A package that in 1962 contained 21 blades in 1964 held 18; another dropped from 6 to 5; another from 5 to 4.

Item: Using more typewriter ribbons lately? A couple of years ago, one typewriter-ribbon manufacturer quietly cut a foot off his standard-size ribbons. Relatively speaking, he deserves more praise than blame, however, for at the same time several of his fellows were cutting a whole yard off theirs. All neglected to mention the change in the printed measurements, and it is unlikely that many outside the trade noticed, for what kind of person measures typewriter ribbons? Answer—a writer with writer's block.

Slack-fill is the descriptive, if impolite, term consumer groups use for one form of packaging to price. Occasionally the slack is simply left slack—the shopper takes home packaged air. But often the packer compensates with some type of "bulking," so that, although the net contents have diminished, the package feels the same to the purchaser. A breakfast cereal has more inner wrapping "for greater freshness." One brand of packaged mints has been made "extra fancy" by inserting colorful cardboard dividers between the mints.

Sometimes the change may even be made to look like an improvement or saving:

Item: The "stylishly thinner" lipstick.

Item: A package of pipe tobacco. The new handy cellophane inner pouch is included at no extra cost to the purchaser—or the packer, since it costs less than the tobacco it replaces.

Item: A frozen TV dinner that has actually dropped a few cents in price. In the name of competition? Hardly. Rather less meat and more potatoes and gravy. Substitution is one of the more popular forms of the game—less chicken, more noodles; fewer meat balls, more spaghetti; smaller peaches, more syrup.

Item: The curious case of the "balloon bread."

In 1947, lobbyists for the California baking industry succeeded in pushing through the state legislature a special bakers' dispensation law which made it legal to bake and sell a loaf of bread weighing only 15 oz. as a 1-lb. loaf, and a 22½-oz. loaf as a 1½-lb. loaf. Changing the legal definition of weights and measures might be considered quite an accomplishment, but during the 1950s the bakers went one better. Through the use of a new and revolutionary process, the dough of the 1-lb. (15-oz.) loaf was whipped with air so the finished loaf was as long, high, and wide as the 1½-lb. loaf. It appeared on grocery shelves at 2¢ less than regular loaves the same size, with the price in large block letters, the weight in almost microscopic print. The balloon technique was soon adopted in several adjoining states.

In 1959, California's Governor, Edmund G. "Pat" Brown, set up the special office of State Consumer Counsel and appointed economist Helen Ewing Nelson to the post.* Mrs. Nelson, as one of her first projects, took on the task of deflating balloon bread. Following an investigation and hearings, the California legislature passed a law requiring that the net-weight statement on bread wrappers be printed in lettering at least a quarter inch high, an important victory

---

* New York's former governor, Averell Harriman, pioneered the idea when he set up a Consumer Counsel attached to his office. Governor Nelson Rockefeller abolished the post, however, shortly after taking office. Several other states now have added or are considering adding similar posts, based largely on the California experiment. The office of the President's Special Assistant for Consumer Affairs, first advocated by President Kennedy, was created by President Johnson, and Mrs. Esther Peterson was appointed to the post in January 1964. The criticism and vitriol heaped on the Mesdames Nelson and Peterson by some advertising and business groups and their political spokesmen and trade magazines helps belie the claim that their efforts are "unnecessary."

which prompted similar legislation in Oregon and Arizona. (The Oregon law went still further and required that the term BALLOON BREAD be plainly printed on wrappers also. Challenged, the Oregon law has since been ruled constitutional.)

Undaunted, the bakers discovered other ways to play the game. One was by eliminating differences. When a housewife sees two loaves of bread, both the same size but one lower in price, it's just possible she'll wonder why and examine the wrapper a bit more carefully. In Oregon the 1-lb. balloon loaf is now priced the same as the regular 1-lb. loaf. California bakers reversed this logic. In California the balloon loaf has been made to appear extra-special. It's now priced 4¢ higher than the regular loaf. The High Cost = High Quality myth dies hard.

Another of Mrs. Nelson's goals has been to restore the lost ounces to California pounds by repealing the 1947 bakers' dispensation law. In a series of hearings in 1964, baking-industry spokesmen argued that it wasn't possible to bake a loaf that weighed exactly 16 or 24 oz. every time, due to the "uncertainties of baking dough." Mrs. Nelson countered by citing one baking company which maintained plants in California, Arizona, and Nevada. She wondered why it could bake 16- and 24-oz. loaves in the last two states but not the first; she wondered, too, why the California loaf should cost the same as the Nevada loaf and more than the one made in Arizona.

Once upon a time there was an expression—"a baker's dozen."

If it appears that only those on the West Coast are privileged enough to be able to purchase whipped air, it should be noted that shoppers in all fifty states have found that a pint of ice cream when melted quite often weighs considerably less than 16 oz.

The extent to which the consumer is victimized by slack-packing depends almost entirely on the concern (if any) exhibited by state governments. Only recently have federal agencies begun to show interest in the subject.

Item: The Papercraft case. In June of 1962, the FTC issued its first slack-pack complaint since the 1930s, charging the Papercraft Corp., Pittsburgh, Pennsylvania, with deceptively packaging its gift wrappings. One Papercraft gift-wrap box, for example, was 24 inches long; along one side of the box there was a transparent acetate "window" through which one could see the roll of gift-wrap paper inside. This was an excellent example of the visual form of half-truth wordsmithing; while the shopper might *assume* the width of the paper was the same as that of the box, 24 inches, the roll was actually only 20 inches, ending just beyond the window on either side, leaving 2 inches of slack at both ends. Papercraft had told no lie; the correct width of the paper, 20 inches, was plainly printed on the box. Deceptive? Papercraft thought not, using as basis for its request for dismissal a long-standing court decision against the FTC which stated that the protection of the "foolish and feeble-minded" was outside the jurisdiction of the agency. Noting that in this instance it was the average shopper who would be deceived—that most people bought gift wrap by sight rather than by actual measurement—and generously finding the average shopper neither foolish nor feeble-minded, the Commissioners found the ruling inapplicable to the present case and, after a year and a half of litigation, upheld the initial cease-and-desist order. One sentence from the order should prove important in future slack-fill cases: "For the seller to package goods in containers which—unknown to the consumer—are appreciably oversized, or in containers so shaped as to create the optical illusion of being larger than conventionally shaped containers of equal or greater capacity, is as much a deceptive practice, and an unfair method of competition, as if the seller were to make an explicit false statement of the quantity or dimensions of his goods."

Slack-fill often occurs in the company of a variety of other deceptions. Item: Mixed nuts. "Anyone who plans to buy ready-mixed nuts for his holiday parties had better be sure that the guests are particularly fond of peanuts or cashews," noted *Consumer Reports* in its November 1964 issue, after Consumers Union shoppers bought four samples of each of thirty-one brands in seventeen cities across the country and checked them. ". . . These two types of nut so vastly exceed all others in most cans that one might suspect on occasion that the Brazil nuts, almonds, pecans, or filberts got in by mistake—except that they were listed on the label." And depicted on many of the labels, too, were tasty-looking heaps of nuts in which those particular types were "curiously prominent." Checking illustrations against contents, Consumers Union found a wide gulf between art and reality. The label on one can showed about 20 percent peanuts; the contents measured out to 65 percent peanuts. Another label depicted 25 percent pecans; the actual pecan content was 4 percent. Under federal law the weight of each type nut needn't be specified on the container; all that is required is that the types be listed in descending order of prominence by weight. One brand confused the order; three didn't even bother to list it. "Seeing double was another failing," the magazine noted; "several brands named pecans or almonds in the plural when there was only one pecan or almond present . . ." One brand, playing it safe, had a label reading "pecans or Brazil nuts or both." A majority of the cans were slack-fill bulked, the nuts inside the tin packed in oversize paper muffin cups. Nutmeat packers defend this practice with the argument that it protects the nuts against breakage; oddly enough, *Consumer Reports* found that the proportion of broken nuts was less in those containers without the paper fillers.

Item: Feminine beauty is quite often a matter of deceptive packaging (and, occasionally, of slack-fill bulking also). Most of us feel that in this area a little artifice enhances reality. The packaging of beauty aids is another matter. One day in the fall of 1962, a Ventura, California, housewife was shampooing her hair when her jar of Clairol Shampoo and Hair Conditioner slipped through her hands, hit the tub and broke. Cleaning up the mess she made an odd discovery: the jar had a false bottom and false sides. She gathered the pieces of glass and sent them to the state Bureau of Weights and Measures. What began as a quiet investigation, with a few sample purchases, quickly became a scandal involving many of the biggest names in the women's cosmetic field. In January 1963, state Attorney General Stanley Mosk revealed that his investigators had found evidence that twenty-three firms were allegedly violating the state's deceptive-packaging statute. California is one of the few states to have such a law; it provides that "no container wherein commodities are packed shall have a false bottom, false side walls, false lid or covering, or be otherwise so constructed or filled, wholly or partially, to facilitate the perpetration of deception or fraud." In a news conference the Attorney General stated that only a few of the firms were guilty of actual shortweighting, but he alleged that all had engaged in deceptive packaging with one or more products, and he showed newsmen a variety of containers—plastic and glass— which held less cosmetics than outside appearances would indicate. The courts later overruled the Attorney General, however, and the charges were dropped, leaving the standing of California's law in doubt.

Clairol was later brought to trial in the Sacramento Municipal Court of Judge James McDonnell, but only on the shortweight charge. Forrest H. Darby, county sealer of weights and measures, testified that during the investigation 174,382 jars of the Clairol product were confiscated, most of them about one-third of an ounce short of their listed weight. Clairol, Darby alleged, was making about

25¢ per jar on shortweight. "When you consider this product is sold on a nationwide basis," Darby said, "25 cents a jar is a lot of money." Clairol pleaded *nolo contendere,* or no contest, declaring in a statement filed with the court that the plea was not a confession but only a convenience to save the government and itself the expense and annoyance of further proceedings. Judge McDonnell fined the firm $276.

The fine is not unusual. Shortweight violations are almost always misdemeanors, with a maximum penalty of $500 and/or six months in jail. The first is so frequent it rarely makes the newspapers, the second rare enough to rate headlines. In the same city one year earlier, county sealer Darby signed a complaint charging Armour and Company with shortweighting packaged frankfurters after a prior warning. Pleading guilty, but claiming the weight difference was due to evaporation, Armour was fined $250. To investigate and prosecute such a case costs the taxpayer a minimum of $2000. Federal penalties are somewhat higher, as are the costs of investigation and prosecution. In 1961, the Quaker Oats Company adopted a new process which expanded the size of their grains of Puffed Rice and Puffed Wheat, but neglected to note the change in weight on their packages. An investigation by the FDA resulted in criminal action on six counts of shortweighting. Quaker Oats pleaded *nolo contendere,* was fined the maximum of $1000 on each count, or a total of $6000. FDA investigators had previously estimated that the shortages "saved" the company some $70,000 in a period of six months. If the FDA estimate was correct, the net result of the incident was a net profit for the company of about $64,000, minus largely tax-deductible legal fees.

In recent years numerous lawmakers have observed that the fine is no longer effective either as penalty or deterrent when applied to large businesses or corporations, yet these are typical cases, indicative of only one area where legislation has not kept pace with modern merchandising. Another thing hasn't changed. In an ordinary robbery or burglary or embezzlement, sometimes a portion of the loot is recovered and returned to the victim. This never happens when a company robs the consumer through shortweight or similar practices. It's a different story, however, when one company steals from another.

During the course of this book, as we journey through this often dishonest land of ours, it seems fitting that we should pause occasionally to look in mirrors or reflective store windows along the way to see just what the vulnerable American looks like. Since intense self-study can be frightening, for the time being we'll stick to brief glimpses, which we'll mold into generalizations or maxims. Being generalizations, many of them may not fit you, though they may describe your neighbors.

Maxim: The most vulnerable American is the semiprotected American who complacently believes he's fully protected by the law, its enforcers, and all the agencies of government.

Because the Food and Drug Administration exists, we believe we are, except in very rare instances, safe from impure food. In October 1964, a typical recent month, FDA inspectors seized 298 tons of contaminated food. Depending on one's point of view, this is either reassuring or frightening. That same month the FDA announced plans to step up food-plant inspections to "at least once a year."

Because the Department of Agriculture exists, we believe that the meat we buy is unadulterated and free from taint. It is doubtful whether more than one out of ten Americans looks for the USDA seal when purchasing meat. Most of us just assume that it is there, that we are being looked after. In reality you may have to visit a number of stores before finding meat with the seal. The reason is simple. The USDA only inspects meat sold in interstate commerce. And more and more of the national-brand packers have diversified their production to regional plants supplying large-population centers, where their products do not have to cross state lines to be sold. There is no federal-state program which requires uniform mandatory inspection of all meat. Bills to set up such a program have been introduced in Congress repeatedly, and just as repeatedly defeated.

Name a federal agency and you will find a similar situation. Our protection, more often than not, depends to a great measure on three things: (1) the standards and reliability of the manufacturer, producer, or seller; (2) the adequacy of state and municipal regulations; and (3) the degree of their enforcement. A breakdown in any one of the three and we are vulnerably exposed.

Maxim: The vulnerable American has a tendency to believe that once an abuse is pointed out, and remedial action taken, the abuse stays corrected.

That great pessimistic-optimist Upton Sinclair admits that he once believed this to be true. When his book *The Jungle* appeared, exposing conditions in the Chicago stockyards, the public hue and cry resulted in sweeping changes in our federal meat-inspection system. Revisiting one of the Chicago packing companies a few years later,

Sinclair saw just how one such change worked. When the federal inspectors examined a piece of meat and found it unfit for human consumption, the butchers dropped it through a hole in the floor, where it was loaded onto a truck and delivered to a local market.

To most of us the term *shortweight* conjures up the image of our gullible grandparents failing to notice the butcher's heavy thumb on the scale. We feel we are separated from such practices by time, laws, and abundant numbers of municipal, state, and federal weights-and-measures investigators. The period clothing needs to be changed for modern garb, and the image made current, for there is more shortweight fraud today than at any time in the past. Time has corrected only one major abuse—rigged scales are rarely encountered, but the change is due as much to the advent of pre-packaging as to fear of detection.* In this area, legislation is not fully concurrent with fraud practices in any state. Even in those few states where the laws are barely adequate, their enforcement is another matter, for there are at present fewer than 4000 weights-and-measures inspectors in the whole of the United States. Badly understaffed and usually overworked (as are most of our "protectors"), they rely primarily on customer complaints (few bother, and most remain blissfully unaware of their loss) and "spot checks." The latter can prove amazingly revealing.

In a recent year, Nassau County, New York, inspectors check-weighed: 39,000 1-lb. cartons of butter—4460 were underweight; 8700 cheese packages—1150 were short of the marked amount; 28,000 packages of prepacked meat—3525 shortweight; and 27,000 quarts of milk—5000 didn't make the full 32 ounces. After a Los Angeles County spot check of 815,000 food containers, nearly 40,000

---

* There has been one recent notable exception. In early 1964 a fraud was uncovered in eastern Colorado which has caused considerable apprehension in weights-and-measures departments across the country. A livestock feeder regularly purchased enormous quantities of feed grain from truckers, weighing the loads in his own scale house. An unidentified person or, far more likely, persons, rigged the scale to operate in much the same way the electronic carport door operates. The electronic device, together with a piece of heavy metal, was placed under the scale house; when activated, presumably by remote control from a nearby car, the metal could be raised or lowered, causing the scale beam to go up or down as a truck moved onto the scales. As many as 30,000 extra pounds might be recorded. The operators fled as soon as the device was discovered. Henry Duff, supervisor of the Weights and Measures section of the Colorado Department of Agriculture indicated why the weight-watchers are so greatly concerned: "If electronic devices can be used dishonestly on big scales, they can also be used on small ones."[3]

were condemned for shortweight, short measure, or slack-fill. In Wisconsin, in a single month, inspectors check-weighed 16,000 packages of meat, poultry, and potatoes—more than a third failed to make the listed weight.[4]

Sometimes protection is nonexistent. Three states—Arkansas, Delaware, and Mississippi—have virtually no weights-and-measures enforcement.[5] In many states the work week of the inspectors officially ends on Friday at 5 P.M., leaving the gypsters inspection-free weekends. The situation is so apparent in one midwestern state that customers have nicknamed Saturday "Thumb Day." And, although less common, occasionally there is collusion. In November 1959, a major scandal erupted in New York City's weights-and-measures department when it was learned that a number of investigators were accepting bribes to overlook violations. One such inspector, apparently well-versed in the traditions of Tammany, had formed a "Butcher's Club," with an "initiation fee" of $75 and "dues" of $50 to $60 each month thereafter.

Let's look at some of the tricks, starting with a limited unit operation—the filling station. The filling-station operator may not start the gasoline pump at zero. He may dispense gasoline from one pump and then charge the unobservant driver the higher toll on the adjoining pump. He may switch octanes. He may rig the pump so it feeds air as well as gasoline. He may fail to push the dipstick all the way down when checking oil, and then put in only part of a quart. In a supermarket, opportunities multiply in ratio to the number of products, with the difference that in cases of fraudulent packaging the victim may never see the person or persons responsible for the swindling.

Item: Way back in the nineteenth century, there was a semi-illiterate, whiskey-soaked rustic known as Daniel (Uncle Dan) Drew. The tale of Drew's battle with Commodore Vanderbilt over the Erie Railroad, and his crooked partnership with Jim Fisk and Jay Gould, are so well known as to need no recounting here. It is with Drew's early years that we are concerned, and with an expression he helped coin. As a young cattle drover, Drew would feed his herds salt, let them suffer awhile, then, just before he was ready to sell them, let them drink almost to bursting. When he arrived on Wall Street, the term "watered stock" came with him.

Drew's trick may be old but it isn't outdated. Shortly before taking his birds to market, a turkey rancher may take a large hypodermic needle and inject water into each bird—increasing the weight by as

much as two pounds. The purchaser, a poultry shopper for a supermarket chain, thus starts out with a shortweight bird. To compensate (and sometimes overcompensate), the butcher or packer has
tricks of his own, some legal, others near-undetectable. If the bird
is to be sold prestuffed, the solution is simple: increase the amount of
the cheaper stuffing. This is quite legal. Present Department of Agriculture regulations require that the label list only the total weight of
the bird with stuffing; by the USDA directive, it is actually illegal
to break down the weight into meat and stuffing. Only New York
State has a law requiring this, and it was recently challenged. On
grounds that the federal law excludes any state regulation, and that
in any event the two laws conflict, with precedence given the federal
law, Swift and Armour in 1964 asked a U.S. District Court to enjoin
New York State from enforcing its law. The three-judge panel ruled
in favor of the state, observing that in certain circumstances a state
has a right to require "a higher standard for the protection of its
consumers."[6]

If you're a housewife, residing in any of the other forty-nine states,
the following will probably come as no surprise. The amount of
stuffing can and often does run as high as 30 percent. A housewife
may plan her Thanksgiving dinner around a 7-lb. turkey to find that
only 5 of those pounds are actual meat.

When the turkey is sold frozen, weight fraud is even cheaper—to
the defrauder. Though a hypodermic injection of water at this stage
would be easily detected, the packer can achieve the same effect by
putting pieces of ice inside the bird; the evidence melts when the
turkey is thawed. Even the ordinary freezing process adds water-
weight to the bird, according to Consumers Union. When a bird is
to be frozen it is first soaked in a chill bath, to make it look plump
and waxy. During this process the bird absorbs moisture; the amount
varies, but as much as 2 lbs. on a 12-lb. 11-oz. bird has been reported.[7]

Almost any meat or poultry product—fresh or frozen—can be
watered to add at least a few unnoticeable ounces. Due to another
odd Department of Agriculture ruling, circa 1960, packers of smoked
meats can play the water game to the extent of increasing the weight
of their product, from purchase to sale, to 116 percent. In buying a
smoked ham, for example, the consumer may pay $1.16 for each $1
of actual meat. This is justified by the argument that the consumer
wants his meat "juicier." Some feel, however, that the order is less
an acceptance of this justification than an attempt to make the best
of a *fait accompli* that only a larger number of inspectors could

correct. In buying ham, water isn't the only extra added expense. The gel surrounding a large canned refrigerated ham consistently accounts for about one-tenth of the weight; with a small ham it is closer to one-fourth.

Item: At least one nationwide supermarket chain forces its meat-department managers and butchers to steal from customers at the risk of losing their jobs, but does this with nary a mention of that offensive word "shortweight." To illustrate how this works, in a simplified example, the meat manager at one of the chain's stores receives from the purchasing supply department a frozen side of beef that weighs 300 lbs. Thawed, it may weigh 265 lbs., and cut up 250 lbs. But the main office of the chain allows only 10 percent for shrinkage. The managers and butchers must make up the difference—in this case 20 lbs.—or be held accountable.

As indicated in Vance Packard's *The Wastemakers,* the packaging-to-price game may be played by altering the quality rather than (or as well as) the quantity of a product. The use of additives to make meat look fresher or better is still common. Early in 1964 the New York City Department of Markets received a complaint that a local packer was adding blood to cheap, fatty, chopped meat and selling it as rich, lean hamburger. After an investigation that required some six months, inspectors managed to catch the offender in the act. The firm pleaded guilty and was fined $100. A similar case a few months earlier, involving a supermarket charged with adulterating and misbranding hamburger, resulted in a $50 fine. Other common adulterants sometimes added to ground meat include coal-tar colors, cochineal, sulfites, nitrites, and ascorbic acid. That some of these—particularly, a salt of sulfurous acid—are dangerous to the consumer doesn't deter the operators. But there are far better (i.e. legally safer) ways to maintain the illusion of freshness. One is simply to use indirect lighting, which bathes vegetables with green light and covers meat with a becoming roseate glow. This is legal in almost all states. "The light keeps the meat from turning," butchers will tell you, completely straight-faced.

In addition to deceptions of quantity and quality, there are those of cost. In 1962, California's Consumer Counsel, Mrs. Helen Nelson, decided to conduct a shopping test to see how a shopper might fare in a typical unarmed encounter with a supermarket.[8] According to a then current DuPont supermarket survey, the average shopper on an average visit bought 13.7 items. Mrs. Nelson drew up a list of 14 items. These were all packaged products, common staple foods and household necessities: white rice, solid-pack canned tomatoes, hot cereal, cheddar cheese, canned tuna, salt, pancake mix, imitation maple syrup, peanut butter, liquid detergent for washing dishes by hand, liquid shampoo, toilet soap, toilet tissue, and dog food.

A typical supermarket in the Sacramento area was chosen and surveyed. Among these 14 items, the store offered a total of 246 possible choices. Five housewives were then selected to participate in the test; though picked at random, they were not average shoppers—each had had some college training as well as considerable family-marketing experience. Their instructions were deceptively simple: to make their selections solely on the basis of the largest quantity at the lowest cost. Each of the five women was given $10 and set loose in the supermarket to buy the 14 items. Though allowed as much time as needed, they were clocked from the time they entered the store until they reached the checkout counter.

The DuPont survey gave an average shopping time of 27 minutes. Only one of the women came in under the wire, at 25 minutes; the other four took, respectively, 35, 40, 55, and 60 minutes.

How did they fare? To understate the results, badly. All five did succeed in picking the lowest-priced package of one item, cheddar cheese, each correctly (and one suspects luckily) choosing the cheapest package. But this was the only one. In the cases of 2 of the 14 products, all five were baffled. In summary, with better-than-average educations, and better-than-average time spent (averaging twice as long as the typical DuPont-survey woman), these five housewives, confronted with 246 separate packages and told to choose 70 (or 14 apiece), succeeded 36 times and failed 34.

Why?

Item: There were 14 different packages of white rice; not one was in a 1-lb. package. The same was true of the 6 packages of salt, which ran a confusing range from $4/10$ oz. to 5 lbs. Imitation maple syrup (7 choices) was available in miscellaneous ounces, pints and ounces, pounds and ounces, and one easily decipherable half-gallon. Toilet tissue was packed in rolls of 650, 800, and 1000 sheets, some single-, some double-ply. Of the 10 cans of tuna, none was 1 lb. or ½ lb., 7 were in fractional ounces. And so it went through the other products: a bewildering array of hungry pounds, thirsty pints and quarts, and vanishing designations.

Item: Of the 25 packages of toilet soap, only 5 bore a statement of weight. The soap manufacturers form a totally "self-regulated" group, free of FDA control. But here it was perhaps best that the shoppers weren't given exact measurements, if only for reasons of sanity, for when later weighed, the 25 packages were found to come in 15 different sizes: $5\frac{6}{16}$ oz.; $3\frac{11}{16}$ oz.; $4\frac{12}{16}$ oz.; $3\frac{12}{16}$ oz.; $3\frac{10}{16}$ oz.; 1 lb. $13\frac{5}{16}$ oz.; 1 lb. $7\frac{6}{16}$ oz.; 1 lb. $\frac{1}{2}$ oz.; $14\frac{4}{16}$ oz.; $14\frac{9}{16}$ oz.; $10\frac{1}{2}$ oz.; $13\frac{9}{16}$ oz.; $6\frac{2}{16}$ oz.; $4\frac{7}{8}$ oz.; $4\frac{9}{16}$ oz.

Item: On most of the products the price range was wide. Per pound, dog food ranged from 9¢ to 19¢, salt from 5¢ to $1.46, tuna from 63¢ to $1.23, pancake mix from 13¢ to 47¢, peanut butter from 40¢ to 77¢. Liquid shampoo went from 79¢ to $3.68 per pint. All of this was hindsight, however, carefully computed later with slide rules, scales, and adding machines. None of the women had access to these aids, nor did they carry a price-computing wheel. Mrs. Nelson is decidedly skeptical of the value of the latter device, some dozen of which are currently available as consumer aids. "How often do you see one in use in the supermarket?" she asks. "The few enthusiastic letters I get about them come mostly from their manufacturers . . ."[9] The reason why is obvious: what woman has the time to make 246 separate calculations to buy 14 commonplace items?

Mrs. Nelson's shopping test did not take into account a number of miscellaneous factors.

Item: Given prices and weights, a computing wheel, and a patient, unhurried, unembarrassed shopper, it is possible to determine the price per pound or quart, but, assuming one is interested, how do you determine the added value of premiums: the peanut butter jar that is also a decorated tumbler; the factory-second wash-cloth in the box of soap powder (displacing just how much soap?); the information on the $275,000 "Check the Values" contest? How valuable are the one, two, and three "value coupons" (good for stainless steel, silverware, or cookbooks); the special offer on mother-daughter dresses (you'll have to buy the package to see, for details of the special offer are inside); the flower seeds and bulbs offer; the offer of three silverplate teaspoons for one boxtop plus 50¢, or the cloth doll for one boxtop and 30¢, or the baby spoon for one boxtop and 40¢? How much is it worth to be charitable—if you send the one-per-package coupon to the Pilot Guide Dog Foundation, Perk Foods Co. will pay 50¢ for each 100 coupons received; or to be hopefully selfish—the chance to win a thirteen-day Caribbean vacation for two? (One might better ask how much such promotional gimmicks are costing you, whether you take advantage of them or not.)

Item: And what if the store also offers trading stamps? How much are they worth as a factor in computing prices?* As a sort of reverse clue, they cost the dealer an average of 20¢ per 100 stamps; though ostensibly free to the customer, he pays for them in adjusted prices. "The only people I know who say that stamps don't raise prices are the people who own stamp companies," says Safeway president Robert A. Magowan. Stephen Mugar, president of the Star Market Co., which has thirty-two supermarkets in the Boston area, says, "I think that stamps, now that all of us have them, have simply added 2 percent to the food-cost index of this country."[10]

Item: How much does the shopper save on free, two-for-one, half-price, 50 percent off, 1¢, and similar sales? Little or nothing, if the seller increases the ordinary and usual price of the article; if he decreases its quality and/or quantity; or if he pricemanships fictitious first prices together with odd sizes, as did one toothpaste manufacturer who offered a special on two Medium-size tubes, computing the "savings" not on the basis of what these two tubes regularly cost but on what the customer would have spent if he had bought the same quantity in multiples of the more expensive Small size.

Take this special offer (on second thought, just consider it):

SUPER WALL LATEX PAINT
$6.98 GAL $2.25 QT
EVERY 2ND CAN FREE

But is it? In several recent cases the FTC thought not, pointing out that since the companies had always sold their paint in this manner, no regular or retail price for the first can had been established, so that the second can was neither free nor a savings.

Item: The "cents off" offer—how much does one save? Careful on this one; if you think the answer is obvious—just what the offer states, 5¢ OFF, 10¢ OFF, etc.—then you may be a vulnerable

---

* Then, too, there is the matter of coupons packaged with the product. The wife who yearns for an Autumn Haze Mink Stole by Renoir would be well-advised to get her husband to switch to Alpine cigarettes, which offers this premium at only 47,185 coupons. If he switches at age 25, and buys a package a day, he could redeem it for her at age 155; if he buys by the carton, however, he'll not only save money but get 4 extra coupons, which will enable him to redeem it sooner, at age 119. If both husband and wife smoked, and both switched at 25, and both bought by the carton, and neither inhaled, she could wear it on her 72nd birthday, assuming the offer was still good.

American. Though it may come as a shock to some economy-minded shoppers, the real answer is, *Quite often you save nothing at all.* Various consumer groups have conducted random surveys to prove this. Their proof was so amazing that the author decided to verify it for himself. Not long ago the manufacturer of a nationally distributed ready-mix whipping cream printed SPECIAL OFFER 10¢ OFF on each can of its product. Checking three neighborhood groceries and two large supermarkets, the author found cans priced at 69¢, 69¢, 71¢, 71¢, 73¢, and 75¢ (one supermarket had the same can at two prices, 71¢ and 73¢). These were the prices the retailers had marked on the cans. In each store, the author asked the manager or owner if the price was the marked amount minus 10¢. In one neighborhood store he was answered in the affirmative. Elsewhere he was told that the marked price already reflected the savings. (This is the usual practice.) Checking revealed, however, that the marked price on the item in all five stores was the same before, during, and after the time the offer was made. In short, only one store honored the special offer; the other four ignored it, and when questioned about it, their representatives, either knowingly or unknowingly, lied.

The cents-off offer is meaningless when the dealer ignores it. It's also meaningless when offered by a manufacturerer on a semipermanent basis. Noticing that the labels on jars of Ehlers Instant Coffee had borne cents-off legends for a rather lengthy period of time, Consumers Union queried the company as to whether its coffee was ever offered at a regular undiscounted price. In reply, the company stated that, while they had used regular labels without the special offer in the past, they hadn't done so for the past several years.

Maxim: The confused American is an especially vulnerable American.

How extensive are these and similar practices? Mildred Edie Brady, Consumers Union's representative, testifying before the Senate Antitrust and Monopoly Subcommittee in 1962, observed "the honestly packaged product has become enough of an exception to the rule that we at Consumers Union are now receiving letters from readers asking us to comment on the event when they happen to find an honestly branded product." Over the past two years, Mrs. Brady said, Consumers Union had received complaints involving over 200 different product lines—kinds of products, not just brands. "Let no one suppose that the companies whose brands are named are small concerns," she added. "This is not one of those situations where a barrel is condemned because of a few rotten apples. The biggest names on supermarket shelves are among the brands most often complained about." She then read a list of forty-nine well-known company names.[11]

How much do these small but common and multitudinous practices cost us? No one knows for certain. One noted food economist estimates that such chicanery probably claims from $3 to $5 of the average family's weekly food budget.

The consumer isn't entirely alone in his confusion. He has numerous allies in what may at times seem to him to be the enemy camp.

The grocer who has to provide valuable shelf space for an increasing number of odd-size packages, as well as tentative answers to basically unanswerable customer queries, is often as disturbed by the plethora of strange weights, cryptic designations, and intentional deceptions as is the shopper.

Several large packing companies have voluntarily acted to lessen consumer confusion by adopting unit-cost labeling for their products, the label plainly disclosing this price for this weight at so much per pound. Some large grocery chains have done likewise. Quentin Reynolds, senior vice-president of Safeway Stores, Inc., recently stated the policy of his chain as follows: "We believe in labeling so the contents are readily understandable by the consumer." It is Safeway policy, according to Reynolds, that prepackaged meats be identified "by clear and concise labeling of the product with exact weight and price per pound." Safeway even disapproves of can-size designations: "We prefer ounces."[12]

Occasionally a trade association will act in the consumer's behalf. At present the package sizes of only a few products are regulated by law. Milk is one, liquor another. The U.S. Treasury Department's Internal Revenue Service, in addition to other assorted duties, is responsible for the regulating of bottle sizes for distilled spirits. By federal law these are standard: one gallon, half gallon, one quart, four-fifths quart, one pint, half pint, one-eighth pint, one-tenth pint, and (brandy only) one-sixteenth pint. Several years ago a number of large distillers, finding their customers unwilling to go along with a proposed price increase, decided to join the packaging-to-price rush. Led by Schenley, the group attempted to build up enough industry pressure to persuade the Government either to (a) eliminate entirely all bottle-size standards, or (b) accept a new scale which included one-third gallon, one-sixth gallon, one-twelfth gallon, and one-twentieth gallon. The move failed when the board of directors of the Distilled Spirits Institute unanimously spoke out against it, saying "Years of public confidence should not be replaced by customer confusion and ill-will."

And there are those in advertising who believe that it is their business to inform as well as persuade the customer.

But, one must unhappily note, these appear to be the exceptions.

The average American may see little difference between the operator who sells books of discount tickets to World's Fair attractions which are ordinarily free or don't exist at all and the manufacturer who offers a "savings" nonexistent except in the realms of word-smithing and pricemanship. But the difference exists, and it isn't simply a matter of semantics. The first is violating the law; the second quite often is obeying it to the letter. Not only is he suited-in-respectability, but he wears over it a coat of near-invulnerability. And he has a strong voice.

Individual consumers constitute the largest spending group in our society. Their annual outlay of some $380 billion makes up nearly two-thirds of our $600 billion gross national product. Yet, ironically, here too size is deceptive, since it is not the number of voices but the way they are amplified that commands attention. For business has something the consumer doesn't have—a number of powerful, highly effective lobbies. The consumer is not without spokesmen, however, and many are highly vocal. When the Senate Judiciary Committee's Subcommittee on Antitrust and Monopoly began conducting hearings on Packaging and Labeling Practices in 1961, the number of speakers advocating increased legislation for greater consumer protection was far larger than the number who spoke out against it. On the consumer's side were representatives of consumer groups, women's organizations, Better Business Bureaus, labor unions, and numerous state and federal officials.

On the opposite side, not necessarily speaking against the consumer, but arguing that additional legislation was not to his best interests, were a smaller number representing the solidly united American food industry.

Which was the more effective? Before answering this question we should look at the bill which came out of the more than two years of hearings.

Introduced in the Senate by Philip A. Hart (Michigan) and in the House of Representatives by Emanuel Celler (New York) the bill had as its stated purpose "to prohibit restraints of trade carried into effect through the use of unfair and deceptive methods of packaging or labeling certain consumer commodities."

Its advocates called it a "Truth-in-Packaging" bill. Its opponents described it as "an unnecessary and unwarranted interference with development," "an undesirable delegation of legislative power," and "contrary to the best interests of consumers."

Just what were the provisions of this "undue" or "long-overdue" piece of legislation?

The bill called for a statement of net-weight content on the front panel of packages and the establishment of standards with respect to the location and type size of the weight declaration. It required that the label bear, in a prominent position, sufficient information about the ingredients and composition of the goods to enable the potential purchaser to make an informed choice. It called for the establishment of reasonable standards of weight and size (outlawing fractional ounces whenever they were avoidable, for example). And it called for the establishment of other quantity declarations (i.e. the meaning of "a serving").

It prohibited the use of quantity descriptive words (such as GIANT, BIG, and JUMBO) in the net-weight declaration. It prohibited deceptive pictures on packages. It prohibited "cents-off" legends as an integral part of a package's label (not prohibiting such offers, but outlawing the meaningless permanent-bargain type). And it prohibited the use of package sizes, shapes, and dimensional proportions which would tend to deceive the average consumer (the slack-filled package, the false-bottomed jar, the heavily indented bottle bottom, etc.).

"What it boils down to," said one national manufacturer, speaking before a group of his fellows on the West Coast, "is whether we run our businesses or whether we let the government run them for us."

"What it boils down to," said *Consumer Reports,* in its May 1963 issue, "is that the package shall not bear false witness."

Who won? When Congress adjourned in the fall of 1965 the bill was still securely bottled up in committee. As this is written, its passage in the current session seems doubtful.

One thing did come out of the long hearings, however, and that was a portrait of the average consumer, that creature we have with less than impartiality chosen to call the vulnerable American. Since we see a different face each time we look in the mirror, it is perhaps not too surprising that there was some disagreement as to his features, expression, attitude, and aptitudes. So much disagreement, in fact, that there actually emerged two portraits. On only one point was there basic agreement. The consumer groups argued that the expression on the face was one of concern; the opposing side didn't disagree—it merely argued that this concern was for entirely different things.

One side pictured him thusly:

The American consumer was intelligent, far more intelligent than the opposing side credited him with being. Not only intelligent enough to see through artifice when it occasionally occurred, but also informed enough to make intelligent choices without governmental aid. His first concern wasn't the exact weight of a product or its price in relation to other products—his first concern was quality. He had taste, discrimination, and decided personal preferences. If, for example, everyone in a household liked the flavor of a certain brand of ketchup, and all the other brands were cheaper, offering greater quantity at less cost, no amount of advertising and labeling could persuade him to buy another brand. More detailed labeling was unnecessary, because more often than not the consumer had already made up his mind long before going to market: he had brand loyalty. Moreover, the consumer rarely, if ever, reads labels. Asked his opinion on this last point, Dr. Ernest Dichter, President of the Institute for Motivational Research, agreed that it was true. "Unfortunately," Dr. Dichter said, "I must report we talked to tens of thousands of consumers and about the only label that a consumer ever reads is the content and proof on the liquor bottle."

So spoke one side. The portrait painted by the opposing side went as follows:

It wasn't so much that the American consumer lacked intelligence as that he often lacked the opportunity to exercise it. Faced with product differentiation, price differentiation, and deceptions of quality, quantity, and durability, offered bonuses of extraneous products or the added inducements of trading stamps, special discounts, and trade-ins, he was asked to choose wisely under circumstances which would baffle even the trained technician. As to his lack of interest in the prices he paid, then to whom were the cents-off deals, the two-for-one specials, the grocery ads with their prices in big black numerals intended? Admittedly, he often didn't read labels, but couldn't this be in large part because he could find little there in the way of helpful reading? True, he did have brand loyalty, but how long would he have it on discovering that the difference between two brands was all too often only a matter of pricing and packaging? As one of America's top package designers, Walter Landor, once put it: "As brands become more and more similar because of almost universal product improvement, package design grows in importance. In fact, increasingly the only discernible difference in brands IS the design of the package."

A third portrait emerged from the testimony at the hearings. Mrs. Brady, Consumers Union's representative, not only painted it in very few words, she managed to include a critical evaluation at the same time:

"The spectacle of some of the country's largest advertisers of consumer goods caught in competitive pickpocket activities is not a pretty one."

Confusion and deception do not constitute fraud *per se*. Taken separately, the wordsmithed commercial, the pricemanshiped bargain, packaging-to-price, shortweight, slack-fill, bulking, ballooning, false coloration, misleading representations, and similar practices are minor irritations. But taken together, layer upon layer, as they exist in the marketplaces of America today, they form a palimpsest for fraud, the climate in which it not only survives but flourishes.

Things *are* seldom what they seem. But sometimes too, sadly enough, they are *exactly* what they seem.

WHATEVER HAPPENED
TO THE OLD-FASHIONED
CON MAN

The United States cannot be called
the native land of the confidence
man, but there is something in the
trusting air of that country that
seems to develop some of the finest
flowers of the species.

Harry D. Söderman
Policeman's Lot

CHAPTER 3

THE MARK IN
THE MARKETPLACE

> Any student of the classic confidence games must be struck by the several parallels they present with some modern big-sell techniques. The confidence man sells nothing but himself, of course, while the salesman peddles more tangible merchandise; but the psychological techniques each employs are remarkably similar.
>
> Pierre Berton
> *The Big Sell*

IMAGINE for a moment, if you will, that the present and the past are coexistent, that each is here right now, no trick so old that somewhere it isn't new, no safeguard so effective that someone can't conceive a novel way to circumvent it, and you will have a satellite-like view of fraud in America today.

Many of the newest tricks are tricks once tried, for a time forgotten, then newly resurrected with only the outer trappings changed, the basic principles remaining the same, while others may contain the principles of several proven tricks, well blended and assimilated. Frauds are like currency. They can be hoarded away for a time and then put back into circulation. And they can be used singly, in part, or in combination. In this and succeeding chapters we'll look at some of these tricks, to see how they were and are now being played on that most trusting of marks, the vulnerable American.

The Bait and Switch

One day during the 1920s, Joseph "Yellow Kid" Weil visited the offices of an olive oil importing firm, introducing himself to the two owners as James R. Warrington, representative of the American Turf Association. Much to the surprise of the two Italians, both wise in the uses of olive oil, the dapper Mr. Warrington told them something about their product they didn't know: that the beautiful sheen on the coats of race horses was produced by frequent rubbings with none other than high-grade olive oil. This was the reason for his visit: the Association was interested in making a small purchase for testing to see if it met their exacting specifications.

How small, one of the partners asked.

Just a sample, Mr. Warrington replied, say five carloads.

The two partners exchanged quick looks. They had never sold as much as one whole carload to a single customer.

Of course, Mr. Warrington added, as though realizing they might think five carloads too trifling to bother with, if the oil proved satisfactory the Association would then place a "substantial" order.

While one partner was showing Mr. Warrington through the warehouse, letting him feel, taste, and smell their finest grades of oil, the other partner, who had remained in the office, noticed a piece of paper on the floor. Picking it up, he discovered it was a newspaper clipping, evidently fallen from Mr. Warrington's pocket.

The clipping was from *The Racing Form*. Under the headline WARRINGTON STUMPS THE EXPERTS/HANDICAPPER MAKES ANOTHER KILLING, was a picture of their visitor and a story recounting his fantastic winnings: race after race he won, through a secret system all his own. When the two men returned to the office and had concluded negotiations for Mr. Warrington's order—five carloads of olive oil to leave Italy on the next available ship—the partner handed Mr. Warrington the clipping, apologizing for having read it, but asking avidly, Was it true?

Mr. Warrington looked at *The Racing Form* story and laughed. No, it wasn't true. He had no "secret system." Because of his high position in the American Turf Association, he did occasionally hear certain reliable "tips." As a matter of fact, he just happened to have one on a race tomorrow. When Mr. Warrington-Weil, alias The Yellow Kid, departed, he took $2500 with him, leaving a promise to meet them at the track the following day. He never did learn what happened to the five carloads of olive oil.

"The switch is an important part of nearly all good confidence games," Weil observes in his rather fantastic memoirs. "The con man starts off on one deal, builds it up to a certain point, then something intervenes and the victim's interest is sidetracked to another scheme, where he is to be fleeced. The strange thing is that the victim forgets all about the original deal."[1]

But not always. Sometimes the original bait is made so tantalizing that the mark doesn't realize for some time that he has already been victimized on the switch. Weil set up one Chicago playboy heir for a rigged horse race, using the old "ringer" gambit. He had two identical horses—or so the mark was led to believe—one slow, the other extremely fast. His plan was to run the slow horse so often that the odds against its winning would rise astonomically; he would then substitute the ringer and make a huge killing. Weil used this particular mark for "cigar money"; he was too gullible to be taken once and let go. Every couple of weeks Weil would tap him $200 or $300 for some essential expense: a water sprinkler to moisten their private training track; a bribe for the jockey; one for each of the judges; a special saddle to conceal an electric-battery arrangement. He kept this up for sixteen months, between his more ambitious frauds, before growing bored with the mark and dropping him.

The modern correspondent of the bait and switch is *bait advertising*, ranked by the BBB as one of the most common of current consumer frauds.

Consider the following ads:

Item: Singer Sewing Machine, completely reconditioned, good as new, with ten-year guarantee, brand-new console, year's supply of free thread (5000 yards), plus free sewing lessons if desired. $19.95.

Item: One-owner 1963 Chevrolet 6 Impala, fully guaranteed, radio, heater, five new sidewall tires. Repossessed; buyer can have by taking over payments still due. $350.

Item: Latest-model famous-name refrigerator. Never used except as showroom demonstrator. Guaranteed $99.99.

Legitimate bargains or bait advertising? You can't be sure unless you visit the store or used-car lot, though one BBB maxim is apt: "If an advertised item sounds too good to be true it often is."

Bait advertising, also known as "switch-selling," can be used in hawking almost any commodity or service (including credit), but it is most prevalent in the area of "noncomparable merchandise," items such as cars, carpeting, aluminum siding, furs, furniture, home appliances, jewelry, pianos, vacuum cleaners, washing machines, radio and TV sets, merchandise about which the buyer is likely to be less than an expert, and satisfactory purchase of which is, at least in part, dependent on the honesty and reliability of the selling concern. Quite often, name brands are used. The bargain is generally just on the edge of believability, though the auto dealer could with no loss whatever offer that 1963 Impala for 1¢, since he has no intention of selling it. It's *bait*.

Once the customer has bitten and been pulled into the place of business, the technique is two-staged:

(1) By one means or another, the customer is dissuaded from buying the bait. Taking the customer into his confidence, the salesman may knock the item: The car is a clinker, the motor ready to fall out, the guarantee good for only seven days and then subject to numerous exceptions. Or the sewing machine is made in Formosa and illegally bears the Singer name—"We have a perfect record on this model; we've sold 812 and had 812 complaints." Or, "This is a late-model famous-name refrigerator, all right. In fact, it's the very last model the Icebox people made before they went bankrupt in the thirties. I'd open it and show you the insides, only the door has a tendency to drop off the hinges, and of course we can't get replacement parts."

Or, if the salesman wants to live dangerously, he may cut short the spiel and simply let the item speak for itself, which it does, eloquently. The woman who sets foot on the treadle and gets in return the sounds of a coffee grinder and a display of blue sparks, and the man who turns on the ignition and is surrounded by clouds of black smoke, usually have in common a hesitancy to rush to sign a contract. The danger in this, so far as the dealer is concerned, is that sometimes there is a rare customer, either simple-minded or an expert mechanic, who still wants to buy the item as is, exactly as advertised. For, as bad as it may seem, the bait (or the "fiddle," as it is sometimes known in the trade) may be worth more than the asking price. Many auto dealers have a standard policy of firing any salesman who is maneuvered into selling the bait; other firms threaten their salesmen with heavy fines if "nailed to the floor" merchandise is sold. In Missouri recently, a woman was so determined to buy a bait-advertised TV set that she finally threw down her money and attempted to carry her purchase out of the store with her. She left instead with a broken arm. Some firms, however, allow for the exception and provide their sales force with an easy out: the sale is made, and the contract signed, "subject to approval of the credit manager."

(2) Once the bait is made to lose its allure, the customer is switched to a similar but more expensive item. *Much* more expensive, at first, for the salesman usually starts high and makes concessions; just how much he will ultimately let the customer "save" depends upon the particular salesman. Almost all switch-selling is done from a par price. When the salesman makes a sale at par he receives a fixed commission, usually 15 percent. On whatever he gets over par, his commission is 50 percent. On anything below par he may forfeit half or all of his commission. Needless to say, the latter type sale is uncommon. Whatever the final price, one can be sure of two things: it will be made to seem a bargain, a special favor on the part of the salesman (usually in the business only because he "likes people," excluding his employer, of course), and it will be higher than if the item were purchased from a reliable dealer.

Once the heat is on a particular swindle, the successful confidence man will usually move to a less warm location or drop the con entirely for a time, substituting another. In his long career Weil never traveled very far from Chicago; however, he had in his repertory literally dozens of big and small cons in which he was proficient.*

The modern salesconman is more conservative, more firmly rooted, less anxious for change, more inclined to try variations on a theme. A heavy attack on bait advertising in the 1950s, by the BBB on local levels and by the FTC on the large interstate concerns, resulted in some changes in the game. An early-rising housewife, reading a bait sewing-machine ad in her morning paper and rushing to be the first customer in the door when the store opened, was apt to find the particular machine already sold out. The man who

* Versatility also has its long-range benefits. Observes Donald MacKenzie in his autobiography *Occupation: Thief,* "Change your field of operation or your *modus operandi* and you throw the [police department's] cross-index system completely out of kilter."

sought the bargain automobile was often told the new owner had just driven it off the lot. The used-car dealer has a certain advantage here, as the advertised item is singular, one of a kind. If the public watchdogs in a community are especially alert, the dealer may cover himself with papers proving a legitimate sale, to a friend or relative or salesman's wife. Quite often the man who is told the car has just been sold will see it advertised again on TV that night, and the next, and the next.

In several states bait advertising, or the refusal to sell advertised goods, has been declared a criminal offense. This has resulted in further changes in the way the game is played. One trend is toward greater use of "automatic bait," bait so obviously bad that the customer does his own switching. Another is to actually sell the bait. Then the salesman knocks the merchandise, *after* the sale, with frightening cautions regarding its use and the pointing out of defects absent from the higher-priced item. If anything, this change is even more effective, for the customer, suddenly feeling he's been gypped, is just as suddenly "saved" by the salesman, who, declaring that he just can't do this to a nice guy, will dramatically tear up the sales contract. Or the customer may be sold the item, then told that due to a backlog of orders, delivery from the factory will be delayed for up to a year. If the customer proves uncommonly patient, he is informed that the model has been discontinued.

Getting a return of the down payment may prove exceedingly difficult: often the guarantee specifies that any refund must be applied to another purchase. Backing out and forfeiting the down payment isn't possible either: the bait advertiser almost always works closely with a finance company, the latter purchasing the conditional sales contract as soon as it is signed. The finance company, of course, isn't responsible for defects in the merchandise or its nondelivery; the customer *is* accountable for the payments. In his heyday Weil tried some remarkable tricks (he once purchased a small island made up of fill in Lake Michigan and tried to form an independent republic so as to make himself eligible for foreign aid), but it is probable that the idea of swindling his victims through time payments never occurred to him.*

---

* One can't be sure, however. As a reading of *Yellow Kid Weil: The Autobiography of America's Master Swindler* will attest, Weil has laid claim to originating about every trick in swindlery. It is true that during his forty years of active participation in the trade (he retired in 1942 and was still living as

The bait-advertising statutes in those states which have them require the advertiser to have on hand a sufficient stock of any advertised item to meet the probable demand, or else be prepared to substitute an item of comparable quality at the same price. The supermarket which offers a "mid-week special" on five pounds of one brand of granulated sugar, for example, must sell the customer five pounds of another brand of equal or better-quality at the same price or be subject to legal action, unless the ad clearly specifies that the supply is limited to x number of pounds. In its *Guides Against Bait Advertising*, the FTC has set down detailed standards which cover the initial offer, the discouragement of purchase, as well as the switch-after-purchase variations. The FTC Guides are not law, but rather statements of policy based on law and on recent FTC decisions, indicating to the merchant practices likely to result in FTC citations. They, of course, only apply to interstate commerce. One important provision in this guide states that "the law is violated if the first contact or interview is secured by deception." Were this principle enforced in other areas, it would cause a revolutionary change in modern advertising.

Bait advertising may also be used in the sale of repairs and services. Recently the FTC obtained a cease-and-desist order against Earl Scheib, Inc., a nationwide chain of automotive paint and repair shops. The Scheib order is typical in that the firm was cited for a number of practices—deceptive pricing, savings, and guarantee claims—as well as for bait advertising. Scheib frequently advertised as "Special This Week" or "For a Limited Time" an offer to paint an automobile at a "bargain price" of $29.95; this also happened to be the firm's regular price. In the bait ads the price was given as $19.95, and the switch was to the $29.95 paint job. Customers who attempted to obtain the lower-price offer were told that the paint was inferior, that it was a flat paint and didn't contain silicones, or they were shown, according to the FTC, "off colors, flash colors, and colors you do not ordinarily see on cars."

The line between legitimate and bait advertising is often thin. The reputable department store which offers dresses or suits at bargain prices, not mentioning that they are off sizes, is a bait adver-

---

this was written) he did try almost every con game imaginable, and most with success. "People say that I am the most successful and the most colorful confidence man that ever lived," Weil writes with typical modesty. "I won't deny it."

tiser by degree if not exact definition, but so long as the items are available for sale it isn't bait advertising.

The "Endless" Chain

"If I can show you how you can have this new car for free; in other words, if I could prove to you that you could have this automobile to use as your very own without digging into your pocket to pay for it, and show you how you could earn extra money besides, would you be interested?"

Every day thousands of Americans listen to the above spiel or one of its variations. The item may be a new automobile, a central-unit home vacuum-cleaning system, an automatic snow-sweeper, a home freezer, a water softener, an aluminum carport, a stereo console, a model home, a wig, or almost any commodity. The pitch may be delivered over the telephone, in a store or auto showroom, or in one's own home. It is the hallmark of referral selling, one of the oldest of all cons, the "something for nothing" scheme, in modern dress, combined with the basic principles of one of the oddest phenomena ever to occur in American history.

During the latter part of April 1935, someone—whose identity will probably never be known—dropped a batch of letters into a Denver, Colorado, mailbox and set in motion a contagious madness that in a matter of days spread from one end of the country to another, halting business entirely in some cities, becoming a business itself in others, and causing millions of Americans with empty pockets to dream fantastic dreams of riches, luxury, and ease. This was the chain-letter craze. Whether billed as a simple way to make a fortune or, more altruistically, as a way to redistribute wealth and abolish poverty forever, the letter usually read:

"This chain was started in hopes of bringing prosperity to you. It is based on a simple geometric progression which, if continued unbroken through six stages, will bring you $1562.50. If continued unbroken through another seven stages, it will bring every single person on earth from a dime to thousands of dollars.

"DON'T BREAK THE CHAIN!

"Within three days send 10¢ to the person at the top of this list of six persons. Then recopy this letter, omitting the name at the top and adding your own name at the bottom, and mail copies to five of your friends. If all your friends and all their friends keep faith and don't break the chain, by the time your name leaves the top of the list you will have received 15,625 replies with a dime in each.

"DON'T BREAK THE CHAIN!!!"

It may be that many people received the full $1562.50. Everyone knew someone who knew someone who had. It may be, too, that the person or persons who started the whole mad fad were of unimpeachable honesty. But if fraud wasn't present at the outset, it entered soon thereafter. Many sent out their five letters, but neglected to send a dime to the person on top. Others started $1, $5, and $10 chains, set up letter factories and mailed out thousands of letters, with their own names in first place. The Post Office Department declared it an illegal lottery and the mail volume tripled. Roosevelt haters found it an easy way to slander and vilify the President en masse. Roosevelt admirers countered with their own chains. Only the mathematicians kept trying to explain that there was no such thing as an "endless" chain, that if it took 15,625 persons to give $1562.50 to one person, then 244,140,625 persons would have to participate for each of the original 15,625 to receive the same amount—and this was more than double the total number of people in the United States.

Looking back, the most amazing thing about the craze was its brevity—it lasted less than two months, from the 26th of April to the middle of June.

Now, thirty years later, it's back. There are some differences: a few are making millions, and it is no short-time fad. But one thing remains the same: no one pays any attention to that simple geometric progression.

The technique varies with the salesconman (or rather with the company he represents, for often the spiel is memorized word-for-word from the sales handbook, and woe to the customer who speaks out of turn and causes the salesman to lose his place, as he may have to listen to it all over again from the start), but often it goes somewhat as follows: The salesman follows the free offer, or "teaser," with a lengthy dissertation on how much American business spends every year for advertising. The soap industry spends so much, the appliance industry spends so much, the food and cosmetic industries spend so much. For each package of cigarettes he sells, the tobacco manufacturer gets 9¢—4¢ of this goes for manufacturing costs, salaries, operating expenses, and his margin of profit; the other 5¢ he spends for advertising. Advertising is one of America's biggest businesses. Eventually (the build-up may take from 15 minutes to a full hour) the salesconman reaches the heart of his "presentation," noting that last year his industry, the automotive industry in this case, spent so much for newspaper, television, and radio advertising. Yet last year the industry also conducted a survey, and they discovered that 45.1 percent of all automobile sales did not cost them a cent in advertising. Why was this? Because these sales were the direct result of one person recommending his automobile to another. The wise men in Detroit thought about this for a long time, and then decided, as an experiment, for a limited time only, to use a portion of their budget to encourage word-of-mouth advertising. Therefore, if you qualify, and if you are the kind of person willing to grab an opportunity when it is offered, as I think you are, and if you would promise to use a new car if you were given one, I'm prepared to make you, as a part of this once-only promotion, a *buyer representative*.

What does a buyer representative have to do, you're asking yourself. You think there is a catch here, that you may have to work hard to earn your "free" automobile, that nothing is "free," that there's a gimmick. But you're wrong—there is no catch. It's as simple as this: All you need do, as a buyer representative, is agree to set up interviews with any of your friends and neighbors who would also like to have a free car under this special promotion. For every friend or neighbor interviewed who qualifies, you will receive $100. For every person your friends and neighbors recommend who qualifics, whether you know him personally or not, you get an additional $50. Now do you see how it works? It's like an endless chain; once it gets started, it keeps going on and on, and the money rolls in . . .

Thus the customer is given a glimpse of the chain. Say I have a dozen friends, and they each have a dozen friends. But he said each had to "qualify," whatever that means. Say only six of my friends qualify, and six of each of their friends . . .

One problem with such logic is that the customer rarely carries his mathematics far enough. Here's how a chain with one person recommending six, and each of the six recommending six more, progresses in pyramid form:

1
6
36
216
1,296
7,776
46,656
279,936
1,679,616
10,077,696

This is a single chain. Multiply the number of chains started in a community by any number you choose, and it becomes apparent that even if you live in New York City or Los Angeles there aren't enough people around to sustain the chains.

Even more to the point is the old adage that a chain is only as strong as its weakest link. If none of the six persons first recommended "qualifies," the chain ends right there.

This pitch is, of course, not the real fraud in the referral method of selling but only the cover or "brush" under which the real swindling takes place. For "qualify" means nothing more and nothing less than "purchase" or "buy," though the salesconman carefully avoids either word. Instead he emphasizes how easy it is to receive the item for nothing and maybe even earn money besides. All one has to do is sign a FRIENDSHIP BOND or ADVERTISING AGREEMENT, which the salesman now produces.

Read it carefully, he cautions, talking on while the customer attempts to do so. It is a simple agreement, seeming to contain just about what the salesman promised. The term BUYER REPRESENTATIVE or EQUIPMENT-OWNING ADVERTISER appears often in the text.

Those are just duplicate agreements, the salesconman explains, if the customer shows signs of literary appetite and attempts to read past the first page: your copy, my copy, the general manager's copy, a file copy. The auto business is just like any other business in one respect, tons of paperwork, he laughs, while holding the papers carefully fanned to make it easier for the victim to put his pen to the signature line at the bottom of each.

And that's all there is to it, the signing of a few papers and one can drive off in his new car, move into his model home, or pick a choice cut of meat from that well-stocked home freezer, all for several telephone calls, maybe an hour's work a day.

This delusion may last for some time. The salesconman usually keeps all of the papers, for approval. A week or more may pass before the new buyer representative arises one morning to find that someone has slipped an unstamped envelope under his door during the night. Though he may wonder for a moment why the letter wasn't sent through the mail, an examination of its contents will soon drive other thoughts from his mind. The enclosed papers can be divided into two categories: the worthless and the costly.

The Friendship Bond falls into the worthless category. On reading it, closely this time, the buyer finds that the advertising allowance will be paid only if the interview meets all conditions set forth in the Interview Procedures Manual. A copy of the manual is also enclosed. As even a cursory reading indicates, there are dozens of loopholes arranged so as to free the seller of almost any obligation to pay the buyer any portion of the referral sales. One condition, in a garbage-disposal referral agreement, required that both the husband and the wife had to be present in the room for the full sales talk; if either left the room for any reason while the sales interview was in progress, the referral agreement was invalidated, even if the couple did buy the garbage-disposal unit.

The costly papers include a conditional sales contract, with long-term credit financing at a high rate of interest, and may also include a mortgage on the buyer's present home, a promissory note, and/or an agreement to let the credit company which purchased the sales contract garnish the buyer's wages if he defaults on a payment. Moreover, the purchased item is greatly overpriced, while the finance charges are the maximum permissible. Usually, in the case of automobiles and model homes, allowance is made for the possibility of one or two referral sales, the commissions packed in with the buyer's price, so that he pays for commissions he may, or may not, get.

A careful reading of all the papers before they are signed would seem to foil this fraud. But not necessarily. Often the salesconman leaves significant portions of the contract blank, such items as actual purchase price and financing charges to be filled in later, after signing. If the customer questions the presence of the sales contract, he may be told that it is there only "to show good faith," a con gambit lifted intact from the old but still reliable "pigeon drop" swindle. If the customer bluntly says, "You're really selling this to me, aren't you?" and obstinately demands an answer, the salesconman may, in shocked offense, deny that it is in any way a sale. "You have my personal guarantee that your referral commissions will entirely cover the cost and probably earn you money besides." The salesconman can promise anything, and get away with it, since unwitnessed verbal promises aren't legally binding. The signed paper is, though.

Over the past several years, the FTC and the Post Office Department have succeeded in breaking up a number of large chain-referral operations. This hasn't greatly affected the racket, however, but has only led to the setting up of smaller companies which operate intrastate and carefully avoid using the U.S. mails in their operations. In 1960 the BBB of Oklahoma City, Oklahoma, conducted a survey of local finance companies and found that the companies admitted to doing at least $4 million annual business in referral-type sales. Oklahoma has since declared referral selling a lottery, as has Ohio, but since only a few states have adequate laws covering the chain-referral method of selling, the nationwide total must be tremendous.

The victim of the chain-referral operator does have one possible out, one way to recover some of the money he has lost. It is a slim out, he may not get a penny back, yet the viciousness of this scheme is such that it puts its victim in a position where he is tempted to compound the fraud. He may call everyone he can think of, attempting to set up sales interviews for the company. Having been swindled himself, he can profit only if others are swindled too.

Once upon a time not so very long ago the "roper" (also known as the "steerer" or "outsideman") was that member of a confidence gang whose job it was to locate prospective victims and set them up for the con game. Today the roper may be your best friend.

Henry Ford, Louis Enricht, and the Great Odometer Mystery

The reporters who gathered on the lawn of Louis Enricht's home in Farmington, Long Island, on the afternoon of April 11, 1916, were there for only one reason: the crazy schemes of crackpot inventors made humorous copy. With England at war with Germany, and the United States each day brought closer to participation, the public was in need of a few laughs. But, contrary to expectations, they got headlines instead.

"Gentlemen," the seventy-year-old Enricht began, "I'll be brief

and to the point. After many years of experimentation I've discovered a revolutionary new process which transforms water into
gasoline." Enricht didn't miss the not-so-muted chuckles. "I realize
you're skeptical," he said. "You have every reason to be. That's why
I asked you here, to let you witness a scientific experiment which
will prove my claims. Now, if you'll just gather around this automobile . . ." The automobile, a Ford, was parked nearby. Enricht
took the cap off the gasoline tank, stuck in a dry stick, then pulled
it out, still dry, to prove that the tank was empty. He let reporters
repeat the experiment and examine the tank to verify this fact.
When they had finished, he took a china pitcher and filled it with
water from his garden hose. One of the reporters was invited to
taste it; he pronounced it good, cold well water. Enricht poured
the water into the gas tank. He then took a small vial from his
pocket and held it up for everyone to see. It was filled with a green
liquid, which Enricht identified as his secret formula. There was
more laughter. Pouring a few drops of the liquid into the gas tank,
he replaced the lid and then asked the reporters to choose one of
their members to drive the automobile. A volunteer ascended to
the driver's seat, Enricht's son turned the crank, the motor sputtered,
caught, and roared. The reporters climbed onto the car and rode
around the village of Farmington. On returning, they excitedly
asked Enricht for additional details. As if aware that a detail a day
would keep the press present, he refused to release any more information at this time, beyond admitting that the ingredients of his
formula were inexpensive and that he could create gasoline at a cost
of about 1¢ per gallon. The then current per-gallon price was 30¢,
and was expected to go much higher in the event that America
was drawn into the war.

Reporters from all over the Atlantic Seaboard were there the following day, and from as far away as the Midwest the day after,
among them William E. Haskell, publisher of the Chicago *Herald*,
a nationally recognized automotive expert. Haskell was frankly
skeptical, and became even more so when Enricht refused to repeat
the experiment, claiming that he feared some of the reporters were
really spies from Standard Oil. With seeming reluctance, Enricht
finally relented. Haskell gave the automobile a far more thorough
inspection than the first reporters had thought of doing, not only
tapping the gas tank to make sure it had neither a false bottom nor
false sides but carefully going under and over every other part,
looking for a concealed fuel tank. When Enricht took out the vial,

Haskell asked whether the chemical was poisonous; assured it was not, he asked if he might taste it. Enricht smilingly agreed. The chemical, Haskell said, had a bitter almond taste. It was prussic acid, Enricht admitted with a laugh, added, as was the green coloring, to disguise the actual ingredients. Again, a few drops in the tank, a twist of the crank, and the engine roared. Haskell went back to Chicago to write a story that was picked up by papers all over the world. Not too surprisingly perhaps, it sparked the most interest in four places: Berlin, London, Washington, and Detroit.

Constantly hounded, Enricht let slip little tidbits of information that only whetted reportorial appetites. Once he even explained how the formula worked, though without divulging its actual ingredients. The chemical itself wasn't combustible, he said; it merely had a passionate affinity for the oxygen in the water. When the oxygen was drawn out of the water the hydrogen atoms were released in what he called an atomic explosion. Ridiculous, scientists said.

One crotchety businessman didn't think so. He sent a brusque order to his eastern representative, who immediately drove to Farmington and handed Enricht the telegram. It read: "Put Mr. Enricht aboard the Wolverine Express and rain or shine deliver him f.o.b. at my office in Detroit." It was signed "Henry Ford."

Enricht politely declined the invitation; he was afraid to take his secret formula with him and he was afraid to leave it at home. Several days earlier he had gone into New York City, intending to buy more chemicals to replenish his nearly depleted stock, but so many people were following him he hadn't dared make his purchase. He *had* provided them with a false lead, he admitted craftily, by buying a half-dozen tubes of petroleum jelly. No, if Mr. Ford was interested he would have to come to Farmington.

The following day Henry Ford and Louis Enricht talked privately in the back bedroom of Enricht's Farmington home. Though every attempt had been made to keep the meeting secret, Ford was identified by reporters leaving the house. He refused to answer any questions. His representative, however, admitted the talks were still in progress. Since Mr. Ford was something of a chemist himself, the representative said, he felt it was safe to say that Mr. Ford had asked Mr. Enricht a number of questions. Somewhat indirectly he indicated the results by saying, "The answers must not have been unsatisfactory or the matter would have been dropped."

The first Ford-Enricht meeting occurred on April 24th, thirteen days after the original demonstration. On the 27th something happened which indicated that the first meeting might also be the last—a New York newspaper exposed Mr. Enricht's past. He was, the paper claimed, a swindler of long standing. In 1890 he had swindled a number of Colorado residents who had invested in his scheme to build a railroad line from Canyon City to Cripple Creek. Finally apprehended in 1903, he got off by pleading bankruptcy. Then there was a matter of mail fraud over his sale of 45,000 acres of the Cumberland Plateau, which he didn't own, despite his claims that his family had been given deeds for the land by Patrick Henry. And there was the case of another "secret formula," which he had sold to an English syndicate for an undisclosed amount, which he had claimed would turn wood shavings into finished railroad ties, change plain dirt into concrete bridges, and accomplish other practical, profitable feats. There was more, almost to the time of his water-into-gasoline announcement.

With evident pleasure, the newspaper tweaked Ford for his gullibility. When reporters visited Ford's office shortly after the paper appeared, he wasn't available for comment. Hiding his face, they happily guessed. But as they should have realized long before this, there was nothing predictable about Henry. He wasn't available for comment because he was on his way to Farmington. The second Ford-Enricht meeting occurred that night. The following day Ford announced negotiations were still in progress; that Mr. Enricht had repented of his past indiscretions, for which he had generously forgiven him; and that he was sending Mr. Enricht a new Ford to use in his experiments, plus funds to cover his expenses. How much? Ford said $1000, but there was speculation that the amount was considerably larger. Everything about the interview indicated that Mr. Ford and Mr. Enricht had reached an understanding.

But this couldn't be true, the newspapers gleefully reported the following day, for, much to Mr. Ford's surprise and chagrin, a representative of the Maxim Munitions Corporation of New Jersey announced that, after long negotiations with Mr. Enricht and a thorough testing of his formula by scientists, who found it measured up to all of Mr. Enricht's claims, Maxim Munitions had obtained exclusive rights to manufacture the gasoline substitute. It was reported, though never officially confirmed, that Enricht had received $1 million in cash and 100,000 shares of Maxim stock, then selling for $10.50 per share.

Ford called in newsmen. He had just talked over the telephone to Mr. Enricht, who had denied completely the Maxim lie and was at this very moment conducting his experiments for the Ford Motor Company. Maxim's treasurer, in turn, announced that apparently there was a misunderstanding on someone's part, for they definitely had an exclusive signed contract with Mr. Enricht. This time Enricht didn't deny it. Maxim Munitions stock promptly doubled in value. And Ford, through his attorneys, brought suit to recover the Model T given Enricht for the tests.

Then came a puzzler. Hudson Maxim suddenly denied that his firm had entered into any agreement with Enricht; he himself was consulting engineer for Maxim Munitions, and he hadn't even met the man. The contradictory announcements have never been officially explained. There was speculation, however. Some felt the doubling of the price of Maxim stock held a clue. Others, considerably later, ventured the guess that Enricht had successfully swindled both Maxim and Ford, but that neither company wanted to admit it publicly. The most common opinion, however, was that Enricht was still working with Maxim, under secret military contract. Enricht refused to clarify the matter; instead he announced that he had discovered a new substitute for metal and was at work on a secret technique for extracting oxygen from the air for use in fertilizers and explosives. This, plus the fact that Enricht had just built a new $20,000 home and had started work on his own laboratory and factory in Farmington, lent support to the view that he was still linked with Maxim. About this time Henry Ford began dreaming of other things, such as the Presidency of the United States.

On April 6, 1917, the United States entered the war. Six days later railroad financier Benjamin Yoakum secretly purchased exclusive rights to Enricht's gasoline formula. Yoakum set up National Power Company to manufacture the gasoline substitute and carried on negotiations with military representatives of both England and the United States regarding its purchase; England, desperately in need of fuel, wanted to place a huge order. All of this was revealed some eight months later, and quite sensationally, when Yoakum publicly charged Enricht with treason. Enricht, Yoakum claimed, had not only refused to turn over the formula, thus sabotaging the war effort, he had also secretly negotiated for its sale to the German Government! Investigators hired by Yoakum had discovered that as far back as July 1916 Enricht had held a number of confidential meetings with Captain Franz von Papen, military attaché to the German Embassy in Washington. There was every reason to believe, according to Yoakum, that Germany's present seemingly plentiful fuel supply was Enricht's doing. Enricht denied selling Germany the formula, though he did admit the meetings with Von Papen, asserting they had concerned a secret formula for making artificial stone. Von Papen had offered him $10,000, Enricht said; he had laughed at the offer. Had Enricht admitted at this point that he had swindled the Germans, he might well have become a national hero; he preferred remaining a con man, however. Yoakum attempted to have Enricht arrested but failed. He did succeed in obtaining a court order to search Enricht's home, factory, and safety deposit box in an attempt to locate the formula. But he found nothing. Enricht declared he had burned his only copy.

Those who like their stories to end neatly will be disappointed with the tale of Louis Enricht. Yoakum died shortly after making his charges, and his case against Enricht was never aired in court. How much Enricht took him for has never been made public; the administrator of Yoakum's estate would only describe the amount as "substantial." As to whether Enricht also swindled Ford, Maxim, and/or the German Government, and if so, of how much, also remains a mystery, since none of the principles was ever willing to discuss it. One may look in vain for mention of Enricht's name in Henry Ford's autobiography. In 1920, Enricht called a press conference to announce that he had a new secret formula for making cheap gasoline, only this time using peat. He formed a company and sold some $40,000 in stock before word got out that the Patent Office had denied him a patent on grounds his process didn't work. Arrested and tried for grand larceny, he claimed that his process did indeed work. To prove it he had his machine and a ton of peat brought into the courtroom. He lit the peat with a blowtorch, but though it made considerable smoke and smell, the machine produced no gasoline. A witness testified that Enricht's more successful experiments in his own factory had been aided by an underground gasoline tank and a hidden hose. In February 1923, the seventy-seven-year-old inventor was sentenced to Sing Sing Prison for seven years. A little over a year later, Governor Alfred E. Smith commuted his sentence to time served. He died shortly after his release. No one has yet offered a satisfactory explanation as to just how he fooled the reporters and Henry.

Enricht's tale has a sort of reverse aptness here, for in one respect things have changed considerably since Enricht conned Henry Ford. The intervening years have revealed an unbelievable amount of swindlery in different parts of the automotive industry, but almost all of it has been perpetrated not by the Louis Enrichts, but by the industry itself upon the American public. Before mentioning a contemporary swindle that, in mystery, estimated losses, overall ramifications, and the very simplicity of its operation shades Enricht's grandest efforts, it might be well to note briefly some of the current tricks of the trade.

When the automobile replaced the horse and buggy, it took over not only public favor but a reputation for shrewd salesmanship. Though bright and shiny display rooms have replaced the barns of the professional horse trader, some of the old atmosphere remains. From the artifices used to disguise the true condition of the merchandise to haggling over price, the climate of mutual deception still prevails. The used-car dealer may turn back the odometer to make it appear that the car he's selling has traveled fewer miles than it has; his customer may do the same thing with the car he's trading in. The dealer is likely to give a used car a cosmetic reconditioning so that it appears better than it really is—steam cleaning the engine, painting over scratches, polishing the exterior, replacing worn seat covers and floor pads; the customer, though usually on a more limited scale, will do the same thing if he feels it will bring him a better trade-in price. Each may make misrepresentations to the other; each may lie; each may go to great lengths in his attempt to disguise major defects. Another thing hasn't changed: the buyer often leaves thinking that he got the best of the dealer; in this, as he soon enough discovers, he's nearly always wrong.

Often the initial deception occurs before the prospective customer enters the sales room, in the firm's advertising. Here are a few simple ads that seem to say one thing but, through wordsmithing and pricemanship, may just as easily mean another, depending solely on the reliability of the selling concern:

"NO MONEY DOWN. NO TRADE NEEDED. With Your Good Credit and Ability to Pay." This may mean there is no down payment; or it may mean that, in addition to the regular financing of the car, the buyer must obtain a separate loan to cover the amount of the down payment.

"$49.95 CASH DELIVERS ANY NEW CAR on Approval of Credit." This may mean that $49.95 is the down payment; or it may mean that $49.95 is the credit charge for the loan for the down payment.

$1 SPECIAL. Any of the Following Optional Equipment May Be Added for Only $1 With Your Purchase of a New Car from Us:

Automatic Transmission, Power Steering, Power Brakes, Radio, Heater, Whitewall Tires, Rear-view Mirror, Tinted Glass, Seat Belts, Padded Dash." This may mean a generous dealer; usually, however, it means that the cost of the item is packed in with the car price.

"NEW '65 MUSTANG HARDTOP. As low as $67 DOWN, $67 PER MO." This one means exactly what it says, except it doesn't say very much. Since the ad fails to mention the number of monthly payments, there is no way for the potential customer to compute the cost of the car or the cost of the credit. This is the most common type of advertising deception; in the auto business, as elsewhere, half-truth wordsmithing has great popularity.

To see how the game itself is sometimes played, let's follow George Smith as he sets out to buy a new car. George isn't totally unprepared for his foray into the land of fraud. He's shopped around enough to know the regular price of the model and make in which he's interested, as well as the "book" price on his old car. He knows many of the tricks of the trade, and isn't about to bite on a bait ad, or be conned into a chain-referral scheme, or pay more than he can afford in finance charges, or be talked into buying accessories he doesn't need. He intends to get a good deal or he won't buy. George is just pulling up in front of an auto agency now. This is his first mistake, for this is one of the least reputable agencies, a so-called "system house," but there is no way to tell this from outside. George actually feels he's made a wise choice, figuring that, since the dealer has a franchise for the make of automobile in which he's interested, it must be a fairly reputable concern.

George enters, is greeted by a genial salesman, looks at the model he's just about decided to buy, and begins talking price. The quoted price for the new car is much too high, George complains; after some haggling, the salesman lowers the price. George insists that he must also get a good trade-in price on his old car. They go outside and the salesman examines it, perfunctorily, seemingly missing several major defects. On the way back inside, he asks George how much he wants as trade-in allowance. George says $1500. The salesman's eyebrows rise. They enter one of the sales offices and the salesman consults the "book," pointing out that $1500 is considerably higher than the official book price on that year, make, and model. After some discussion, the salesman writes down $1100 on the purchase order, another victory for George, as this is more than he expected to get. This brings them to the financing. The salesman gets out the "rate chart" and suggests a monthly payment rate.

George argues for, and gets, another more in line with his budget. This too goes down on the purchase order. The salesman reviews the details of the transaction and gives George the purchase order to sign, cautioning him to read it carefully first, which he does. At about this point the salesman suddenly remembers another appointment. Since only a few details remain, would George mind if another salesman completes the sale? He doesn't mind. The second salesman, a very likable fellow, explains the warranties, insurance, etc., and gives him a credit application to sign. George's credit rating is checked and proves acceptable. Now comes the big test (the salesman sighs)—getting the general manager's approval. He has to approve all deals, and the salesman only hopes he's in a good mood. George waits nervously. Finally the salesman returns, with a wide grin. You're in luck today, he remarks, handing George the conditional sales contract for his signature. George signs. The papers are processed and, with handshaking all around, the transaction is completed. George, feeling rather proud of himself, drives home in his new car.

George Smith isn't a vulnerable American; he's a damn gullible American, as he begins to realize on arriving home and reading his copy of the contract. He discovers that, although the down payment is $1100, he has been allowed only $500 on the trade-in of his old car and has signed a note for the balance, plus interest charges. He discovers, too, that the price of the new car is about $200 higher than agreed upon. There are other surprises still to come, but since it will be awhile before George discovers them, we'll leave him screaming over the telephone (ineffectually, alas), retrace our steps, and see where he went wrong.

George is not unintelligent. He would never fall for such an old ruse as the "handkerchief switch" (where the newly arrived immigrant is persuaded to tie up his savings in a handkerchief for safekeeping, his well-intentioned adviser helping him tie the knots) or the "bait and switch" or the "shell game." Yet he has fallen for a trick that differs from them more in degree than kind. System houses work on the "take-over" or "turn-over" system. The first salesman sets up the mark; the second, or "T.O." man, together with the sales manager, knocks him down. To George the first salesman is the enemy, he fights him and wins, the signing of the purchase order being akin to unconditional surrender. In reality, the first salesman is a decoy, the purchase order merely a piece of paper on which he scribbles down George's demands, and the signed document no

more legally binding than a peace treaty signed by the victor but
not the vanquished. The second salesman delivers the *coup de
grâce*, in two stages. He knows exactly how to handle George, since
he has monitored the whole transaction; the salesrooms of most
"system" houses (as well as those of some reputable agencies) are
wired for sound. Both the T.O. man and the "general manager"
often listen in, so that either or both can enter fully informed at any
strategic moment. George has no idea how much personal attention
he has received. Relaxed, his guard down, George signs the "credit
application" and conditional sales contract more or less automatically. Because he sees no mention of the terms agreed upon in the
purchase order, he thinks of them as supplementary documents and
overlooks the blank spaces, which are filled in after he has signed.

The technique can be varied to fit the customer. George has been
a victim of *low-balling*, the practice of making a highly attractive
offer and then, through various stratagems, switching to another,
far more expensive deal. One such trick is *bushing*, increasing the
quoted price of the car after the customer has agreed to buy.

If George had been more cautious, his swindlers might have tried
high-balling instead. There is a provision in most sales contracts
which permits reappraisal of the trade-in car at time of delivery.
If there is a difference between the contract-signing time and the
delivery date of the auto (if, for example, the dealer can't deliver
the new car immediately), this provision covers the dealer against
the possibility that the trade-in car may be wrecked or damaged in
the meantime. High-ballers make an attractive offer, stall for weeks
on delivery, then use this provision to back out of their original
trade-in offer, on the assumption that, although this may make the
customer extremely unhappy, he'll probably think he has already
wasted too much time to back out. This also keeps him from shopping around.

Most auto-buying customers share a common delusion. They feel
that if they get more for their trade-in than the official "book" price,
or have to pay less than book for the car they purchase, they have
made a good deal. The only trouble is, there is nothing "official"
about book prices. They are only guides, and are taken much more
seriously by the public than by the trade. As *Consumer Reports* has
frequently noted, book prices are largely computed from reports
from dealers, some of whom inflate the sales price they report for
their own specific makes, apparently hoping to give potential customers the impression that their particular cars are the best buys in

terms of future resale value. Firms have also been known to have
more than one book, although this practice is now rare. It isn't
necessary, for one thing, because there are easier ways to do it,
such as *packing*.

Packing has a multitude of forms, ranging from simple deception
(lumping the insurance rates and credit charges together in the
contract so the customer can't tell the true cost of either) to outright
fraud (leaving parts of the contract blank to be filled in after signing, as in George's case). One of the most common forms of packing
is raising the selling price of a car to compensate for a higher trade-in
allowance. But its most effective forms are in the realm of financing.
Here the line between the reputable and the disreputable dealer
often grows thin, sometimes disappearing entirely.

As in many other businesses today, the greatest profits in the auto
industry aren't in the buying and selling of automobiles but in the
sale of debt. The least welcome customer in an auto showroom is
the man who wants to pay cash or arrange his own financing.
There is good reason for this: the finance charges on an automobile
are usually more than one-fifth and may run to as much as one-fourth
of the cash price, and a good share of this goes to the dealer.

The practice of selling cars on credit (or, put another way, selling
credit on cars) dates back to just before World War I. As Hillel
Black notes in his book *Buy Now, Pay Later,* in 1914 the average cost
of a new automobile purchased at the factory was $762, while the
annual average wage that year was $627. Then, as now, automobiles
were expensive, costing more than the average man could afford to
pay at one time. Yet if the automotive industry was to survive, and
thrive, some way had to be found to make the automobile available
to that average man. The obvious answer was to sell automobiles
on a time-payment plan. Yet the automobile manufacturers didn't
want to wait for their money; they wanted cash on delivery. And
the automobile dealers, the retailers, couldn't afford to buy the automobiles from the manufacturer at a huge outlay and then wait for
the payments to dribble in. As a result, a new branch of the industry
came into being, the sales-finance company.

In many respects, the role of the sales-finance company is much
the same now as it was when it first came into existence fifty years
ago. It lends the dealer the money to buy his cars from the manufacturer. This is known as "floor-planning money," and is lent without interest. In return, the dealer sells the sales-finance company
most of the installment contracts he makes with his customers. At

first the dealer made no profit on this part of the transaction. He also carried full liability if the customer defaulted on payments. In the mid-twenties, due to competition among the sales-finance companies, the rules gradually changed, with the companies finally assuming the full liability and also kicking back to the dealer a portion of the finance charges. Over the years this kickback, or rebate, has increased in both size and importance, until today about *half* of dealers' profits come from this source. This makes for a most vulnerable consumer, for whether the dealer is reputable or disreputable, it is to his best interest to see that his customer pays the highest possible finance charges.

One way he can do this is by disguising the actual finance charge through various types of packing. Another is through the use of duplicate rate charts. The customer is rarely aware that the rate chart he is shown—which computes his financing in terms of so much down, so much per month for so many months—is only one of a half-dozen or more charts the salesman can use. Hypothetically, the higher-rate charts are supposed to be used for those customers who are the worst credit risks. In practice, however, it is often the gullibility of the customer, rather than his credit status, which is the deciding factor. The difference between the use of one rate chart and the use of another may add several hundred dollars to the cost of the automobile.*

The way in which the sales-finance companies handle the kickback, or rebate, makes the temptation to use the higher charts almost irresistible, for the higher the rate the higher the *percentage* that is kicked back to the dealer.

Although many states have set maximum finance rates, only two states, Ohio and Michigan, have laws regulating the size of the dealer's kickback.

Temptation also confronts the dealer when it comes to the sale of tie-in insurance, for the auto dealer receives commissions of between 25 and 30 percent of the premiums paid on collision policies and 15 to 20 percent on credit-life and personal-accident policies.

This by no means exhausts the possibilities of deception and fraud. There may be fraud in hidden service charges, in warranties and

---

* True annual interest rates on auto financing generally range from 12 to 34 percent. As we'll see in Chapter 6, however, the true annual interest rate is almost never quoted. Instead, various deceptions are used to represent the interest as being 4 to 9 percent. In 1961 the Chicago BBB reported a case in which the interest on a loan for a used car was 270 percent.

guarantees, in the computing of taxes, in the sale of accessories, etc. One further trick of the disreputable dealer deserves special mention. This is the *balloon note.* The customer is offered what seems a very reasonable rate, so much per month for so many months. Multiplying one by the other, and then subtracting the cost of the car, it would appear that the finance charges are very low. What isn't mentioned is that there is a final payment many times larger than the monthly payments. In a typical case reported by the BBB, a woman was offered a new car for only $90 down and only $35 per month for 23 months. No one mentioned the balloon note that came due on the 24th month, for $1400. Use of this device not only enables the dealer to quote a lower monthly rate than his more reputable competitors; since most of his customers can't make the unexpected payment, he gets a big chunk of the refinancing.

The sad thing is that, even if George Smith had read his contract carefully, had made sure that all the blank spaces were filled in, had been given exactly what he was promised by the first salesman, he still could have lost almost as much through credit trickery. As it is, he lost both ways.

Lest the foregoing give the impression that fraud is universal in the auto industry, it should be mentioned that there are honest automobile dealers who disavow such chicanery. It doesn't necessarily follow, however, that by patronizing a reputable dealer, and getting the fairest of fair deals, the automobile owner won't be the victim of fraud, for we come now to that contemporary swindle mentioned earlier, what the *New Republic* has dubbed "The Great Odometer Mystery."

Three years ago a Canadian who was in the United States on a business trip and had to go from Washington, D.C., to Florida, let a leading rental-car agency put him in the driver's seat of a new automobile. A methodical man, he noted the mileage reading on the odometer at both the start and the finish of his trip. He found that the odometer had registered more miles than he could possibly have traveled. He filed a complaint with Florida's Division of Standards.

Since the complaint seemed legitimate, and since it wasn't the first of its kind, an investigation was begun. Officials obtained 36 rental cars and tested them. In every car except one, the odometer overregistered the mileage. Of the 36 cars, 10 showed an error of 6 percent or more, the error in some running as high as 14 percent. On learning of this, the National Bureau of Standards, through its Office of Weights and Measures, began its own investigation. This time 48 cars were selected at random from various rental agencies in the District of Columbia, including both compact and standard sizes, and tested under exacting conditions. The result—an average overregistration of 3.5 percent.*

At this point the reader may, like the Canadian, be pointing the finger of accusation at Hertz, Avis, and the other rent-a-car companies. The logical suspect is the person with a motive, the individual (company or companies) who stands to profit from the commission of the crime. But this, remember, is a mystery, and in most mysteries the first suspect is rarely the guilty party. As soon became evident, nothing was quite what it first seemed. Though the rental-car agencies did profit, they were apparently not the guilty parties. Nor were the victims alone those who first appeared to be—that comparatively small number of people who use rental cars. The victims were everyone who owns and drives a late-model car as well as many people who have never owned or driven a car in their lives. For it was found in subsequent tests that the odometers registered high on *all* new U.S.-manufactured cars and trucks.

Just what did this mean?

It meant, in the rent-a-car field alone, and excluding trucks, that —computing the annual rental-car mileage at roughly 1.26 billion miles, the average overregistering at 3.5 percent, and applying the usual 10¢-per-mile rate—customers were overcharged at least $4.25 million last year.

It meant, according to an Internal Revenue Service estimate, that the United States Government was losing $40 million a year in tax revenues from allowing 10¢-a-mile deductions on miles never traveled.

It meant that, unless the local licensing bureau in a community was especially diligent, users of taxis were paying for an unestimable number of extra miles.

It meant that, since the odometer is connected to the speedometer and causes it to read high also, many Americans arrested and fined or jailed for speeding weren't guilty of speeding at all.

It meant that if, on moving from one community to another, a family paid by the number of recorded miles, they overpaid.

It meant that, since the mileage of a car is one of the prime considerations in determining the trade-in value, a great many Amer-

---

* Rental trucks, also checked, overregistered an average of about 1 percent.

icans were being cheated out of dollar value on the sale of their property.

It meant that they were being cheated on their automobile warranties.

It meant that they were being cheated on their tire warranties.

It meant that they were changing their oil before it was necessary.

It meant that they were getting fewer miles per gallon of gas.

There was no trouble discovering who was guilty. The automobile manufacturers admitted a collective guilt, though they didn't call it that. The Society of Automotive Engineers, technical advisory group to the automotive industry, admitted that odometer specifications on new cars called for a setting of between 0 and plus 5 percent. These specifications admittedly date from 1962, but may go back further. How much further is a part of the mystery.* The biggest question, however, is why?

The industry gave two reasons: (1) It was impossible to set odometers at 0 because of engineering problems. Experts advising the Bureau of Standards, however, found that a relatively minor, inexpensive change—putting more teeth on the gears that pick up revolutions from the transmission—would result in accurate readings. The industry in later arguments, in effect, admitted knowing this all along. (2) The high setting was made in part because of considerations of safety. As William Sherman, head of the engineering and technical division of the Automobile Manufacturers Association explained it, "Since the odometer is part of the speedometer, it was better at 60 miles an hour to have the speedometer read a little high so if the fellow is misled, he's misled on the safe side." This prompted James Ridgeway to ask in the *New Republic*, "If, in fact, speed really were a prime consideration, why not stop making autos that go faster and faster?"[2]

In essence, the industry argued that no fraud was committed, that this was, at worst, a slight case of honest, well-intentioned, and unavoidable deception.

Conventional mysteries end with the solving of the crime and the punishing of the guilty. This isn't always the case in real life. The Bureau of Standards solved the odometer mystery in 1962 and at that time began trying to have odometers set back to 0. The Auto-

---

* *Consumer Reports* began receiving complaints regarding rental-car overcharging as far back as the late fifties. The magazine also reported that when complaints were made to the rental agencies an immediate refund was nearly always forthcoming.

mobile Manufacturers Association set up an Odometer Subcommittee to negotiate. When nothing came of the negotiations, the Bureau called a Conference on Weights and Measures. The decisions of such conferences, which are made up of state and local weights and measures officials, have the force of law in forty-three states. The conference ruled that odometers should be set for average error o. In June 1964, the AMA Subcommittee agreed that, as of January 1, 1965, the odometers of all vehicles made for rental use would meet the new standards. The change would be made on other new vehicles soon thereafter. It was agreed that the cost of making the change on older vehicles would be prohibitive.

If your automobile is an American make of the years 1962, 1963, 1964, or 1965, chances are you are being defrauded every time you drive it. This may even be true if you are driving an older-model car, since one of the unanswered questions in the great odometer mystery is just when the "deception" first occurred. The other puzzler: who's to blame?

Periodically, throughout this book, this same question will be asked in regard to other cases. Often, as here, there will be an all-embracive answer, an admission of collective guilt by a whole industry or a group of companies, or a single company policy. The absence of a personal villain is one of the hallmarks of the biggest of modern frauds. We know that some man or men at some time and place made a decision which led to the odometer deception, but we will probably never know who or when, since in this case (as in many) the inquiry ended with the admission of joint responsibility.

Maxim: Collective guilt ultimately becomes singularly absolving.

Maxim: A little deception can go a long way.

CHAPTER 4

STORMING THE CASTLE

> The poorest man may in his cottage
> bid defiance to all the force of the
> Crown. It may be frail; its roof
> may shake; the wind may blow
> through it; the storms may enter,
> the rain may enter—but the King
> of England cannot enter; all his
> forces dare not cross the thresh-
> old . . .
>
> William Pitt

As IT once was, so is it still, in principle. Man's home is his castle. Representatives of the country, city, or state cannot enter, without permission of the court. Policemen cannot make a search without a properly executed warrant. By law, the sanctity of one's home is inviolate.

In practice, however, the American home is as vulnerable as its occupants. Not only vulnerable but subject to planned, deliberate, repeated assault. At this very moment an army of more than 1.5 million is massing to invade the American home. Representing some 3000 direct-selling companies, these salesmen and saleswomen this year will not only cross our thresholds but recross them carrying more than $3 billion in loot. Most will leave behind something of value, as the majority of these invaders are personally honest (if persistently bothersome) and represent reputable concerns. But there will be swindlers in their ranks. And even some of the best represented will use artifice and trickery to gain entry, for honesty and reputability are relative too.

One of the most amazing things about many of these invaders is their steadfast denial that they are selling anything. In this field of battle the words *sell* and *cost* are rapidly becoming obsolete. Products aren't sold; they're *placed* or *introduced*. But they aren't placed for money; they're placed for *a consideration*. And those who place them aren't salesmen or saleswomen, they're *manufacturers' representatives* or *product consultants*.

Following are some of the keys currently being used to open the doors of American homes to deception and fraud:

The Survey Sell

"Mrs. Smith? I wonder if I might have a few moments of your time? I'm not selling anything. I'm conducting a survey for *Parents' Magazine*'s Cultural Institute. This, as you perhaps know, is an educational research organization. I'm an educator and . . ."

So began the typical opening pitch of the sales representative of a firm which sold encyclopedias, books, and magazines. What followed was summarized by the FTC in its recent complaint against *Parents' Magazine* Enterprises, Inc., and its wholly owned subsidiary, *Parents' Magazine*'s Cultural Institute. According to the FTC, contrary to their statements and representations:

"These encyclopedia salesmen were not engaged in making surveys;

"Printed questionnaires were not used in making surveys but were used solely to gain entrance to prospects' homes;

"Salesmen and representatives were not necessarily teachers or representatives of an educational system but were essentially and primarily salesmen whose sole objective was to sell publications and services;

"The quoted price of encyclopedia sets was not an introductory or reduced price but the regular price of the sets;

"The *New Wonder World* encyclopedia set was not obtainable in exchange for a testimonial regarding the set, plus a small introductory price of the set, but was obtainable only at the regular price;

"Special offers were not made to selected persons, but the offers were made indiscriminately;

"The 'free' items offered to prospective purchasers who would 'buy now' were not free but were included in the purchase price of the publications and services; and

"Books purchased and received from the concern were not bound with soft pliable backs as were the samples but were bound with rigid covers."

In November of 1963 the two firms signed a consent order with the FTC, agreeing to halt these false, misleading, and deceptive practices. In so doing they joined a long list of distinguished encyclopedia firms whose practices have drawn FTC citations in recent years: the Americana Corporation, publishers of the *Encyclopedia Americana* (cease-and-desist order for fictitious price-reduction claims);* *Encyclopaedia Britannica* (cease-and-desist order for misrepresenting the regular selling price of its goods and services); the Crowell-Collier Publishing Company and P. F. Collier & Sons Corporation, publishers of *Collier's Encyclopedia* (cited in 1960 for allegedly falsely representing that the encyclopedia was "free" if the yearly supplements were purchased, and miscellaneous other misrepresentations, final action on the complaint still pending); American Education Society, Inc., publishers of the *Universal World Reference Encyclopedia* (consent order for various deceptive practices, including survey selling, fictitious pricing, bogus claims that a portion of the sale price went for charity or college scholarships, and misrepresentations that the salesman was calling at the suggestion of the person's minister or pastor).

"The encyclopedia industry was formerly a quiet outpost of the book trade," observes Ralph Lee Smith, former editor of the National Better Business Bureau's monthly service *Do's and Don'ts in Advertising Copy*. "Its sober, conservative selling tactics matched the dignity of its merchandise. After World War II, however, encyclopedia publishers began to 'think modern.' Specifically, they began to realize that the commodity in which they were dealing—knowledge—might have many more commercial possibilities than they had realized, if only it were sold according to contemporary methods."[1] The FTC citations are one result of this new approach; another is reflected in total U.S. encyclopedia sales, which jumped from $125 million in 1954 to $330 million in 1961.

---

* The FTC order was issued in 1947. The misrepresentations continued, however. On November 30, 1960, the Americana Corporation was found guilty of violating the FTC order and fined $16,000 in a federal court.

The Sympathy Sell

"Hi. I'm collecting votes for a medical scholarship . . ." In trade this is known as the "college-boy gag," and is one of the hallmarks of the youthful bogus magazine salesman. Another popular approach begins: "Gee, you gave me a shock! You know, you look just like my Mom!" Once inside, tricks include placing a number of *journals* (the word *magazine* is psychologically unappealing) in exchange for a *donation* to a charity or educational fund; misrepresenting the number, duration, and prices of subscriptions; package deals, where one or two desired magazines are sold with a number that are unwanted; and accepting subscriptions for magazines the salesman isn't authorized to sell and later switching the customer to other magazines as provided for in a "substitution clause" in the contract. In October 1964, postal inspectors arrested a Phoenix, Arizona, man whose company, operating nationwide, allegedly took 34,000 persons for an estimated $342,000 for magazine subscriptions which the Post Office Department charged were never delivered. Of late, the check-raiser has joined the sales ranks: picking the ill and the elderly as his principal victims, he offers them assistance in writing their checks, leaving enough blank space so he can later raise the amount. To combat such fraud, the Magazine Publishers Association has a "central registry" which provides credentials for approved magazine salesmen. Printing is cheap, however, and the bogus operator often presents an abundant number of authentic-looking documents, which may even include a card certifying his company is licensed by the BBB, which of course licenses no one. "Always hand them your credentials upside down," advises one door-to-door sales manual. "By the time they have them turned around, you can be well into your sales pitch." The sympathy sell shouldn't be confused with

The Pity Sell

Seemingly crippled, maimed, or deformed persons are used in this approach, which is usually tied in with a charity pitch that often is as well made up as those who present it.

The Charity Sell

The California Missionary Army, now defunct after an exposé of
its operations by the San Francisco *Examiner*, went door-to-door
asking for donations of $1 or $2 to help place free Bibles in hospitals,
prisons, and the homes of the poor. Even though the "home missionaries" kept 50 to 60 percent of collections, the firm grossed
$100,000 within a few months in just one metropolitan area, while
giving away at most some 300 Bibles. As one of the leading "min-
isters" told *Examiner* writer Clint Mosher, who was working undercover as a missionary-collector, "I could go from house to house
asking for donations for the Salvation Army and come back with
$45 or $50 in no time."[2] A check on eleven of the missionaries by
the Sacramento Sheriff's office revealed that six had police records,
which included charges of robbery, burglary, auto theft, assault,
battery, and forgery. The Army was active for about a year before
the BBB and police were able to accumulate enough evidence to
bring charges against its leaders. Two fled. The third, a thirty-seven-
year-old ex-convict, was apprehended, tried, and convicted of grand
larceny and given sixty days in jail and two years' probation.

The Party Sell

For years reputable companies used this particular sales gimmick
to sell cookware, silverware, and household appliances. In return
for inviting her friends to her home for a cooking party, the company
would provide the housewife-hostess with ingredients for the re-
freshments, plus a free pressure cooker or similar item. Of late, this
device has been taken over by the gypsters, the "wig party" being
one of their current tricks. The hostess is promised one or more
free wigs—on a referral-type agreement. Outright fraud is common.
Quality wigs with fine, real hair are shown and sold on an order
basis, for $300 or more; cheap wigs, worth $50 or less, with coarse
or synthetic hair, or sometimes yak hair, are delivered. Cases have
been reported where substances used in the wigs were so toxic they
caused the wearer's own hair to fall out. Promissory notes are presented as "credit applications." A young government clerk in Washington, D.C., bought two wigs at a "bargain" price of $700; she later

found they could be purchased in a beauty salon for $169 each. According to columnist Sylvia Porter, fully 10 percent of the $150 million in annual wig sales involve deceptive practices.[3] A check on the background of some new "beauty consultants" in the nation's capital revealed that prior to the "wig boom" these men had been used-car salesmen, bookies, "boiler shop" stock operators, and cemetery-lot salesmen.

The Bargain Sell

The offer of a bargain by a door-to-door salesman is nearly always synonymous with deception, since there are few, if any, real bargains in this type of selling. Contrary to the well-fostered myth that the door-to-door salesman can offer merchandise cheaper than the established retail merchant, who must pay rent, utilities, salaries, etc., is the fact that the sales person receives a high percentage in commissions on anything he sells. At best, products offered door-to-door are priced competitively or slightly higher than similar products in retail stores. Sometimes they are much higher. The trade magazine *Chemical Week* recently reported of one product, "Door-to-door specialty salesmen get a high commission—as much as $100/sale. Consequently, this form of direct selling can add 30–40 percent to the final price of a water-softener unit."[4]

The Free Sell

The something-for-nothing pitch is the key which opens many doors. "Two *free* USDA choice New York cut steaks or two Rock Cornish Game Hen dinners," promises the text under the full-color, mouth-watering illustration in the newspaper ad or mail brochure. "No obligation. Just call and request information on our special, money-saving family food-freezer plan." The telephone call brings the frozen dinners, together with a salesman. This isn't all that is free, he effuses: if you take the introductory offer of 307 pounds of choice meat, at wholesale prices, you get the freezer itself free! The average family, he explains, spends $28 per week on perishable and nonperishable foods. Yet, because the company buys and sells in quantity, this plan is being offered at a tremendous saving: only $8.95 a week! In addition, you can buy any brand of frozen food you want at wholesale or less. There is a five-year guarantee on this latest-model freezer. There is a warranty which pays you for any food spoilage. You pay nothing until you've had your order for at least forty-five days. And if you sign now, on this last day of the special offer, you will receive as a free bonus twenty delicious beef filets.

It has been estimated that fully one-third of the food-freezer plans now in operation involve some degree of fraud. Over the past two years the FTC has cracked down on more than a dozen large "food plans," operating out of New York, Maryland, Illinois, Texas (141 dealers), Minnesota, Iowa, and North Dakota. Here are a few things their salesmen misrepresented or neglected to mention. The freezer is not free; it is sold on an installment plan, the payments separate from the quoted food payments. (Not only not free but costly. According to the FTC, one huge East Coast outfit, the Tenax Corporation, charged $999.95 for freezers which sold elsewhere for $275 to $300.) Often the freezer isn't new; the warranty is on parts which never wear out; and the buyer pays extra for food-spoilage insurance, the policy so wordsmithed as to render claims near-uncollectable. Prices charged are rarely, if ever, wholesale; the cost of frozen foods, due to hidden finance charges, is often double or triple the retail price, and sometimes only off brands are available. No mention is made of the fact that the quoted price is just for the first shipment of meat, which is generally exhausted in three to four months— though the payments go on. Nor is any mention made that the stated meat weight is precutting weight, that often there is both a cutting and a delivery charge, that even then the shipment may be short in weight and long on the least desired cuts, and that while the two "free" steaks are USDA choice, the rest of the meat isn't.

Home-improvement Schemes

This year, for the fourteenth year in a row, the National Better Business Bureau reports that complaints regarding the home-improvement industry led by a large margin any other type of consumer complaint. Estimated losses to the American public for this year alone are expected to run into the hundreds of millions.

On the West Coast a team of three men, operating under an impressive company name, took residents of one community for $25,-000 in less than one month on shoddy, overpriced painting, roofing, and alterations. Specialists, they concentrated on bilking the blind, having them sign "building-permit applications," which turned out to be mortgages or deeds of trust to their homes.

On the East Coast thirteen home-improvement firms and forty-five men were indicted in a $4 million swindle, charged with fraudulently soliciting alteration jobs from home owners at prices greatly in excess of costs, trapping scores of people in debt-consolidation schemes, causing many to lose their homes. Among those indicted were five "respectable" bankers; all were charged with fraud, three were also charged with bribery.

Similar scandals have recently erupted in many parts of the country—in Pennsylvania, Maryland, Nebraska, Texas, Ohio, Illinois, California, Washington, New York, the District of Columbia,* Maine, New Jersey, Kansas, Michigan, Louisiana, Arizona—some involving itinerant, "fly-by-night" operators, others involving some of the largest companies in this field.

M.O. (Modus Operandi) of the Fly-by-Nights. These operators, working singly or in teams, drive through neighborhoods in overloaded pickups or trucks, spotting houses in need of repairs. Usually they underbid reputable contractors, not because, as often claimed, they have materials left over from the last job and want to get rid of them cheap, but because they do only cover-up work. Sometimes they start the job, then ask for cash payment in advance of completion, to buy needed supplies or to pay their men before the weekend; then they skip, leaving the job uncompleted. These customers are often best off, as the completed job may be worse than no improvement at all. Scrap lumber may be used for building extra rooms; factory-reject storm windows installed which don't fit; inner walls blown full of insulation not only worthless but in some cases highly combustible; exteriors covered with interior paint, which fades in sunlight; or roofs "tarred" with a mixture of burnt lubricating oil and lampblack, which runs when it rains. A large family group of more than 100 members, known as the Terrible Williamsons, has pulled these tricks and others of similar genre in the East and Midwest for years. Bothersome as they are, and as costly as their operations may be to some, damage by the itinerants is small compared to that inflicted by their highly organized fellows who go in for company names and credit fraud.

* After an extensive survey, the Washington, D.C., *Star* estimated that as many as 30 percent of the contractors in that area were "of questionable integrity."

M.O. of the Company Men. Currently the undisputed leaders in home-improvement fraud are the aluminum-siding gypsters. Contacting their victims through bait advertising, referrals, telephone solicitation, or door-to-door canvassing, they offer "special deals" or "bargain prices" on aluminum home siding, storm-screen windows, carports, or patio covers. Usually working in pairs, they often never mention the name of their firm, preferring well-known manufacturers' names—such as Alcoa or Aluminum Corporation of America—albeit without permission of these companies. The "hard sell" is frequently employed, the sales spiel, often given at night, lasting two to five hours, adding exhaustion to their weapons.* They have one basic credo: "Promise them anything, so long as they sign." The papers may include a lien contract, with the home as security, a promissory note, a mortgage or deed of trust. In some instances the home owner is persuaded to sign a "hold check" as down payment on the work, with the understanding that the check won't be cashed, that it is merely a "show of faith" to be held until credit is approved and supplementary financing arranged. The check *is* cashed, however, almost immediately; should it bounce, the operators use the threat of criminal action as a club with which to intimidate the signer. Often a "completion note" is included, in which the buyer certifies that the work has been satisfactorily completed—before it is even started.

Once he has put pen to paper, the buyer never again sees these particular men, who in reality are neither manufacturer's representatives, home-improvement experts, or contractors, but simply hard-sell salescommen. They immediately sell the signed contract at a discount to a bank or a loan or finance company, using a portion of the money received to pay a local contractor for the work. (Some eliminate the last step; others give the contractor only a down payment, the home owner later discovering that he must pay twice for the same work.) Since the contractor who will do the job at the lowest possible cost is always the one chosen, the resultant work rarely deserves to be called an "improvement." In one week not long ago, a crew of ten salesmen sold 400 aluminum-siding jobs to families in one Los Angeles neighborhood. Each salesman pocketed an average commission of $1200 per job, as much or more than a regular contractor would have charged for the whole project.

* The weary signer may have second thoughts on awakening, but it will do little good. Most of these contracts contain a cancellation penalty clause amounting to 30 percent of the contract.

If the home owner argues that he can't afford the work, that he already owes money, often the improvement deal is tied in with a debt-consolidation scheme. In a typical case, a home owner was not only short on cash but had debts amounting to $4000. The salesconmen paid off his creditors, arranged to have $1000 lent to him for immediate expenses, and signed him for $7000 in home improvements—the whole package for no larger monthly payments than those he was already making. The excessive interest charges were hidden in the number of payments, the years the man would be obligated. Even without debt consolidation, the cost can be fantastic. A Westchester County widow, mother of four children, whose only property was the home her husband had left her, signed a $5000 note for a loan to pay for aluminum siding and a minor porch-renovation job. Though the contracting firm was one of the largest in the area, the work was shoddy, and she will be paying the loan company for it at the rate of $64.20 every month for the next seven years. The San Francisco BBB reports one case where a home owner signed up for a siding job with "low monthly payments" that extended over fourteen-and-a-half years.

The Model-home Sell. A referral-selling variation. The householder is offered a chance to have a model kitchen, bathroom, or siding job installed "at little or no cost" in exchange for giving the contractor permission to show the work as a model to prospective clients. Should the couple seem reluctant to have a parade of strangers passing through their bathroom, the gypster offers the deal on the basis of before-and-after pictures or a single "TV visit" ("We now take you to Mr. and Mrs. Joe Jones, in their bathroom in Anytown, U.S.A."). This is also known as the "showcase gimmick."

Crew-switching. The salesmen divide into two crews, each taking a bogus company name. Crew "A" fans out over one part of town, crew "B" over another, each going door-to-door offering improvements at fantastically inflated prices. The crews then switch territories and company names, offering lower prices than their "competitor," whom they characterize as a gyp outfit.

The Fear Sell. The two uniformed men, whose papers identified them as Government Building Inspectors, emerged from under the house holding a piece of rotten wood. "Dry rot," one explained. "If you don't have this taken care of immediately there is a good chance some night soon your house will come tumbling down, crushing you and your kids. It could go anytime." At another house the men found that termites had undermined the foundations. The wiring was dangerously overloaded in another. Bricks came crashing down the chimney of still another as they applied their crowbars and discovered the chimney was infested with mortar mice.* While in another home the men found that, due to leakage from the sewer system, the drinking water had been dangerously contaminated.

Their impressive credentials and uniforms to the contrary, the above men were not official inspectors but salesmen. And in each case there was nothing wrong with the house before they examined it. Their aim was to get the home owner to sign a contract for unnecessary repairs and services: a chemical solvent for the dry rot ($412); pest removal and replacement of supports, which weren't replaced, only painted over ($1122); rewiring, or rather recovering, the old wiring with new friction tape ($843); a new chimney, alias the old chimney rebuilt with a few new bricks on the side where they show ($195); and the installation of a $125 water softener and "purifier" ($700). These are a few examples of the "fear sell." There are more, and worse.

A bad fire in a community will often bring, before the ashes have cooled, a team of "fire inspectors" whose scare tactics include horrifyingly realistic home movies designed to convince the home owner that for the safety of his family he cannot afford to be without a fire-alarm system or ample extinguishers. The systems, once installed, are usually no better than extra-loud doorbells. The extinguishers quite often put the family in greater jeopardy than before, as many are types too dangerous for private use, for example those filled with methyl bromide or carbon tetrachloride, both of which explode with heat, the latter also producing a dangerously toxic gas.

Even more common, and more frightening, since they offer not only fire but lethal gases and silent suffocation, are the bogus furnace inspectors.

Following is the actual spiel of one of these men, as delivered in the home of a San Francisco widow on the afternoon of January 15, 1960. Two days earlier, the same man had visited the woman's home, partly dismantled the furnace, and declared that it "leaked" dangerously and had to be replaced without delay. He picked the wrong woman, however; putting him off, she called the local BBB, who in turn called in an inspector from the Pacific Gas & Electric Company (PG&E), who found the furnace thoroughly safe and in

---

* If presented with this pitch, ask the inspectors to catch one of these rodents for you. Since biologists have yet to see one of these creatures, it should bring a good price.

need of neither replacement nor repair. When the salesman made his follow-up call, there was present a BBB representative, who secretly tape-recorded the following:

". . . The flue pipe instead of taking all of the smoke and fumes up the flue, a good percentage of them are going up in the house . . . See where she's burnt out over there . . . that's going right up into your house . . . The warm air plenum is above here, which means that the smoke and fumes go up in here, and then that fan turns on back there . . . Now, there have been several articles written by this Dr. Sox [San Francisco Director of Public Health] . . . I'm not saying this to scare you, I'm just saying it to impress upon you . . . This is worse than the raw gas, because, see, the raw gas you can smell. This you can't smell. This is carbon monoxide . . . This is no different than if you took the exhaust pipe from your automobile and ran it in here . . . I'll tell you one thing, if we were back East, we could shut that furnace off as a menace. We can't out here because of the PG&E . . . I would actually be doing you a favor . . . by shutting your furnace off . . . I'm not doing that to sell you a furnace, I'm just trying to be honest with you . . . it's not healthy. I would replace it and I would do it now . . . it's leaking . . . We can allow you $28.50 as junk for that old furnace."[5]

The man who delivered this fraudulent pitch was not a fly-by-night operator. He was an accredited representative of the Holland Furnace Company of Holland, Michigan, the largest seller of replacement furnaces in the United States, a firm with some 500 offices, more than 5000 employees, and an annual business income of over $30 million. Nor was this instance unique; according to the FTC, Holland had been similarly victimizing customers for thirty years. Among the cited tactics were that workmen posed as official inspectors; that they sprayed gasoline on pipes while the home owner wasn't looking, then lit it to prove there was a leak; that they substituted burnt-out parts to prove the furnace needed replacing; that they would dismantle furnaces and then refuse to put them back together "because we don't want to be accessories to murder." When the home owner still proved obstinate, some threatened to file a complaint with the police, fire department, or appropriate agency, charging that the furnace was a menace to public safety. In July 1958, the FTC obtained a cease-and-desist order forbidding the company to use misrepresentations to gain entry into homes and expressly forbidding these and other fear-sell tactics. Holland ap-

pealed to the courts, which, in August 1959, not only upheld the
FTC order but, appraised of new complaints, took the unusual step
of issuing a temporary injunction against Holland's use of the cited
sales tactics. As the 1960 case of the San Francisco widow and similar
complaints later introduced in evidence indicated, not all of Holland's representatives took the threat of criminal charges for contempt of court too seriously. Perhaps they had grown immune to
fear.

In January 1965, Holland Furnace and its former top management were found guilty of criminal contempt for violating the federal
court's temporary injunction. The corporation was fined $100,000;
the ex-president was sentenced to six months in prison; and two
former vice-presidents were each fined $500. This marked the first
time the officers of a *major* corporation have been held criminally
responsible for the misdeeds of the company's salesmen.

The BBB and the FTC aren't the only groups active in combating
home-improvement fraud. Various trade associations, such as the
National Established Repair, Service and Improvement Contractors
Association, which represents some 200,000 industry members, have
worked unusually hard to drive the swindlers from their field.
NERSICA, on the other hand, strongly opposes the licensing of
contractors as a solution, and to date only five states require this
elementary partial safeguard. In some communities, the Chamber
of Commerce, like the BBB, will help the confused consumer separate the fair from the fraudulent. Even more active is the Federal
Housing Administration, which keeps a blacklist of more than 7000
names of dishonest firms and salesmen, and prohibits lenders from
providing FHA home-improvement financing to anyone on the list.
However, as one of the BBB pamphlets points out, "The gyp contractor often thinks up a new name and address every spring."[6] And,
though a good watchdog, the FHA operates on a short chain, protecting only its own yard. As *The American Home* noted in an unusually penetrating article on this subject, FHA home-improvement
loans account for only 25 percent of the home-improvement financing
in the U.S. today. Observes the magazine, "There are virtually no
consumer-protection controls over the remaining 75 percent of the
private nongovernment home-improvement financing."[7]

Fighting these swindlers individually is a wearying, time-consum-
ing, and often frustrating experience. There is, however, a single
way to reduce their ranks appreciably. For years, Cleveland, Ohio,

was a prime target for these gyp operators, both the itinerants and the company men. Today Cleveland has less of this type fraud than probably any other major American city. Much of the credit goes to two organizations: Cleveland's Better Business Bureau, one of the most effective BBB's in the country, which has made the stamping out of home-improvement fraud a special crusade; and Cleveland's highly active Home-Improvement Council, headed by the real-estate editor of the Cleveland *Press*. What they did was simple— they went after the co-conspirators. Persuading Cleveland banks and savings-and-loan associations to stop dealing with the phony home-improvement firms, they cut off local financing, without which these swindlers could not operate.

Unfortunately, Cleveland's example is near-unique.

Meantime, the door-to-door army is still marching, its ranks including the honest and the dishonest and every in-between shading. There are ways in which the occupant of the castle can fight back. Putting a sign on the door reading NO CANVASSING OR SOLICITING isn't one of them: "Consider this a personal challenge, a dare to all your powers of persuasion," reads the sales manual of one encyclopedia firm. Even the sign NIGHT WORKER, DAY SLEEPER, DO NOT DISTURB is ineffectual. One such person, tired of the interruptions of apparent illiterates, would take the sales person's home telephone number, promising to call him back on his lunch hour—which he did, at 3 A.M. In his most entertaining book *The Big Sell*, Pierre Berton devotes a special chapter to instructions on how to be a hard head; many of the techniques are the creation of his friend, television cartoonist George Feyer. One begins:

"SALESMAN: Good afternoon, sir. I represent the Family Counselling Division of the National Home Service League.

"FEYER: Is that a Communist front organization? . . ."[8]

Others include reciting miscellaneous facts to the encyclopedia salesman in an attempt to prove that it is he who really needs the set; feigning violent insanity; refusing the "free gift" because you never accept charity; telling the young magazine salesman collecting points for a college scholarship that you disapprove of all kinds of education; surveying the surveyors; interrupting sales spiels with funny stories; insisting that the vacuum-cleaner salesman clean the whole house in his demonstration; and selling the salesman something of your own. These are only a few of Mr. Berton's suggestions.

Purchase of his book is a must for those who desire to live dangerously.

Most of us, however, are too timid for such tactics. We just close
the door as soon as it is humanly possible, and yearn for the good
old days of the moat and drawbridge.

CHAPTER 5

THE INVISIBLE CON MAN

> Making something appear what it
> isn't is a con man's stock in trade.
>
> Joseph "Yellow Kid" Weil

B Y LEAVING the TV dark, the radio silent, the newspaper unread, the car idle, and the telephone and doorbell unanswered, chances of being swindled can be reduced appreciably. Yet even these extreme tactics don't provide immunity to the invisible con man. This year he and his fellows will rob vulnerable Americans of an amount that can only be estimated as "in the hundreds of millions," by means of one of the oldest and yet still most effective types of larceny—mail fraud.

In most of the swindles and frauds previously mentioned, the American is vulnerable because of inadequate laws or ineffectual law enforcement. This isn't true of mail fraud. The Postal Fraud Statutes, 18 USC 1341 and 39 USC 4005, are not only comprehensive, they carry stiff penalties. And they are backed by one of the best qualified law-enforcement groups in the country—the United States Postal Inspection Service. Entrance requirements for the job of postal inspector are second only to those of the FBI in severity. The convictions record of the service is second to none. During fiscal 1962, for example, postal inspectors arrested an average of 888 persons every month. *Over 99 percent of those brought to trial were convicted.*

Yet mail fraud flourishes, has increased at a phenomenal rate since World War II. Why? For the answer we must look at mail fraud from the swindler's point of view, as a trade, with a number of highly attractive features:

(1) It is profitable. Investment is low, returns are high. Business expenses often do not exceed advertising, printing, and postage costs.

(2) Working conditions are ideal. The mail-order swindler doesn't have to go out and look for victims: he need only buy a mailing list or run an ad. He can work whenever he pleases, wherever he chooses. It isn't even necessary that he remain in the country, if he utilizes the services of a mail-forwarding firm.

(3) Unlike Claude Rains, he finds invisibility a most advantageous state. Never seen by his victims, he can't be identified by them. Distance and anonymity separate him from their dissatisfied wrath. The only clue to his identity, his mailing address, is often no clue at all. Usually it is only a mail drop. Using a series of runners, he need never be personally connected with it.

(4) The time gap works in his favor. If he's a hit-and-run promoter, working on the low-unit high-volume principle, he may open a business, use it, close it, and be engaged in a new promotion before the Post Office Department receives its first complaint. If the amount swindled from his individual victims is low, complaints will be few. Chief Postal Inspector H. B. Montague estimates that probably only one out of every ten persons fleeced by mail is sufficiently well informed to file a complaint through proper channels. (Yet during 1964 the POD received 119,092 mail-fraud complaints.) One "business-of-your-own" gypster, with a large sales force that covered a number of states, was able to operate for six years because his victims were unaware that his operations came under the jurisdiction of the POD. The mail-order swindler often considers his victims ignorant; often he's right. Ignorance, like vulnerability, being relative, all of us are ignorant to a degree. Wise enough to see through the most sophisticated con games, we may still be unaware of just what protection we are offered by the mail-fraud statutes. The man who reads a fraudulent ad in a newspaper or magazine, goes to the place of business mentioned, and is there swindled, probably wouldn't think himself a victim of mail fraud; nor would the housewife swindled in her home by a door-to-door salesman who accepted her check for goods or services never to be received. Yet both could be—if that newspaper or magazine was sent through the mails, and if that check went through the mails in clearing the bank. The mail-fraud statutes are broad; such little-understood provisions are often used to catch criminals otherwise untouchable—

but the average citizen, ignorant of them, isn't likely to seek their protection.

(5) Last, but by no means least, the mail-order swindler is partly protected by the laws themselves. The same statutes which protect the privacy of our letters protect the mail con man. If a postal inspector suspects that a letter is being used as part of a swindle, he can't open it or refuse to deliver it. (Few of us would have it any other way, however great the fraud.) He may, however, answer a questionable ad, posing as a customer, to gather evidence. But considering the number of such ads and the number of inspectors— less than 1000, many assigned to matters other than fraud, such as mail theft and pornography, the odds are in the favor of the swindler, especially if he moves fast. And, as former Chief Postal Inspector David H. Stephens once observed, "We can't begin to check the schemes promoted through the use of mailing lists."

Nor is the mail-order swindler discouraged by those remarkably high conviction statistics, the awareness that in recent years more than 95 percent of those brought to trial have been convicted. For he knows the key phrase here is "brought to trial." The high conviction record of the POD is easily explained: lawyers for the Department make sure they have a solid and well-prepared case or they don't go to trial. A majority of the mail-fraud cases never see the inside of a courtroom.

As contrasted with the Federal Trade Commission and the Food and Drug Administration, which are regulatory agencies responsible to Congress, and which have only administrative powers, the Post Office Department is an executive agency, responsible to the President, having both administrative and judicial powers. This means it can act to halt mail fraud in several ways.

Taking the judicial course, it can instigate charges in a federal court to stop the fraud and punish the defrauder with a fine or prison sentence or both. Without considering appeals, this can, and often does, take a year or longer.

Taking the administrative course, it can move faster. Like the FDA and FTC, whose practices are also governed by the Federal Administrative Procedures Act, it can act to halt a fraud without subjecting its perpetrators to criminal penalties. In brief, Mr. Invisible Con Man has all the same outs as Mr. Cheap. He can obtain a hearing before an impartial hearing examiner, and, if he has been careful in his promotion, his chances of winning are good, for there are loopholes in the mail-fraud statutes as broad as the statutes themselves are wide, the largest of which is a single word—"intent." Postal inspectors must not only prove that people were defrauded, they must also prove that the scheme was contrived with "deliberate intent to deceive." Too, unlike the FTC, which can act on deceptive or misleading advertising, the POD is limited to cases of outright fraud.

Assuming the swindler wasn't careful, and the hearing goes against him, a Fraud Order is issued. A Fraud Order has more bite than the FTC's Final Order: by its provisions, any mail addressed to the swindler is returned to the sender unopened and marked "Fraudulent." But even without complications, delays, and appeals, the hearing procedure will usually give the swindler three to six months to continue playing his game. And then he can simply open a new company at another address.

But here, too, the quickest way to end the fraud is through compromise. If the swindler is willing to stop immediately without contesting the charges, he can sign an Affidavit of Discontinuance, which is similar to the FTC's Consent Order, i.e., he agrees to stop doing what he doesn't admit he's done. This has resulted in an interesting situation in the past. The more dangerous the promotion, and the more anxious the POD to halt it immediately, the more likely the swindler will suffer no worse punishment than a gentleman's agreement.

Of late, the game has grown a bit rougher, with the POD placing greater emphasis on criminal prosecutions. In July 1964, a significant precedent was set when postal inspectors, discovering a pair of mail-order swindlers had fictitious-name accounts in six New York-area banks, successfully filed an involuntary bankruptcy petition to freeze the accounts. As a result, 275 victims of this particular fraud received refunds of $15,904. Although the POD is able to return money in only a small number of cases, during 1964 a record high of $9,259,-250 in restitutions was made.

These are a few of the breaks of the game. In the ABCs of mail fraud, which follow, we'll look at some of the ways the game is played. Since the pitch varies, it seems appropriate to mention not only the common but also some of the uncommon gyps, starting off with one that may well be unique:

A is for ADOLF. When Gustav Huber of Bristol, Tennessee, died, his landlady found some odd papers among his effects. So odd that she turned them over to postal inspectors, who were not long in discovering that the late Mr. Huber had been the victim of a fraud.

The papers included a batch of money-order receipts and a packet of letters. The receipts were made out to a man whose various occupations included preacher and private eye. The letters were signed "Adolf Hitler." Investigation disclosed that the swindler had convinced the pro-German Huber that Hitler, Eva Braun, and a number of Nazi generals were living on a nearby mountain, busily engaged in digging a tunnel to Washington, D.C. When finished, the group would come up under the White House and take over the U.S. Government. Over the years, Huber had shelled out $11,000 for such items as picks, shovels, and a new dress uniform for Hitler's triumphal march up Pennsylvania Avenue. In return he had received personal thank-you notes from Adolf, plus the designation "Führer No. 2." Unwilling to point out the entrance to the tunnel, the con man was convicted of mail fraud.

A is also for the AGED, the victims of a large percentage of mail frauds. Though no one likes to be reminded of it, today there are eighteen million Americans over age sixty-five. According to a 1961 White House Conference on Aging, 75 percent of these people have incomes of less than $1000 a year, and 15 percent less than $500. One would think the swindlers would pass them by: on the contrary, the elderly are the primary targets for the numerous work-at-home, business-of-your-own, investment, retirement, life and health insurance frauds, for though their average annual income is only about $2000, their overall spending power is $38 billion a year. It has been estimated that $1 billion of this amount is taken from them by fraud. Senator Harrison A. Williams (New Jersey) believes this figure is "much too low." Observes the Senator, "It could be that elderly people are wasting ten cents of every spending dollar on fraudulent, useless or grossly misrepresented products and services."[1]

B is for BARGAINS and BANKRUPTCY. Using an impressive letterhead, with a name such as American Claims Adjustors, brochures are sent out offering a variety of merchandise, from "Norelco-type" shavers to "American Radio Corporation" transistor tape recorders, supposedly the stock of bankrupt companies which must be liquidated at a loss. The bait, the bankruptcy, and the bargains are generally bogus. The merchandise is cheap and, despite its American brand name, usually foreign-made; the bargain price is exorbitant; and often the ordered item is packed with an unordered item and the whole package sent C.O.D. During 1963, some dozen of these companies grossed an estimated $11 million; there is reason to believe the amount has since doubled. That year a single firm sent out ten million brochures. To get names, these firms often rent the mailing lists of credit-card companies.

B is also for BUG EXTERMINATOR. That this is one of the oldest mail-order swindles hasn't diminished its popularity. "Guaranteed to kill bugs of any kind . . . absolutely safe . . . can be used around pets and children . . ." For $2 the sender receives a small block of wood, a little wooden mallet, and these simple instructions: "Catch the bug, put it on the block, and hit it with the hammer."

C is for a number of things:

CLIPPING SERVICES. This is one of the many "work-at-home" schemes directed at the elderly who live on small pensions or savings and hope to supplement their meager incomes by part-time work at home. The ads promise "big profits" from setting up your own clipping service. All you need do is read the newspaper every day and clip out pertinent articles, which can then be sold to individuals or companies for $1 each. Instructions for setting up such services may cost from $2 to $50. All neglect to mention that there is little demand for the articles once they have been clipped.

COINS. "$1000 For a Lincoln-head Penny!" Every month, with predictable regularity, the POD's *Postal Enforcement Action* bulletin lists the apprehension of several of these gypsters. In many instances, the advertiser isn't interested in buying coins, only in selling coin catalogues or appraisal services at a high fee; but an increasing number offer inflated prices for rare coins, then, once the coins have arrived, skip without making payment.

C.O.D. You didn't order anything sent C.O.D., but maybe someone else in the family did. After paying the postman, you open the package to find you've bought a piece of land all your own (dirt or sand) or a trash-can liner (last week's newspaper). The C.O.D. for the absent neighbor is a popular variation; the relative-who-is-away gambit is far more sickening. There are those who scan the obituary notices, then send out cheap Bibles, rosaries, or crucifixes addressed to the deceased. The acceptance rate on this particular swindle is high. Sometimes the C.O.D. gambit is abandoned for the much simpler technique of sending a bill addressed to the deceased for an amount allegedly due.

CONTESTS AND CREDIT CHECKS. The contest, sponsored by a local merchant, looks so easy you're sure you'll win. And you do! Not the first prize, the new automobile, but one of the second prizes, a "credit check" or "gift certificate" which may be worth as much as

$50—when buying a specific type of merchandise with a prepacked price that allows for your winnings, the cost of the promotion, and a sizable profit for the merchant.

COUPONS. Among your "junk mail" is a letter with a coupon, redeemable for a "free" permanent wave or car wash. In either case you may find the rinse is extra, in fact just about what the whole operation would ordinarily cost. An improvement on this is the coupon book; for from $2 to $10 you receive a whole book of coupons, each good for free merchandise or services at various establishments—for instance, two dinners for the price of one at a local restaurant. Some of these promotions are legitimate. Lately, however, the gypsters have moved into this field in great numbers, launching huge quickie promotions, selling more books than agreed to by the participating merchant, or listing establishments without permission, leaving the purchaser with a book of nonredeemable tickets (a fact he may discover embarrassingly, when presenting his coupon after having dinner for two). Two men, operating in upper New York State were recently convicted after clearing at least $10,000 in this scheme. Deception is common even to many of the "legitimate" promotions. Often an examination of the coupons discloses limiting conditions not mentioned in the enticing ads: the movie tickets good only for matinees, the lube job free only with a complete motor overhaul.

D is for DEATH. As Jessica Mitford makes plain in her remarkable exposé *The American Way of Death,* you can't escape fraud by dying: death, or its prospect, makes you all the more vulnerable. This specialized branch of fraud offers certain advantages to the swindler: the man who buys a nonexistent cemetery lot or prepays $637 for a $96 coffin, believing the cost covers the funeral too, and the woman who pays for perpetual care and gets immediate neglect aren't likely to complain, nor do they make good identifying witnesses. Back in 1933, Cleveland's Director of Safety, one Eliot Ness, formerly of Chicago, broke up an unusually large bogus cemetery-lot swindle which had been victimizing that city's immigrant population for years (in one block, Slovenian families had paid out $86,000). In 1940, due largely to the efforts of the BBB and POD, more than 100 separate companies operating nationally were closed down. They're back now, no longer preying on naive immigrants but offering equal interment to all. Exceptionally well organized, they often use a double company. Obtaining a cheap piece of land, they approach prominent local citizens with a plan for creating a "memorial park" whose beauty will be a credit to the community and, of course, to the prominent citizens who will serve as honorary trustees, directors, or sponsors. The actual selling and swindling is done through a second company which, when it accumulates enough funds, liquidates, leaving the first company without assets but with full responsibility.

D is also for DOGS. Anyone who buys a pet of any kind through the mails is gambling on disappointment. Some years ago the POD succeeded in catching and jailing one particularly sick practitioner of this gambit, the court finding no merit in his defense that he hadn't claimed the dogs were live. The current trick is less offensive and more profitable, a part of the increasingly prevalent "no-send" or "failure-to-furnish" fraud. The swindler takes out an ad in a specialized publication, such as one devoted to dog breeding or training; posing as a kennel owner, he advertises a special type of hunting or show dog, claiming an impressive pedigree, maybe even using photographs. When enough money comes in, he skips.

E is for EMPLOYMENT. Though this con is worked on the domestic level, the foreign-employment scheme is currently the most popular. Excellent jobs overseas, high pay (up to $1500 a month), special bonuses, paid travel allowances, favorable living conditions, and no taxes are some of the promises common to these ads. In exchange for a fee or cash bond, the hopeful applicant may receive a free government brochure which lists foreign job opportunities or a page of classified ads from a newspaper. A California-based employment service netted $3500 in three and a half months on this promotion; more than $5600 in $22.50 fees poured into a Denver post office box; while a single Baltimore outfit took in $150,000. The operators of each also netted prison terms, but only after the promotions had been in effect for some time.

F is for the FAILURE-TO-FURNISH racket. As in the "no-send" cases already mentioned, there is no way to detect this scheme from the ads themselves, which usually appear in reputable publications and may offer any type merchandise. The take can vary from hundreds of dollars to thousands, depending solely on how much time passes before one of its victims files a complaint. Often the swindler will increase his operating time by sending out postcards reading "The merchandise you ordered is temporarily out of stock. Please accept our apologies for the delay. We expect to make shipment shortly." Be sure to save the card; often this is all you will get for your money. Last year, no-send items included antique firearms, treasure maps, wheelchairs for amputees, hearing aids, sailboats, air-craft engines, surplus jeeps, Tom Dooley medals, and mushroom spawns.

G is for GENEALOGIES. Perhaps it's inaccurate to list this as a fraud, since the customer is often sent just what he wants—an impressive genealogy that gives him royal lineage or his own coat-of-arms or heraldic device.

G is also for GOLD BRICKS and the GULLIBLE. Believe it or not, the POD still reports cases of the latter purchasing the former. Just as the fallout of the first atomic bomb included a shower of phony uranium stocks, the current world gold crisis has led to a revival of this old reliable.

H is for HEIRS. If your name is Edwards, you probably know all about this swindle, which has been going on for 120 years. Even its m.o. is the same as on its first appearance in 1846. A letter arrives, bearing the letterhead of a legal firm. It begins:

"Dear Mr. Edwards:

"We have been informed that you may be related to Thomas Edwards who lived in New York City in 1705. If this is correct," you may own the Woolworth Building, the Transportation Building, the Western Union Building, City Hall, the New York Stock Exchange, Fraunces Tavern, Battery Park, and almost everything else on the southern tip of Manhattan Island, that is, if the Edwards-Hall legend is true. In 1705, Queen Anne deeded a large piece of Lower Manhattan Island to Trinity Church. Legend has it that the property didn't belong to the Queen but rather to Thomas Edwards, son-in-law of a Dutch seaman, Thomas Hall, who was said to have been given the land by the Director General of New Netherlands in 1642. The case against Trinity Church, as it is often called, has been brought to court many times, but there is still no authenticated evidence that anyone named Edwards owned property in Manhattan prior to 1821. There is considerable evidence, however, that a large number of Edwardses have parted with amounts ranging from $100 to $1000 for each member of their immediate families as filing fees necessary to establish their claims.

I is for INSURANCE. Although artifice and trickery can be found in every phase of the insurance business (see Chapter 15), the mail-order insurance field is especially fraught with fraud—from fly-by-night companies that collect premiums, then fold before payments are due, to long-established firms, whose policies are wordsmithed to the extent that it is literally impossible to collect on a claim. Currently the most prevalent of these schemes is the offering of health, accident, and life insurance policies to elderly "uninsurables" who can't ordinarily obtain coverage. Bait-advertised promises to the contrary, many of these policies are fantastically expensive and are filled with trick exemption and coy cancellation clauses.

"Reputable" insurance companies refer to such operators as "insurance's fraudulent fringe," yet it is the reputable companies that are largely responsible for the existence and number of these operators, since the insurance industry as a whole has not only done very little in the way of policing itself, it has also made it all but impossible for the federal government to act. Up until 1945, the industry maintained, successfully, that the sale of insurance was neither "commerce" nor "interstate" and thus didn't come under federal jurisdiction. That year the Supreme Court, in the South East Underwriters Association case, found this argument specious. To forestall federal regulation, the insurance lobby, with the help of Senator Pat McCarran (Nevada), introduced a bill in Congress providing that the federal government could regulate insurance companies "only to the extent that such business was not regulated by state law." The bill passed both houses with a comfortable margin. The lobby then concentrated on pushing regulatory laws through the state legislatures. Most states now have an insurance licensing agency; in all but a few states, however, these agencies are little more than token bodies, unable to offer more than a semblance of policing of the practices of the often monolithic companies. As a result of this legal legerdemain, the FTC presently has authority over only those mail-order insurance companies which do business in a state and are not licensed there, or are licensed there but have no agents there. The FTC has successfully obtained only one cease-and-desist order, and that a consent order, in the health insurance field in the past seven years.

K is for the KNITTING-MACHINE CON. Another of the work-at-home schemes, the bait ad offers earnings of $15 to $25 weekly for knitting garments which the company promises to buy. The victim may put out $450 plus finance charges amounting to $100 or more to obtain a cheap West German-made knitting machine worth less than $50, only to find that, no matter how fine the knitting, the company considers the work "below acceptable quality." *Changing Times* reports that one firm took in $64,275 in just five months on this promotion.

L is for LOTTERIES. There are all kinds, and they are all illegal by U.S. postal laws. In July 1963, a self-ordained "bishop" was given a year in the custody of the Attorney General of the state of Florida for selling "blessed numbers" in the form of Bible verses, guaranteed to win in local lotteries.

M is for MATRIMONIAL SCHEMES. The POD breaks this category into three subheadings: men fleecing women; women fleecing men; and fraud artists fleecing both sexes.

N is for NURSERY PRODUCTS. The false advertising of trees, shrubs, flower bulbs and seeds, and other nursery products is another multimillion-dollar business. Since plants can be obtained much more economically dead than live, these operators often send the former without guarantees. The hit-and-skip operator doesn't mind making guarantees, however, as he knows that by the time the flowers are supposed to blossom or the trees bear fruit his company will be safely defunct. Yet the promotion may prove so rewarding that the gypster will stick with it, aware that his profits will more than offset the inconvenience of a fine or, at worst, a short jail sentence. One such operator, whose mail-order nursery operated from an Illinois address, ran weekly ads in some 950 newspapers offering ever-bearing strawberry plants and red African violets. In response to orders, he sent out dead sticks. Complaints and returns yielded more dead sticks. When postal inspectors filed criminal charges against him, he had more than 100 employees filling an average of 25,000 orders a day. His profits are unknown, but some indication of them can be deduced from his advertising budget, which ran to $2 million a year. Convicted of mail fraud in July 1954, given a year's sentence and a $32,000 fine, he kept up business as usual until October 1956, when the U.S. Supreme Court finally refused to review his conviction.

Wordsmithing is also common in this fraud. The Ailanthus, made famous by Betty Smith in her best-selling novel *A Tree Grows in Brooklyn*, is often sold by mail, with synonyms such as "tree of heaven" or "super-growing shade tree." The most popular synonym, "Skunk tree," is never used, nor do the ads mention that this is a "trash" or "weed tree" whose planting is prohibited in many communities, including Brooklyn. Author Pierre Berton, who for many years wrote a widely read syndicated column for the Toronto *Star*, once devoted a long column to exposing the nursery racket and identifying as gyps the Ailanthus, the Golden Crown (the dandelion), Pink Magic (the common bur), the Skyscraper Plant (the great mullein), and the Incredible Snowstorm Plant (the milkweed). "This did not stop one couple from mailing me a check for $3.95 for six Incredible Snowstorm Plants," Berton sadly relates. "I returned the check, explaining what the column was all about and pointing out that I had tried to make this clear. I received, in reply, a torrent of abuse for my fakery, together with a cancelled subscription and the promise that they and their friends, who were also planning to buy the Incredible Snowstorm Plants, would never again believe another word I wrote."[2]

P is for PATENTS. One especially glib swindler took an elderly Rochester, New York, industrialist for nearly a half million on the patent dodge, by convincing him that a movie company which had gone broke in the crash of '29 actually owned the basic patents on sound movies. If they could buy up the stock in the defunct company—so his enticing spiel went—they could sue the major studios for more than twenty-five years of patent infringement. The industrialist shelled out $400,000 for the stock, plus $25,000 to rent an armored car to bring the $200 million "settlement" from California. Needless to say, it never arrived.

PHOTOGRAPHY. The photography gyp has several forms. "Send us your favorite snapshot and we'll send you a *free* 8 × 10 hand-tinted enlargement." The ad neglects to mention that it is to be sent C.O.D. in a $10 frame. Far more expensive is the letter which begins, "One of your friends has written us saying that you have a beautiful child who should be in pictures. Our business, as you know, is finding child stars . . ." The letter goes on to recall the great child stars of the past—Baby LeRoy, Baby Sandy, Shirley Temple, Deanna Durbin, Elizabeth Taylor—dwelling on their earnings, implying but not quite saying that the company in question was responsible for each of their successes (neglecting to mention, of course, that there is little demand for child stars today, or that Baby LeRoy retired by reason of old age at four, that Baby Sandy was a has-been at two). Such fortune may await your child, the letter promises, if you'll let our talent scout call on you. "There is no obligation." There is, however, as the proud parents discover, a large outlay for photos, coloring and retouching charges, a fee for a full-page listing in the model-agency's directory, etc. Names for such promotions are purchased from maternity hospitals, diaper services, and toy shops.

PORNOGRAPHY. It is illegal to send pornography through the U.S. mails or to receive same. This simple fact has been the basis for a very profitable racket. Using suggestive or *double-entendre* words and phrases in girlie magazine ads or personal mailings, pseudo pornographers broadly hint that the photos and books they are selling are obscene. When purchased, however, at exorbitant prices, they prove to be quite innocuous. This was, for a time, a near-perfect racket, as customers were most reluctant to complain to postal inspectors that they had attempted to order pornography and had been gypped, while the POD in turn couldn't arrest someone for not sending pornography through the mails. A recent change in postal regulations, however, has made it unlawful to "offer to sell" pornography.

S is for SONG WRITING. Does a catchy tune keep running through your head? Do you have a bit of inspired verse that would sound good set to music? For a price you can realize your dream. It's usually a high price, on an installment basis, with fees for collaboration, arrangements, sheet-music printing, recording-studio rental, etc. The business of "song sharkery" is old and well established. Some years ago a Los Angeles promoter was arrested and given a fine and prison sentence for bilking the public of at least $1 million in fees. Last year his son was arrested and given five years' probation for similarly collecting $453,000.

U is for UNORDERED MERCHANDISE. The mail brings merchandise that you haven't ordered and don't want, often tied to a religious or charity pitch: the cheap dresser scarf is made by a handicapped person (a grotesque, nightmare-inducing wheelchair photo is enclosed); money received for the tin St. Anthony's medal will help support an orphanage (starving-child photo enclosed); or the sheet of stamps is from an institution that rehabilitates wayward boys (throw them away without a contribution and you not only feel cheap and uncharitable but you may even be contributing to the delinquency of a minor). Although the name of the charity may be unfamiliar (or vaguely familiar, for many use names similar to those of long-established charities), many people yield to this pitch. Perhaps, to them, the feeling of self-righteousness is worth a dollar or so. Many, however, apparently pay out of the vague feeling that even though they didn't order the merchandise, they are now somehow responsible for it, and they haven't the time to rewrap and remail it. As a conscience-easer, it should be noted that millions of dollars are taken in annually by such operators, with only a token payment, if anything, actually going to charity.

Although a recent POD study of the unordered-merchandise field disclosed hundreds of cases of fraud and near-fraud, there is no law which prohibits a company from doing business in this manner. But there is also no law which says you must either pay for or return unsolicited merchandise (including the stamps sent to your children "on approval"). What to do with it? If you haven't destroyed the wrappings, you can rewrap the package, mark it REFUSED, and drop it in a mailbox. This is what the POD recommends. There are other ways to play, however, which the POD discourages, and which the author of course isn't recommending, but which some find add a certain satisfaction to the game.

One is to keep the package until the first dunning letter arrives, then reply with a bill for storage charges. No matter how legal-sounding the name on the letterhead, you needn't return the merchandise until the bill is paid. If, as sometimes happens, the letters become threatening, you can turn the correspondence over to the POD for possible criminal action. If you tire of the game after a while, you need only write the company that unless your bill is paid within thirty days the merchandise will be sold for storage charges or destroyed.

Some go a bit further, mailing the company their own merchandise, odds-and-ends of junk that have accumulated around the house, which are sent sans postage and return address (this, by the way, is illegal). During the 1964 presidential elections, one San Francisco liberal, tired of receiving pleas for funds from a group that called itself "Democrats for Goldwater" and discovering that the postage-paid envelopes enclosed with such pleas would hold four pounds of lead, succeeded in collecting several hundred of these envelopes from fellow Democrats, which, mailed back to the group, cost it $2.40 each.

V is for VANITY PRESSES. The advertisements appear in many magazines, most newspapers, and some writers' publications. Manuscripts wanted by major publishing firm. Object: publication. The would-be author hopefully mails off his manuscript. For a change, the reply isn't a rejection slip but an excited letter of acceptance. The manuscript, writes the publisher himself, has occasioned the most enthusiastic readers' reports in many a month; the firm would be proud to publish the author's book. A contract will follow. It follows, by several days, leaving the author just enough time in between to inform all his relatives and friends of the good news. The contract is a "cooperative publishing agreement," the author to pay all costs of the first printing. To offset this discouraging development are all the tempting clauses which refer to high royalties, movie rights, TV rights, foreign translations, book-club sales, autographing parties, etc. To make a long, sad story short, the author may pay from $600 to $6000 to see his work in print, only to find that book reviewers don't review vanity-press titles, bookstores don't carry them (some of these firms don't even have salesmen), the only advertising is a small ad in the author's hometown newspaper, and the total number of copies sold only slightly exceeds the number purchased by the author himself. Even then, the publisher may charge the author storage on unsold copies. Though the brochures for these firms cite many famous authors who have paid to have their own works published, few are contemporary, and a letter to the firm asking them to recommend one satisfied author will draw an evasive reply. The FTC has cited nearly all of the now operating vanity presses for misrepresentations, the POD has obtained fraud orders against several, but they continue to operate, promising a little less but still taking in substantial amounts in excess of what an ordinary printer would charge to print and bind a book. An allied fraud is the so-called "literary agent" who charges a fee to evaluate the author's work. Often he works in collaboration with the vanity publisher, receiving $250 or more for each author he recommends who succumbs to the vanity pitch.

VENDING MACHINES. The vending-machine racket leads by a comfortable margin all the other business-of-your-own investment gyps. Retired people are the chief victims of this fraud. "Business opportunity," reads a typical ad. "Applicant must have car, references, $600 to $1200 working capital which is secured by inventory, and must be willing to work 8 to 10 hours a week for guaranteed profits of $200 to $350 a month . . ." Another ad promises "Your net profits approximately 100 percent. On some of our machines, the net profit may be 200 to 300 percent!" The m.o. of this fraud is simple. The investor is sold cheap vending machines at exorbitant prices (one New York company sold its coffee-dispensing machines for *1600 percent* above cost), together with directions for their servicing, plus "exclusive" areas or routes. The promised returns are almost always inflated, the machines are expensive to maintain, and the territory (more often than not) has more than enough machines already. During the past year the POD has reported dozens of cases involving amounts ranging from $30,000 to $200,000, taken from people who failed to heed the BBB's elementary advice: "Investigate before you invest."

Interestingly enough, even skilled con men have found the

vending-machine business risky. "Yellow Kid" Weil, who had a perfect record of failure in every legitimate business venture he entered ("The notion that any swindler would be a great success if he
turned to legitimate channels is indeed erroneous"), once lost a
sizable sum on a then revolutionary idea that chewing gum could
be distributed through vending machines. He designed his own
machines and had a chemist compound a new flavor of gum. As the
Kid tells it, he sold the machines at a loss to a man who made a
fortune from them, while the gum formula was sold for a pittance
to an outfit called Wrigley's, which marketed it under the name
Spearmint. The Wrigley Company, however, tells a rather different
story of the gum's origin.

W is for WORK-AT-HOME SCHEMES.

"Women wanted as longhand addressers to mail advertising for
our firm. Good pay for part-time work. No typing, no selling, no
canvassing. We furnish everything . . ."

The above ad, appearing in the Help Wanted columns of newspapers across the country, netted its advertiser $300,000. To ap-
preciate its effectiveness, it should be noted that each of its victims
lost only $3, the cost of a mimeographed sheet of instructions for
setting up an envelope-addressing business at home. For many, however—the aged, who are the principal targets of this fraud—$3 was
more than they could afford to lose.

The work-at-home gyp began to bud during World War II; in the
fifties it blossomed; today it is in full bloom, netting its operators
as much as $50 million annually. The work varies—mushroom rais-
ing, chinchilla breeding, bootie knitting, bead stringing, plastic
laminating, photo coloring, home importing, and artificial-flower
making are just a few of the most common types—but the basic
pitch, the promise of good pay for part-time work at home, is consistent in all these schemes and has a strong appeal to bedridden
invalids, shut-ins, and the elderly retired. The ads either state or
imply that no experience is necessary, that there is a ready market
for the goods or services, and that there are large profits. They
neglect to mention that instead of pay there is payment, for exor-
bitantly priced goods and equipment. There is only one element of
truth in the work-at-home pitch. You *can* make big money with a
minimum of effort—if you're a swindler.

Often a single company will run up a sizable profit in a short
period of time. One Ohioan set up an envelope-addressing scheme,
charging $1 for a sheet of mimeographed instructions and $6 for

a starting kit. From August 1957 to December 1958 alone, he took in $65,000, according to postal inspectors, who found it difficult to pin down his operation, however. Not until December of 1963 was he convicted of mail fraud, given a suspended sentence, and placed on two years' probation. One of the earliest of these operators was at one time operating forty-four known companies, their promotions ranging from Angora breeding to a vanity literary agency for movie scenarios.

The most successful of all the work-at-home operators, according to the POD, was Nels Irwin. Irwin entered the mail-fraud field in 1952 with a firm known as Coast Industries, operating out of Gardena, California. Beginning with a sure-fire method of applying a velvetlike finish to any product, he soon branched out into silk-screen painting (Screen Print Co.), miniature trees (World-Wide Miniature Tree Nurseries), molding machines for making plastic novelties (Plasti-Form Co.), tropical fish and other enterprises (Mail Order Distributors). Irwin's fees rarely exceeded $100; his estimated gross over a six-year period totaled $3 million. Although the POD began its investigation in 1953, not until 1963 were Irwin and his general manager convicted on sixteen counts of mail fraud. Irwin was sentenced to three years in prison with four years' probation, while his assistant was given the same probation and nine months in prison. In investigating the numerous complaints, the POD was unable to find a single customer who had made a cent on any of Irwin's promotions.

"Field hopping" is not uncommon in mail fraud. Undisputed champion of such swindlers is a man we'll call Richard Davis, who since World War II has been involved in a fantastic number of separate companies selling such things as the Ailanthus tree; a "transistor" pocket radio that was a crystal set; a battery additive, composed mainly of Epsom salts; a fuel converter ("run your car half on gas, half on air"); several skin foods ("grow a new skin overnight"); a "lose a pound a day" reducer; a car cloth which would "end car washing, waxing, polishing forever"; powdered heat pellets ("end snow shoveling forever"); and a "miracle fertilizer" to restore "unsightly brown grass," actually a green dye.

Since Davis's actual participation was often hidden behind three or more dummy corporations and ad agencies, law-enforcement officials won't even guess how much money he took in on his various promotions, or how many promotions there actually were. When finally convicted by a federal jury on eleven counts of mail fraud in connection with the fuel-converter scheme (which took in a third of a million in a single year), he left behind him a long string of FTC and FDA cease-and-desist and consent orders, POD fraud orders and discontinuance agreements, and the shells of more than two-dozen abandoned companies. He was sentenced to a year and a half in prison and given a $3000 fine.

Perhaps it's time for a really truthful ad:

JOB OPPORTUNITY: Mail-order swindlery. Low investment. High profits. Ideal working conditions. Full or part-time. Short unpaid vacation every ten or fifteen years optional.

CHAPTER 6

THE FALL OF THE CASTLE

> If everyone started spending only
> what he earned it would be worse
> than a depression, it would be a
> catastrophe.
>
> Dewey D. Godfrey
> President, International
> Consumer Credit Association

T HIS is a short chapter about a simple, but costly, deception.

If you lend money to a bank or savings-and-loan association—i.e., put money in a savings account—you will be told the truth about the interest paid. Your interest will be quoted at the true annual rate.

If you borrow money, or buy on time, the lending agency—whether it is a bank, finance company, small-loan company, auto dealer, or retail store—will deceive and perhaps even defraud you. Your interest will be computed in a way that makes it appear far less than what you'll actually be paying.

Basic to the working philosophy of the modern American credit industry is what Senator Paul H. Douglas (Illinois) calls "the golden rule of the lending business"—*Always represent the cost of credit as being 6 percent or less.*[1]

This figure wasn't arbitrarily chosen. To most of us, 6 percent seems a reasonable interest rate. So it also seemed to most of our forefathers, for this rate has been with us so long as to achieve universal acceptance. Former Under Secretary of Commerce Edward Gudeman, testifying before a Congressional committee, once traced the origin of the 6 percent rate to medieval church doctrine, which set this as the maximum interest rate that ought to be charged to consumers. "Since such borrowers normally needed credit only because of some natural catastrophe or similar occurrence which threatened them with starvation or other such adversities," Gudeman related, ". . . charging a rate of interest to consumers in excess of 6 percent was regarded as unfair profiteering at the expense of the needy, the desperate, or the unfortunate."[2]

Thus a habit was formed, backed by the force of religious dogma —acceptance of 6 percent as the dividing line between fair and fraudulent interest rates, between good business and usury. As time passed, the habit became so ingrained that when, well into the twentieth century, merchants and lenders decided that 6 percent was too low a figure to cover expenses and risks and still make a reasonable profit, the habit was found to be too strong to break. So alternatives were taken, ways devised to circumvent it. Through various polite deceptions, the borrower was made to think that he was paying only 6 percent, despite the fact the lender was actually receiving a higher, often much higher, rate.

Today most banks and businesses are playing the game of *false percentages*. Though, as in wordsmithing and pricemanship, the rules vary, depending on the players and the playing field, there are five basic variations which have proven especially popular. Some of them are rather cute; all of them can be, and often are, quite costly.

(1) *No Interest Rate Is Quoted.* A federal employee in New Mexico purchased a television set on time. Priced at $285.55, it was to be paid for at the rate of "about $14 a month." No mention was made, either verbally by the salesman or in writing in the contract, of the interest or finance charges or even the number of months the customer must make payments. After paying $147.30 over ten months, the man decided to pay off the balance and found that to do so would cost him an additional $206.22. Only then, by some simple addition and subtraction, did he discover that his credit charges amounted to $67.97, or more than 33 percent annual interest.

This is probably the most common type of interest deception. Emphasis is placed on the low payments—"$10 down and $10 a month" or "pennies a day." It is quite legal in many states. It is widely practiced in many states where it is not.

(2) *The Add-on Rate.* A clerk in a small community in upstate New York wanted to borrow $100, to be repaid in monthly installments over a period of one year. At the local bank he was told that

the finance charge on the loan would be $6. The $6 was added to the $100 and then divided into twelve equal monthly payments. There appeared to be no deception here, and the rate certainly seemed to be 6 percent. Actually, it was more than 11 percent, for with each payment the man had use of less money, so that the average amount of his loan over a period of one year was only about $50. But he paid a full $6 on $100. In other words, the interest rate was quoted on the original amount of the debt and not on the declining or unpaid balance, as is the custom in business credit or government loans. This, too, is very common.

(3) *The Discount Rate.* A Colorado cowboy also borrowed $100 from a bank. He, too, was told that his finance charges would be $6 on $100, or 6 percent. But that mythological phrase "6 percent" is highly relative. The cowboy paid a slightly higher rate of interest than the clerk, since in his case the $6 was deducted from the $100 when the loan was made. Loaned $94, he had to repay $100.

(4) *The Add-on or Discount Rate Plus the Fee System.* This is "packing," as mentioned in Chapter 3—the adding on of all sorts of extraneous and often exorbitant fees, for such things as credit investigation, loan processing, late-payment service charges, and that very effective sentimental gimmick, credit life insurance ("If you die your wife won't have to pay off the balance of your debt").

Such packed charges not only add to the cost of the item but compound the camouflaging of the actual finance charges. Auto dealers and their finance companies are best at this game, but small-loan companies, debt proraters, and others often run a close second.

(5) *The Monthly-rate Gimmick.* A housewife in Michigan purchased a new electric skillet at a local department store on its revolving-credit plan, paying the low interest rate (sometimes called a "service charge") of 1½ percent. A receptionist in Minnesota bought a new dress under the same type plan, her interest rate 2 percent. A telephone operator in Texas bought a girdle, at 3 percent. A teenager in Florida hopefully bought a size 28AAA bra, at 4 percent. Or so each was told. The interest charges quoted, however— and this trick is common to small-loan companies as well as to retailers offering revolving-credit plans—were by the month. The true annual interest rate is 12 times the quoted figure, or, in these cases, 18, 24, 36, and 48 percent per year. The teenager was lucky, paying only 48 percent; interest on some of the currently popular teen credit plans and junior credit cards runs as high as 94 percent.

Question: How do most Americans react to being victim to these deceptions?

Answer (and here's the wonder of the game, the only reason businesses can continue playing it): They don't, for most never become aware that they are being conned. In four of these basic tricks the borrower-buyer finds it nearly impossible to compute the true rate. One, however, converting the monthly rate into the annual rate, is so simple that even a child can do it. But, apparently, many adults lack either the curiosity or the simple know-how, for even here a remarkably large number are unaware of just how much they are paying. "We live in a world in which our children can compute and recite the batting averages of their favorite ball players," observes Senator Douglas. "Young university graduates are well versed in the complex mathematics of inter-space flight. Yet the great majority of our citizens are unaware of or are unable to decipher the rates of interest they are charged with respect to ordinary consumer credit transactions. In fact, too often the average borrower does not even receive the necessary information from the lender to be able to perform the simple arithmetic involved in determining the true annual interest rate on credit transactions."[3]

Recently two economists associated with the National Bureau of Economic Research proved this in a study of consumer sensitivity to finance rates. As in Mrs. Nelson's packaging survey, the participants were atypical, chosen from among the subscribers to the magazine *Consumer Reports*. As a group, these people were well above the national average in education, income, and ownership of goods. As readers of the magazine, they were far more likely to have been exposed to information on credit costs than the general public. The 840 interviewees had several things in common with more representative Americans, however: all had borrowed money on the installment plan during the past two years; all thought they knew the interest rate they had paid; and most didn't. Considering just one portion of the findings, a total of 234, or nearly 28 percent of those interviewed in this special group, thought their interest rate was 6 percent. But only 6 of the 234 had paid even close to this mythological rate. In reality, 96 of the 234 who thought their interest rate was 6 percent were charged somewhere between 9.5 and 19.49 percent, while 63 were charged between 19.5 and 49.9 percent, and more than a few were paying 50 percent or more.[4]

Maxim: The vulnerable American may, without contradiction, be both unusually intelligent and remarkably ignorant.

Such ignorance can be expensive. Offered a variety of credit plans or different forms of financing, but denied the information necessary to comparing them and choosing the most economical or least costly, the average American finds it impossible to shop intelligently for credit. Having chosen, however, by whatever means or manner, he often remains in ignorance as to the extent of his obligations. In recent years consumer debt has risen astronomically, as have personal bankruptcies. The bankruptcy rate today is more than twice as high as in either 1930 or 1935. From 1950 to 1962 bankruptcies increased almost fivefold—from 33,000 cases filed in 1950 to 148,000 filed in 1962. Nine out of ten of these bankruptcies were nonbusiness, or personal, in nature. Between 1958 and 1963 alone, personal bankruptcy filings increased from 64,617 to an estimated 132,135—a gain of almost 110 percent. Causes are numerous, the blame attributed alternately to the consumer's desire to live beyond his means or to the merchant's desire to help him do so through the extension of "too easy credit." Yet probably everyone concerned would agree that the consumer's ignorance as to the extent of his obligations and indebtedness is a significant factor.

Five little tricks. One hesitates to call them "frauds," for, as practiced by "respectable" bankers and "reputable" merchants—not as occasional artifices but as basic day-to-day tools of the trade—they have the sanction of accepted usage. Five little tricks, which would seem to be the least important forms of credit deception, since from here trickery branches out into the realms of complex and high finance and unmistakable fraud. Five little tricks that nevertheless help explain why our national credit system has been described, so fittingly, as "a model of contrived confusion."[5] Just how important are they?

Several years ago Senator Douglas, together with nineteen other senators, introduced a "Truth-in-Lending" bill in Congress. The result of numerous complaints and a long series of hearings, this bill had a simple purpose, "requiring the disclosure of finance charges in connection with extensions of credit." It provided that anyone engaged in the business of extending credit at the retail level would have to disclose fully in writing the costs of the credit to the borrower before the credit transaction was signed. This written statement would include the total amount of the finance charge, expressed both in dollars and cents and in true annual interest rate. In short, the lender or retailer would have to disclose the cost of the credit, just the same as the cost of goods. The bill did not regulate credit. It did not set, or even suggest, a maximum chargeable interest rate. It simply required that the truth be told.

First introduced in 1962, and consistently reintroduced in each new session of the Congress since then, supported by Presidents Kennedy and Johnson, their top financial advisers, credit unions, consumer groups, trade unions, and many savings-and-loan associations, the bill, to date, has yet to make it out of committee. Major opponents of the bill—the American Bankers Association and most retailers' associations—have advanced a number of arguments against its passage, many remarkably similar to those advanced against the "Truth-in-Packaging" bill: that it constitutes unwarranted interference in business and states' rights; that it is unnecessary, the consumer having little interest in interest rates; that the consumer's major concern isn't learning the intricacies of financing but having credit available when he needs it. In-trade arguments, however, have been franker and might be summed up in the statement of a spokesman for the National Association of Retail Clothiers and Furnishers, quoted in *The Financial Post*, "If a store offering credit at 1½ percent a month had to tell customers this means 18 percent per year [it] would create an undesirable psychological effect on the American consumer's buying habits."

Though opponents of the bill have publicly minimized its importance, they have fought it with unusual determination, causing California Consumer Counsel Helen Nelson to remark, "The fierceness of the continuing battle nationally and on the state level to prevent this law from coming into existence is the most convincing proof that this is the fortress of credit abuse. No other piece of credit legislation has been fought so hard by so many retailers and financial institutions."[6]

The bill would, perhaps needless to say, eliminate those five little tricks.

Meanwhile, the game is still being played, to the benefit of some and the distress of others, those whom David Caplovitz, senior study director of the National Opinion Research Center, calls the new "urban sharecroppers," while every day new anomalies are added to a national credit system whose workings have come to resemble a kind of acceptable madness.

Today many merchants make more money on the extension of credit than on the sale of goods. The least welcome customer in many stores is the man who insists on paying cash. One mail-order house recently announced in its catalogues, "Credit orders only! No cash or C.O.D. orders accepted." "Today," writes Richard Phelon in *Dun's Review,* "few lenders will turn down a loan application on grounds of a past bankruptcy. Indeed, there are even some credit merchants who advertise their willingness, at a price, to give the bankrupt another chance."[7] Addressing the New York University Graduate School of Business Administration, Rudolph A. Peterson, president of the Bank of America, the world's largest commercial bank, told students that "Debt performs a vital function in our economy and it must grow in order for the economy to prosper." Remarking that the connotations of the term "debt" have, or should have, changed tremendously over the past few decades, Peterson said "we must rid ourselves of the semantic problems arising from the association of the word 'debt' with other more virulent four-letter words."[8]

Today debt prorating, or consolidation, has become a big business. The debt proraters take charge of the individual's finances, paying off all his debts, keeping him out of bankruptcy court but adding to his indebtedness one more debt, the prorater's fee, which, depending on the state, can lawfully amount to from 12 to 48 percent of the total of the debts prorated.

In the realm of auto financing the situation has reached the stage of the ludicrous. Until the early 1960s there was, in auto financing, what was known as the "36-month wall." Auto dealers and their finance companies universally agreed that payments on a new or used car shouldn't be extended over a period greater than 36 months. And for a very good reason, one quite obvious now that the wall has fallen and payments are spread out over 49 months and longer. The moment a new-car buyer drives his $3000 Super Savage Tiger Special out of the salesroom it depreciates 20 percent in value. After three years' time, depreciation will have reduced its value to about one-third of its original cost, say to $1000, making it worth considerably less than the payments still to be made. It therefore becomes sounder economically, rather than continuing payments, to let the finance company repossess the car, then apply future payment money toward the purchase of a new model. This practice has now become so common, observes one credit man, that it has little if any effect on the individual's credit rating.

Viewing with some alarm the growing indebtedness of the American public, financial columnist Sylvia Porter asked a number of credit experts, "How much debt is too much?"

Their shocking, if frank, answer: "We don't know."

"It well may be that the old rules-of-thumb for safe borrowing and lending are obsolete," Miss Porter concludes. "It well may be that worries about how much debt is too much are unwarranted. But the central fact is that we do not know, and just our ignorance gives thoughtful observers a queasy feeling. The quicker we are given warning or reassurance, the better for all of us."[9]

There is a popular story told in credit circles, said to be based on fact, of a woman who refused to meet her payments to a loan company. Examined by her physician and pronounced mentally ill, she was committed to a mental institution, from whence she regularly sent money to the company. Once she was pronounced cured and released, the payments stopped.

CHAPTER 7

CAMELOT REVISITED

> Don't be frightened. I want to be
> your friend. Do you want to be
> mine?
>
> —Suggested psychological ap-
> proach for use with a shy student,
> from a dance-studio teaching
> manual

IF YOU have a desire, however commendable or base, there are
frauds to match it. If you have a dream, be it noble or small, there
are specialists to exploit it. If you have a weakness, some would find
it and turn it to their profit. Love can be made a racket, loneliness a
gyp, hope a high-priced commodity. A sampling of such frauds
follows.

Computing the X-factor

Imagine a good fairy entering the "system house" of that auto
dealer who gypped George Smith in Chapter 3. With a flick of a
magic wand the automobiles vanish, leaving in their place desires
and illusions, intangibles which can be felt but not seen, and yet,
even more miraculously, can be sold. Another wave of the wand
and the auto display room is transformed into a grand ballroom, the
sales cubicles stretch into the shape of smaller ballrooms, and the
salesconmen are suddenly metamorphosed into handsome, debonair men and beautiful young women. Only music and glamor are
added. The initial deceptions and high-pressure sales techniques

remain, as do the "bugged" salesrooms, the time-payment contracts, the finance company in the background, and, often, a final disillusionment as expensive as it is heartbreaking.

The result, which we'll call Melodyland, is not unique. It could be any one of hundreds of dancing studios which have discovered the magic secret. The secret is simply this: only a limited number of people will pay to learn to dance, but an unlimited number will pay, often far more than they can afford, to overcome personal fears and weaknesses.

The "free lesson" gimmick is the usual bait. Through lucky-buck contests, zodiac puzzles, and telephone quizzes ("Name the last three Presidents of the United States . . . Johnson, Kennedy and Lincoln . . . Wonderful! You got two out of three and that means you win!") potential students are lured into the studio to receive one or more free lessons. Unknowingly, from the moment they enter the gilded door to the time they put pen to contract form, they are players in a drama as well rehearsed as it is attractively staged. It matters little whether the scene is Washington, D.C., or Pocatello, Idaho. Many of these studios, particularly those belonging to national chains, use near-identical teaching and organizational manuals covering every detail of their operations, from answers to every possible objection to signing up for additional lessons to the step-by-step buildup to Lifetime Membership.

To the prospective student, the atmosphere seems relaxed and informal. But every minute of the first "free" hour-long lesson is carefully plotted. During the first thirty minutes the student is taught several basic steps, while, at regular intervals, the teacher explains that Melodyland is not so much a school as a private club (not everyone can join) or a family (Mr. Melody, who heads the chain, cares about each pupil as he would a son or daughter). The three-minute break is even more carefully charted. "Tell me all about yourself," the dance analyst asks with breathless expectancy. If the student hesitates, there are helpful questions, and an interest in the replies so total as to draw confidences from even the most reticent. During the next twenty-seven minutes the student's dancing ability is evaluated and a possible plan for future lessons drawn up. Invariably, the student receives exceptionally high marks for Rhythm and Cooperation, but slightly lesser marks, indicating the need for more training, in such things as Poise, Style, Precision, Leading or Following; the plan, which is only tentative and has to be approved by the Head Registrar, indicates that the student shows so much promise that a four- or five-lesson course might be in order.

The routine is so firmly fixed that a casual customer, interested in brushing up on the latest steps, can't walk into the studio and "buy" lessons, not without first going through the buildup. Some studios even refuse to reveal their per-lesson price. The student must buy the whole Melodyland way of life.

On arriving for the second lesson, the student is greeted by name and immediately exposed to the infectious excitement of studio life. There are introductions to other students, enticing mentions of frequent nightclub parties, outings, and contests with prizes, followed by the teaching of a few more steps, plus more probing questions. These rarely concern the student's financial situation. In many of the larger studios it is standard operating procedure to begin a discreet but thorough credit investigation of each potential student following the second lesson. There is another reason for this curiosity, beyond the teacher's natural interest in anyone so talented and charming. By the end of the second hour the analyst is supposed to have discovered the student's "X-factor."

There are differing explanations as to what the X-factor actually is. The creation of a motivational research organization which has worked with many of the dance chains, it has been described as "the pupil's personality background and emotional needs for dancing lessons." It is assumed, interestingly enough, that the student is not in the studio merely from a desire to learn to dance but because of some deeper emotional problem. It may be loneliness, insecurity, a desire for social status, a need for acceptance and belonging. One former dance instructor, interviewed in a national magazine, frankly defined it as "some weakness." "We are instructed," the teacher is quoted as saying, "how to appeal to people's desires to overcome their handicaps, such as false teeth, hair pieces, their inability to socialize, crippled members, withered arms, that sort of thing."

Usually the X-factor is discovered during the first or second lesson,* while the third and fourth lessons are spent in using this knowledge as a lever to overcome the student's objections to signing up for additional lessons. A favored technique, suggested in many studio manuals, is the "picture story," the teacher offering the tale of a person whose problems were exactly the same as the student's,

---

* It may be known even before the student sets foot in the studio. As revealed in a state probe, one national chain bought mailing lists of persons who had at some time or another ordered crutches, braces, or other aids for the handicapped.

but who overcame them through dancing to become a sought-after member of the Jet Set.

By the third lesson, the soft but persistent sell is well underway, never to let up as long as the student visits the studio. At first the student may contract for a minimum course, for example, 10 hours for $49; before these lessons have reached the halfway point, however, he is being readied for advanced courses, the "300-hour atmosphere." Most of this selling is highly emotional. Lessons are never offered bluntly; they are always tendered conditionally, obtainable "only if enough progress is shown" or "only if approval for a more advanced course can be obtained from the Head Registrar." Frequently approval is initially denied. The traumatic effect on a student whose X-factor is a basic insecurity needn't be imagined—it has been described in several of the state hearings on dance-studio practices. The possibility that he may not be one of the chosen few can reduce an adult to a child suddenly told he won't pass, that he must remain behind while his class goes on to a higher grade. Given a second chance, his gratitude at being allowed to buy more lessons is sometimes pathetic enough to make a sensitive teacher adopt another trade.

On signing his first contract the student is assigned a regular teacher; as time passes their relationship grows extremely close, the teacher literally befriending the student, arguing against the Registrar, the Superintendent, and the various dance boards that the student really does possess dancing ability and is ready for more advanced lessons. To some the world of the studio becomes the only real world, and the teacher-pupil relationship the most meaningful of their lives.

Lest this relationship appear one-sided, there is usually a way for the student to show his appreciation. Periodically, throughout the year, there will be intrastudio contests, the "best teacher" being chosen on the basis of points given for the number of hours his or her students have signed for in the advanced courses. More effective, a proof of even broader loyalty, is an annual group-selling effort in which teachers and students alike participate—Dance Days.

Once a year all the studios in the Melodyland chain will hold a gigantic campaign, with each studio competing to be the leader in number of hours sold. During this period, special discounts are offered on lessons, and the students become salesmen, attempting to sign up their friends in the hope that their own studio may win the grand prize, an especially engraved loving cup. According to one ex-student, "Dance Days was like Mardi Gras stretched over six weeks, a constant party, with the tension building up to an unbelievable pitch in the last week, a kind of mass hypnotism that was so emotional everyone would alternately sob with disappointment or relief. There were huge charts on the walls. It was like election night, the telephone ringing constantly as District Supervisors would call in new returns, or Mr. Melody himself calling to offer congratulations or encouragement. For an hour St. Louis might be ahead, and then we'd pass them, and then Dallas would pass us, and we'd fall far behind, and then later, through a real effort, we'd surge way ahead.

"Many of the students took their vacations at this time so they could stay at the studio. When it finally ended you were emotionally drained, too tired to even think about how you were going to pay for all those extra lessons you'd signed up for."

Not all are so anxious to make the studio the focal point of their existence. For many a student there comes a moment of decision, when he frankly states that he doesn't want or can't afford more lessons. There are numerous techniques expressly designed to overcome such objections. One is "relay salesmanship," another form of "T.O. selling." Sometimes a half-dozen teachers and supervisors will talk in turn to a student, even pursuing him to his home, attempting to convince him that to discontinue would be a terrible waste of talent. Sometimes this massive emotional assault isn't necessary, the simple "switch sell" being quite effective. A male student who fails to respond to the persuasion of his willowy blonde instructress may be switched to a more amply endowed brunette and taken into a private ballroom and taught a close embrace known as "the old renewal step." While most of the studio heads deny that sex is ever used to sell lessons, some of the teachers and more than a few disillusioned students have told different stories—of suggestively unbuttoned blouses, intimate hints of varying subtlety, corsages, gifts, candlelight dinners. Since the teachers usually obtain from 3 to 5 percent of all monies collected from lessons they sell, occasional instances of these and even more entangling involvements would appear to be inevitable, though, for the record, most studios strongly condemn such practices and hold the threat of instant dismissal over any teacher found guilty of out-of-studio fraternization.

But while some students may hesitate and take two steps back, there are others whose only desire is to waltz on forever. To make this possible, several of the chains formed Lifetime Clubs, designed to appear the most *in* of *in* groups. As the student progresses step-by-step through the various courses, earning in turn various medals of accomplishment, the lifetime club, with its champagne parties and other ultra-exclusive social events, is depicted as the ultimate symbol of belonging, all the more tantalizing in that membership is never offered. To belong, the student must personally request membership, pass a number of qualifying boards, be voted on by the lifetime club members, and finally write a personal letter to Mr. Melody asking to belong. The first letter is nearly always rejected, and sometimes the second also. Any reservations the student may have harbored up to this point vanish in a wave of disappointment and anger. But there is a last appeal. As the student and teacher wait in acute anxiety, the supervisor will place a person-to-person call to none other than Mr. Melody himself, who will listen to each plea in turn. Should the student's progress and ability be exceptional enough, the recommendations strong enough, and the student's desire sincere enough, the voice from the father studio just might grant acceptance. Though there is some variance, depending upon the chain and the student's financial situation, the average cost of a lifetime membership is about $12,000.

A widowed Albany, New York, tourist-home operator paid a local studio $11,800 for her lifetime membership. She was seventy-nine at the time. Another widow, sixty-nine, was persuaded by a Baltimore, Maryland, studio to sign eight separate contracts for dancing lessons, at a cost of $34,913. A Yonkers, New York, cigar-stand operator paid $9000 to a studio on assurances that he could become a professional dancer. He was blind. A shy middle-aged bachelor paid $51,000 to a Calgary, Canada, studio: $36,000 for dancing lessons, plus a $15,000 loan.

Probably none of these "privileged few" would have complained had the studios lived up to their promises. Instead, like many other lifetime members, they suddenly found themselves unwelcome in the studios. Lessons would be postponed or interrupted without notice, teachers once friendly became insulting, parties were held to which they were not invited. In con lingo, it was the "kiss off." But it is also proverbial that "Once a mark, always a mark." During the 1950s someone came up with the double-lifetime membership.

Lest it appear that the studios were able to bestow the boon of immortality, it should be noted that such memberships ran concurrently. There is a legend sometimes voiced by irreverent teachers that the double-lifetime club was the creation not of a teacher but a lifetime student who missed the sales pressure. With a sort of inevitability, one middle-aged Canadian widow purchased four life-time courses, in return having a ballroom named in her honor.

Though many of these practices date back to World War II and earlier, it was not until the late fifties that federal and state agencies began paying them serious attention. The Consumer Frauds Bureau of New York Attorney General Louis J. Lefkowitz's office began its investigation into the operations of various dance studios early in 1958, giving special attention to practices employed to obtain memberships from the aged, the crippled and infirm; the workings of the lifetime clubs; and the credit techniques used for collecting on dance contracts. Lefkowitz discovered that several of the larger chains maintained their own credit companies. Following the investigation, Arthur Murray Inc., Dale Dance Studios Inc., Fred Astaire Inc., and several other large studios signed a code of ethical conduct agreement with the Attorney General's office, agreeing not to engage in some of the most often cited abuses. In an attempt to correct the others, particularly the sale of more than one lifetime membership per person, a bill was introduced in the state legislature. It passed the lower house but, after an extensive lobbying campaign, was defeated in the senate.

Meantime, California's Attorney General Stanley Mosk had begun his own investigation. After a long and extremely bitter fight, during which he was opposed by one of the state's top lobbyists, Mosk succeeded in obtaining a consent agreement, which was followed by the passage of a state law in 1961, covering the activities of all dance studios operating in California, and prohibiting various forms of bait advertising, the use of coercion or fraud in obtaining contract signatures, and, in the most damaging blow thus far struck against the lifetime racket, limiting the sale of lessons to no longer than seven years and no more than $500 per individual. The Attorney General fought hard for an additional provision enabling students who signed for lessons and subsequently became crippled, senile, or otherwise physically or mentally unable to continue the course to obtain a full refund on unused lessons, but had to settle for a compromise token return. Although the bill went into effect in 1961, some studios in Southern California ignored it, continuing to sign up students for amounts over $4000. Legal action had to be taken to enforce compliance.

By this time the FTC had issued a complaint against the nation's largest dance-studio chain, Arthur Murray Inc., and its three leading officers—Arthur Murray, Kathryn Murray, and Murray's brother, David A. Teichman. The complaint covered a number of alleged abuses: the phony quiz or contest gimmick; the offering of a "free lesson" when a substantial portion of the lesson time was spent not in teaching the student to dance but attempting to sell additional lessons; and "using in any single day 'relay salesmanship,' that is consecutive sales talks or efforts of more than one representative, with or without the employment of hidden listening devices, to induce the purchase of dancing instructions." The complaint also cited the practice of using "analyses," "tests," "studio competitions," "dance derbies," or similar artifices to induce the purchase of lessons, and it cited the use of partly blank contracts and misrepresentation as to payments and financing terms. On July 5, 1960, the respondents signed a consent order agreeing not to engage in these practices in the future. The agreement was made binding not only on the named parties but also on their agents, representatives, and employees, thus covering the more than 500 Murray-franchised studios. A cease-and-desist order (not a consent agreement) was subsequently issued against Fred Astaire Inc., Washington, D.C., and its officers, covering similar tactics, plus the practice of running want ads for teachers whose condition of employment was later revealed to be the purchase of regular dancing courses. Since Mr. Fred Astaire's only connection with the chain was the use of his name and photograph, he was not personally cited in the complaint. Neither of the FTC orders affected lifetime memberships.

In 1963 the New York bill was rewritten to include a $500 ceiling on dance contracts, reintroduced, and this time passed. To date, fewer than half a dozen states have this limitation, and, as this is being written, an attempt is being made to revoke the California statute.

Recently eight employees of a St. Louis, Missouri, dance studio were convicted of fraud, two given prison sentences and the others probation. According to the Post Office Department, "During the period July 1957 to May 1962 an estimated 6000 victims were defrauded of at least $833,872 through fraudulent representations in the sale of various dance courses." During the trial a former staff member testified that "Our new market is widows who have insurance money and inheritances." Once contracts were signed, he said, these students were "phased off" in favor of new prospects. This is the first conviction obtained in a dance-studio fraud to date. It has since been upheld by the U.S. Court of Appeals.

Although the above actions have helped curb some of the most objectionable practices, they have by no means eliminated them. Still a major problem are the contracts themselves, which often compel the students to pay for lessons even though they may desire to quit or be incapable of continuing. Although U.S. courts have found these contracts near-invulnerable, one London, England, court recently found a way around the problem. After hearing the case of a woman who had been induced to sign a long-term health-studio contract when she was only eighteen, the court gave her seventy years to pay, at a rate equivalent to about 14¢ a month.

Jet-age Aspirations

For some the dream is of something far more practical than learning to dance, though not necessarily less glamorous or exciting or romantic. For a twenty-two-year-old Ohio miss it was the longtime dream of becoming an airline stewardess. After signing "enrollment papers" which obligated her for $800 in installment-paid "tuition," studying her correspondence-course lessons for months, and passing each of the tests with exceptionally high scores, graduation day finally came. Proudly carrying the diploma which the registrar (salesman) had promised would gain her immediate employment with the airline of her choice, she applied for work at TWA, United, and Delta, only to learn that although she met nearly all of their qualifications—she had a nice personality, a high school diploma, was between twenty-one and twenty-eight, and exactly the right height —she failed to meet one essential requirement. She weighed 312 pounds.

Young men dream too. More than 3000 paid from $400 to $600 each to enroll in a California-based mail-order correspondence-course school after being promised that on graduation they would obtain high-paying jobs as jet-aircraft mechanics. Like the numerous stewardess schools recently cited by the POD and FTC, this school failed to mention that most of the airlines have their own personnel-training programs. No mention was made either that jet-engine manufacturers had said the lessons were next to worthless or that the promised employment opportunities were inflated or bogus. Convicted of mail fraud in 1962, the "dean" of the school was sentenced to seven years in prison and his chief "registrar" to three, unusually stiff sentences considering that most of these operators net nothing worse than consent orders.

The young are not the only victims. Though for a time it looked as if the phony-correspondence-school racket had run its course, in the last several years such schools have begun to multiply, along with the more solidly based but equally fraudulent operations. The increase in automation and attendant job displacement has brought about the change and made vulnerable an older class of students. Many of these new educational establishments—which offer in addition to the more glamorous occupations such as modeling, TV acting, medicine, nursing, criminology, and the law, training in such diverse skills as cosmetology, audiometry (the fitting of hearing aids), motel management, horticulture, and invisible weaving—have found they can operate almost indefinitely on the edge of the law as long as the extravagant job promises made by their salesmen do not appear in the enrollment contracts. Here, too, there is usually a finance company in the background which buys the contract as soon as it is signed. Aspirations, too, bring a good price.

Not all of these schools operate by mail, nor are all of them fly-by-night operations, though, like one West Coast stewardess school which offered "the prospect" of on-campus swimming pools and established sororities but which operated out of a two-room office, this type predominates. In October 1964, a long-established, nationwide modeling school, Patricia Stevens Inc., entered into a consent agreement with the FTC covering false misrepresentations of employment available to its graduates. In investigating one California school charged with various fraudulent claims for its courses in automotive repairs, refrigeration and air conditioning, TV repairs and electronics, even seasoned FTC investigators paused for thought on discovering that the school was owned and operated by a Los Angeles church.

The Widow of the Unknown Soldier and Other Sad Short Stories

During 1964 benevolent Americans dug deep into their pockets and brought out a record $11 billion for charity. In 1950 the average American gave 1.8 percent of his total income to philanthropic causes; by 1964 this had risen to 2.3 percent. Such statistics are heartwarming. They help restore confidence in man's innate goodness. They can be cited as proof that the individual American feels a responsibility for his fellow man and is willing to shoulder that responsibility.

Some draw different conclusions from the same evidence, feeling it only proves that the average American is a sentimental mark, a vulnerable sucker for any half-carefully-contrived plea.

It may be both are right.

According to a New York *Times* estimate, another record was set in 1964—as much as $300 million of that $11 billion is believed to have gone to charities that were partly if not wholly fraudulent. Equally distressing to many is the awareness that probably one-fourth to one-half of that $11 billion wasn't used for the purpose for which given. It went instead to cover advertising, salaries, rent, special promotions, and other costs of the big business of fund raising. The latter estimate is admittedly vague. But there is no way to be more exact, since when it comes to telling the public where its charity dollars go, even the largest and best-known charities are frequently guilty of evasive artifices ranging from half-truth word-smithing to complex deception bordering on fraud.

For example, one of the most respected of American charities, whose fund raising is largely accomplished by a single annual campaign, until recently listed the cost of running that campaign at a low and quite reasonable 15 percent; this was done by putting 40 percent of its fund-raising costs under the heading "Health Education."

In 1959 the Rockefeller Foundation decided to make a study of the leading United States charities. A committee composed of prominent leaders in the fields of government, business, education, and medicine was appointed. After a detailed investigation, its report was issued in 1961. Besides revealing a huge waste of funds and personnel by organizations with overlapping functions, it observed that of the fifty-six leading agencies "a vast majority" were practicing some form of public deception. Many failed to report total income, many reported "net" for "gross" proceeds, accomplishments were wordsmithed and falsified, achievements claimed for which the agencies were not responsible. Much of this contrived confusion and intentional deception related to fund raising.

The fund-raising story can be briefly told. By World War II, competition for the charity dollar had grown so intense that many of the leading agencies were engaged in an undeclared war of their own. Some eventually agreed to a compromise armistice, joining forces to make a united appeal on a profit-sharing basis. Others, deciding that the old ways of soliciting funds were no longer the most effective, contracted with outside companies utilizing modern big-sell techniques, often choosing not necessarily the most reputable firms but those promising the greatest returns. Promises being the stock in trade of the con men, many accepted this *carte blanche* opportunity and went into the fund-raising business.

In 1948 a national charity, which shall go unnamed here, contracted with two mailing firms for its solicitations. These firms utilized the unordered-merchandise gimmick, sending out personalized name stickers and ballpoint pens. The gimmick paid off. Between 1948 and 1953 the public donated $3,978,000. This was revealed by a New York State legislative subcommittee in 1954 when, against considerable opposition, it conducted a pioneering investigation into charity fund raising. The committee also revealed that of the nearly $4 million collected, $3,252,000, or 82 *percent*, had been spent on fund raising; another 10.5 *percent* went for administrative expenses and a small reserve; while only $302,000, or 7.5 *percent*, actually reached the charity.

Fraud? Not at all. No charges were ever filed against anyone in conjunction with the promotion. The charity was a reputable organization, as were its officers, and as was its advertising agency. As for the two firms hired to handle the mail-order fund raising, the charity once characterized them collectively in a brochure as "one of the most respected fund-raising agencies in the United States." The men who headed them had been connected with major charity promotions in the past. None of them were criminals—i.e., had criminal records. What they did have was a long list of fraud orders, affidavits of discontinuance, cease-and-desist orders, and records of remarkably high profits in almost every charity promotion with which they had been connected. One of these men deserves special attention. We'll call him Mr. King, for over the years he has earned the right to be designated King of the Charity Con Men.

As is common with such operators, Mr. King tried a variety of mail schemes before discovering that charity begins at home. Entering the field in the early forties, he was one of the first to use the miniature-license-plate gimmick. Contracting with a well-known veteran's organization for the use of its name, in return for a portion of the profits, King launched one of the largest mass-mailing campaigns in the history of fund raising. It was phenomenally successful, at least for Mr. King, who retired after four years with a like number of millions, another $1,335,000 for the sale of the fund-raising setup to the charity, plus a monthly consultant's fee of $1000, which he continued to receive for another seven years.

By this time King was a confirmed Company Man, working simultaneously behind the names of more than a half-dozen different fund-raising corporations and advertising agencies on a variety of promotions. Below is a mere sampling:

A. A veteran's organization. In two years $2.1 million was collected, $1.9 million of which went for fund-raising costs.

B. Another veteran's organization. Some $2 million netted in three years, almost all of which went for fund raising. The charity folded.

C. A crippling-disease charity, once one of the most respected in the country. In a single year $1,272,000 was collected, only $250,000, or about 20 percent of which reached the charity. In all, in this promotion alone, King and his associates are believed to have netted, over a period of seven years, close to $11 million as their share.

Although frequently investigated and several times tried for charges arising from his various promotions, King was in the charity business for over twenty years before being convicted of fraud. His conviction is currently on appeal.

At what percentage does fund raising become fraud? No one is quite sure, least of all the charities themselves, who, often apparently more concerned with profits than purpose, must bear more than a little responsibility for turning con men into kings. From deceiving to defrauding the public is a short step indeed.

But in assigning blame, the well-intentioned public deserves its share, for its lack of selectivity and concern. We give, we give generously, and, much too often, we give unthinkingly. In order to prove this point to New York City police some years ago, an accused swindler stood on a Manhattan street corner and in a few minutes collected $15 for The Fund To Aid the Widow of the Unknown Soldier.

Camelot Revisited

For many, the dream is of a place of one's own, a homesite, or vacation cabin, or retirement haven, far away from the pressure of crowded buildings, rush-hour traffic, and current events, close to nature but with all the modern conveniences, where the climate is fresh and free of artifice and fraud.

Call it Eden or Camelot, it is an ageless dream. Yet it has an especially strong emotional appeal to the not so young, to whom retirement often represents the pot of gold at the end of the rainbow.

Thousands thought they had found such a place in what we'll call "Heavenly Acres," located, according to the colorful promotional brochure, in "the lush valley of the Rio Grande in New Mexico," depicted, in the picture on the front cover, as a paradise of verdant grasses, swollen streams, and tinted hills. The pictures inside were even more appealing. One showed two very pretty young girls laughing and playing in the snow; in another there were fast-moving trout streams, with Dad pulling in the trout as Mom fried a skilletful over the outdoor fire; while others showed attractive ranch-type homes, with large shade trees and rolling lawns fronted by paved streets. And the price was modest—two and a half acres of this heavenly paradise for only $10 down and $10 a month, or, if this seemed too high, half an acre for only $5 a month, or, for those who desired not a homesite but an estate, five acres for only $15.

Pictures, it is said, don't lie, and these were truthful enough. The scenes were real, only they were from other parts of New Mexico. "Today in clear, bright trout streams," read the copy, "it seems that a man can reach out and touch the fish." In some places perhaps, but not in Heavenly Acres, not even with the longest arms, for as the brochure pointedly omitted mentioning, this was arid land, miles from the nearest water. It failed to mention, too (as Senator Harrison A. Williams' Subcommittee on Frauds Affecting the Elderly brought out), that there were no facilities for electricity, natural gas, or telephones, nor prospects of any in the near future; that the nearest stores, shops, and schools were in a community nine miles away. But these were minor sins of omission. Most important, it failed to mention that the land was on top of a 1400-foot-high mesa, inaccessible to ordinary cars because the winding dirt road was too narrow. Even to reach the top was difficult, to build a house there absurdly and undesirably expensive.

Yet the brochure was representative of an increasing number of such prospectuses, believed to be netting their promoters up to $500 million annually in the sale of cypress swamplands in Florida, unclimably steep rocky hillsides in California, dustbowl land in Kansas, tracts under the waters of the Great Salt Lake, cactus country in Arizona, and Death Valley desert. Often the initial bait is a "free lot," offered as a prize in a local newspaper contest which everyone wins. "Free" except for "closing costs," which may range from $40 to $250, usually far in excess of the value of the land. In many instances, as in the case of "Scenic Land Hawaii," closed down by the POD, the promoters don't even have clear title to the land they're selling. Sometimes there is a degree of subtlety to the bait: one Florida operator informed potential buyers that under no circumstances would he part with more than half the oil, gas, and mineral rights.

If the "ranchero racket" offers a realizable dream to its victims, it offers the prospect of big profits to the fast-moving con man. Observes John McWhirter, Florida land sales board director, "A land promoter could distribute a half million misleading brochures and the land could be sold before a prosecuting attorney would even know of the offense."[1] One West Coast company collected $3 million in sales of building lots in the desert before any of its victims realized that, since the brochures were sent through the mails, this might be considered mail fraud and alerted the POD.

In 1962, BBB investigators, real-estate commissioners, representatives of thirty-one states, and the federal government held a national conference on interstate land sales, in an attempt to deal with this growing fraud. As a result of the conference, several of the western states have adopted more stringent land-sale regulation, while to date some dozen states have outlawed the use of the "free lot" gimmick. In general, however, most of the recommendations of the conference have yet to be realized: stronger state subdivision and disclosure laws; speedier prosecution of offenders (one case has now been in the courts eleven years); adoption of BBB-type voluntary advertising codes; and an amendment of the Securities Exchange Act to require the same investigation and public prospectus for interstate real-estate promotions as for securities and stocks. As one official at the conference noted, "We could stop this overnight, if the public would refuse to buy land 'site unseen.'"

Such is the stuff that dreams, and vulnerable Americans, are made of.

CHAPTER 8

FOOL MEDICINE

> *foolproof,* adj. So simple, plain, strong, or the like, as not to be liable to be misunderstood, damaged, etc., even by a fool.

Do you suffer from irritability, low vitality, stunted growth, soft bones, fragile bones, malformed teeth, premature aging, senile dementia, arthritis, neuritis, digestive, nervous and mental ailments, cirrhosis of the liver, coronary heart attacks, strokes, diseases of the kidneys, constipation, wrinkles, and/or premature ejaculation?

"Are you troubled with migraine headaches, diabetes, intelligence loss, memory defects, severe agitation, cancer, leukemia, itchy piles, and/or pernicious anemia?

"Do people avoid you at parties because of your dandruff, obesity, baldness, flat chest, poor posture, bad breath, body odors, and/or socially offensive flatulence?

"Want to keep your blood neutral and well coagulated, put iron in your spine, stimulate your personality glands, extend the prime of life, increase the intelligence quotient, prolong the sex act indefinitely, improve your vision, develop new graces and character traits, and live longer and better?

"If so, there is a single pill which will do all these things for you, a unique nutritional discovery containing a secret formula composed of . . ."

The spiel of an oldtime patent medicine man? On the contrary, such promises are being made today in every part of the country, and, incredible as it may seem, thousands are being taken in by them.

Not the sophisticated, of course. They carefully purchase a medication whose advertising reads: "Medical tests have proven that, if used correctly, Brand X can be of significant value as an aid in the temporary relief of . . ." The very qualifications seemed to lend authenticity to the claims. The irony is, both promises may be equally false and the two seemingly different products one and the same. Although this fact is not widely publicized, a large number of drugs, of both the prescription and nonprescription varieties, are not manufactured by the "drug companies" or "laboratories" which package and sell them but are ordered in bulk from a manufacturer who, using a standardized formula, its ingredients cleared with the Food and Drug Administration for purity and safety, may sell the same compound to a dozen or more packagers, to appear under as many different labels with as many different claims, each semantically directed to the credibility of a particular market.

Who, then, is the least vulnerable American?

Such modern merchandising makes fools of us all, and leaves us especially dependent upon the honesty of the seller and the vigilance of those who regulate his activities.

Yet, in the field of medical hoaxstering there is an even stronger bond between the perceptive and the gullible—*need.* The man in pain, be he a third-grade dropout or a Harvard graduate, will, if approved methods fail, try almost anything for relief, while the woman with a lumpy soreness in the breast may resort to the most transparent quackery to avoid the possibility of confirming her dire suspicions.

Be it pill, food, machine, or soothing medical manner, if the product or treatment is based on a valid need, no matter how patently phony the pitch, the fraud will find some victims. A Denver man sold bottled dirt as a cure for stupidity in children. A Los Angeles health practitioner treated a thirteen-year-old girl, a victim of cancer, via "sexual therapy," with the knowledge and apparently tacit approval of the girl's desperate mother. More than a million people bought a book which claimed arthritis could be cured by doses of cod liver oil. One mechanical-minded swindler sold hundreds of people a machine which he promised would, among other things, grow new fingers and toes. A simple newspaper article reporting the Food and Drug Administration's seizure of a product which bogusly claims to break the cigarette habit will invariably result in a rash of requests for the product.

Fraud is the filling of vacuums, the creating of a supply to match each demand. So long as a gap exists between human suffering and medical knowledge, the swindler won't have to seek out his victims —they'll look for him. The pain of the arthritic, for example, is beyond imagining. Because there is as yet no cure for arthritis, and no medication which offers more than partial temporary relief to its twelve million sufferers, the Arthritis and Rheumatism Foundation estimates that at least 60 percent of all arthritis victims already under medical treatment *also* resort to the use of worthless preparations.

The health swindler is not content with merely capitalizing on existing needs, however. By turning a desire into a need, or convincing the public that a need exists where none does, he multiplies the possibilities of fraud. Human nature being what it is, this is not especially difficult.

Fear helps: the scare sale is by no means restricted to the peddling of furnaces. One reason the cancer quack can claim so many cures is because many of his patients didn't have cancer in the first place. Displaying one or more symptoms, susceptible to suggestion, afraid of surgery or X-ray, neurotics seek out the quack and—miraculously —are cured. The well-meaning, if misguided, healer who attempts to get his sassafras-tea cancer cure authenticated by the American Medical Association or the National Cancer Institute often finds that the most difficult requirement to fulfill isn't that the patient must have survived for a substantial period after treatment, but proving, through biopsy, with tissue obtained from the tumor, that it was ever cancerous.

Fear helps, but vanity helps even more. Few people are satisfied with themselves as they are. Most would like to be taller or shorter, heavier or (far more often) lighter, have clear youthful skin, full heads of hair, radiant toothsome smiles, the alleged sexual capacities of a teenager (memory also plays marvelous tricks). The nostrums purchased just for "the curing, preservation, and beautifying of bodies," as Frank Gibney so tellingly puts it, defy credibility.

The FDA seized one "height improver," which consisted of a device for hanging from the ceiling with weights on the feet to stretch the spine and neck (the reason for seizure in this case wasn't false claims; used as directed it would have done exactly what it promised).

But such buyers aren't purchasing credibility. Scoff, if you will, at the claim that Nutri-Bio will prevent measles, mumps, and chickenpox; only remember that a few years ago the idea that a drop of liquid on a sugar cube could prevent polio would have sounded even more ridiculous. Laugh at the magic Sonus Film-O-Sonic machine, which will both diagnose and treat diseases; only don't forget the X-ray. Wonder how anyone could really believe, as hundreds of thousands apparently did in 1959, that "royal jelly," the food prepared by the drones for the queen bee—supposedly endowing her with longevity and extraordinary fertility—would for humans be a veritable Fountain of Youth? Then think about hormones.

Modern medical science has made anything *possible*. The swindler could ask for no more preprimed marks.

"Medical quackery," says National BBB president Kennedy B. Willson, "is probably the most widespread exploitation in our country today." "Health swindles," observes Chief Postal Inspector H. B. Montague, "lead all other categories of mail fraud." Such frauds are unquestionably the cruelest and most vicious of all types of swindlery. But far more important, from the point of view of the con man, be he individual or corporate, they are usually the most remunerative and safest.

The Scary Mythmakers

The U.S. Department of Health, Education, and Welfare estimates that the American public spends at least *$1 billion* a year on falsely promoted, worthless, or dangerous drug products. Of this, $100 million goes for phony cancer cures, $250 million for misrepresented arthritis remedies. But the largest portion, over $500 million, goes for what the AMA calls "the largest and most lucrative confidence game in history": nutritional quackery.

This shouldn't be too surprising. We're all food faddists to a degree. In addition to our inherited superstitions—carrots are good for nighttime vision, oysters are a love food, fish and celery are brain foods—each of us has decided preferences and prejudices, feels that certain foods are better for us than others, even though there may be no scientific nutritional basis for such beliefs. And often, our psychological makeup being what it is, whole-wheat bread may be better for us than ordinary white bread, if we feel that strongly about it. Then, too, the average American is abnormally health conscious, aware that "an ounce of prevention is worth a pound of cure." We may not actually need that multiple-vitamin capsule we take before each meal, but "better safe than sorry." And, unless we take such preparations in lieu of needed medical treatment, most of this nutritional faddery is harmless, even though it may be expensive.*

At the same time, there exists a highly organized group of myth-makers whose efforts to make the most of these and similar beliefs is of more than passing interest, if only because they help to create the climate which has fostered some of the more spectacular frauds.

In 1963 the Food and Drug Administration announced that it planned a major overhaul of existing dietary food regulations; among other things, the project would spell out the specific labeling information deemed necessary to facilitate intelligent purchase and use, taking into consideration scientific progress made in this area since 1941, when the rules were last changed.

Within a week after this announcement, both the FDA and Congress were deluged with thousands of postcards. In often identical words, their writers objected strongly to the FDA's attempt to put vitamins and minerals on the prescription list, ban the sale of "natural" or "organic" foods, and drive health-food stores out of business. Since the proposed rule changes would have done none of these things, it is interesting to see just what they did propose to do. In essence, they were "more truth"-in-labeling changes. By already existing regulations, for example, the packager of a vitamin and mineral preparation is required to state on the label the name and quantity of each ingredient in his product. This was one of the most important features of the original Pure Food Act of 1906, which ended a number of dangerous abuses. In recent years, however, an opposite abuse has flourished. Numerous manufacturers of such preparations have added scores of different ingredients for which no nutritional need has been established (so-called "shotgun" formulas),† or have increased the quantity, potency, or strength of ingredients far above what is deemed necessary ("loaded" formu-las). Such a product may be no better for the user than one con-taining only the twelve recognized essential vitamins and minerals, but it makes for an enormously impressive label. One of the pro-

---

* Some of it can be dangerous, however. Speaking at the 1963 convention of the AMA, Dr. Charles Pease, of Children's Memorial Hospital in Chicago, de-scribed the cases of seven children whose bones were malformed because their mothers had given them overdoses of Vitamin A. "Some people," the doctor said, "are convinced that if one capsule gives a child the Minimum Daily Re-quirement, then three pills will make him grow even better."

† Products whose labels list 50 to 100 separate ingredients ("all the vitamins, minerals, and trace elements from the land, the sea, and what used to be the bottom of the sea," reads the label of one) are not uncommon.

posed FDA changes would require that such labels state clearly and conspicuously the lack of proven need for any such ingredients listed.

However misguided the postcard pressure may have been, it was seemingly effective. The FDA has shelved the proposed changes for further study.

Behind this and similar instances of mail-order lobbying are a number of highly organized food-faddist promotional groups, operating out of Southern California, Massachusetts, and Texas. Advocates of so-called "natural foods" and various "nature cures," and declared opponents of all processed foods, the use of commercial fertilizers, and the fluoridation of water, these groups are most active in disseminating, via the familiar scare sell, what the FDA calls "the four basic myths that underlie all nutritional quackery."[1] These are:

(1) *The myth that all diseases are due to faulty diet.* It is the promise of this myth that the average diet lacks essential nutrients which can only be supplied by use of food supplements or special food products, such as yoghurt, blackstrap molasses, and kelp tablets. But according to the U.S. Department of Health, Education, and Welfare, "Americans have to go out of their way, nutritionally speaking, to avoid being well nourished. The normal American diet now includes such a variety of foods that most persons can hardly fail to have an adequate supply of the essential food constituents. Deficiency diseases which have plagued our nation in the past are now almost unknown. Overweight has become a more common product than underweight." Yet the myth persists, even though doctors today have trouble finding cases of rickets and pellagra for case study, and even though yoghurt has much the same nutritional value as milk, the "minerals" in blackstrap molasses are mainly impurities that get in from the sugar-refining process, and the iodine in kelp tablets is adequately supplied by seafoods and iodized salt.

(2) *The myth that soil depletion causes malnutrition.* This myth postulates that chemical fertilizers poison the land and the crops grown on it and that only "organically grown" foods, using natural fertilizers, are safe and contain pure vitamins and minerals. According to the AMA, the only disease in man known to be associated with any deficiency of soil or water is simple goiter, due to lack of iodine in certain geographical areas. The deficiency of this essential element is remedied by the use of iodized salt.

Since the publication of Rachel Carson's *Silent Spring*, a great many Americans have become concerned about the dangers accruing from the misuse of chemical pesticides. These organizations have now taken up this concern and have made it an important part of their scare argument.

It is of interest that in examining some of the so-called "organic farms," the Department of Agriculture found several where both chemical fertilizers and pesticides were in use. "Organically grown" fruits and vegetables, sold through health-food stores, are of course more expensive than similar produce available through regular grocery outlets.

(3) *The myth of overprocessing.* There is just enough truth in this myth to make it entirely credible. Some methods of food processing and cooking do result in removal or reduction of vitamin and mineral content. On the other hand, sufficient vitamins and minerals are added to many of these products to make up for the loss (Enriched, Fortified, etc.), while a well-balanced diet usually supplies, through other products, more than the minimum daily requirement. The FDA recently seized for false claims a number of $195 pressure-cookers which were alleged to "vaporize" food so that it retained all its nutrients; the only difference from ordinary pressure-cookers, according to the FDA, was that the $195 ones were more cheaply made.

(4) *The myth of subclinical deficiencies.* According to this myth, if you feel tired or run-down or have any sort of ache or pain, you have a subclinical deficiency of some vitamin or mineral and need a food supplement to remedy this lack. This may be true in some cases—pregnant women need extra calcium, babies and small children need additional vitamins C and D; it probably isn't true in most cases; and in any case, only a doctor can say. One thing is sure: this myth does sell a lot of unnecessary vitamin preparations.

The sad irony of the foregoing is that those who are undernourished, who most need supplementary vitamin and mineral products, are those least able to afford even a well-balanced diet, let alone supplements.

Undoubtedly, many of those responsible for disseminating these myths believe in them. Their motives may be nothing more than the wholly sincere desire to convert others to the true gospel. Yet this persistent campaign to undermine public confidence in the nutritional value of staple foods not only makes good business for the food faddists and fringe promoters, it has also set the stage for some rather spectacular promotions, such as that of Nutri-Bio, which former FDA Commissioner George P. Larrick has called "one of the

biggest misbranding operations ever encountered by the Food and
Drug Administration . . . a classic case of food faddism gone wild."[2]

In chemical composition Nutri-Bio (the name derived from the
slogan, "Better Nutrition Through Biochemistry") was little different from many another "food supplement" or "multivitamin product." Its components were harmless, and mostly unnecessary. Of
its thirty-seven listed ingredients there were twenty-one for which
no nutritional need had been established, while the others were
more than adequately supplied in any well-balanced diet. But packaged in promises and sold through a remarkable con gambit wherein
the victim became the salesman, it became, for a time, a fad of epic
proportions.

To date, the whole Nutri-Bio story hasn't been told. There is still
some mystery as to the identity of the genius behind the promotion,
Nutri-Bio's commander-in-chief as it were, since the organizational
setup of Nutri-Bio's sales forces owed much to the U.S. Army. Although the parent company, Nutri-Bio Corporation, was based in
Beverly Hills, there were manufacturers, dealers, and distributors
all over the United States and Canada, linked by an involved chain
of command.

When Nutri-Bio first appeared, it was possible to buy a week or a
month's supply in a local health-food store. But as purchasers soon
learned, to do so was to miss out on a good thing. For there was a
way not only to have it at a much lower price, but to make money
besides. Purchase of a six-month supply at $24 from a distributor
brought a discount of 35 percent and the rank of Private in the
Nutri-Bio hierarchy. The excess over one's own needs could then
be sold to friends, at a profit. Thereafter, the larger the purchase, the
higher discount and rank became, until the individual who purchased
$25,000 worth in any single month became a General, entitled to a
62 percent discount on all future purchases. Nor was this all. Should
any of one's customers also want to become distributors, the individual could become their "sponsor," and from that point on he
would receive a percentage of anything they sold. The resemblance
to the chain-letter fad and referral selling was not purely coincidental.

Nutri-Bio was launched in 1958. By July 1960, total sales had
reached $1.8 million. By July 1961 they had jumped to $8.2 million
and continued rising. Some of the credit for this spectacular rise
was due to the handsome and talented movie star Robert Cummings,
who spoke enthusiastically of Nutri-Bio on his TV show *Love That*

Bob. If Nutri-Bio was the secret of Cummings' perennial youthfulness, the American public wanted Nutri-Bio. And Cummings had no reason to be unhappy with the public's response. In a preliminary prospectus filed by the Nutri-Bio Corporation with the Securities and Exchange Commission in October 1961, Cummings was listed as Senior Vice President in Charge of Nutritional Research, a director of the firm, and its second largest stockholder. His Nutri-Bio salary for the fiscal year ending July 31, 1961, was $78,641, plus $7453 set aside under a company profit-sharing plan. During the same period, his wife was paid $76,141, and an agreement reached wherein, beginning August 1, 1961, each of the five Cummings children would receive $166 per month for use of their names.*

Although the POD, BBB, FTC, and FDA began investigating Nutri-Bio almost from the start, they encountered difficulties every step of the way, not unlike those anyone would meet who sets out to fight an army.

Most of the sales pitches took place in private homes, out of sight and hearing of snoopy investigators. Even if an FDA man did arrange to be present, and did hear a distributor sell his product with promises that it would eradicate juvenile delinquency and prevent or cure cancer, heart attacks, diabetes, multiple sclerosis, gangrene, tooth decay, asthma, hemorrhage of the eyes, arthritis, bursitis, mumps, measles, chickenpox, and 75 percent of all other diseases, who could hold the Commander-in-Chief, or even the Vice President in Charge of Nutritional Research, responsible for what one of the Privates said? The parent company merely disclaimed him, in effect drumming him out of the ranks.

When the FDA seized cartons of Nutri-Bio which bore fraudulent health and therapeutic claims on the labels, tracing responsibility back to the parent company through the maze of distributors and dealers proved near-impossible. It was discovered that many of the shipments made from Beverly Hills had been undeceptively labeled for interstate commerce, then relabeled by the dealers who received them. A similar problem was encountered in connection with much of the promotional material ("the largest collection of pseudo-scientific health literature ever assembled," according to former Commissioner Larrick). The books, pamphlets, very professional sales kits, leaflets, records, and film strips abounded in fraudu-

---

* The Cummings family severed connections with the Nutri-Bio Corporation in 1962.

lent claims, but again the FDA ran up against the elusive chain of command. As a result, the FDA was citing lots of Privates, Corporals, and other enlisted personnel, and even a few Generals, and seizing tons of mislabeled Nutri-Bio, but not until November 1961 was it able to cite the parent company itself in one of these seizures, leading to some labeling changes and to the withdrawal of some of the promotional aids.

Since all seizures of the product went uncontested, the FDA did not even succeed in obtaining an injunction banning distribution of the product. However, by 1963 it was apparent that the promotion had peaked, and in January 1964 the Nutri-Bio Corporation declared bankruptcy. One might credit the hard work of the FDA investigators, but more than anything else this decline and fall was probably due to the weakness inherent in any referral scheme: there just weren't enough people around to sustain the "endless chain." There were, however, more than 75,000 salesmen, who had accumulated an awful lot of Nutri-Bio. The basement of one Chicago General yielded more than fifty tons.

So came and went the Nutri-Bio fad, without so much as a single injunction or criminal charge.

The Case of the Vanishing Fat

While many are profiting on the malnutrition myths, others have made their fortunes by capitalizing on a very obvious truth: Americans are fat.

According to Peter Wyden, in his book *The Overweight Society*, 79 million Americans are carrying around excess poundage, while at any one time at least 2 million of them are attempting to do something about it—i.e., diet. That they're (correction: *we're*) mostly unsuccessful is due to the fact that most of us want to eat our cake and lose fat too. In this special milieu, the magic pill or product which will erase unwanted pounds all by itself—without will power, exercise, the reduction of caloric or carbohydrate intake—has become for many as desirable as and often synonymous with regaining one's youth. Thus, when we learn of an "AMAZING NEW MEDICAL RELEASE," a "no-diet reducing wonder drug" which promises to do just this, as did Regimen, we huff and puff with unaccustomed speed to the nearest drugstore counter.

With Regimen one could have avoided the exertion, for it had actually been on the market in various forms and under different names more than twenty years before being given the big-sell treatment in 1957. Until then, however, it had lacked an entrepreneur talented enough to make the American public spend millions to buy it.

Unlike the case of Nutri-Bio, there is no secret about the identity of the genius responsible for the Regimen success story. He is John T. Andre (alias John T. Andreadis, alias Timolean T. Andreadis), whose long experience with federal agencies and false claims eminently qualified him for this particular venture. As early as 1948, one of Andre's firms had been the subject of a postal-fraud order for its Hollywood Two-Way Reducing Plan. Turning briefly to a different but no less profitable field, in 1955 Andre signed an affidavit of discontinuance with the POD for two of his firms regarding false arthritis and rheumatism cure-claims in their promotion of the drug Sustamin. Another Andre product, Man-Tan, a preparation for coloring the skin to simulate sun tan, was the subject of a 1959 postal-fraud order, later withdrawn when Andre agreed to reword his claims. Two other postal-fraud orders, issued in 1957 in connection with the sale of Propex reducing tablets, were later withdrawn on technicalities. In all, Andre had been associated with nineteen firms in the weight-reducing business before launching Regimen.

This he did spectacularly, early in 1957, with an initial advertising budget of $1.5 million, much of which was spent on network television. These were no ordinary commercials. In addition to authenticated medical reports of Regimen's amazing effectiveness in scientific tests, viewers were given "live proof." In an improvement on the ancient Before-and-After gimmick, women were "weighed in live" before the cameras each week on programs such as Dave Garroway's *Today Show* to show exactly how much weight they had lost. The makers of Regimen claimed, and the TV evidence seemed to prove beyond a doubt, that the user of Regimen could eat whatever he or she liked, including potatoes and desserts, and, with no will power whatsoever, lose twenty-eight pounds in twenty-eight days. In a very short time Regimen was America's most popular nonprescription reducing drug.

There were, as always, a few skeptics. The same year the Regimen campaign started, the National BBB issued a nine-page bulletin listing fraudulent claims for the drug; it was billed as a fraud by medical witnesses before a Congressional subcommittee; two of the

Regimen firms signed a POD fraud order, agreeing to halt its sale through the mails; and the FTC issued the first of several complaints (later withdrawn pending criminal action).

Basically, there are two kinds of reducing aids: "bulk-formers" such as Metrecal, which give the user the feeling of fullness with a minimum of calories, and so-called "appetite depressants," drugs such as Dexedrine mostly available only on prescription, which *may* help curb the appetite. Regimen supposedly fell in the latter category, since its major ingredient was phenylpropanolamine, which when taken in large enough doses may act to curb the appetite. In such doses it may be dangerous, however, and so is available only on prescription. What made the Regimen claims most amazing, the investigators agreed, was that there wasn't enough of the drug in the colorful Regimen pills to do anything, nor were any of its other ingredients conducive to weight loss. Yet the TV viewer almost saw the pounds disappear, and by 1959, despite the mail ban, over-the-counter sales reached $6½ million, while the product was among the top fifty national TV advertisers.

In February 1960, following a long investigation, the FDA made its first Regimen seizures, later resulting in a permanent injunction prohibiting interstate distribution, and in June a New York State grand jury returned a 130-count indictment charging conspiracy to publish untrue, deceptive, and misleading advertisements. In January 1964, a federal grand jury returned a 58-count indictment, charging conspiracy to ship misbranded drugs in interstate commerce, using the mails and television to defraud, and false advertising claims. What made these two indictments extremely important was their break with precedent, for not only were Drug Research Corporation and its president, John T. Andre, named, but also the New York advertising agency handling the Regimen promotion: Kastor, Hilton, Chesley, Clifford & Atherton. The earthquake jolted Madison Avenue, but its aftershocks were to be even more disturbing.

The New York State case came up first. In return for the prosecutions dropping most of the counts in the 130-count indictment, Andre pled guilty to 3 counts of false and misleading advertising claims, and the drug company and advertising agency pleaded guilty to 7 counts each. On February 7, 1965, Chief Justice John M. Murtagh of the Criminal Court of the City of New York fined the promoter $1500, the manufacturer $3500, and the ad agency $3500.

The federal case followed immediately, and it was during this trial that the Government explained just how the magicians had accomplished their tricks, including the live on-camera weigh-ins.

Although the two women weren't typical housewives, as claimed, but professional actresses, their weight problem was real and both did lose weight. However, contrary to their repeated assertions that they hadn't suffered a minute and had eaten what they liked, each admitted, during the trial, that she had been on a near-starvation diet and had suffered so horribly that she had found it necessary to consult a doctor for medication. Even at that, one of the women didn't lose weight fast enough, until given a prescription drug issued in the name of her boy friend.

The medical test results were much more easily obtained. Two doctors, both well thought of in the research field, both recipients of various research grants, had supplied fraudulent test results for as little as $1000 and $4000, as they admitted under questioning.

During the six-week trial the ad agency tried valiantly to prove that it had prepared the advertising in "good faith," while the Government contended that it had deliberately planned a fraudulent campaign.

On May 6, 1965, a federal district jury found Andre, Drug Research Inc., and the firm of Kastor, Hilton, Chesley, Clifford & Atherton each guilty of more than 25 counts of criminal fraud. The ad agency was fined $50,000, the drug company $53,000, and Andre $50,000. In addition, Andre was given eighteen months in prison. All three sentences have been appealed.

Most New York advertising agencies refused to comment on the decision, but according to the New York *Times* they were speechless more out of shock than reluctance to talk, for this was the first time an advertising agency had been held criminally responsible for advertising it prepared. The Advertising Federation, the largest trade group in the industry, did issue a statement to its members, warning them that, as a result of the Regimen decision, advertising agencies might have to refuse to handle advertising "about which they don't have all the facts and which has any feature or claim whatsoever which would seem to be exaggerated or unprovable."[3] No action was taken against the three networks that aired the commercials; and, of course, aside from the fines, none of the $16 million which the FDA estimates the Regimen fraud cost the American public will ever make its way back to its still chubby victims.

The Musical Cancer Cure and Other Devices

Our faith in the effectiveness of pills and potions is probably equaled only by our reverential regard for the capabilities of the machine. The magical device which will diagnose and cure all ailments is one of the staples of medical hoaxstering. Recently a man sold a vacuum cleaner guaranteed to "suck up all the germs in a room," while a woman paid $28,600 to be psychoanalyzed by a "curative computer."

Pseudo-scientific-device quackery in America is said to have begun in Connecticut in 1795 with the appearance of Dr. Elisha Perkins and his marvelous "tractors." Perkins, an accredited doctor as well as a successful mule trader, announced that two pieces of dissimilar metals placed in contact with the skin would "draw out a surcharge of noxious electric fluid that lies at the root of all suffering." The mysterious and fascinating properties of electricity were just becoming known: it sounded possible. Though other doctors cried "fraud" and "fake" and said the device had been "gleaned up from the miserable remains of animal magnetism," Dr. Perkins' metallic tractors became a national fad, which later spread to Europe. For his humanitarian efforts Dr. Perkins was ousted from the Connecticut Medical Society, but for compensation he had the knowledge that he had conned the Father of Our Country, as George Washington is said to have purchased a set.

Something positive can be said for this and the multitude of diagnostic-treatment devices which followed: patients who relied on them may have died, but the devices themselves enjoyed uncommonly long lives.

In 1962, FDA investigators seized and destroyed 1093 Micro-Dynameters. Selling for $875 apiece, these devices had been represented as capable of diagnosing and treating cancer, TB, rheumatism, nephritis, and a host of other ills. Stripped down—minus the fancy console, the flashing lights, the knobs and dials (many of which weren't even connected)—the ultra-modern machine consisted of a string galvanometer, a simple device for measuring electrical current which utilized a pair of probes fastened to the patient's skin. All that had changed since it first appeared in 1795 as Dr. Perkins' tractors was the name, the packaging, the salesmanship, and the price.

In 1915, just as the age of radio and electronics was being inaugurated, there appeared a man whom the FDA has called "a genius of pseudomedical science," "an electronic miracle man," and "the dean of all Twentieth Century charlatans": Dr. Albert Abrams.

To call Dr. Abrams' San Francisco headquarters a clinic would be a disservice. It was a laboratory of Frankensteinian proportions from which emanated healing waves supposedly capable of reaching and curing people on any part of the planet. It was a college of quackery whose students, and their students, dominate the field today. And it was a gadgetry workshop-factory out of which appeared some of the most amazing and durable of all pseudomedical devices.

Dr. Abrams was the originator of "Radionics," a system of treatment based on diagnoses of blood specimens. Local practitioners obtained blood samples from the ears of their patients and mailed them to San Francisco, where they were placed in an electronic machine called a Radioscope. Readings from this machine were then sent back by postcard, revealing the diseases the patients were supposed to have and the type of treatment they should be given by other machines—available from the Abrams College of Electronic Medicine, same address.

These machines included: the Oscilloclast, based on Abrams' theory of Electronic Reactions (E.R.A.), which postulated that each diseased organ or tissue emanated characteristic electronic waves or vibratory rates which, when played back into the body, would cure the disease; the Reflexophone, with which Dr. Abrams could diagnose disease in a patient thousands of miles away by examining his written signature; and the Short Wave Oscilloclast, which effected "distant therapy" or "absent healing" through a sort of high-frequency prayer.

Just tracing the subsequent history of the more than thirty Abrams devices during the years since the inventor's death in 1924 would necessitate a book-length history of quackery. Suffice it to say that nearly every bogus medical device in use today is related to one or another of the Abrams models, while the pseudoscientific jargon accompanying their use is often straight out of Abrams pamphlets.

One of the most colorful of the Abrams-type devices was the Spectrochrome (also known as the Dinshah Machine), a colored-light projector distributed through a healing cult organized by Dinshah P. Ghadiali. Approximately 10,000 members paid dues to local chapters called "planets." Group leaders who ran the machines were called "normalizers." Treatment could be given only during certain phases of the moon with the body in a north-pointing position. In accordance with Ghadiali's Spectro-Chrome Metry, or the Science of Attuned Color Waves, various colors were shone on affected parts for psychic healing. Ghadiali was convicted after a six-week trial, fined $20,000, and placed on probation for five years. Immediately upon its expiration, he resumed his activities, and in 1958 was brought before a federal judge and permanently barred from further medical-religious activities.

As fully in the Abrams tradition was the Sonus Film-O-Sonic 105, also known as The Musical Cancer Cure. The inner mechanism of this device was actually the playback mechanism of an ordinary dictating machine. Moistened pads were connected to the "trouble spots" on the body and the music supposedly played through these for curative effect. "Smoke Gets in Your Eyes" was played for cancer, "Holiday for Strings" for arteriosclerosis.

During Dr. Abrams' lifetime there was no device law on the books. Not until the passage of the Federal Food, Drug, and Cosmetic Act of 1938 did medical devices come under the authority of the FDA. Meanwhile the Abrams College of Electronic Medicine had become the Electronic Medicine Foundation, which took over the marketing of the original Abrams models. In investigating the Foundation, FDA agents sent in blood from animals and dead persons, as well as colored water, receiving in return diagnoses and instructions for treatment, proving that the machines could not distinguish between the quick and the dead, animals and humans, or blood and coal-tar dye. In 1958, after a long series of reversals, the FDA finally succeeded in obtaining a federal court injunction permanently barring sale of thirteen Abrams inventions. On July 9, 1961, Foundation president Fred J. Hart, former Republican candidate for Congress from California, sold a Short Wave Oscillotron to a Reno chiropractor; in 1962 he was found guilty of contempt of the court order and fined $500, and the Foundation was dissolved. Mr. Hart is currently president of one of the "natural food" organizations.

Despite the efforts of the FDA, everyone of the aforementioned machines is in use somewhere in the U.S.A. today, together with such ageless hoaxery as the *Le Joi* devices (sexual nostrums, ranging from stimulants, substitutes, elongators, and props to sensation-deadening salves such as Longo, Retardo, and Sta-On) plus the more modern products of the atomic age: the Wonder Glove, a mitten said to be lined with uranium ore, for arthritis; the Rado Pad, a mattress with bits of uranium in the ticking, for sinus pains; and Ferguson's Zerret Applicator, a plastic dumbbell-like device containing two tubes of "Zerret water," alleged to produce the "Z-ray, a force unknown to science," which by expanding the atoms in the body will cure all diseases. In analyzing Zerret water, FDA investigators found it identical to Chicago tap water, and W. R. Ferguson, its inventor and manufacturer, received a two-year prison sentence, while its distributor was sent to jail for a year. These were strong sentences, considering that over 90 percent of the convicted health swindlers receive probation and/or a fine, the latter usually less than the cost of one cancer-cure machine. Most often they fare no worse than a consent order or a mail ban. Medical hoaxstering is one of the safest of all branches of swindlery, if one has the stomach for it.

From the point of view of the swindler, that is. The victim is often less fortunate.

Sometimes the quack treatment is in itself dangerous. Often the treatment will disguise symptoms, making it difficult for a regular doctor to make a correct diagnosis even if he is consulted in time. But much too often the treatment will do nothing except soothe the fears of the patient, while the condition progressively worsens past the point of no return. Some years ago a Spokane housewife went to a "sanipractor." Diagnosing her ailment via an Abrams radionics device, he overlooked the obvious: that she weighed only 108 pounds and was coughing blood. His prescription: hot and cold water compresses and a ten-day fast. On dwindling to 60 pounds she died, but not before infecting her husband and child with TB.

How do you recognize quackery? Here are some guidelines supplied by the Department of Health, Education and Welfare:

—Is the formula or treatment secret?
—Does it promise a quick cure?
—Is it advertised by case histories or satisfied-user testimonials?
—Does its sponsor claim medical men are persecuting him, fear his competition, or trying to suppress his wonderful discovery?
—Are the recognized treatments belittled?

A single Yes answer is adequate cause for suspicion.

There is only one thing wrong with such logic. The time when we most need to apply it is also the time when we are least likely to do so. No one functions best when sick or afraid. Often the pain or discomfort of an illness make it impossible to think clearly. At our weakest and most vulnerable to suggestion, this is the time when we need "maximum protection." It is also the time when we are least likely to get it. Ralph Lee Smith puts it bluntly: "The United States Government is substantially unable to defend you and your family against health huckstering."[4]

Why?

Too many promotions, too few regulators. Overburdened and undermanned as the federal regulatory agencies are, their plight is in many ways less acute than that which exists on the state level. For example, in the most populous state in the Union, California, the total number of agents assigned to investigate medical frauds is six.

Again there is the time gap. Months or years may pass between the time a quack healer starts treating patients, or a fraudulently represented product appears on the market, and the time the FDA or appropriate agency can complete an investigation and take action. It took the FTC *16 years* to enjoin the manufacturers of Carters Little Liver Pills from claiming that their product was good for the liver. This is an extreme example, but in the case of a cancer patient who puts his faith in a bogus remedy, even six months may be too long.

Moreover, some of the most effective types of advertising are untouchable. Our constitutional guarantees regarding free speech being what they are, there is little the FTC or FDA can do about best-selling books from reputable publishers promising miraculous cures for just about every ailment through the use of such folksy medicines as honey and vinegar or cod liver oil and orange juice.

Moreover, in most instances the FDA can only deal with a *fait accompli*, often after substantial damage has been done. Though medical-device quackery in America dates back to 1795, contrary to the case of drugs, there is still no law on the books that requires FDA premarket testing of all new diagnostic, therapeutic, and prosthetic devices to determine effectiveness and safety.

Moreover, the offender retains a distinct advantage: the burden of proof is always on the accuser. The maker of a food supplement who claims his product will "kill germs, heal wounds, and exhilarate the mentally depressed" doesn't have to prove his claims are true— but the FDA does have to prove that they are not. This takes time. In the case of the unlicensed healer (or the licensed healer gone wrong), obtaining evidence is often extremely difficult. "We're up against four stonewall factors," observes Joseph F. Bottini of the Cali-

fornia State Bureau of Food and Drug Inspection. "One, the victim
is reluctant to testify. Two, he is ashamed to admit he has been
bilked. Three, he believes in the treatment. Four, he is dead."[5]

Even when the bogus healer is brought to trial, conviction is by
no means certain. Juries are no more immune to the spell of the
con man than his victims. And more than one jury has been swung
to acquittal of a cancer quack by the plea that he is more saint than
sinner in that he offers his patient something a regular doctor cannot, something to make his or her last days brighter: hope. Which
may be true. Although it is equally true that the quack doesn't
distinguish between the early-cancer patient who may still be cured
if given legitimate treatment and the one who is past saving.

Even when convicted, the quack usually needn't worry about being taken out of commission even temporarily. In most states he is
subject to prosecution only for the misdemeanors of practicing
medicine without a license or petty theft, and subject to felony
prosecution only if he takes more than $200 from his victim.

"Medical quackery has taken more lives than all other forms of
criminal activity put together," asserts one of the few medical pros-
ecutors in the United States, Los Angeles County's John W. Miner.

"Except for the public executioner," Miner told a Senate subcommittee recently, "only the medical quack is permitted to earn his
living by killing people. How shocking that there is only one case
in Anglo-Saxon law of a murder conviction where death was caused
by such fraud."[6]

Miner secured that conviction, of second degree, which is on
appeal.

*   *   *

*In the sampling of deceptions, swindles, and frauds mentioned
in the preceding eight chapters, one mark has been readily identi-
fiable—the American consumer.*

*But there is another mark here, another vulnerable American, less
obvious but no less victimized—the reputable businessman. The
butcher who weighs his meat honestly pays a tax on that honesty
when his competition short-weighs. The national manufacturer who
insists that the true merits of his product be stressed in advertising
is penalized for his frankness when his competitors inflate their
claims. Fraud is often unfair competition, measurable not only in
dollars and cents but also in loss of reputation, since on learning that*

a number of companies lie, cheat, and steal we are inclined to believe that everybody's doing it.

In the following chapters we'll look at the other side of the coin to see how businesses are being swindled by individuals.

Keep in mind that this is the same coin, however, and that, heads or tails, it comes out of the same pocket.

CAVEAT VENDOR AND THE
STILL VULNERABLE
AMERICANS

Do it unto others as they'd like to
do it unto you, but do it first.

David Harum

CHAPTER 9

TURNABOUT

> They didn't offer Green Stamps or
> discounts or anything.
>
> —South Bend, Indiana, housewife
> to police after being arrested for
> shoplifting.

THE noon rush had just ended when two men entered the store and approached the cash register. Something about them—their manner, their distinctive dress, perhaps their Jack Armstrong boyishness—made the cashier guess that they were FBI agents, and she wasn't far wrong. As one opened his wallet and showed her his identification, she found that they were agents of the United States Treasury Department—Secret Service.

"The manager just left for lunch," she explained.

"That's all right," said the older of the pair. "I'm sure you can help us, Miss—?"

"Jones. Betty Jones."

"You see, Miss Jones, we've been trailing a gang of counterfeiters and have reason to believe that they may have passed you some bad bills. May we see your twenties, please?"

She quickly scooped them out of the register and handed them to the young, handsome, unmarried-looking agent. Examining them carefully, he separated them into two stacks. Moistening his thumb, he felt the upper right-hand corner of the bills he'd picked out, then held up his thumb for Betty to see. It was covered with green ink!

"Seven of them," he told his partner, who nodded solemnly. The older agent began copying the serial numbers on an envelope.

"Now, Miss Jones—Betty," the young agent smiled, taking a notebook and pencil from his pocket. "I want you to try to remember everyone who gave you a $20 bill this morning." While Betty was trying hard to recall the people and describe them, the older agent put the seven counterfeits in the envelope and sealed it. Turning the envelope on its face, he asked her to initial over the seal. She did so, after which both agents did the same. She remembered four people, which the agents agreed was remarkably observant.

"As you probably know," the older agent said, handing her the envelope, "we can't take these bills without a court order. So we want you to keep them in the cash drawer until my partner comes back for them later this afternoon."

Betty nodded, putting the envelope and the other bills in the drawer, pleased that it was the young agent who would be coming back.

"You've been very cooperative, Betty," he said, and again he smiled, in a nice personal way. "We hope it won't be necessary for you to have to identify these people or to testify in court, but if it should be, could we count on you?"

She assured them that they most certainly could. Wait until she told her girl friends about this!

She didn't tell them, however. It was much too embarrassing, especially the part where the manager, contrary to the explicit instructions of the "agents," tore open the envelope, revealing the strips of newspaper inside.

This short con is known as the *count and read*. Net loss: $140 and one dream.

The woman had been waiting for at least fifteen minutes, with the $5 bill and the scarf in her hand, trying to attract a clerk who wasn't busy, when the personable young man appeared.

"I'm sorry we kept you waiting. Now may I help you?"

She gave him the scarf and the bill.

"I'll wrap this and bring you your change."

She had a still longer wait, for she never saw him again.

Net loss: $5. The scarf was found on one of the counters. The young man, after all, wasn't a shoplifter, only a *phony employee*.

The man paid his lunch check for $1.60 with a $20 bill. The cashier smiled politely and counted out $18.40 in change.

The little old lady next in line handed her a bill and her check; the cashier mechanically thanked her and gave her her change.

The cashier had waited on several more people when the lady returned, looking perplexed and upset. "Miss," she said, "I'm afraid you made a mistake in my change. I gave you a twenty and you only gave me change for a five."

The cashier, very politely, assured the woman that she was mistaken, but opened the cash drawer just to be sure. The ones, fives, tens, and twenties were each in their separate compartments. Her work had become so automatic that she was sure if she had made the wrong change she would also have put the bill in the wrong compartment too. She was always careful on taking a bill to leave it on the shelf above the drawer until after making change, but the little old lady had left and then come back.

Again she told the woman she was sure she was mistaken.

"No," the lady insisted, a little more desperately. "It was a $20 bill. I'm positive it was."

By the time the owner noticed the commotion, the woman was almost hysterical. The cashier explained what had happened, as did the little old lady: "I'm very careful with my money. I cashed my Social Security check just this morning, and I paid my bills, and I had just this twenty left over. I know it was a twenty," she went on breathlessly, "because I met my daughter-in-law on the street and she told me her new telephone number and we couldn't find any paper to write it down on, so I wrote it on the bill until I could get some paper and copy it . . ."

"You wrote her telephone number on the bill?" the owner asked.

"Yes," she foraged a moment in her purse and brought out one of the restaurant match folders. There was a telephone number written across the face. "See, I copied it on this."

"Just a moment." He rang open the drawer. There, right on top, was the $20 bill, the same telephone number written across it.

"I'm terribly sorry," he apologized, handing her the bill. "These mistakes happen." He glared at the cashier and she apologized too. The woman left without a word.

A whole minute passed before the cashier realized that the woman wasn't supposed to get the whole twenty back, a minute more before she felt brave enough to risk the owner's wrath by telling him. By the time he was outside, the little old lady was nowhere in sight.

Net profit to the mother-and-son team: $20, $5 of which was unexpected.

"In retrospect, it is easy to see through a confidence game," observes Alan Hynd, who has probably chronicled as many of these frauds as anyone. "Oftentimes a victim will look back upon the steps that were taken by a swindler and wonder how he could possibly have been victimized. But when a confidence scheme is in actual operation, everything is different. Every little act of the confidence operator, every shadow of phraseology, every flicker of facial expression is so thoroughly artful that it mirrors integrity. Then, too, when a confidence scheme is in process of perpetration the victim is usually kept at such a high emotional pitch that reason rarely has a chance to function."[1]

This is true whether the game is a million-dollar stock scheme or one of the multitudinous *short cons* which are the subject of this chapter. A short con has been defined as any confidence game in which the mark is not placed "on the send," or sent for funds; in short, he is taken, usually quickly, either for money on his person or for money to which he has immediate access.

The foregoing are all short cons—they are also very old tricks, absent for a time, newly resurrected. The count and read, for example, infrequently used since World War II, when swindlers posing as government inspectors took businesses for hundreds of thousands of supposedly counterfeit ration stamps, is again having a brief vogue. There is a whole new generation of potential marks. These particular short cons are also known as *pushover rackets*, that is, swindles or frauds which are worked over the counter of the victim's place of business. In the second example, that of the woman and the bogus clerk, it was the woman who was defrauded. The store lost nothing except the time of the manager, the store detective, the clerks who attempted to track down the missing sale, and, almost assuredly, the future patronage of the woman. But the phony employee might just as easily have walked to a cash register, rung up the sale and made change like any other clerk, while pocketing from the drawer as many bills as he could palm. This is markedly successful in large stores which have frequent turnovers in personnel or take on part-time or temporary help during busy seasons or for special sales. Playing the executive helps. A man may wander from department to department, carrying a piece of paper, ostensibly checking prices, executive-looking enough so that the clerk would hesitate asking his business, circumventing any queries with "Please straighten that merchandise" or "Polish that counter."

Some additional pushover rackets:

Short-change tricks (also known as *laying the note, hipe racket,* and *ringing the changes*). These come in an innumerable variety, adaptable to the occasion, but having in common fast action. The transaction moves so quickly and is so confused, that an hour or more may pass between the getaway and the dawn. Often these are worked by a pair, both making small purchases and getting change, handing back coin for paper, paper for coin, small bills for larger bills, adding another item to the purchase, subtracting one already paid for—*either, or,* but often *all* of these—until the multiple transactions, accompanied by a constant flow of questions, leave the clerk mathematically exhausted. Many banks publish small booklets on the proper methods of handling cash for the use of tellers and retail clerks. Most advise: "Concentrate on each transaction. Let nothing distract you. If distracted or confused, stop the transaction, return the money to the drawer and start your count again. When in doubt, recount." Often, by the time the clerk is able to halt the play, the $5 or $10 or more has already been palmed and pocketed.

Sometimes, however, the game is played so simply and unhurriedly that the clerk doesn't suspect it is a bogus transaction. A woman brings a five-dollar item to the counter, pays with a $5 bill and the exact coins for sales tax. Then, after the clerk has wrapped the item, the woman has second thoughts. "I forgot. I wanted to keep that $5 bill. Would you mind giving me the five for five ones?" The clerk gets out the five and the woman counts out the ones, carefully, since they are new and seem to be sticking together. As the bills are being exchanged, the woman says suddenly, "Come to think of it, I'd rather have a ten, if it wouldn't be too much trouble," handing back the five. More often than one might believe, the cashier will put the five and the five ones back in the drawer, hand the woman a ten, and forget the whole transaction. Net loss: $5.

Till-tapping tricks are also quite diverse. The practice of leaving the bill on the ledge of the cash register until change is made does decrease the number of change complaints, but it can also reduce the cash intake if the customer distracts the cashier and the bill is within reach of a confederate. A number of Illinois stores fell victim to this trick in 1962, much to the puzzlement of police, who found that even leaning across the counters they couldn't reach these particular cash registers, until the 6-foot five-inch former college-basketball star took just a second too long.

Most successful till-tapping is focused on the one-clerk or owner-clerk store and consists of various means of separating the clerk and the cash register, by having him called to the phone in the store next door, asking him for an item on display in the window and luring him outside to point it out, or asking for more of an item than is on display so that he has to go to the stock room—while a confederate till-taps. The line between theft and fraud is often invisible.

Once an old short con is brought back from desuetude, it may spread contagiously. On July 4, 1964, the San Francisco *Chronicle* reported an uncommon swindle that had occurred in nearby Napa the previous night. The assistant manager of a large local grocery store was preparing to close for the day when the store's unlisted telephone rang. "I'm holding your wife and two children hostages," an unrecognizable male voice said. "You can kiss them goodby unless you do as you are told." Warned that his every move was being watched, the grocer was ordered to put $1000 in small bills in an envelope and to place the envelope in a designated spot behind the store, while the caller held the phone. The grocer did as he was told. The caller, still on the line when he came back, told him he was not to call home for thirty minutes, then hung up. By the time police arrived, the money was gone. The grocer's wife and children had spent an uneventful evening watching television.

On August 29th, the *Chronicle* ran another story, this one date-lined Sacramento. A cashier in one of the Bank of America branches had received a telephone call at the bank informing her that her one-year-old daughter was being held hostage. Warned that she would never see her little girl again if she spoke to anyone of this, she was told that in a few minutes a man would approach her cage. She was to give him all the money in her cash drawer. She too did as she was told, handing over $3200. The call was a hoax, the child safe.

The friendship con. For some reason, service stations are the principal victims of this fraud. The con man learns the name and working hours of the manager or owner, then waits in the vicinity until he sees him leave for the day. The con man then comes in and asks for him by his first name, Franz. On being told that he has gone, the con man panics. One of their best friends, Les, has been arrested for not paying his traffic tickets. He has all of the bail —here he pulls out a large roll of bills—except for $50, which he was counting on Franz to put up. Franz, of course, can't be reached, as usual having stopped for a few drinks en route home. If the attendant doesn't make the logical suggestion, the con man will, usually offering to put up a worthless ring or watch for security. One of the best ways to inspire confidence, the Yellow Kid has observed, is to appear to have more money than the mark. Not only does it create a trusting awe; for some reason, people seem to feel that a man with money has no need to be crooked.

Leaving a ring or other article as security is known as the *simple simon*, one of the oldest of the short cons. One variation is now all but obsolete. A well-dressed man and woman would appear at an automobile agency, wishing to buy a car. They lacked sufficient cash for the down payment, but the woman was wearing an impressive diamond ring. Could that serve as collateral until they could bring in the balance? The salesman should feel free, of course, to have the ring appraised before deciding. Which he did, promptly, finding it to be worth more than the entire price of the car. Just as the deal was consummated, the woman would ask if she might see the ring on her finger just once more, for sentimental reasons. At which time the diamond would be expertly and discreetly switched for a zircon or glass double.

There was a certain risk inherent in this game—including the possibility that the salesman might pull his own switch first—but it wasn't this which caused this con to disappear so much as the fact that today few auto dealers are interested in diamonds or currency; credit is their best friend.

A related short con is the *lost and found*. A well-dressed man in an expensive automobile drives into a service station for gas. While the attendant is waiting on him, the man makes sure that the huge diamond ring he is wearing is noticed. While the car is being attended to, the man gets out and stretches. Later, as he's driving off, he halts the car suddenly, jumps out and begins frantically searching the area around the pump. He's lost his ring! The attendant helps look. When they fail to find it, the man gives the attendant his card, writing on it the name of a local hotel and a room number, offering a $100 reward for the ring. A few minutes after the man has driven off, a seedy-looking hitchhiker appears, asking for directions. Leaning over, he picks up something which he pockets surreptitiously. Asked if he has found a ring, he replies defiantly "What of it? Finder's keepers." For $50, he is eventually persuaded to part with the ring. On calling the hotel, the service-station attendant then learns that no such person as the man named on the card is registered there. The "diamond" is glass.

There is a rather moribund variation on this, which has been worked in various retail stores in different parts of the country in the past. While talking to the clerk, the "customer," noticing his shoe was untied, would lean down to tie it. When he straightened up, the clerk would observe, to his horror, that his customer had lost an eye! The routine was the same from this point on, with the reward being offered for the lost glass eye. That this trick isn't often heard of is probably due to the limited number of one-eyed con men.

The original form of the *clip* is now also rare. A man would enter a busy barbershop with a young boy. He would have his hair cut, then, while the boy's was being cut, leave for a minute to get a cigar. When after some time he still hadn't returned, the barber would remark to the boy, "Your dad must have been delayed." To this the boy was apt to reply, "He's not my dad. He just met me on the street and said he'd give me a dollar if I'd get a haircut."

For all the conning required—persuading a young boy that he needs a haircut—it hardly seems worth the effort, but the modern form of the clip, no longer played in a barbershop but in a retail store, can be most lucrative. It works like this:

A middle-aged woman and a man young enough to be her son enter a store at about the same time. While the young man browses, the woman selects a large quantity of merchandise, which she carries to the counter. Looking back impatiently in the direction of the young man, she tells the salesgirl that she can't wait any longer, she's late for an appointment. Picking out one of the items—something expensive but not as expensive as many of the other items selected—she says, "I'll take this with me. Please wrap up the rest. My son will pay for them if he ever finishes deciding." Taking leave, she speaks briefly to the young man; he glances at his watch, says something, nods, and continues browsing. On coming up to the counter and paying for his own purchase, he is told that he is to pay for his mother's also, including the item she took with her. "My Mother? I never saw that woman before!"

"But I saw you talking to her!"

"She just asked me the time."

To play this singly requires considerable gall—the alleged son may walk out at any time; playing it doubly is equally dangerous—the young man will be marked well before he's permitted to leave the store. But it often works, for the same reason the old barbershop clip usually worked, the salesgirl, like the barber, being afraid to offend the customer by asking for payment. Seeing the large quantity of merchandise piled up before her, and mentally weighing the risk of losing a single item against losing the whole sale, she takes a chance. It's a gamble, with her employer's merchandise, but it's a gamble he may encourage and sometimes force her to take. Confidence operators, including credit artists and check passers, find that the easiest retail stores to swindle are those where the salespeople work on either a quota or commission basis. The greater the pressure to sell, the greater the vulnerability to fraud.

The *switch* operator specializes in making his or her own bargains. Wanting an $8.95 book, he pays $3.95 for it, by switching dust jackets. Desiring an expensive new dress, the female of the species switches tags with one lesser priced. Price tags on clothing are usually affixed so they can be removed easily, without tearing the garment. Add one new or part-time salesgirl, unfamiliar with the merchandise, and the store has had an undeclared bargain day.

Following are a few recent examples of an even more popular sport, the *refund racket:*

A twenty-two-year-old New York man specialized in swindling New Jersey hardware stores with a very simple technique. He would enter a crowded store, pick up a gallon of paint from the back of a shelf, and bring it up to the counter.

"I bought this paint here and later found I didn't need it. It hasn't been opened. I'd like a refund please."

In many stores he got the refund. In others the personnel were less cooperative—many refused to give a refund, some even said they could tell from the markings that it had been purchased from another store. When refused a refund the man would walk out in a huff, with the can of paint.

Shoplifters like the refund racket because it means they can get full value for their thefts, often only minutes after they take place. All that is required is an assortment of wrinkled store bags plus a little daring. The right bag, together with the item, will get a refund in most large stores. To swindle those stores which also require the sales slip be produced requires only a little more preparation, the purchase of some cheaper item. When asked for the sales slip the customer produces it, then says "Oh, I must have saved the wrong slip!" It usually works, the nonexistent slip and the real slip somehow adding up to a pair, which in the clerk's mind indicate one regular customer who might be offended if refused a refund. To beat a "hard-head" store requires only a bit more advance work. Many customers, particularly men, aren't concerned with saving their receipts; often they leave them on the counter or drop them on the floor nearby. Picking these up requires no great art, and with a good collection of assorted prices the cheat can match the slip to the merchandise.

In 1960, New York City detectives arrested two men and a woman who, they said, had swindled Macy's, Gimbel's, B. Altman, Saks Fifth Avenue, and other large stores of more than $100,000 over a period of a year and a half. The woman would enter a store late in the afternoon and purchase a number of expensive outfits, paying with a bogus check. The following morning one of the men, posing as her husband, would bring the clothes back for a cash refund, the whole transaction being completed before the check had time to bounce. Success encourages repetition, however, and like most retail swindlers they were arrested after hitting the same store several times. In this case they were recognized by an alert clerk in Saks.

Many stores do not give cash refunds, only credit. This doesn't eliminate fraud. The shoplifter may steal an item that is easy to boost but hard to pawn or resell, then use the credit for something harder to lift but with a better resale value. Too, credit slips are often easily altered, by adding a digit or two, or counterfeited altogether. A number of stores no longer issue gift certificates, for these very reasons.

One form of fraud engaged in by an even larger number of people is *diddling*. Women diddle more than men, buying an expensive coat or dress to wear on a special occasion, returning it the following day as unsatisfactory or because hubby thought it too expensive. "He didn't even let me try it on!" she may say—despite powder marks on the neck, opera tickets in the pocket, or cigarette burns along the hem. Oddly enough, the better the store and the more expensive the garment, the more chance the return will be accepted without comment. Except, perhaps, for a small initialed "U.U." at the bottom of the credit slip, meaning Utterly Unreasonable. The limit of patience varies from store to store.

Pickup and delivery tricks. These are generally classified as robbery or theft, but because they often contain elements of deception and artifice, many are on the borderline of fraud. One warm July afternoon in 1964, a man in a green pickup truck drove up to the loading platform of the Gubser Garlic Company in Gilroy, California. "I've come for the ton of garlic," he told the warehouseman, who groaned and dutifully began loading the forty-four 50-lb. sacks onto the truck. Not until some time after the man had driven off did the warehouseman learn that no one had ordered a ton of garlic. Police were unable to pick up the scent.

Two "deliverymen" entered a Chicago department store, went to the rug department, rolled up the most expensive rug on display, put it over their shoulders and carried it out through the store. They did not escape unnoticed, however. An alert floorwalker stopped them and insisted they take the rug out through the shipping door in the rear. The men obligingly complied.

A sports-minded thief once picked up an aluminum kayak in one of Manhattan's larger department stores, hoisted it over his head, carried it down six flights of stairs, past a half-dozen store guards, out through Herald Square, and down several blocks to his parked car, where he was tying it on the roof when police Captain Daniel J. Campion—who had followed in astonished wonder—asked to see his sales receipt.

Charles Stivers, a friend of the author's, was co-owner of a San Francisco folk-singing bar known as The Drinking Gourd. One morning, when only the janitor was in the bar, two burly men in movers' uniforms arrived and said, "Charlie sent us for the piano." It still hasn't been recovered.

One of the more ancient delivery tricks, the *in and out*, now nearly obsolete, went as follows: A swindler would call a store (often a jewelry store), using the name of a well-known person from out of town, and order something expensive, such as a pair of diamond cuff links, with directions that it be sent to his hotel room C.O.D. The arriving messenger would be met by a man identifying himself as Mr. So-and-So's secretary, who would take the parcel, walk into the next room to get the money—and continue walking, through the other door, down the corridor, down the stairs, through the lobby and down the street. This elaborate artifice is rarely employed nowadays. It isn't necessary. Many stores will charge and deliver merchandise regardless of whether a customer has an account, provided the amount is less than the store's "floor limit." (This remarkable phenomenon, how to charge without having a charge account, will be discussed in Chapter 13.)

There is a dodge similar to the above, aged in usage but still current. A man posing as the secretary of a prominent person visits a jewelry store, where he selects for his employer an expensive necklace, to be wrapped as an anniversary gift. The necklace is to be charged and delivered to Mr. Such-and-Such's residence between one and three that afternoon, while Mrs. Such-and-Such is out at her weekly bridge game. (The name, address, and social engagement of the mistress of the house are real, having been learned by prior canvassing of the social columns.) Before leaving the store the "secretary" obtains the card of the salesman, in case anything should go wrong. He is assured that nothing will.

Nothing does. When the delivery truck pulls up before the residence shortly after one o'clock, the swindler is watching from a nearby car. A few minutes later he drives to a phone booth and calls the house. Posing as the manager of the store, he says he fears a mistake has been made, a package delivered in error. Has, by any chance, a package from his store been left there? The maid confirms that one has. Noting the name and title on the salesman's card, he says, "Our assistant manager, Mr. Kendall Phelps, will be over shortly to pick it up." The swindler arrives, shows the card, apologizes profusely for the inconvenience, picks up the package and departs. Usually no one is any the wiser until Mr. Such-and-Such receives his bill.

Shortly before Christmas each year, some large community is hit with a large-scale variation of this trick. A gang of four or five swindlers will go through the society pages picking out several dozen of the more prominent names. Assuming, usually correctly, that most of these people have accounts in the city's best stores, the swindlers make a number of separate calls per name, ordering an expensive gift be sent to Mr., Mrs., or Miss This-and-That at a certain address. The send-names are fictitious; the address is real, that of an apartment—known as a *drop* or *reception center*—especially rented for the occasion.

Whatever the type store, there are short cons specifically directed to fleecing it. A sampling:

Cigar Stores. Old but still common is the *punchboard racket*. A persuasive salesman convinces the owner of a cigar store that he can make a good profit and attract new trade by putting a few punchboards in his establishment. The cost, per board, is only $2. Each board has 500 punches; if all are punched, at 10¢ each, the merchant will take in $50. There are $25 in prizes—a $20 Grand Prize and $5 in miscellaneous small amounts. Minus the initial purchase and the prizes, the merchant stands to make $23 per board.

The merchant takes one, to try it. A day or two later a man comes into the store and makes five or six punches, with no luck. Starting to leave, he discovers he has an extra dime. "I might as well lose this too." Instead, he punches out the $20 Grand Prize.

Bunco detectives claim that, no matter how many times this con is pulled, there are some who still never connect the two men.

Cleaning Shops. A man brings in a new suit for cleaning. On the day it is due, a woman identifying herself as the man's wife comes in to pick up the suit. Unfortunately, her husband left for work without leaving the receipt and he must have the suit to wear that evening. She describes the suit accurately and the cleaner gives it to her. Later the same day the man returns with the receipt and asks for his suit. The cleaner tells him that his wife has already picked it up. "*Wife*, what do you mean *wife?* I'm not married." Cost to the cleaner, or his insurance company: the price of one new suit.

Florists. A man and a woman enter a florist shop, the woman weeping copiously, the man attempting to comfort her. They wish to buy flowers for their mother's funeral, the man explains, about $30 worth. As they are shown sample wreaths, the woman's mood begins to brighten—"What beautiful flowers! Oh, Mother would love these! George, wouldn't it be nice if the rest of the family bought their flowers from the same shop? Then we'd know they'd look just right." The florist, also in a happier mood, delivers a short lecture on the importance of floral symmetry, concluding, almost apologetically for being commercial on such an occasion, that there would be an appreciable savings on a large order. There's one problem, the man explains—the rest of the family won't be arriving until tomorrow and the funeral is on the following day. If they all came in tomorrow afternoon, could he still have them ready in time? He assures them that he could, and as a token of appreciation, he charges them only $25 for their own order.

The man gives him a check for $75. Made out to Sam White, drawn on a law firm, and marked "From the estate of Mrs. Esther White," it looks authentic. But the always-careful florist excuses himself and goes into the back room, where he checks his obituary clipping file. Yes, there is a clipping from the morning paper, giving the name, date, and mortuary, with Mr. Sam White listed as one of the surviving kin. The list of kin, he notes happily, is quite long. The check is cashed; it bounces. This is known as the *deceased-mother racket.*

Garages. A man brings in a late-model car for a complete overhaul. He also wishes to leave the car in storage for a month while he is away on business. He pays with a larger-than-amount-of-transaction check, but the garageman doesn't mind; he has more than enough security in the automobile. The check is bad, the car stolen.

Jewelry Stores. Precious stones are beautiful, expensive, and have a decided psychological effect on feminine emotions. They are also anonymous, have a consistently high resale value, and are easily concealed. More than sufficient reason why so many swindlers have made gem acquisition their primary endeavor and why, even though the jewelry industry has one of the most vigilant of the trade-protection associations, the Jewelers Security Alliance, gem theft remains a multimillion-dollar-a-year business.

Alliance files contain a catalogue of more than one hundred separate confidence tricks. Nearly all are derived, however, from two basic techniques—the straight steal, and the switch (or subsitution trick).

Of the first type, the *gum-wood swindle* is one of the oldest. A well-dressed woman would enter a fine jewelry establishment and ask to see a selection of unset diamonds. As the salesman placed the tray of gems on the counter before her—always aware of the exact number he was showing and holding to the old safeguard of never showing too many at one time—and the woman, very much at ease, discussed them with him knowledgeably, a confederate would enter the store and create a disturbance. The moment the attention of the salesman was diverted, the woman would take one of the stones, put it in a wad of chewing gum, and stick the gum under the edge of the counter. (This required much less time than it takes to describe it.) The woman would then leave, without making a purchase. Immediately noticing the loss, the salesman would quickly have her apprehended. While she was being brought back into the store, perhaps furiously indignant, perhaps sobbing hysterically, a second confederate, who had been in the store all the time, would remove the gum and stone from under the counter and leave. Amidst protestations of innocence, the woman would be searched, but nothing found. She could then, if she so desired, file a whopping suit for false arrest. Such suits declined appreciably once the Alliance's master file system came into being in the 1930s, listing with descriptions and photographs all known jewelry-confidence operators, while glass counters and alert clerks have almost completely retired the gum-wood fraud. A host of other gambits have taken its place.

Substitution, or switch, tricks usually call for a fine eye for detail and a talented counterfeiter of stones. On several visits to a jewelry store a particular ring is studied and, later, an accurate counterfeit or facsimile made; the two are then switched. One of the basic rules of the game is that the swindler in his "studied shopping" never shows the slightest interest in the ring that is to be stolen. It is always another ring in the same tray that he examines, discusses, and almost buys.

Familiar as many of these tricks now are, jewelers still find themselves vulnerable. Late on Saturday afternoon in January 1964, a woman walked into Tiffany's 57th Street and Fifth Avenue store. While examining diamond rings she pulled the old-fashioned switch, taking a 3.69-carat marquise-shaped diamond ring worth $19,800. In its place she left not a bogus diamond but a 2.75-carat marquise worth about $7500. The switch wasn't detected. It would appear, at this point, that Tiffany's had been defrauded of about $12,300. Actually, the store had begun to show a profit.

The woman then crossed the street to Harry Winston's. While Tiffany's sells a variety of select merchandise, Winston's sells only valuable jewelry. Only a few customers are admitted to the main salon at a time. Each sits at an elegant black-and-gold table, with two salespeople in attendance. Winston's clerks are taught to appraise their customers. The woman who came in at 5 P.M. that day was about forty, elegantly dressed in a charcoal suit with Persian-lamb collar. She was attractive and poised. The salesman showed her a tray of twelve rings. Apparently undecided, she left at 5:25 P.M., promising to return.

As a clerk was returning the tray of diamonds to the safe, he noticed that the price tag was missing from one. Examining that ring carefully, he saw the word "Tiffany" engraved inside. By the time security police reached the street, the woman was nowhere to be seen. Missing was a 5.30-carat marquise diamond ring worth about $38,500. Left behind, however, was the 3.69-carat ring. Richard Winston, nephew of the store's president, thought the woman might have made the switch inadvertently. Hurrying across the street, Winston found Tiffany's safe had just been closed and, due to the time lock, couldn't be opened until nine o'clock Monday morning. All weekend the jewelers remained in doubt. On Monday their fears were confirmed—a switch, or rather two switches, had been pulled. In exchange value, the woman made $31,000; Winston's lost $38,500, for the $19,800 ring was stolen property and was returned to Tiffany's; and Tiffany's, who first appeared to have been swindled of $12,300, actually made a $7500 profit on the transaction.

One of the most successful of the switch artists, a man we'll call Williams, knew more about cowhide than precious gems, yet managed to accumulate some $1.5 million of the latter in less than five years. Williams would following traveling jewelry salesmen, paying special attention to their luggage; he would then duplicate their sample cases and switch them. Later he simplified his technique even further by waiting until the salesmen had checked their luggage in railway depots, claiming it with bogus but identical claim checks.

The atomic age has made one phase of gem swindlery easier. During the early years of the Cold War, a foreign diplomat alighted at New York's Idlewild Airport. When his luggage was checked through Customs it passed automatically under a Geiger counter. The needle zoomed up to read near-100 percent radioactivity. Though fearing the very worst, the components of an atom bomb, FBI and Customs officials could do nothing but follow the man to his embassy, since diplomatic immunity prevented either search or seizure. For months the official and all his associates were watched. It was then found, by means still unrevealed, that his intentions were not sabotage but fraud: the equipment he had been carrying was part of a newly developed process whereby poor-quality industrial diamonds were subjected to intense heat and bombarded with a radioactive substance which changed their color, for about a month, to a pure blue-white. The scheme was exposed before any of the stones could make their way onto the market.

Today there are synthetic diamonds which will pass all but the most exacting of laboratory tests; beautiful "reconstructed" rubies made by electrically fusing powdered fragments of natural Burma rubies and adding coloring; star sapphires, created industrially, which virtually duplicate the composition of real stones; and jade, "colored" or "treated," which has fooled even the experts.* Yet even today the swindler must often still rely on an engaging manner and sleight-of-hand.

Three classic jewel frauds are worth mentioning. One, which dates from the 1930s but is still among the unsolved cases in the files of the Alliance, is a novel take-off on the ancient *in and out*.

A woman visited a large East Coast jewelry store in quest of a wedding gift for her niece. At the clerk's suggestion, she finally

* For an entertaining account of this and related frauds, such as the practice of attributing modern carvings to ancient dynasties, see Richard Gump's superb volume *Jade: Stone of Heaven*, Doubleday, 1962.

decided that a diamond bracelet would be appropriate, but couldn't choose among the three most expensive. She would have to consult her brother, she said, mentioning his name, which the clerk immediately recognized as that of a prominent psychiatrist. The problem, however, was that he had a very full schedule and she was uncertain as to whether he would have the time to come in. The salesman advanced a suggestion. With the manager's permission, he would accompany madame to the doctor's office and show him the three bracelets. Minutes later, the clerk and the woman were en route to the doctor's office in her chauffeur-driven limousine. On their arrival, the receptionist greeted the woman cordially and told her to go right in. She took the three bracelets with her. When, after a lengthy wait she still hadn't returned, the salesman, growing suspicious, asked to see the doctor. The reception he received was totally unexpected.

For some time the woman had been consulting the psychiatrist about the problems of her "brother," who, she said, had a phobia about diamonds. Once he began talking about them, the more hysterical he became. The doctor had told her to bring him in. Several times she had started to the doctor's office with him, only to have him change his mind at the last minute. This time, she told the doctor, she had succeeded; her brother was waiting outside. He was a little disturbed, however, and she suggested that the doctor wait a few minutes before seeing him, until he had calmed down. The doctor agreed, and the woman left by another exit.

There was no question that the man was disturbed. He not only confused relationships—asking where the doctor's sister had gone— he suddenly screamed "The diamonds! She's stolen the diamonds!" "Yes, I know," the doctor replied, "and isn't it nice weather we're having?" The man wouldn't be pacified, however, and finally became so hysterical that the doctor was forced to have him removed to a hospital under restraint.

One day in June 1919, Nicky Arnstein, associate of Arnold Rothstein and husband of comedienne Fannie Brice, entered Tiffany's, where he asked to see a ruby on display in the window. It was a perfect 12-carat pigeon-blood, beautiful against the white velvet cushion on which it rested, and Arnstein was not in the least disturbed by the $60,000 price tag. In fact, he liked the gem so much that he asked for another exactly like it, the two to be made into a pair of earrings for his wife. The startled salesman explained that that wouldn't be possible—the gem was one of a kind! In that case,

Arnstein said, he wasn't interested. As he started to leave, the clerk had a hurried consultation with the manager, who called Mr. Arnstein back. He explained, as had the clerk, that this was an exceptionally rare stone; however, Tiffany's had agents in all parts of the world. It was just possible that a matching stone might be found, perhaps in Burma, but it was only a possibility, not a guarantee, and the second stone would undoubtedly be more expensive than the first.

Never a haggler, Arnstein took out his checkbook and wrote out a check for $70,000—$60,000 for the first stone, and $10,000 as a deposit on the second.

Some months later, Tiffany's agent in Rangoon was engaged in conversation with a newly met acquaintance in the lobby of his hotel when the man mentioned that he too was very interested in precious stones, that in fact he had a ruby he was trying to sell. The agent, with polite but cursory interest, volunteered to look at it. The man had it removed from the hotel safe. Examining it, the agent had trouble suppressing his excitement: it was a perfect blood-red 12-carat stone, so close a twin to the first stone that he doubted if anyone could tell them apart. Yes, he might be interested, he said calmly, if the price were right. The asking price was high, $135,000, but the agent cabled Tiffany's New York, which in turn contacted Arnstein. The return cable read simply "Buy it." The stone was sent to New York on the first ship.

At the time it arrived, Arnstein was having differences of opinion with the law, and some time passed before Tiffany's was able to contact him. When finally reached he informed the store, sadly, that he had undergone unforeseen financial reverses; he couldn't afford to purchase the stone at this time; he understood, of course, that he would have to forfeit his deposit.

Since early in its colorful career, Tiffany's has adhered strictly to a policy of anonymity regarding its customer transactions. Though the Arnstein story has been widely circulated, Tiffany's will neither confirm nor deny that one Nicholas Arnstein took the firm for $65,-000 by selling it back its own stone. No charges were ever filed, though it is said they were for a time considered. Tiffany's, according to underworld rumor, wasn't the only party taken. Arnstein's partner in Burma is said to have skipped with the whole $135,000.

The following is not, as it first appears, a business swindle, yet it is too good to be left unrepeated. Though, like the Arnstein story, this tale has been told in so many different variations as to make one suspect it is apocryphal, it actually happened to Cartier's in New York some years ago.

A middle-aged man, accompanied by a young and very beautiful blonde, entered Cartier's late one Friday afternoon, the man asking to see something special in the way of jewelry for his companion. He was shown a variety of extraordinarily lavish pieces, one in particular, a massive throatpiece of diamonds, causing the young lady to gasp aloud. Holding up the necklace so the young lady could try it on, the man asked, "Do you like it?" She liked it more than words could say. "I'll take it," the man told the clerk, without even asking the price. When told it was $100,000, he nonchalantly wrote out a check for that amount. It was late Friday afternoon, however; the bank was closed and the man unknown to the establishment. As tactfully as possible, the clerk said that it would be necessary to go through the formality of clearing the check. The man understood; giving the clerk the girl's name and address, he suggested they have it delivered on Monday after the check had cleared. The pair left the store, the girl almost melting into the man's arm.

Monday morning Cartier's put through the check. It bounced. The man did have an account, but his funds were far from sufficient to cover the paper. Cartier's promptly called the man at his office and informed him that the check had failed to clear.

"Yes, I know," was his now classic reply, "but I had one hell of a wonderful weekend."

To turn from the grandiose to the comparatively mean, *shoplifting* is theft, not fraud, but since it contributes significantly to the "gyp tax" the customer pays, a brief mention seems in order.

Hypothetically, shoplifters come in two kinds: the *booster* and the *snitch*, the professional and the amateur. In recent years, however, it has become increasingly difficult to distinguish between the two. While once the difference was apparent in the amount stolen, the frequency of the thefts, or the methods employed, the dividing line today most often is whether the shoplifter intends to use the item or resell it.

Losses, it is generally agreed, split about evenly between the two groups. Less equitable is the division of the sexes. Among both groups females predominate, perhaps because women do more shopping than men, one private detective service, Willmark Service Systems, Inc., estimating that as high as 83 percent of the amateurs are women.

Why do people shoplift? Whole volumes have been devoted to

motivations.* Law-enforcement officials are inclined to doubt that many of these people, of either sex, are true kleptomaniacs, believing that this term is more common in courtrooms than in psychiatrists' offices. The "impulse" theory of shoplifting is also in bad repute, since the average shoplifter steals two or more items. The "need" theory is also open to question, since the amateur usually steals not necessities but luxuries, and more often than not has enough money on his or her person to pay for the items stolen. Of late, the "revenge" or "get-even" motive seems to be an increasingly popular justification, the customer stealing to right some real or imaginary wrong. Joe Lincoln, chief of security of New Jersey's General Supermarkets, Inc., observes: "They may steal from you because the roast they purchased last week wasn't tender enough; or perhaps they found the eggs broken when they got home; or possibly because a shopping cart scratched their car in the parking lot."[2]

Professionals often use special aids such as "booster boxes," seemingly sealed packages with hinged flaps that spring open to receive goods, or special clothing—belts with hooks, worn under a coat or dress; roomy "booster bloomers"; "Jane Russell bras." An Oakland, California, booster team of a man and two women recently came up with a basketball variation. The man, an exceptionally tall Negro, walked around the main floor of a department store, carrying a giant-size, newly purchased wastepaper basket on his shoulder, while his accomplices dropped items into it from the mezzanine. The most important recent innovation in professional boosting, however, is the wig. Today the female shoplifter can alter her appearance in seconds.

In ingenuity the amateurs deserve equal billing. One "pregnant" supermarket customer in Michigan gave birth to a pound of butter, a chuck roast, two packages of cube steaks, a package of dried beef, a large bottle of pancake syrup, and assorted packages of candy, toothpaste, and hair tonic. Some current supermarket snitch tricks: substituting butter cubes for margarine; dumping the contents of cereal boxes and replacing them with two or three cartons of cigarettes; putting phonograph records in frozen pizza pie packages, nylons between the pages of a magazine; loading up baby carriages; rolling today's groceries out the back door of the store using yesterday's receipt.

---

* An exceptionally good study—minus the hysteria common to many such volumes—is Mary Owen Cameron's *The Booster and the Snitch*, Free Press, Glencoe, Ill., 1964.

Store owners and managers have their own countertricks, such as conspicuously placed mirrors that may or may not be two-way, closed-circuit TV systems, strolling guards, private detectives who are supposed to look like shoppers. There are also numerous preventive measures. In supermarkets, small high-priced items, such as razor blades and lipsticks, are kept near the check-out counter, often encased in plastic bubbles mounted on out-size cardboard. Only bulky items are placed in "blind" corners. Phonograph-record jackets are cellophane sealed, so an extra disk can't be slipped in. Vegetables and fruits are dumped out when they're weighed, then re-sacked. After-the-fact techniques, designed to persuade the shoplifter to dispose of the item before leaving the store, range from the subtle to the extreme. Among the former is use of a "spook": the manager, without explanation, drops a second item, identical to the one seen stolen, in the customer's cart. This not only eliminates the risk of false accusations, but is said usually to result in both items being returned to their proper place. Some stores utilize more drastic measures. When a shoplifter is spotted in the act, the public-address system may blare out, "There's a jar of caviar missing from shelf 3B. Will an attendant please replace it." The psychological effect of such an announcement on other customers—who may or may not have guilty consciences—would make an interesting study. One detective service was recently quoted in the press as saying that stolen items were usually secreted in pockets, with purses running a close second; shortly afterward, one store manager instructed his employees that they were to consider all women with purses and slacks, or purses and coats with pockets, as probable shoplifters. Some stores are so shoplifter-obsessed that they offer their employees "bounties" on each shoplifter apprehended. Most who have tried this method don't recommend it. Remarked one store owner who adopted this procedure, then dropped it in less than a month, "After a week everyone looked like a thief, even our oldest and best customers. Moreover, they *felt* the suspicion. Business has never been so bad." The bounty in this case was $3.

Apparently some feel the situation extreme enough to warrant extreme tactics. According to the FBI, shoplifting is one of the fastest-growing of all crimes, reported arrests up 81 percent in the past six years.[3]

A major cause for the increase, experts agree, is the widespread adoption of self-service merchandising. Larger displays of more easily accessible goods plus fewer clerks equals Opportunity, so say the experts, or, in the words of an old proverb, "Opportunity makes the thief." Observes the manager of one chain of retail stores, "We try to tempt people in buying and at the same time tempt them into stealing!"[4]

Such statistics lend themselves to any number of interpretations. They may be used as evidence of the decline in American morality —i.e., more people are shoplifting. Or they may simply mean that more shoplifters are being caught. Or more who are caught are being reported to the police. Attitudes toward the shoplifter have changed during the past several years. Revisions in the laws have made the apprehension of shoplifters easier, and have added to arrest totals. Though the booster knows better, the snitch often believes in a myth: that he can't be arrested unless he takes the goods off the premises. Though once true, this is so no more. Forty-seven of the fifty states now have laws permitting in-store apprehension if the shoplifter is observed in the act of stealing. There is also a growing "shoplifter consciousness" on the part of retail-merchant groups. Until recently, most stores were unwilling to prosecute apprehended shoplifters, content merely to recover the goods and issue a warning. The old attitude, as summarized by a spokesman for the Super Market Institute, was that prosecutions were "either bad publicity, too risky from the point of view of false arrest charges, or simply not worth the effort it takes to bring a pilferer to justice."[5] Today many merchants have come to the conclusion that such publicity isn't necessarily bad but may be preventive,* that the ominous cry of "false arrest," though often voiced, rarely results in a suit, and that it *is* worth the time required to prosecute cases. A number of large retail chains now have a policy of prosecuting each and every apprehended shoplifter, whatever the age or circumstance. Some, slightly more flexible, prosecute only known repeaters, but require each shoplifter to sign a confession which, together with the name, address, description, and sometimes a photograph, are made accessible to other stores.

And a few communities have made an all-out assault on the problem, with some success. Oakland, California, was for many years a

---

* Many stores once reluctant to discuss the subject now make public their arrest totals. During 1961, Sears Roebuck and Company apprehended 2500 shoplifters in its Eastern Division alone. The same year, Alexander's four New York City stores caught 5700; in 1962, the pre-Christmas total was 6500, with another 1000 apprehended by year's end. Of the 7500, about 3500 were teenagers.

booster's paradise, leading most other American communities its size
in known losses. Early in the 1960s, the Oakland Retail Merchants
Association, working in close harmony with local police and community officials, adopted a number of antishoplifting measures,
which included special court handling for juvenile offenders, stiffer
sentences for adult repeaters, more beat patrolmen in the downtown
areas, crime-prevention clinics and retail-security training schools
attended by both law-enforcement officers and merchants. Police
also set up a master shoplifter file, enabling a merchant to learn in
minutes whether a person had been apprehended previously. A
store-detective group, sponsored by Retail Merchants, issues circulars with mug shots and descriptions of professional boosters and
bad-check passers known to be operating in the area. Today the
pros avoid Oakland. Between November 1962 and October 1963,
shoplifting arrests decreased 5.2 percent over the previous year. The
percentage of recidivists, or repeaters, among juvenile offenders is
so low as to cause other communities to study Oakland's methods.

But Oakland has gone against the grain. Nationally the number of
arrests has risen. Also risen is the value of items stolen. In supermarkets, this has nearly tripled in just four years. According to the
Super Market Institute, in 1961 the average item pilfered had a
value of $1.11; in 1965, it was estimated at $3.06.

What is the national loss to boosters and snitches? As with fraud,
nobody knows. One leading law-enforcement official estimates it at
$78 million. An expert in the field of shrinkage prevention believes
the amount to be close to $5 billion. (Some of his fellows set it at
$2 or $3 billion.) A rather wide difference of opinion. According
to a representative of the National Retail Merchants Association
(NRMA), estimates vary greatly, "depending on whether you talk
to someone in the protection field or a top-management executive."
The problem of computing "accurate estimates" is as much one of
bookkeeping as detection. Most stores lump together under the heading "stock shrinkage" not only losses to shoplifting but also losses to
employee theft, bookkeeping and system errors, and damaged or
shopworn merchandise. It is not improbable that these figures may
even sometimes be increased for tax purposes.

What is undebatable is the steady increase in such losses: NRMA
figures for all U.S. stores show a rise in stock shrinkage from 1.16
percent of gross sales in 1959 to 1.39 percent in 1963. Small enough,
it would appear, but according to an expert in this field, a reduction

of *one-half of a percentage point* in shortage figures related to
sales volume can have the same effect on profits as a:

$1,428,570 increase in sales for a $10 million store
$5,454,540 increase in sales for a $20 million store
$6,250,000 increase in sales for a $50 million store, and a
$7,258,000 increase in sales for a $75 million store.[6]

Only the percentage hasn't been reduced; it has steadily risen.

Although the experts may not agree as to who steals and why and
how much, on one point there is unanimous agreement, the identity
of the ultimate victim. It is the customer who picks up the tab for
retail fraud, whether it be shoplifting or some ingenious short con.

It has been estimated that the average supermarket must make
$264 in new sales to offset just a $2 theft, $6.60 in new sales to offset
the loss of a single nickel candy bar. By such reckoning, it would
seem that all but the most booming businesses would be fated to
bankruptcy or eternal debt. There is an alternative, however, which
almost all stores find preferable: passing the cost on to the customer.

"In shoplifting, as in bad-check writing, it is the poor shopper
who foots the whole bill," observes Philip L. Ennis, manager of the
Oakland Retail Merchants Association. "Retail stores cannot afford to
assume the loss. They have no choice but to pass it on—in its entirety
—to the customer."[7]

Moreover, the customer pays not only for the theft but also for the
special detectives, shrinkage-prevention experts, lawyers, two-way
mirrors, closed-circuit TV systems, theft insurance, bonding-com-
pany fees, special packaging, and other personnel and equipment
used to prevent or detect it.

The full cost may be in doubt, but all agree it is high and growing
higher. "What's more," notes Sylvia Porter, "it imposes a mounting
'hidden tax' on all honest customers, for retailers pass on the cost to
us in prices they charge."[8]

Who pays? We—the customers, consumers, and most vulnerable
Americans—do.

Maxim: Turnabout is not necessarily fair play.

CHAPTER 10

EVERYBODY'S DOING IT

> In the opinion of the men who
> operate the shopping services, al-
> most every employee will steal if
> afforded the opportunity. There is
> no "trusted worker."
>
> *The Investigator's Handbook*

THE advertising monitors of the FTC aren't the only men who
spend their working hours watching television. In a teakwood-
paneled office at Red Devil Paint Company's factory in Mt. Vernon,
New York, company president Donald L. Greene spends up to four
hours each workday watching a 12-inch TV screen. The program, a
continuous daytime serial, isn't listed in *TV Guide*, but if it were it
might be titled "Suspicion," as the screen is linked to a closed-circuit
camera focused on the activities of some forty employees in Red
Devil's shipping and receiving department.

"Before we installed it last May, we were losing $5000 a year in
paint," Mr. Greene told Lee Berton, a staff reporter for the *Wall
Street Journal*. "But a June inventory check showed not a can of
paint missing."[1]

One of the largest department stores in the San Francisco Bay
area has two-way mirrors in its restrooms and dressing areas. "Employees had a habit of secreting merchandise inside their clothes before going home at night," observed an executive of the store,
unidentified by request. "We pretty well broke that habit." Asked
how many actual arrests had been made because of this measure,
the executive said he had no exact figures on theft, but he could get
figures on the number of men who had been arrested for loitering or

engaging in homosexual practices. These cases, he admitted, outnumbered the theft cases. "Of course, in the shoplifting or pilfering
cases, we don't mention the mirrors in court." Why not? "Because
our attorneys advised us against it." Anticipating the next question
before it was asked, he volunteered, "We use only female detectives
in surveillance of the lady's rooms and changing areas. There is
really no question of invasion of privacy." Having made this clear,
he then related a humorous incident he had recently witnessed involving a woman and a girdle.

Every day, in retail businesses the length and breadth of the
United States, and even in the air above it, thousands of "customers"
in the employ of "shopping services" such as Willmark Service System, Inc., Commercial Service Systems Inc., the Dale System, and
Harvey Burnstein, are trying to catch employees in the act of committing a crime.

In a drugstore in Los Angeles, a nondescript woman approaches
the counter with a $5 item. "That will be $5.20 with tax," notes the
cashier. "No, don't bother wrapping it—I'm in a hurry," remarks the
woman, putting down the exact amount and hurrying out even before the clerk has a chance to ring up the sale and give her a receipt.
From nearby another "customer," equally nondescript, watches to
see if the clerk, given the opportunity for theft, takes it.

A young man buys a ticket at the cashier's window of a motion-
picture theater in Boston, gives it to the ticket taker, and enters the
theater—to leave shortly thereafter by another exit. He isn't interested in the movie, only in whether the cashier produced the ticket
from the machine or had it in her hand, whether the ticket taker
tore the ticket in half and handed back the stub or whether he kept
and palmed the whole ticket.

In a jet en route from Chicago to New York, a handsome young
executive traveling first-class, after preliminary pleasantries, asks the
stewardess to have dinner with him that evening at '21. On another
flight another "passenger" tries to persuade the stewardess to accept
a $5 tip for rendering such excellent service.

These are ordinary, day-by-day duties in the life of shopping-
service agents, who are hired by employers to spy on their employees. Detecting theft is only one concern of these operatives. Many
are hired to watch for violations of company policy or to evaluate
employees on conduct or efficiency. Usually it is a package deal.
Following each of these encounters the "shopper" will fill in a long
form, which not only covers all details of the transaction but may

ask whether the employee was courteous, indifferent, or rude; was neatly or sloppily dressed; stood up well or poorly under stress; had clean or dirty fingernails; had bad breath; was smoking on the job; wore an excessive amount of cosmetics; spent more time talking to other employees than helping customers; etc.*

Often this "observation," to use the polite phrase, is extremely specialized, as in the case of the Playboy Clubs, which use the services of Willmark. Willmark agents, posing as Playboy keyholders, are instructed to observe the Bunnies to see if their "tails are in good order"; that they wear name tags and don't wear jewelry, have runs in their hose, medium or short heels, underwear that shows, or crooked or mismatched bunny ears. They also watch to see if, when a show is in progress and a comic on, Bunnies laugh at his jokes. These and other revealing insights into Bunnydom were collected by Gloria Steinem, while serving as an undercover Bunny in the New York Playboy Club for *Show Magazine,* and were contained in a letter from Hugh Heffner to Willmark shown to all new Bunnies. Informing employees that they are being watched, and what they are being watched for, is strongly recommended by most of these shopping services. The Playboy Clubs have an admittedly special problem: maintaining the illusion of lascivious living without the reality of actual sin. "Use your most attractive and personable male representatives to proposition the Bunnies, and even to offer . . . as high as $200 on this, 'right now' for a promise of meeting you outside the club later," the Heffner letter instructs Willmark. Here, as in most other businesses, employees claim that they can often spot the spies. As one Bunny told Miss Steinem, they never have more than two drinks. Then, too, she realistically confided, "Nobody but a schmuck or a Willmark man would offer you the money *before.*"[2]

The suspicion business is big business, though just how big most of these shopping services are reluctant to say. Not too long ago two books were published which chronicled the increasing use by business and government of closed-circuit TVs, special mirrors, hidden recorders, lie-detector tests, company spies, and other privacy-reducing devices and techniques. Both books—*The Naked Society* by Vance Packard and *The Privacy Invaders* by Myron Brenton—

---

* Not long ago a "shopper" in a San Francisco bookstore accidentally dropped her form. When she returned and began surreptitiously looking for it some time later, the cashier without comment handed it to her—after having thoughtfully filled it in, rating himself rather low for Appearance but giving himself the highest mark for Helpfulness.

were published early in 1964, raising an indignant cry from the spied-upon public and causing a Congressional investigation. Apparently not everyone had the same reaction, however. Blonder Tongue Laboratories, Inc., Newark, New Jersey, a producer of closed-circuit TV used in spotting plant thievery, reported sales from January through June 1964 up 250 percent from a like period the previous year.

Extreme measures admittedly,* but, as in the case of shoplifting, those who adopt them see the threat as even greater, the difference between profits and losses, even business and bankruptcy. "To many of us it isn't a question of 'privacy invading' but 'self-defense,'" remarks one retail-store owner who has fired eight cashiers in two years for thefts. According to fairly reliable estimates, this year, as in years past, some 200 businesses will go into receivership consumed by the multitudinous small and large bites of employee theft.

"Carelessness about pilferage losses and lack of inventory controls can break a company," observes Max L. Schulman, president of J. W. Mays, Inc., an East Coast department-store chain. In 1963, Mays' losses to employee theft were about 1 percent of sales, or $750,000 a year. The company then adopted some simple nonextreme preventive measures in its five stores: guards at the exits were boosted from twenty-three to thirty; cleaning of the stores was shifted from overnight to early morning and early evening; spot inventory checks were increased; and all trash leaving the premises was examined. Result: eleven employees have been fired for stealing, and pilferage losses have fallen "way below" $50,000 a year.

Nationwide losses to the trusted employee, alias the internal thief, are even more difficult to determine than losses to the booster and snitch, for such cases are only occasionally reflected in conventional criminal statistics. These statistics don't take into account the cases of those who were caught but not prosecuted because they agreed to make partial restitution. They don't reflect the cases of those who were fired but went unprosecuted because of the fear that court appearances and attendant publicity might reflect on the corporate image. Or those borderline cases which just might, with a sympathetic jury, go against the store, with the resultant possibility of a civil-damages suit. Professor Jerome Hall of Indiana University esti-

---

* Extreme enough in some cases that the courts have interpreted them not as "detection" but "entrapment." One shopping service recently advised member subscribers: "Put an extra $10 bill in your cash register. See if your cashier reports it at the end of the day."

mates that 98 percent of all detected embezzlement cases are handled without public prosecution. This reluctance to prosecute hides true losses. It also disguises the criminal's identity: the fact that the "respectable middle class" is responsible for more extensive crime commission than is generally acknowledged. And it helps create an air of permissibility: when confronted with evidence that she had stolen more than $27,000 from her employer's accounts-receivable department, one woman asked, "Is this going to cost me my job?"

How high? The Insurance Information Institute states that theft by bonded employees alone (less than 15 percent of all businesses bond their employees, and usually only those who handle cash),* totaled $73 million in 1963, a rather large jump from the 1960 total of $45 million. Investigations, Inc., the fact-finding division of Norman Jaspan Associates, a leading management-consultant firm, after a detailed study, sets the loss in cash and goods alone at $4 million a day, $1 billion per year. Many consider this conservative.

It depends, again, on how you break up those inventory-shrinkage figures. "Employee theft, it is generally agreed, is a large component, probably greater, perhaps much greater than shoplifting itself," remarks Mary Cameron in *The Booster and the Snitch*.[3] Norman Jaspan believes inventory shrinkages break down to about 70 percent employee malpractices, 25 percent honest clerical errors, and the remaining 5 percent shoplifting and related practices. As for that 70 percent, this is how Jaspan puts it in dollars:

Type of Store	Total $ value of sales	Loss resulting from employee dishonesty
Department stores	16 billion	140 million
Supermarkets	50 billion	100 million
Hardware stores	9 billion	90 million
Discount houses	4½ billion	25 million
Variety stores	4 billion	60 million
Drug retailers	6 billion	50 million
Others	135 billion	140 million

If, by some still unfathomable magic, employee theft were to totally disappear, Jaspan believes our general price level could be reduced by as much as 15 percent. Just employing elementary safeguards would, he asserts, reduce this amount significantly.

* *New Yorker* writer St. Clair McKelway once likened bonding to a gambling game, with the bonding company betting that the employee wouldn't steal and the employer betting that he would.

Who is this thieving employee who has declared himself a silent partner in his employer's business?

"Of the more than 400 million dollars in losses uncovered by my firm in just the past ten years," Jaspan says, "about sixty percent can be traced to employees on the supervisory or executive level." Theft by store managers, claims Jaspan, is "far more substantial than malpractices by rank and file workers and makes what customers steal seem penny-ante by comparison."[4]

According to John Delaittre, a member of the Federal Home Loan Bank Board, which supervises the savings-and-loan industry, between 1958 and 1962 embezzlement in associations insured by the Federal Savings and Loan Insurance Corporation involved more than $4 million. Of the 435 defalcations in that period, nearly 70 percent involved lower-echelon employees; these cases accounted for only 20 percent of the losses, however. The chief officers embezzled 56 percent of the money.[5]

In their book *The Thief in the White Collar* Jaspan and Hillel Black describe the "typical white-collar thief" as being above average in intelligence and usually the hardest worker in the establishment. "Once involved in fraud, he seldom suggests new methods of business operation for fear that a radical change in procedure would result in his exposure. Except in rare instances, his home life is exemplary . . . Often he is the first employee in the office and the last to leave. He may even eat his lunch at his desk. In short, his fate is a constant damnation, for he is inexorably tied to the scene of his crime."[6]

Heading the National Association of Bank Auditors and Comptrollers' list of rules for thwarting and detecting bank embezzlement is the dictum, "Insist that each officer and employee take a full and uninterrupted vacation away from the bank."

It is sadly ironic that the honest employee who conscientiously cares about his job, who may even give of his own time to make sure that he has done the best job possible, is liable to be the first employee suspected when a shortage occurs.

Why does the trusted employee steal? Sociologists and criminologists offer a host of reasons, always carefully noting that they are at best generalizations and that no crime can ever be reduced to a single motive. The classic case of the Pennsylvanian who for more than twenty years served as superintendent of schools and taught Bible lessons at the Presbyterian Church—while at the same time embezzling at least $125,000 from school funds to keep a pretty redhead in minks, diamonds, automobiles, and a luxurious apartment —is classic because it is the exception rather than the rule. The once popular theory that a man stole because he gambled, drank, and/or liked to live high with low women may still be true in some cases, but today few would advance it as a general rule. Extravagant living standards still rank high among the more modern causations, but it is usually of a more mundane sort: as Vance Packard puts it in *The Status Seekers*, people may steal to attain and maintain status. Abnormal family expenses and inadequate income are other frequently cited causes. One bonding-company pamphlet states frankly: "Good environment is conducive to the honest performance of duty. Employees who are underpaid, overworked or abused, often steal from their employers without compunction. *They feel they have it coming.*"[7] The blame shifts: some cite "misplaced confidence" as a significant cause, others believe it is "a lack of real trust on the part of the employer, sensed by the employee." Some believe the equation to be "weak moral fiber plus opportunity." For those who prefer their sin original, a leading shopping service headed a recent subscriber bulletin: "*Anyone*—repeat, *anyone*—will steal if two basic factors are present: 1. Opportunity & 2. A better than average chance that they [sic] won't get caught."

Dr. Donald R. Cressey believes it is often due to a "nonshareable problem." "Trusted persons become trust violators when they conceive of themselves as having a financial problem which is nonshareable, are aware that this problem can be secretly resolved by violation of the position of financial trust, and are able to apply to their own conduct in that situation verbalizations which enable them to adjust their conceptions of themselves as trusted persons with their conceptions of themselves as users of the entrusted funds or property."[8]

Dr. Cressey observes that often the verbalization or rationalization is motivation enough in itself. Among the more common examples:

(1) "I was only borrowing it." The much-loved Virginia lady who in her quarter-century as assistant treasurer of a local building-and-loan association used her grandmotherly script for one of the all-time highs in currency embezzlement was said, upon apprehension, to have used this excuse. She embezzled $3 million.

(2) "The firm owes it to me." A stock clerk in a piece-goods establishment in Passaic, New Jersey, was refused a $5 raise. The next week and each week thereafter he took home $5 worth of cloth.

At the end of six months he again boosted his salary, and took home
$10 worth. He kept this up for several years. He was caught when
his employer began wondering why he had never again asked for a
raise. A bank employee who felt he was receiving $1500 less per
annum than he thought he was worth, carefully took exactly that
amount. Later, when given a raise bringing his salary over the
amount he thought he deserved, he paid back the excess. Though
undetected while stealing the money, he was caught while returning it.

(3) "Some of the most respected businesses in America got their
starts by doing things a lot shadier."

(4) "I don't like my boss." One California paint-shop foreman
admitted that every day for seventeen years he had stolen something, a light bulb, a roll of toilet tissue, something. It was his form
of protest.

(5) "Everybody's doing it." In the files of Investigations, Inc., is
the case of a stock-control clerk who, rendered sleepless by his
troubled conscience, finally went to the office of his superior, the
credit manager, and blurted out a confession of his petty thefts.
The manager carefully closed the door and said quietly, "I'm not
going to turn you in. Forget this conversation. And don't discuss it
with anyone else. You see, this department just can't afford a scandal
—I've been embezzling for years, myself. We're in this thing together."

Is everybody doing it? Of course not, but each year apparently
more people are, for an ever increasing amount—enough to give the
employer the feeling that he can't afford to pay the high cost of
trust, enough to give the individual the feeling that he alone is paying a tax because of his honesty. And enough to create a strong
climate of mutual distrust.

Though it is obviously impossible to list all the "tricks of the trade,"
a representative sampling of some of the arts and artifices should
assure those who fear the decline of American values that good old
Yankee ingenuity, know-how, and imagination have not altogether
faded from the American scene:

The *carryout* is probably the most common form of employee
theft—merchandise, office supplies, tools, precision parts, small articles that are pocketed or pursed and leave with the employee at
day's end. Many firms, however, deal in larger commodities. In 1951
the FBI broke up a Ford Motor Company employee theft ring estimated to have stolen between $5 and $10 million worth of auto

parts. The smaller parts they carried out in their lunch boxes, the larger ones under the hoods of their own automobiles. This was the third large-scale employee-theft operation uncovered at Ford. Another ring of thieving employees stole some 500,000 pounds of lead from the ACF Industries, Inc., plant in Buffalo, New York. They did this by melting the lead down, casting it into shapes that would fit around their bodies, then wearing it out under their clothes.

A Western mining company discovered that it was losing large quantities of gold from its refining plant, but not by the carryout method. Workers were stripped for examination at the end of each shift. Investigators finally discovered that the gold was put into containers which were then flushed out of the plant through its sewage system and picked up downstream.

The *mailout* is not uncommon. In Kansas City, Missouri, an employee in the shipping department of the Western Auto Supply Company mailed packages of merchandise to his roommate via parcel post. When apprehended, the loot, worth some $20,000, included enough TV sets, radios, tape recorders, typewriters, tires, tools, and electrical appliances to fill a 3-ton truck.

All day long the pneumatic tube in the large midwestern department store went "Whoosh" as it carried the containers of cash and receipts from the sales clerks up to the cashiers and back. One of the store's maintenance men found the sound particularly irritating as the tube went through the top of his supply room. Maybe, in the beginning, he merely meant to reroute the pipe. Soon, however, he was enjoying the sound, which had become something like the grain of sand in an oyster. With only a few minor adjustments, he added a stovepipe branch to the pipe. During his lunch hour he would divert every other tube, extracting the cash and sales slip, stamping the slip with a date stamp from office supplies, returning the slip with change when necessary, and, of course, pocketing the amounts of the sales. Over the years he stole an estimated $181,000, and would have stolen more had he not been reckless enough to go on vacation. A relief worker discovered the extra pipe and change trays. Since he wasn't caught in the act and refused to confess, the store's surety company, knowing the case would be difficult to prosecute, made a deal. The man paid back $71,000 out of his "savings" and was allowed to keep his $65,000 home, his new automobile, and new power cruiser. He now lives in Florida, in retirement.

Stealing is usually easy; it is concealing the theft that is difficult. One eastern department-store employee managed quite well, even though his loot included twenty-eight refrigerators, fourteen gas ranges, and numerous other bulky items, and the store had periodic inventories of the warehouse where he worked. He did it by nailing the empty storage crates to the warehouse floor.

Sometimes a means for detecting fraud is used to effect it. A manufacturer of wooden doors and frames who found he was losing his merchandise had a meter installed to count automatically the number of units produced. At the cost of exactly one penny, employees bought a pencil which, when correctly inserted in the meter, enabled them to change the production figures. Unimaginative crooks would have lowered the figures and resold the extra doors and frames. These employees, however, eliminating all that bother, raised the totals, and collected $175,000 in fraudulent incentive earnings.

As these employees discovered, you can rob the boss without actually stealing goods or currency. In February 1964, a Pine Bluff, Arkansas, man pleaded guilty to mail fraud. As agent for an insurance company, he obtained old policies from policyholders by telling them that the company was going to issue new, wider-coverage policies at no additional cost. He then forged the holders' signatures, sent the policies to the company, and received the cash-surrender value, amounting to $12,572. In November 1962, a Pittsburgh, Pennsylvania, purchasing agent pleaded guilty to defrauding his employer of $25,000 by causing fraudulent invoices to be mailed to the firm and receiving checks in payment, which were mailed to post-office boxes he had rented. In July 1964, a Haddonfield, New Jersey, man pleaded guilty to mailing fictitious orders to his firm in the names of numerous legitimate firms, for which he received substantial commissions. He was a salesman for antitheft devices.

In *The Privacy Invaders*, Myron Brenton describes still another way to steal without stealing. "There has been a marked increase, in recent years, in con artists who apply for high-salaried, top-level positions. Such men are smooth talkers and know their way around, but are totally unqualified for the job. Their talent lies in bluffing. They know that sooner or later their masquerade will be exposed, and that is precisely their game. They play for time. Even if the company catches up with him after a year or so, the con man will still be as much as $30,000 or $40,000 plus expenses ahead."[9]

There is an even simpler way to play, but it took a decidedly unconventional man to think of it.

If a survey were taken asking, "What do you consider the most disagreeable of all tasks?" a majority of those questioned would probably reply "Job hunting." Joseph Sherman made job hunting his occupation. For over two years, Sherman applied for countless jobs that he neither wanted nor was qualified to hold. While on the East Coast he applied for jobs in the West; while in the West, in the East. Object: travel expenses.

The fifty-six-year-old former resident of Turtle Creek, Pennsylvania, wrote such remarkable job resumes that prospective employers, usually engineering and electronic firms, often wired him the money to come immediately. After all, most companies could use a senior design engineer and departmental manager (as he called himself in one application) with a *cum laude* degree in electrical engineering, prior employment at Applied Science of Princeton, Westinghouse, Douglas Aircraft Aviation, and the Martin Company, especially considering he was "personally responsible for the origination and development of new circuitry and ideas for sophisticated applications into complex military systems and apparatus such as: radar, telemetry, microwaves, guidance and control, etc."

Sometimes Sherman would simply trade the resume for the cost of a round-trip airline ticket across-country; often, however, he appeared for the interviews, received the jobs, and obtained advances on salary plus moving expenses for his family.

He had a flaw in his character, however, one traditionally associated with genius: he was absent-minded. Once, after applying to the Avco Corporation under two different names, he appeared for an interview and forgot under which name he had been summoned. And he was eventually caught by the POD in 1963 (and sentenced to twenty months in prison) after RCA discovered they had given him expenses for three separate job interviews.

Altering records so they not only make possible theft but also disguise it is exceedingly common. When inventory shrinkage in a large retail store jumped from $2000 to $40,000 in one year, private detectives were hired. Suspicion focused on the store's manager, who was living far above his income even by credit-society standards. But watching him every minute of the day, they could find no evidence of wrongdoing. The none-too-subtle surveillance got on the man's nerves, however, to the point where he broke down and confessed his technique. Each night, after the store had closed and he remained there alone, supposedly counting the day's receipts, he would take the tape which recorded the sales out of one of the cash registers, put in a fresh tape, and re-ring all of the day's sales, except some $150 worth. Pocketing the difference, he then destroyed the original tape.

86ing is simpler. In many retail stores, when a clerk makes a mistake or misring on the cash register, he is instructed to re-ring the sale correctly, mark "86" on the incorrect sales receipt, and put it in the cash drawer. When receipts are later counted, the amounts on these 86'd slips are subtracted from sales totals. To effect fraud, the clerk need only pick up a sales receipt left by a customer, 86 it, and pocket the amount. If he is consistent in his thefts, and keeps the amount low, he may eventually be fired for inefficiency but probably not for theft.

Most employee theft is solitary. When several employees work in collusion, losses can skyrocket. The elevator operator of an East Coast electrical-appliance-company plant stole some $50,000 worth of merchandise in four years. Well acquainted with local bars, he supplied several with company catalogues. The bartenders would then take orders from their customers for any item in the catalogue, at one-third off. On receiving an order, the elevator operator would pass it on to his accomplice in the particular department; loaded onto the elevator, the item would be taken to the basement, to be reloaded onto a company truck and delivered. Service was excellent.

It was less so in the rug department of one large California store. Customers often cancelled their orders because delivery was so slow. This was puzzling because the carpet installers put in so much overtime. Eventually the owner discovered that he had a competitor in his own place of business. Once an order for carpeting was received and exact measurements taken, the manager of the rug department would delay installation until the customer in exasperation called and cancelled his order. The manager would then promptly call him back, posing as another company, offering immediate installation of the same carpeting but at a lower price. He could do this because his overhead was negligible: the materials and labor belonged to the store. By the time the manager and his sixteen installer-accomplices were arrested and convicted, the store was out $250,000 in merchandise, $200,000 in overtime pay, and an undetermined amount in profits.

In April 1964, Arthur Keller, general manager of Mainbocher's Fifth Avenue dress shop, was arrested for trading on the feminine mystique. The price tags on Mainbocher dresses start at $750 and go up. To conceal this fact from their husbands, women would often pay part of the cost of a dress in cash, then have the store bill their spouses for the less shocking balance. Keller used this common deception and the involved bookkeeping it entailed to camouflage a little deception of his own, at least $166,000 worth. Observed Assistant District Attorney Leonard Newman after Keller entered a plea of guilty, "This is a case where the exact details of the defendant's manipulations may never be known," a remark which probably caused more than a few women to breathe easier.

When Dolly Gee was arrested on Christmas Eve of 1963 in San Francisco's Chinatown, the shock was felt in every Chinese settlement in America. The sixty-four-year-old Miss Gee was something of a legend, in international banking circles as well as among Chinese-Americans. As manager of the French-American Bank, her father, Charles F. Gee, had been Chinatown's leading banker during the 1920s. Dolly had gone to work for him at sixteen, becoming manager of the bank on his retirement in 1929, and continuing in this position when the bank was merged with the Bank of America. Considered one of the most valued employees of the world's largest bank, she was credited with having built the Chinatown branch into the sixtieth largest among the Bank of America's some 800 branches. Once when the bank's founder and president, A. P. Giannini, made a thoughtless statement, coming out in favor of Chinese exclusion laws, Dolly had healed the breach and avoided a run on the bank by its Chinese-American depositors. Less than a year from her retirement, after nearly fifty years in banking, Miss Gee confessed to bank officials that she had been juggling the bank's books for more than a quarter of a century. The confession touched off one of the most complex individual bank investigations in the United States, according to federal banking officials, for Dolly Gee *was* the Chinatown branch. Many of the bank's records, dating from the 1920s, didn't exist outside her head.

The story as it unfolded was remarkable enough that one San Francisco newspaper dubbed her "Robin Hood of Chinatown." It began in 1919. That year her father arranged for the French-American Bank to be a correspondent for the China Specie Bank Ltd. of Hong Kong. On Gee's suggestion, Chinatown depositors invested heavily in the bank. In 1923 the China Specie Bank folded, and the deposits of the Chinatown families—some $100,000—went with it. Charles Gee couldn't bear to let them suffer the loss. Instead, he didn't tell them and, by borrowing money from dormant foreign accounts in his own bank, eventually paid off the depositors. When Dolly went to work for the bank she discovered her father's secret;

CAVEAT VENDOR

when he retired she inherited it. Over the years the dormant accounts accrued interest that amounted to hundreds of thousands of dollars. The exact amount is still in doubt; at the time of Dolly's trial in 1964, it was estimated at $340,000. Pleading guilty to embezzlement, she was sentenced to two five-year terms, to run concurrently, one of the conditions of her sentence that she would explain to bank officials just how and what she had done. She was paroled after sixteen months.

Considerably more self-seeking were the motives of the assistant cashier of a Pennsylvania bank who embezzled $600,000 so he could buy a controlling interest in the bank and elect himself president. His plan miscarried, wrecking the bank and buying him a ten-year sentence instead.

Lawyers sometimes tell the tale of one of their more unscrupulous fellows who, before the advent of the Federal Deposit Insurance Corporation, helped embezzle a large midwestern bank. A young cashier from the bank appeared in the lawyer's office one day seeking legal advice: he had embezzled $100,000 from the bank, he admitted, and the bank examiners were due momentarily. He knew it was probably useless to ask, but was there anything he could do? The lawyer gave the matter some thought and came up with explicit, if surprising, advice. Go back to the bank, the lawyer advised, and steal another $125,000, then bring it to me. Perplexed but feeling he had nothing to lose, the cashier did as he was told. On receiving the money, the lawyer called the president of the bank and asked for an appointment. Once in his office, he came right to the point. His client, the young cashier, had embezzled $225,000; if word of the theft became known it would almost certainly cause a run on the bank. He was prepared to offer a compromise. If the bank would agree not to prosecute, the cashier would pay back $100,000 and no word of this would ever reach the public. After consulting with his directors, the banker reluctantly agreed. The bank got some of its money back, the young man went free, and the lawyer pocketed the remaining $25,000 as his fee.

The story may be fictional (though it probably isn't), but its lessons are apt and true. If a thief has the foresight to steal big and set aside a good portion of his loot as "detection insurance," he stands a better-than-average chance of receiving a light punishment or no punishment whatsoever. When given the choice between retribution and returned funds, many firms and their bonding companies unhesitatingly prefer the latter. Too, the more the thief steals the less severe is apt to be his penalty, if for no other reason than that he can afford the services of a good attorney. As Cato the Censor put it more than a few centuries ago, "Small thieves be in towers fastened to wooden blocks; big ones strut about in gold and silver."

Who pays for employee theft? Needless to say . . .

It is probably true, as Norman Jaspan and others assert, that the employer must shoulder much of the blame for the situation as it now exists, that "management's lack of awareness of what actually takes place in its own bailiwick serves as prime cause of much white collar crime."[10] It is probably true too that those businesses which have found it necessary to revert to such extreme measures as restroom-peeping largely created the situation they so fear, through the lack of adequate "preventive management." It may be that with tightened inventory controls, unscheduled audits and inventory checks, better management-employee relations, and similar cares and cautions, employee theft can be reduced drastically. It may even be (though one reserves the right to be skeptical) that one day man will create a fraud-free society. In the meantime, it is difficult to disagree with Mary Cameron when she asserts, "When an abundance of highly attractive consumer goods is displayed on the open shelves of relatively unguarded stores, and when low-paid employees daily handle millions of dollars in money belonging to impersonal corporations, it is inevitable that a certain percentage of people will try to obtain merchandise or money by the simple and direct method of appropriation. Together, the impersonality of the corporation and the needs of the middle class, family oriented man or woman combine in an atmosphere conducive to rationalized theft; snitches, embezzlers, and till-tappers alike come out of the acquisitive corporate society; and so, too, though through somewhat different processes, do boosters, other professionals, and the criminal subculture which nourishes them."[11]

The coin *is* two-headed. Advertising deceptions and business frauds against the consumer are basically violations of trust; so is employee theft. The employee who sees his company picking the public pocket, whether through lying ads, shortweight packaging, or income-tax chicanery, can't be blamed for not taking too seriously company rules regarding honesty. He can be blamed, however, for becoming too much of an organization man, one who even apes his company's morality.

Apparently, even the United States Government believes that

employee theft is not only inevitable but that we should make the best of it. The U.S. Department of Internal Revenue, in the latest edition of its official booklet, *Your Income Tax*, reminds us: "Embezzled funds are income to the embezzler in the year the funds are misappropriated."

IV

THE SPECIALISTS

CONTROL OF 8 BANKS
IN COLORADO COST
CON MEN $65,000

Deadline, Denver *Post*
April 29, 1965

CHAPTER 11

PAPERHANGING MADE EASY

> It's foolish to use a gun to get
> money when hanging paper is so
> easy. I'm afraid of guns and knives,
> and I guess that's why I turned to
> paperhanging.
>
> —Professional bad-check passer
> awaiting sentencing in Pueblo,
> Colorado.

Bank Bilking

IT WAS so tempting. And temptation breeds ingenuity. There were those stacks of bills only an iron grating away. Legend says that it was an English lord who first rolled a coin across the teller's counter onto the floor, then, when the teller stooped to retrieve it, stuck his gum onto the end of his walking stick, pushed the stick through the grating, and extracted with it a bill.

With a hooked wire you could remove a whole package of bank notes.

With a good location on the balcony above the teller's cages, an acute sense of timing, and a fishing pole, there was no limit to the catch.

Banks are said to have first kept their cash in view to prove that they were solvent; today they keep it out of sight—and reach—to stay that way.

But frustration, too, breeds ingenuity.

In the 1940s most American banks adopted a "foolproof" system for reducing forgery losses. Unless the person cashing the check had an account with the bank, it was necessary for a bank official to approve and initial the check. Foolproof the system may have been, but geniusproof it was not. William Hamilton Harkins, whom the William J. Burns International Detective Agency, official forgery and check-fraud investigators for the American Bankers Association, has called "the greatest lone-wolf bank bilker the world ever produced,"* promptly devised a way to beat the system. When he worked it on the Hotel New Yorker branch of the Manufacturers Trust Company, he used three checks—the first a legitimate cashier's check for $12.75, purchased in the bank sometime earlier; the second and third, identical forged cashier's checks made out on a Boston bank, for $1401 each.

Entering the bank, Harkins approached the bank officer directly, handing him the $12.75 check and explaining that he had bought it the previous day but found he didn't need it and could he get his money back? The officer initialed the check automatically. Returning to his hotel room, Harkins copied the initials onto one of the $1401 checks. He was now ready.

The following day he returned to the bank and presented the uninitialed $1401 check at one of the cashier's cages for payment. The cashier politely told him that it would have to be approved by one of the bank officers. While walking across the floor to the officer's desk, Harkins switched checks. "You O.K.'d this for me yesterday," he explained, handing the man the $12.75 check, "but I was in a hurry and didn't have time to cash it. I assume it's still good?" The official assured him that it was. On his way back to the cashier's cage, Harkins again switched checks, only this time he presented the initialed $1401 check, which the cashier promptly cashed.

Bank officials revised and improved their system, using different-

---

* Horace Crowe, manager of Burns' criminal division and the man responsible for sixteen of seventeen of Harkins' arrests, once described him as "the perfect bank swindler." His forgeries were so expert that many have never been connected to him, leaving his total take in doubt. "Some claim a million dollars," Harkins once remarked, "but the more conservative say five million." Questioned under lie detectors and truth serum, he beat both. Imprisoned in various institutions and asylums (by pretending insanity he received lighter sentences), he conned his way out of some, used one as his case of operations and alibi while passing checks nearby, and escaped from six others, including San Quentin. For a more detailed account of his career see "The Great Bank Bilker" by Charles Lanius, in Alexander Klein's anthology *The Double Dealers*, J. B. Lippincott, Philadelphia, 1958.

colored inks for different banking days. Harkins noticed and profited. Then they started using different positions on the check for the
initials, like hours on the dial of a watch, so a check initialed in the
morning would have to be approved a second time if presented in
the afternoon. When Harkins next presented his small check for
initialing, the bank officer looked at his watch and Harkins guessed
why. A half-dozen small checks, initialed at different times in different banks, and he had the new system down pat. When the banks
switched to another system, whereby the placement of the initials
indicated the amount, Harkins was ready. He had thought of this
a long time before and was only surprised the banks had taken so
long to come up with it. Today, in many banks, when you attempt
to cash a check and haven't an account, a bank guard accompanies
you, carrying your check, from the teller to the officer and back, a
tribute to the skill of William Hamilton Harkins.

While modern banking practices have made obsolete many of the
old tricks, some reappear occasionally in new guise. In 1849, Ah
Toy, California's first Chinese prostitute, appeared in Recorder's
Court in San Francisco, asking that the judge issue warrants for the
arrest of a number of prominent San Francisco males who had paid
her in brass filings rather than gold. One day in March of 1964, four
men entered separate banks in Fresno, California, a few minutes
before closing time and cashed $180 worth of 50-cent coin rolls.
Examined later, each roll was found to consist of one 50-cent piece
at each end and thirty-eight brass washers in between.

Over the years, bank bilking has undergone some significant modifications. Simple theft remains, as does simple embezzlement, and
periodically some nearly forgotten swindle is dusted off for a brief
comeback, but the more spectacularly lucrative frauds often involve
complex and extremely sophisticated falsification of records, with
the result that the records not only make possible the fraud but
also effectively disguise it. Preventive measures have become equally
involved. To circumvent a particular fraud, safeguard A is introduced; safeguard B is then set up to prevent tampering with A, and
C to protect B, and so on.

Such systems, however, have a built-in weakness: they are run
by people. In researching his thesis on embezzlement, Dr. Donald
R. Cressey interviewed several hundred convicted embezzlers. A
number told how in learning to detect fraud they, of necessity,
learned how to commit it. "In school they teach you in your ad-

vanced years how to detect embezzlements, and you sort of absorb it," observed one former accountant. "In my case I did not use any techniques which any ordinary accountant in my position could not have used; they are known by all accountants, just like the abortion technique is known by all doctors." Another embezzler put it even more simply: "The whole thing was second nature. I knew the procedure backward . . ."[1] He merely reversed the procedure.

These men were caught and convicted, however, not because they failed to learn their lessons well but because they learned them too well, and never considered that there might be other ways of doing it. The most successful swindlers often have in common the ability to see things freshly. Rather than observing a chain in which to cover up a fraud, safeguards A, B, C, etc. must be altered accordingly, they find a different way to commit the fraud. They see not what everyone else sees, but what they have overlooked. Often it is the obvious.

Some years ago Burgess Smith, often described as "Sherlock Holmes of the laboratory," invented a special "safety paper" for checks. When altered with bleach or ink eradicator, the paper would reveal a telltale VOID. Forgers tried all manner of chemical combinations to beat it but failed. There was a much simpler way, one group discovered: posing as bankers, they purchased reams of the special paper from bank-supply houses and made their own checks. Blank-check stock is now as closely guarded as printed currency.*

Until a few years ago, deposit-slip forms were available on the counters in all banks. With the advent of automation in the late fifties, many banks switched to a new system designed to speed up the recording of transactions and to eliminate human error. Each checking account was given its own IBM-type number; customers were issued both deposit slips and checks, on which the account number appeared. Knowing the force of habit, one enterprising young swindler opened an account with a small deposit and in due course received his checkbook. Tearing out the deposit slips, he scattered them on the bank counter. In less than one hour all the slips had been used and a sizable amount automatically credited to the swindler's account, which he promptly withdrew.

* A similar fraud has grown up in the theft of airline-ticket stock, which is as negotiable as cash. In 1964 the International Air Transport Association, to which most world airlines belong, formed a special fraud-prevention unit to investigate this multimillion-dollar racket.

The Paperhangers

Once upon a time such ingenuity and imagination were characteristic of one particular branch of swindlery, paperhanging. The annals of rascality are rich with the successful coups of forgers such as William Hamilton Harkins. There was James Townshend Saward, alias Jim the Penman, who in a twenty-five-year period, from 1831 to 1856, nearly broke the Bank of England. Saward, according to Murray Teigh Bloom, was "the greatest forger of them all," the man to whom credit is due for first organizing forgery as a business, by using thieves and con men to obtain signatures and handwriting specimens of the rich and prominent, along with passers to hang the spurious paper he so deftly penned. Saward's depredations were so huge that London bankers formed a Committee for Protection from Forgeries and Frauds. That it took a quarter of a century to catch the elusive penman and deport him to Australia was due in no small part to the fact that Saward, a barrister, was serving on the Committee.

There was Alex Thiel, who learned the art by copying signatures from the Declaration of Independence and who, in his debut in 1930, forged $162,000 worth of negotiable checks on a New York multimillionaire, checks so perfect they fooled not only the bank but also their victim. Thiel possessed the ability to look at a signature once, then reproduce it from memory as long as forty-eight hours later.

There was Charley Becker, "the prince of forgers." When the system of protecting cashier's checks by perforating the figures was first tried, Becker bought a bank draft for $12, chewed the paper soft, restuffed the holes, and punched out new ones, making a quite passable check for $22,000.

There was Jacob Sackstein, a specialist in upping the amount on checks, who was so expert that in his later years, with both arms so crippled with arthritis he could barely move them, he still succeeded in writing passable paper; and Frederick Emerson Peters, who specialized in using illustrious family names such as Franklin Delano Roosevelt III, who bounced his first check in 1902 and his last the day he died in 1959, and in the intervening years took the preacher who married him with a higher-than-amount check.

Measured against these colorful con men of the past, the modern paperhanger is drably disappointing. Once known as a bad check "artist," he is now almost always referred to as a bad-check "passer," for quantity has replaced quality, and repetition art. His scores aren't large, but small and numerous, rarely exceeding $50 unless he deals in government or payroll checks. As for the perfection of his trade, even with years of experience he usually remains a bumbling amateur, since the ease with which the crudely bogus is acceptable discourages the development of expertise. Often he doesn't even master the rudiments. In its check-cashing rules, one large New York City bank instructs its tellers: "When seeking an endorsement, place the check face down and secure it with your thumb. Often the bad-check passer cannot remember the name he is using and will have to look at the face of the check or his ID before signing."

But one thing can be said for the modern check passer, though less to his credit than to the discredit of the merchants who accept his checks. He is successful. The loss to check fraud is estimated, conservatively, at $800 million a year, or roughly $2 million a day or $1500 a minute.

Mostly because it is so simple. Few other trades are as easily mastered. Becoming a bad-check passer requires no skill, little practice, a minimum of preparation and expense, and only a small amount of daring. As for obtaining the tools of the trade, it is possible to open a checking account in most banks, receiving ten or more blank checks immediately, with (1) a single piece of easily obtained identification, (2) a single dollar bill, and (3) the promise that a large deposit is forthcoming. Passing the check is no more difficult. The amateur swindler need only frequent a half-dozen stores in a given neighborhood over a period of a week or two, buying some small item each time, paying with cash, then buy a larger, resalable item, paying for it with a check made out for more than the amount of purchase. "That check must be good!" asserted a young female clerk, on being told that a check she had accepted was bogus. "That man is one of our regular customers!" The passer had been in the Chicago drugstore twice, buying a package of razor blades one time, a tube of shaving cream the other.

High marks in Palmer Penmanship may be helpful, but they aren't essential. Nor even is literacy. An aged resident of Roanoke, Virginia, who could neither read nor write, was arrested eighteen times in ten years for passing bad checks. He would ask the store clerk to fill out the check for him, then scribble an illegible signature at the bottom. In an attempt to limit his activity, local police slipped in among his identification cards one which read: "I am a bad-check man. If I attempt to cash a check in your store, call the police department immediately." He used the card several times as ID, with ill luck, before being wised up by a fellow cellmate. Nor is the ability to copy a signature accurately absolutely essential. One thirty-eight-year-old man was apprehended in 1955 after having cashed 150,000 worthless checks over a period of seven years. His technique was to go into a new town, learn the names of its more prominent citizens, and write checks made out to himself, each for less than $100. He made no attempt to obtain copies of actual signatures, figuring, apparently correctly, that most merchants would be as unfamiliar with them as was he.

It is not the check passer alone who has changed. While once banks and individuals were the primary victims of the check swindler, today the retail merchant is the most vulnerable American —assuming 90 percent of all losses. Many merchants don't take too kindly to this development, some even going so far as to charge the banks with contributory negligence amounting almost to complicity.

The Bouncers

Check bouncing is minor-league fraud. ("Bouncing a check occasionally is a good way to see if your patronage is really appreciated," explained a man in Los Angeles' small-claims court recently.) It's also a simple way to borrow money without paying interest. And it can be done with some safety.

The gypster who bounces a $25 check on his corner grocer will often promise to make it good, paying $5 now and promising the balance next week. The $5 takes him off the hook. In most states the law says that if part payment is accepted on a check no criminal action can be taken. The merchant's only recourse then is a civil suit, rarely worth the expense, or a collection agency, which if successful will take 20 to 50 percent. Knowing this, the merchant usually holds onto the check and hopes. This is all to the good of the gypster. In many states, if the loss is $99.99 or less, the passer can only be convicted on a misdemeanor; $100 or more, and it becomes a felony. However, on a second offense, an accumulation of several checks can be used to total $100. Unreported bad checks quite often make the difference between whether the passer is in jail or still busy paperhanging.

Roughly 80 percent of all returned checks come back marked *n.s.f.* (not sufficient funds), *account closed,* or *refer to maker.* Not all are totally bad. Many are collectable, eventually. These include checks with unreadable signatures or endorsements, incorrect dates, discrepancies in the amount. Some are the result of honest error on the part of the maker. Some are the result of bank error. And some are fraud, as above. That other 20 percent represents an almost total loss. These are stolen, forged, and fictitious checks.

Robbery with a Pen

Much current forgery isn't of a whole check but only an endorsement. In 1964 an all-time record of $5 million in United States Government checks were stolen and cashed, up more than 50 percent since 1959, up 11 percent since 1962. Social Security, veterans' allowances, federal retirement and tax-refund checks, the technique was usually the same: the check was lifted from a mailbox or the mail drop in an apartment-house entryway, the endorsement forged, and the check cashed with bogus identification. The cost to the actual payee was largely in time and worry, as the Government makes good such losses. Retail merchants, who cashed some 90 percent of these checks, paying 100 pennies to the dollar for their trust, were less fortunate.

The whole-check forger usually obtains the basic tool of his trade, the blank check, by simple theft, but occasionally artifice is used. Some years ago a gang of paperhangers came up with an interesting variation. An advance man for the gang would arrive in a city, learn the name of the largest local industry and its payroll dates, and, buying one of its checks from a local fence or an obliging bartender, discover the name of its printer. A telephone call to the company would give him the name of the head payroll clerk. A second call, to the printer, would put the swindle into operation. Posing as a clerk, he would explain that the company needed 500 more checks immediately. How soon could they be ready? Since the printer already had plates and the firm was his top customer, he might promise delivery that afternoon. An accomplice disguised as a messenger would appear at the specified time to pick up the checks, and on payday 500 forgeries would be in circulation.

Overuse retired this dodge, but the vacuum was soon filled. When a business is burgled, one of the first things police ask is whether any pads of company checks are missing. If so, merchants are then alerted to watch for checks bearing the missing numbers. Not long ago one check gang came up with its own refinement, since much copied. They would break into the office of a company, rifle the desks, steal the stamps and petty cash, maybe even smash and loot the Coke machine. All evidence would indicate this to be the work of juveniles. Checking the check pads, the cashier or accountant would quickly determine that no checks had been stolen. Many had, however, though the companies wouldn't learn of it until much later. Instead of stealing whole pads of checks, the thieves would take some dozen checks out of the middle of the highest-numbered pads. Another gang, picking up and improving on this, obtained a rubber stamp and stamped IMPERFECT on the stubs of the checks they'd stolen.

Although they make bulky and strong circumstantial evidence, many professional check-passing gangs have their own protectographs. Others simply use those of the companies they rob.

While companies are often lax in providing security for their blank checks, most individuals are careful not to leave their checkbooks lying around. But they file away without further thought in any convenient place their cancelled checks and bank statements—far more useful to the housebreaking forger, since they provide perfect examples of the person's handwriting and signature, as well as a good estimate of how much money is kept in the account.

Mailbox thieves are also partial to bank statements, which banks usually mail out in easily recognizable envelopes. In the spring of 1964 a gang of swindlers, playing the same game but on an international scale, bilked six New York banks out of $221,000 in less than three weeks. Members of the gang planted in post offices in Buenos Aires, Argentina, and São Paulo, Brazil, would intercept bank statements sent from American banks to wealthy South American depositors. When a sufficiently large amount was discovered, the gang photocopied any useful information, including the depositors' signatures. This was then sent to accomplices in Paris, Brussels, and Zurich, who would open accounts in the names of the Latin Americans. Letters, with the forged signatures, would then go to the New York banks instructing them to transfer specific amounts of money to the European accounts. By use of the forged signatures, the money would be withdrawn shortly after the transfer occurred.

Although the counterfeiting of blank checks calls for some technical skill, usually the services of a printer, it is the most popular form of check fraud currently in use by the professional paperhangers. A legitimate check, such as a payroll check, is obtained and duplicated in large numbers, together with bogus driver's licenses and other phony identification. The checks are then passed more or less simultaneously in a concentrated area, usually on a weekend or bank holiday. One West Coast-based gang, utilizing its own airplane to fly its passers to chosen communities, at its peak passed more than $50,000 a day. Occasionally a photograph of a check is used. One paperhanger, posing as an oil man from Santa Fe, took a number of banks and businesses in California with photographs of a $180 certified check issued by a bank in Ogden, Utah. The photocopies were so expert that one was accepted by a bank vice-president. According to one merchant who was stuck, "They looked so good that in running your fingers over them you'd swear you could feel the embossing."

Law-enforcement and Treasury Department officials are reportedly viewing with some apprehension the current photocopier boom. When these machines first appeared—from Xerox, Kodak, 3M, and other companies—they caused little concern, because they reproduced only in black and white—and, as any good check passer knows, checks printed on white paper are the hardest kind to pass. The new Xerox model now reproduces an accurate color facsimile on any type paper stock, and both sides of a sheet of paper may be used. Treasury officials fear this may mean not only a boost in bad checks but a whole new era in currency counterfeiting.

The color of a check, incidentally, does affect its passability. In February 1962, members of the Northern California Check Investigators Association had as their featured luncheon speaker a professional forger then under indictment on check charges in Marin County. Speaking from thirty-seven years of experience, he told the group that the color of a check makes a big difference. "Gold and yellow checks are the easiest to move," he said. "Blue is questionable, and white is impossible." The size of the check makes a difference too. "Thirty-five-dollar checks are best. Twenty-five is a little too pat, and people tend to shy away from anything higher than thirty-five." Backing up his statement was his own record, which showed he had passed more than a thousand $35 checks on branches of one California bank. By way of a luncheon *hors d'oeuvre*, he walked into a San Rafael bank and conned a teller out of a book of blank checks.

Checks are sometimes drawn not only on nonexistent accounts but nonexistent banks. Two classic examples are on display in the FBI offices in Washington, D.C. One is drawn on "The East Bank of the Mississippi" in "Slippery Rock, Mississippi" and is signed "U. R. Stuck." The other, a $1775 check accepted by a used-car dealer in Wellington, Kansas, is signed "N. O. Good." A drugstore in a small town in southern Colorado once cashed a check for a man who signed himself "I. P. Standing." These three checks had more than humor in common: all were blank counter checks which the merchants had thoughtfully provided.

Is there any way a merchant can avoid bad-check losses? "Yes," says a New York City check-squad detective: "Don't accept checks."

Elementary precautions will minimize losses, however. Examining both the check and the identification carefully is primary: it would appear almost too commonsensical to need mentioning that the endorsement on the check should correspond with the payee's name, the handwriting on the check with the specimen signature on the identification; that any description of age, height, weight, nationality, and sex, or any photograph should fit the person passing the check; that a pre-endorsed check should be re-endorsed in the cashier's presence; that any endorsement which varies from the person listed as the payee is unacceptable; and that any attempt to hurry the cashing of a check is suspect—yet the absence of such common sense characterizes most bad-check passing.

One hesitates to suggest that merchants are often stupid in their cashing of checks. But it is difficult to otherwise explain the Secret Service's statement that many stolen Old Age and Survivors' Insurance checks are cashed by teenagers.

Just how serious the bad-check threat may be to a particular business is something only its owner can decide. Many firms have extremely lax check-cashing procedures, citing the fact that only 1 check in 2000 is bad, blissfully unaware that once the word that a store is "easy" circulates, the odds for that particular store change appreciably. As a setup, such an establishment is second only to the store whose owner approves the cashing of large checks because he has more currency than he wants to keep on hand over the weekend.

Rules vary. Knowing your endorser and refusing to accept out-of-town checks will cut losses, yet many businesses find either or both rules impractical. Though firms which refuse to accept checks for more than the amount of purchase sustain the lowest of all check losses, many businesses feel that the benefits of customer service outweigh the risk. Those firms which make a practice of cashing payroll checks choose to assume that risk and generally price their merchandise accordingly. It is a good practice in any business, of whatever size, to limit the number of people who can authorize the cashing of a check, and to train them accordingly—but few businesses do.

Whatever rules are adopted regarding identification, there is always the possibility that the ID may be in part or wholly fraudulent. One large midwestern department store cut its bad-check losses $100,000 a year by requiring two pieces of identification instead of one. This isn't a particularly safe rule: two pieces of fake ID can be obtained almost as easily as one. (See Chapter 12.) A little better is asking for more identification than the customer offers. A hunting or fishing license is worthless as ID, as is a Social Security card. Every male between eighteen and thirty-nine should have a Selective Service, or draft, card. How reliable it is as ID is something else. When apprehended by the FBI, forger Courtney Townsend Taylor had in his possession fifty-seven bogus draft cards plus nearly as many Social Security cards and driver's licenses—all made by himself. Ironically, bank credit cards are not considered good identification by many merchant groups "because they are issued too indiscriminately."

Growing losses have caused many to view the threat more seriously than in the past. Many metropolitan police departments and retail merchants groups now conduct periodic seminars on check cashing. In January 1963, California's Bank of America inaugurated a Merchant's Loss Prevention Clinic, which tours the state with exhibits and films to instruct merchant customers in suggested procedures for cashing checks and making change. By March 1965, the clinic had visited every major community in California, reaching some 30,000 merchants. Growing losses have also caused some stores to take more drastic steps. A number of supermarket chains have installed cameras at their check-out counters to photograph everyone who cashes a check. Just the presence of the camera, film or no film, probably reduces losses. Some markets use clear ink pads to take an invisible fingerprint on the back of the check, which shows up under ultraviolet light. Others use Scotch tape—taking the print on the sticky side and affixing the tape to the check. They do this even though law-enforcement officials state that a single fingerprint is almost valueless in apprehending a criminal.

Almost everyone concerned with the bad-check problem agrees that, if elementary caution were used in the cashing of checks, losses would be nowhere nearly so great. Yet the crime will remain major, many merchants say, as long as the banks make it so easy for the paperhanger to operate.

Co-conspirators?

Some put it more bluntly. In an only slightly fanciful Alice-in-Wonderland vein, an officer of the Retail Merchants Association of a large East Coast community remarked, "Some day some little merchant is going to get stuck with a bad check and, instead of just shrugging and saying 'This is one of the risks of the business' and adding it to a large stack of similar checks good only at income-tax time, he's going to get mad and swear out two warrants—one for the check passer and the other for the president of the bank on which the check was cashed, charging conspiracy to defraud. He'll have a damn good case. Then, and only then, will banks begin to realize that they have some responsibility to their customers."

Similar complaints can be heard in many parts of the country, usually, though not always, directed at the practices of the so-called "new banks" in metropolitan and suburban areas. The specifics are that the banks supply the swindler with the blank checks from which he makes his snowstorm of fraudulent paper, all too often with few or no questions asked, and that they do little to hinder or stop him once he's started. "Repeatedly, we've appealed to the banks to keep someone in the bank after hours to verify accounts and certify checks," complains the president of a Washington State retail dry-goods firm. "We've even offered to pay the salary involved. They've not only refused; many of the banks will no longer even verify whether the check is good over the telephone."

There is a reason for this new caution, and it apparently has little to do with recent cries of privacy invasion. Up until a few years ago, almost all banks would permit a merchant or credit agency to call and establish the approximate balance of a customer's account, using a code similar to the following:

L-2: Low 2 digit—under $35.
M-2: Medium 2 digit—$35 to $65.
H-2: High 2 digit—$65 to $99.
L-3, M-3, H-3, etc.

Some banks still permit this, but many now refuse—to avoid liability. A swindler, for example, can buy a $500 piece of jewelry at noon, the bank verifying by phone that there is an adequate amount in his account to cover the check, then go to the bank at 12:15 and close his account before the check has cleared. "Every time the banks put a new rule in force," the dry-goods merchant commented, "it decreases their liability and increases ours."

Edward M. Toothman, Chief of Police of Oakland, California, and former chairman of the International Association of Chiefs of Police, commented on the problem in an October 1963 bulletin to merchants in the Oakland area. Citing the recent case of a man who had opened twenty-two separate accounts, fourteen on branches of the same bank, Toothman said: "In all of this the banks blame the merchants and the merchants criticize the banks. Of course the police are in the middle of this squeeze. They are the 'fall guys'— fighting the proverbial windmill . . ." In February of 1963, the Oakland Police Department conducted a survey of eight representative banks in the area, relating to their procedures for opening and closing checking accounts. The findings give a rather clear indication of some of the reasons why check passing has become such a popular trade.

Among the questions asked were the following:

(1) What information is required to open a checking account? Each of the eight banks required the filling out of a signature card which asked for name, address, telephone number, occupation and employer, birthplace, father's name and mother's maiden name, and a list of previous bank accounts. All required the customer to show at least one piece of identification—but one would suffice. Some form of military identification was considered best, a Social Security card worst, but even a library card was acceptable.

(2) What background investigation is conducted? Some made a cursory check of former accounts, but most didn't. If for some reason the new account seemed suspicious, it was flagged and watched, but even a suspicious account was rarely refused.

(3) What is the minimum deposit required? Most of the banks expected $25 or more, but almost all admitted they would open a checking account for $1 if the customer said he was expecting a higher amount shortly.

(4) What was the procedure for issuance of checks? All eight banks issued checks immediately, whatever the deposit, with personalized checks to follow in about ten days. The average number of checks first issued varied from ten to twenty-five.

(5) Were new accounts ever refused? All answered "Rarely." As one banker explained it, "Banks are competitive." Accounts were refused if the person couldn't produce a single piece of ID.

(6) Were records kept of refused accounts? The majority of the banks didn't keep such records.

(7) When were accounts closed by the bank? Most closed new accounts if they were overdrawn. Otherwise, each case was handled separately on its own merits. Several of the banks closed accounts if an insufficient balance was being maintained; most simply charged the customer a service charge.

(8) Who was notified when an account was closed? In all cases, no one outside the bank was notified, not even other branches of the same bank.

(9) What were the markings on returned checks? Going along with the national trend, five of the eight stamped their returned checks simply *refer to maker*. Banks favor this all-purpose noncommittal designation over the more explicit *n.s.f., account closed, unable to locate,* etc. because it avoids civil liability in case the bank has erred and the check is good. Merchants place this high on their list of grievances, complaining that it is cryptic, that when a check is returned so marked they have no way of knowing whether it is bogus or has an illegible signature.

(10) Do the banks maintain any form of central clearinghouse on bad-check information? No.

Though the conclusions are fairly obvious, they bear stating. There was no real background investigation of new accounts. Bank officials relied too heavily on limited identification and their ability to judge character. Almost anyone except a child could open an account for $1 and immediately receive ten to twenty-five checks. Though such things could prove extremely important, not only to law-enforcement agencies and merchants but to the banks themselves, there was no standardized procedure for closing an account, no records kept of refused accounts, and no sharing of check-fraud information.

To the charge that they are not carrying their share of the liability, the banks point out that, while they do offer merchants the fullest possible cooperation in check-cashing matters, the initial decision whether or not to accept a check can be made only by the merchant. "It is not a matter of shirking responsibility," one California banker pointed out, "but rather a matter of defining it. Of course, no one is happy with the bad-check situation, but we have our own problems in this and other areas, and they aren't small by any means."

Flying Kites

Two frauds to which banks are particularly vulnerable are check kiting and double pledging. Observes the American Bankers Association of the former, "Check kiting is one of the most dangerous practices imposed on bankers today and can wreck a perfectly good institution in a short time."

Check kiting is simply covering a bad check with another that is worse, and this with another worse still. In simplified form it works as follows:

With small deposits of about $25 each, the swindler opens checking accounts under different names in a number of widely scattered banks. At bank C he cashes a check for $100 drawn on bank A, depositing $25, pocketing $75. He covers the bank A check with a $250 check on bank B, depositing $125, pocketing $125. The check on bank B is made good with a $500 check on bank C, $300 deposited, $200 pocketed. And so it goes, on through the alphabet or back through the cycle.*

Here the old dictum "Time is money" is literally true. All the swindler need know is the number of days it takes for a check to clear from one bank to another; this he can learn with a few test checks, passed on various days of the week. Taking into consideration weekends and banking holidays, and always allowing for the unexpected, a clever swindler can run up a huge profit before letting the checks he's kited (sailed from one bank to another) fall to earth.

---

* It is rarely this simple or transparent, however, often involving dozens of other legitimate transactions which provide cover for the operation.

A gang of swindlers, operating in different cities, often under the guise of legitimate businesses, can greatly multiply the time and the take. Wiring funds to cover the checks and other refinements will further increase the operating time. In a recent month, the Post Office Department reported kited-check manipulations with losses of $11,000, $25,000, $39,000, and $342,000. (Since checks are mailed from one bank to another in clearing, this brings check kiting into the jurisdiction of mail fraud.) In a matter of a few weeks in early 1964, a fashionably dressed woman of about fifty-five, who always carried a French poodle (symbolically neatly clipped), took banks in Louisiana, Illinois, Washington, Idaho, Colorado, and Texas for more than $26,000. One three-member ring, broken up in September 1964, succeeded in bilking banks and businesses for more than a half million.

Even amateurs can play. In fact, there are probably more "respectable" people kiting checks than professionals. A white-collar worker, running short toward the end of the month, can kite checks in the interim and cover the last with his paycheck. A business operating on a short cash supply can meet its expenses and payrolls by kiting against expected income. In these instances the banks are simply loaning the money—although interest-free and without their knowledge. The "respectables" remain that way until, through some miscalculation, the kite crashes.

Check kiting not only pits the swindler against the banks but may play bank vs. bank to the benefit of the check kiter. Even when a bank discovers that it is being used as part of a check-kiting operation, it may not bring it down—at least not immediately, and certainly not on its own head. Banker A, discovering an overdraft on his books, and finding a pattern of kited checks in the account, may keep his suspicions to himself until after the fraudulent buck has been passed. Bankers recount, privately, tales of bank officials tossing back and forth huge batches of checks, saying "You take them, they're yours," "No, you take them, they belong to you."

Double pledging is similar to check kiting, but usually played on a grander scale with false collateral on loans and generally with the complicity of someone in the bank. The mortgage on a piece of property, for example, may be sold to several different banks; several loans may be made on real or wholly fraudulent insurance policies; or a man may obtain an automobile with a small down payment, then, with a batch of forged pink slips, secure a series of separate loans.

One type of check fraud on which banks and issuing companies assume total liability is the misuse of traveler's checks.

It would appear that no form of fraud would be simpler, no "double your money" investment surer. Since these checks will be replaced in case of destruction, theft, or loss, all the gypster need do is buy a book of checks, claim to lose them, obtain a full refund, and, cashing the "lost" checks, double his or her money. Actually, losses to this gambit are remarkably low, in part because each of these companies maintains its own police agency for its "checks that never bounce," going to absurd lengths to track down such swindlers and giving their apprehensions and convictions maximum publicity. Forgery is more common—and may become even more common as photocopying machines increase.

At a recent convention of the American Bankers Association, a speaker described the automated bank of the "very near future." Through the use of a network of master computers, checks would clear banks not in days or weeks but minutes. The day might even come, the speaker said, when people wouldn't have to handle money. Using a coded identification card, a person could make a purchase in a department store, service station, or neighborhood grocery, and in moments the amount of the purchase would be transferred automatically from the individual's to the store's account.

The word "foolproof" wasn't mentioned, but the speaker did say, "Bad checks and similar frauds will be unknown."

Odds, anyone?

CHAPTER 12

CREDIT CARD SWINDLERY:

A NEW AND

MAGICAL WORLD

> All the Carte Blanche application said was that it would open a new and magical world to me. Other ads seemed to grow out of every corner of the city saying you should go now, pay later—live it up and charge it. I couldn't believe it was as easy as that, but I wanted to find out.
>
> Joseph Miraglia
> *Life* Magazine

FROM earliest times, magicians have warned the uninitiated not to trifle with magic powers. Wondrous as they seem, their possession is fraught with great danger, and one must ever be on guard against the strong temptation to misuse them.

During the past decade, some twenty million Americans have been given the modern equivalent of a magic wand, but rarely if ever is it accompanied by this elementary caution.

"I had always dreamed of taking a big trip to all the fancy places, of living it up like a millionaire's son—just once,"[1] admitted Joseph Miraglia, a nineteen-year-old, $73-a-week clerk from Queens. One day, while having lunch in a restaurant, the good-looking, clean-cut teenager noticed a stack of Hilton Hotels' Carte Blanche application forms on a nearby table. He picked up one and filled it out (it didn't ask his age) and dropped it into a mailbox. A few weeks later he received an envelope containing a small plastic card. Skeptical of its power, he decided to test it. Taking a cab to the Waldorf, he checked into a $55-a-day suite and ordered two bottles of champagne, which arrived properly chilled. The following morning, after a luxurious breakfast in bed, he checked out.

"When I went down to pay the bill with the credit card, they looked at me like I was some kind of special guest," Joe recalled with awe. It *was* magical, and dreams *can* come true. He was on his way.

Flying to Montreal, because Napoleon was one of his heroes and Canada the closest thing to France, Joe checked into a two-bedroom, two-bathroom, two-TV suite at the Reine Elizabeth Hotel. Later in the lobby he met a pretty little blonde, blue-eyed with a page-boy haircut; that evening they dined at one of the city's finest restaurants, La Tour Eiffel, Joe sampling for the first time champagne cocktails, vichyssoise, beef in wine and crepes suzettes. The next day he bought his new girl friend a $675 silver-mink stole. "It was the most money I had ever spent. All of a sudden, the credit card was just like an Aladdin's lamp and you didn't even have to rub it. I realized that if you could buy mink stoles with it, you could probably buy almost anything." It was no idle boast, Joe discovered, that Carte Blanche was known as The Prestige Credit Card. "That card gets you power and authority and respect," he marveled. "And I was given those things wherever I went—oh boy, was I given them!"

When Joe flew out of Montreal several days later, he was accompanied by a cocker-spaniel puppy named Candy who, adorned with an $18 rhinestone-studded collar, and comfortable in a large traveling kennel, was to be his companion for the rest of his magical travels; he left behind the warmly clad blonde and some $1000 in charges for hotel and restaurant bills, a Hertz-rented car, and valet services.

He landed in Las Vegas. Frank Sinatra made way for him at the dice tables—"Let the kid roll"—and with luck, Candy, and a new girl friend at his side, he came away winners. Evenings he gambled, partied, and scattered $10 tips; afternoons he shopped with his magic card, buying, among other things, a pair of white silk pajamas for $35 and $200 worth of new clothes for the vivacious brunette showgirl.

As a mere clerk in Queens, he had never had a chance to do New York in style. On flying back, he charged nearly $2000 worth of clothes in a single day—eight hand-tailored silk shirts in a store where Cary Grant was said to have his shirts made, four pairs of slacks, two sport jackets, a tuxedo, an evening hat, garters, five pairs of shoes, a Rex Harrison hat, three more pairs of silk pajamas, a gray smoking jacket, a silver-tipped walking stick, luggage—all of which was delivered to his $60-a-day suite at the Henry Hudson. The suite itself, Joe later recalled, had a living room "as big as a football field," a couple of bathrooms, two bedrooms, a private bar, three air conditioners, and a color TV. Although there was still about $400 left from his Vegas winnings, he was curious to see if, by some magic, credit could be transformed into cash. It could. He cashed a check for $150 at the Plaza Hotel, using the card as identification.

A little bit jaded now, he was trying to think of something new to do when he remembered something from a movie which at the time had seemed to him the epitome of luxury: in one scene an actor had paid $1.25 for a cup of coffee at the Fontainebleau. Together with Candy, he flew to Miami Beach and checked into the hotel.

Here, for the first time, someone was suspicious of his largesse. The manager of the Fontainebleau took his credit card, promising to return it in three days. Paying his bill in cash and regretfully leaving his magic wand behind, he flew to Havana. By now his purchases had grown so cumbersome that he needed the services of two porters to take his luggage into the Habana Hilton Hotel, where he rented another large suite, with two balconies that overlooked the ocean.

More than a little of the magic had rubbed off. "I thought I would have to watch my expenses without my Carte Blanche," he admitted. "But when I said that I had once had a card, that was good enough for them. They told me it would be fine if I paid my hotel bill by check and said I could cash $250 worth of checks in case I needed some change." When no one held him to the amount, he was as liberal with his pen as with the credit card, using as his sole identification a receipt for some shoes he had bought in Miami on his Carte Blanche.

In addition to the suite, he rented a cabana, complete with shower and telephone, and ate his breakfasts beside the pool. Breakfast that first morning consisted of veal scallopini, chef's salad, mashed potatoes, string beans, and rum and Coca Cola. Then there were clothes, hairdos, and pedicures for the pretty Dominican girl who kept him company, and filet mignon for Candy. Without any credit card or identification, except the shoe-store receipt, he spent nearly $1000 in three days.

Returning to New York with just 40¢ in change, Joe decided to replenish his pocket money. He had no trouble cashing a check for $100 at the Statler Hilton, but when he attempted to cash a similar check at the Plaza the once-stung cashier recognized him and alerted hotel detectives. Five wonderful weeks, $2000 in bad checks, and more than $10,000 in charges after it had all begun, his credit-card spree was at an end.

It should come as no surprise that the current credit explosion, based in part on trust but also in part on deception, hidden interest rates, wordsmithed promises, and simple and compound misrepresentation, should in turn open whole new vistas of individual fraud and bring into being new specialists in swindlery, among them the credit-card con men.

Although it can be said that the Enjoy Now, Suffer Later form of credit is as old as Adam, Eve, and the apple, the credit card itself is a fairly modern manifestation. One of its original progenitors was the old-fashioned "letter of credit" issued by banks to businessmen and tourists traveling abroad. Each time funds were withdrawn, the foreign banks would make a notation of the amount and stamp their seal on the letter. When the last of the money was drawn, that bank would return the letter to the issuing one, which would then make payment. Needless to say, forgery abounded. Another ancestor was the Traveletter System, less fraud-prone because quite short-lived. Introduced in this country in 1894, it was used mainly by traveling salesmen and was good only for food and lodging. But both these systems required money or suitable collateral on deposit in advance. The first large-scale innovation of credit-card trust came in the 1930s when the oil companies introduced their petroleum credit cards, then good only for the purchase of gasoline in a few scattered service stations, now widely accepted for the purchase of almost anything short of a whole automobile. But successful as they were, it can be said, with only slight exaggeration, that the beginnings of the modern credit-card boom can be traced to something more commonplace: a man's forgetfulness.

One evening in February 1950, Frank MacNamara, a thirty-five-year-old commercial-credit specialist, was working late in his Manhattan office. Breaking off for dinner, he went to a nearby restaurant, ordered, ate his meal, then discovered that he had forgotten his wallet. Two hours later, after waiting for his wife to drive in from Long Island, he was able to pay his bill.

The next day MacNamara mentioned the incident to his attorney, Ralph Schneider; out of the discussion came the idea of Diners' Club. As Hillel Black notes, "In the credit card industry, Mac-Namara's dinner is now fondly referred to as The First Supper."[2] Only a dozen New York restaurants and a hundred cardholders signed up the first year. The second year the pair went $58,000 into debt, but their billings for the goods and services charged on the card passed the $1 million mark. By 1960, Diners' had total billings of $165 million, and that year showed a profit of $2 million. By then, too, they had imitators, in the dozens. Two have proved especially strong competition, Hilton Hotels' Carte Blanche and American Express. The trio are now known as the Big Three of the all-purpose credit cards.

Today, twenty million Americans carry some seventy million credit cards, entitling them to wining, dining, lodging, traveling, entertaining, clothing, telephoning, hospitalization, and goods, gifts, and services of nearly all kinds. You can rent or buy an automobile with a credit card or obtain berthing for your yacht or fly via thirty-five airlines to a hundred-odd countries where American credit cards are honored by some 170,000 firms. You can rent geishas for a party in Tokyo; eat bird's nest soup in San Francisco's Chinatown or Shrimp Arnaud in New Orleans; drink in Hemingway's haunts in Paris, or, if less literary-minded, see the Folies Bergère; buy a case of the finest Scotch in Hoboken; go on safari in Africa or polar-bear hunting in Alaska; buy jade in Hong Kong, saris in India, or Bayer Aspirin in Bombay; contribute to the political party of your choice; have immediate credit recognition at over 1300 hospitals in all fifty states (Carte Blanche); buy your vitamin pills by mail order at special prices (Diners'); give your wife—but not your girl friend—a specially embossed "Hers" credit card (Carte Blanche); tour Yugoslavia (Diners'); buy lesser-known works of the famous masters, specially selected by Vincent Price (Sears Revolving Charge). With the Bell System Telephone Credit Card you can add something different to your next party with a long-distance call to the Kremlin. BankAmericard, The Card with Buying Power, offers "the convenience of 38,000 charge accounts"; Carte Blanche, "the services of over 100,000 member establishments"; and your Diners' card "is honored everywhere for nearly everything." An unbelievably magic world is open to the credit-card holder—be he legitimate or fraud. Ah, there's the rub, for in the last several years the boom has begun to develop some ominous thunder. Those financial editors who viewed the early success of Diners' and marveled "Where will it all end?", not really expecting an answer, have begun to receive one nevertheless. Although, except for the first several years, Diners' has shown a clear annual profit, its largest competitors have both had their bad moments. Each of the Big Three has had to raise its annual membership-card fee (from $5 and $6 to $8, and then to $10 and $11). Several of the oil companies have had to decrease the purchasing power of their cards. Of the numerous bank credit cards launched between 1952 and 1962, more than two-thirds have failed, including one of the largest, Chase Manhattan's Charge Plan (CMCP), which the bank sold in 1962 for about $9 million, the amount of its uncollected customer accounts. A large number of members does not automatically equal success; for many of the card plans it has meant total failure.

To increase profits, the credit-card companies must also increase the number of memberships or the number or size of purchases by existing members. Each of the Big Three has widened the base of goods and services available with its card, one even for a time considering (though finally rejecting) a pay-before-you-go funeral plan. But, as the companies are discovering, attempts to solicit more members can create even weightier problems. "By extending credit privileges to an ever-widening group of people eager to live on the cuff," Hillel Black observes, "the risk of loss mounts. Each time someone does not pay the tab he has charged with a credit card, it is not the restaurant owner or merchant who absorbs the loss but the credit-card company."[3] In 1959, Diners' losses came to about $1 million, equal to almost half of the company's net profits. This despite the fact that Diners' had upped its membership-rejection rate to about 40 percent of all applicants.

The easier the credit, the more vulnerable the company issuing it and the greater the opportunities for fraud. Dollar losses from the misuse of stolen credit cards alone increased eightfold from 1958 ($266,850) to 1962 ($1,915,000). Add to this the loss from bad debts, forged cards, checks cashed by merchants who view the credit-card holder as a man of proven honesty (forgetting how easily they got their own cards), and it becomes evident that the new field of swindlery is yielding a rich harvest.

Just who are the credit-card cons?

They range from the naively innocent to the professionally fraudulent, with all shadings in between.

There is the "deadbeat," the man (or woman) who on first obtaining a credit card intends to pay his bills, but once in possession of this "symbol of power and inexhaustible potency" (as one motivational research analyst calls it), gets carried away and finds himself in deep debt, lacking the power to swim back. He may be honest; he may mean well; he may even be described as the violated rather than the violator, seduced by the constantly repeated theme "buy now, pay later." But whatever his justification, once his purchases exceed his ability to pay, he is, to his creditors, a deadbeat, a source of loss. A recent survey of all members of the American Petroleum Credit Association revealed that the second worst offender in the domain of credit-card fraud was the card owner who "suddenly went haywire," spending more than he could afford. *Restaurant Management,* trade magazine of the restaurant industry, in a survey that was ten months in preparation, revealed that credit-card holders found their magic so potent and so deceptively easy to use that they spent an average of 25 to 30 percent more than customers who paid cash. *Life,* in another survey, found the average even higher—up to 35 percent. While most people wouldn't consider the deadbeat a crook or criminal (he applies for the card under his own name), the credit-card companies believe he is often something other than what he seems. The easiest way to get away with credit-card fraud, they point out, is to avoid any indication of fraudulent intent. A jury won't convict a man for fraud if they believe his only crime is bad financial judgment.

The chiseling proprietor is another of the credit-card cheats, and of late his numbers have been increasing. In the first flush of the credit card's success, restaurateurs were near-unanimous in proclaiming that its use would inaugurate a whole new era of profits. Many have since had second thoughts. When a customer charges a meal on his card, the restaurant bills the card company, receiving in return the amount charged minus a certain percentage. Diners' deducts 7 percent; American Express, between 5 and 7 percent; Carte Blanche, 4 percent.* Many restaurateurs consider this excessive,

* Hotels pay an average of 3 to 5 percent, specialty shops as much as 10 percent. As these affect prices and rates, both cash and charge customers share these credit-card costs also.

Bank credit cards—which are a combination of the credit card and the revolving-credit plan—operate differently. The card is issued without cost to the pointing out that the average restaurant profit is only from 3 to 3½ percent. *They also admit, frankly, that it is the customer who absorbs most of the charge, in higher food and beverage prices—be he cash or card-carrying.* The credit-card companies counter with the argument that use of the card increases business. At any rate, some of the less scrupulous have found a way around the deduction. As *Time* noted in 1962, "Nowadays when a customer flashes his credit cards, many restaurants and hotels that subscribe to the plan bill him directly, to avoid the 5–7% commission charged by the clubs."[4] The worst they can expect for this, if caught, is to be dropped from member listing.

Since the card companies make good on all charges on legitimate cards, swindlers have found still another gimmick which cheats the company of far more than 7 percent. Working with credit-card thieves, they take stolen cards and make up bills for fantastic charges. In one season, a Miami Beach ring ran up more than $75,000 in fraudulent sales. One place billed Diners' $500 for a single dinner, another $700 for the same. The first establishment was a pizza parlor, the second a Chinese restaurant.

The company-card cheat is another source of loss, though not to the credit-card companies. Like the restaurateurs, many large businesses welcomed the advent of the credit card, believing that its itemized bills would bring to an end the padding of expense accounts (long known as "swindle sheets"). They were soon to find that it only made such fraud easier, for larcenously minded employees, including executives, were not long in discovering that many waiters and maître d's were quite happy to make out bills for higher than the amount of the lunch or dinner (often doubling the charge, or adding nonexistent guests), then splitting the difference in cash. A New York advertising executive shared $3000 in split charges with various filling-station operators on his card issued by the Esso Standard Oil Division of Humble Oil and Refining Company, before someone began to wonder why he was buying a new set of tires every two weeks. And more than a few companies have, and are, treating their employees to more exotic pleasures.

---

customer. The bank collects an advance fee from member merchants and an average of 6 percent on each charge. If the customer pays his bill in twenty days there is no charge to him; if he doesn't, there are carrying charges. These are set up on a revolving-credit basis. The claimed cost for the credit is usually 1½ percent per month, or 18 percent per year. The actual cost is always higher. (See Chapter 6.)

One fairly large New York City call-girl operation offered its customers charge privileges on any of the major credit cards, up until the time it folded in early 1964. Charges were made on a fashionable Manhattan restaurant and itemized as food and beverages, the restaurant owners collecting a 15 percent commission from the madam. Similar operations, involving establishments listed as babysitting services, secretarial services, and public-relations consultants, have also proven popular.

(The credit-card companies offer their customers three billing choices: company account—bill sent to office address; personal account—bill sent to home address; and personal account—bill sent to office address.)

In most fields of criminal endeavor, there is a wide line between the amateurs and the professionals. As yet this isn't true with credit-card fraud. An amateur with a single stolen card may net as much before being apprehended as the professional whose arsenal includes all the weapons of forgery and impersonation. Amateur Joseph Miraglia ran up $10,000 in charges and passed $2000 in bad checks in a little more than one month on his first—and, one hopes, last—time out. One of the best of the professionals, a thirty-five-year-old Canadian who, with his cultural English accent, pince-nez, sandy gray hair, clipped mustache, fashionable wardrobe, and silver-handled malacca walking stick, bore an amazing resemblance to the young "Yellow Kid" Weil, made some $20,000 in bad charges and laid $15,000 in bouncy paper on a fraud binge that took him across most of the Northeast and Canada. The Canadian was in operation five months, averaging less per month than Miraglia. He was a pro, however, in that he lasted five months instead of one. He made his own checks, identification, and credit cards. When arrested by the FBI at his suite in New York's Hotel Beverly, he had in his possession a check-writing machine, reams of check paper, engraving tools, inks, glues, an assortment of credit cards, and a portable printing press.

Credit-card fraud is another of the easier trades. No apprenticeship is necessary. All that is needed is the ability to look and act like a status carrier (Joe, you'll remember, dreamed he was a millionaire's son), an appreciation for expensive things, a talent for bluffing, and no objections to travel (the credit-card con man is highly mobile). With imagination, it isn't even necessary to steal a card or apply for it fraudulently. During the late fifties, one credit-card company made up a cardboard display poster for use in hotels and restaurants advertising the magic of its particular card. Printed on the poster was a facsimile card, made out to John Doe, Anytown, U.S.A. Using a razor blade, a swindler cut out the facsimile; posing as Mr. Doe, he ran up $5000 in charges.

As a number of swindlers have unhappily discovered, since the application for a credit card and the bills charged on it are sent via the U.S. mails, credit-card fraud is also mail fraud and means pursuit by the Post Office Department. Among the numerous credit-card cases reported in recent issues of the POD's *Enforcement Action* were the following:

A twenty-five-year-old Miami, Florida, man lifted the wallet of an acquaintance and used the three credit cards it contained to run up $5000 in charges in less than ten days. An Iowa farmer sent his hired man into town to make a few small purchases, giving him his credit card to use as payment; when he was apprehended three months later in Hawaii, the charges exceeded $4000. An Albany, New York, man, using fictitious names, obtained a number of oil-company credit cards; operating nationally, he obtained some $30,-000 worth of automotive accessories, which he resold.

While high living probably accounts for the better part of credit-card fraud, definitions of what constitute high living vary. In November 1964, New York City police arrested a thirty-five-year-old man, who must rate special citation as the sickest of the credit-card thieves. According to police, for some eighteen months the man had been living high in various East Coast hospitals on stolen Blue Cross cards. He would, they alleged, check into a hospital, take an expensive room, demand and receive the best in food and attention, and, when bored, prowl around other rooms stealing more Blue Cross cards.

Neither high living nor profit provided the motive of another credit-card operator. To his amazement, Marion G. Neff, an Indiana state policeman, suddenly began receiving strange gifts in the mail. The outlandish array of items he hadn't ordered included sixteen live Maine lobsters, twenty-five poplar trees, a rug from Iran, sweaters from Ireland, title to two lots in Hawaii, and a guitar with lessons. Postal inspectors discovered that all the items had been ordered by mail and charged to phony Diners' Club accounts, but, aside from handwriting samples, they were without clues. One day in January 1963, policeman Neff arrested a South Bend, Indiana, architect for driving with a suspended license. His face was familiar:

Neff had arrested him twice before—once for speeding, once for drunken driving. His handwriting awoke even more vivid memories; under questioning, he admitted that he was responsible for sending some twenty-five packages to Neff. Revenge by credit card.*

On the way to her car in the parking lot of a Los Angeles supermarket, a housewife is the victim of a fast-moving purse snatcher; in a crowded hotel lobby in Kansas City during a stockman's convention, a Wyoming rancher has his wallet lifted by a pickpocket; in Dallas a traveling salesman is mugged and robbed.

These three victims have several things in common: each is understandably upset but believes his or her ordeal to be over; each is wrong; each has just become an especially vulnerable American.

In Rochester a woman leaves her Charga-plate on the counter in a department store; a Birmingham man, a wee bit in his cups, doesn't notice that the waiter has neglected to return his Diners' Club card after taking the charge; a lawyer drops his Air Travel card in John F. Kennedy International Airport in Washington.

These three—because they aren't aware of their losses and may not be for some time—are even more vulnerable than the foregoing trio.

Of the 70 million credit cards in circulation in the United States, 1.5 million are lost each year; of these, about 60,000 have been stolen. This type of larceny, combined with fraud, has grown so extensive that the FBI has created a new "wanted" category: Most Wanted Credit Card Thief. There is no shortage of candidates. This has resulted in an interesting change in some of the oldest criminal professions. While the purse snatcher, pickpocket, and robber were once quick to pocket the cash and dispose of any incriminating identification, the identification today is often worth more than the currency. Sold to a fence, in turn resold to a lone swindler or gang, the credit cards, together with driver's license and other ID, may be in use within hours.

"Not generally appreciated by the public is the speed with which in this jet age a freshly stolen credit card may be put into circulation in a city thousands of miles away," observed Evan McLeod Wylie in a study of credit-card theft which appeared in the New York *Herald Tribune*. "Airmailed to a confederate, a card stolen on the West Coast can be in use in any Eastern city the next day. By

*Although swindlery wasn't the point in this case, notice that all this merchandise was sent on the strength of a fictitious credit-card number.

courier, a batch of stolen cards can be shifted from New York to Chicago or Dallas in a few hours."[5]

Although several attempts have been made to smash Mexico's bordertown business in credit cards and credentials, in 1965 even an amateur swindler could buy in Tijuana the following at these average prices:

Telephone credit card: $10.*
Department store Charga-plate: $40.
Diners' Club card: $50.
Carte Blanche card: $50.
American Express card: $75.
Air Travel card: $700. (This is the most coveted of the credit cards, as it is good for immediate transportation to almost any part of the world. A card sometimes sells for as high as $1000. One reason it is so expensive is that a deposit of $425 is required of the cardholder.)

All the above are legitimate, though stolen, cards. One could buy in addition any three pieces of perfectly forged identification, description to match that of the passer, for $50.

Recently a Charga-plate stolen from a woman's purse in San Francisco on Tuesday afternoon was flown to Tijuana, resold, and back in San Francisco in circulation when stores opened Wednesday morning.

Often stolen credit cards prove more valuable as identification than for charges. Operating from a hotel room just off Times Square, a forger organized his specially trained associates into two battalions: one stole credit cards and personal checks; the other traveled around the country via jet "laying paper." An exceptionally well-organized ring, they operated on a near-perfect timetable, visiting as many as eight cities in seventy-two hours. Hotels were their targets. Arriving in a new city, they would register at every one of the major hotels and, with their credit cards, establish check-cashing privileges. Once this was done, they would retrace their route, cashing checks. Their planning was exact. Advance men scouted the hotels, evaluating the cashiers for alertness and learning when they went on and off shift; "blockers" were posted in the lobbies in case of pursuit; taxis were always kept waiting outside, and getaways

---

* Discussed separately in Chapter 14.

were coordinated with airline departure times. Before being stopped
by the FBI, their take reached $100,000.

A smaller Canadian group netted more in less time. Duplicating
Diners' Club cards, and using them solely for identification, they
succeeded in passing more than $250,000 in bad paper, mostly on
banks.

Who picks up the tab for credit-card fraud?

Those who accept bad checks, whatever the identification, are
stuck with them.

The credit-card companies assume most of the loss on counterfeit
cards (excepting only the most crudely bogus), all the loss on unpaid accounts, all the loss on fraudulently obtained cards, and *part*
of the loss on stolen cards.

That other part can and often does come as a costly surprise to
the victim of the credit-card thief, who suddenly finds himself in
double jeopardy. For if you have a card, and it is lost or stolen,
chances are that you will be held liable for any charges made on
the card up to the moment the card company is notified of your loss
—and sometimes even after.

Just above the signature line on the application for Hilton Hotels'
Carte Blanche is the statement: "If this application is accepted and
a credit card issued, the applicant shall be deemed to have agreed
to the terms and conditions accompanying the card." One of these
is: "Lost or stolen cards should be reported immediately by wire or
letter to the Hilton Hotel Corporation . . . The cardholder will be
responsible for payment of all amounts charged by use of his card
until written notice is received by Hilton Hotel Corporation." Diners'
Club uses the positive approach in one of its invitations to join:
"No need to worry if your credit card is lost or stolen. You simply
notify the Diners' Club in writing and upon receipt of notification,
your liability ends and the Diners' Club assumes full responsibility
should any unauthorized charges be made to your account." Most
other credit cards are similarly conditioned. Air Travel cards are an
exception—the cardholder is liable for all charges made up to thirty
days after the loss is reported.

Because the question of liability is one of ticklish legality, for a
time the credit-card companies were reluctant to test it in court.
During 1964 the issue did make its way into the courts in two states,
California and Colorado. Colorado found the cardholder liable; California ruled he was not.

The Colorado case had some interesting features. "The events which give rise to this lawsuit could well find their setting on a theater stage instead of a judicial tribunal," noted Denver District Judge Mitchel B. Johns. The events were these:

In April 1962, a man whom we'll call Angelo Greco appeared in Denver and contacted officials of the Commerce Investment Corporation, an equipment-leasing firm. Greco was a mystery man, no one knew anything about him—who he was or where he was from. "He was tall, dark—I wouldn't say handsome—and suave," said Nathan Kobey, Denver attorney and company president. "He had good manners." He also had letters which indicated that he could obtain $1 million worth of credit from the International Insurance Company of Nassau, the Bahamas. The Denver company, in need of capital, promptly elected Greco vice-president, and the following month he turned over to them a $200,000 check drawn on the Bank of the Bahamas. Then, just before the check bounced, he disappeared.

Just what Greco intended remains a mystery, as he reportedly collected no money from the company. All that is known is that, at about the time he disappeared, a United Air Lines credit card, issued to the company in the name of Kobey, disappeared also. Then the charges began coming in, all made by a man fitting Greco's description—Houston to Miami to Nassau to New York, San Francisco to Sydney to London to Paris, back to London, then back to the United States . . . On some flights more than one ticket was charged. The tour lasted from May 31 to July 23, during which time $7631.57 in charges were made on the card. When recovered by a ticket agent (the user promptly disappeared), it bore a forged signature. Kobey, like many other credit-card holders, hadn't signed his card on receipt of it. (A remarkably large number of people never sign their credit cards on receiving them, believing this is safer and circumvents forgery; actually, it only makes it easier, leaving the swindler a blank space in which to sign the name in his own handwriting.)

United attempted to collect for the charges; the company refused to pay for them, arguing that they were unauthorized. In February 1964, United took the case to court.

Greco wasn't one of the defendants, but during the proceedings his name came up more often than any of those who were. By now a little of the mystery had dissipated, but only a little. It was learned that, while Greco was in Denver, he was still under indictment by a federal grand jury in Miami for securities fraud, mail fraud, and conspiracy. He returned to Florida in 1963 long enough to plead guilty and to be placed on probation, before again disappearing.

Judge Johns ruled in favor of United: "As between two innocent persons victimized by the wrongdoings of a third person, he who was responsible for setting the machinery in motion which made it possible for the wrongdoer to benefit must suffer liability," he said. It was the company which ordered the card and which put Greco in the position of authority which gave him access to it, he stated; thus, United was "at the mercy" of the cardholder, and "the only legal conclusion" was that the firm was liable for the $7631.57, plus $3500 for attorney's fees.

Kobey, speaking for himself and the company, promised to appeal the case to the Colorado Supreme Court. "I don't think forgery creates rights in anybody," he said.

Due to the special circumstances surrounding the case, the decision casts little legal light on the question of the liability of the ordinary cardholder. However, it does illuminate how important that "thirty days after notification" clause can be. Credit-card bills are sent to cardholders once a month. Not until the first of these bills arrived did the company realize the card was missing and notify United. As a result, the company was liable not just for thirty but for the whole fifty-four days the card was in use.[6]

The California case involved an unreported stolen card. Though the first judge ruled in favor of the card company, finding the cardholder liable for failing to report the loss, an appellate court reversed the verdict, ruling that cardholders are "not absolutely liable" in every case. This is, however, only one partially qualified decision in one state.

If you have lost your credit card, Consumers Union strongly recommends that you call or wire the issuing company, following this immediately with a registered letter. You are legally liable until the company is notified "in writing."

Light as the credit card may seem in pocket or purse, its owner is carrying a heavy load of possible liability. The average in bad charges run up on a stolen all-purpose credit card is about $500.

Since the advantages of taking up credit-card fraud as a trade have been depicted, it might be well to point out some of the disadvantages of this particular avocation. It is not for the idle. The swindler must work fast and enjoy the loot while he can, for, as careers go, this one is decidedly short-lived: it is a rare credit-card con man who goes uncaught for as long as six months. The opposition is formidable: postal inspectors; FBI agents; state and local police; the security forces of the credit-card companies; plus the fraud-prevention groups of the various trade associations, which include retail merchants, retail credit, hotels, and airlines. Also to be considered by anyone intending to steal now and pay later is the interest rate: since the advent of Diners' Club, a number of states have passed or have under consideration laws dealing explicitly with credit-card abuses. The most severe to date is a law passed in Texas in 1959 which offers as maximum penalty for the "misuse" of a credit card a $10,000 fine *and* ten years in prison. Too, during the past several years the major credit-card companies have adopted a "get tough" policy of prosecuting every case involving a stolen or fraudulently obtained card. One company recently spent $5000 on a chartered plane to fly witnesses across the United States to testify at a trial involving a loss of less than $500.

Company safeguards against credit-card fraud, and techniques for stopping it once it has started, are closely guarded secrets, but some have slipped out. They range from the use of colored fibers, embossed emblems, and nonerasable paper (used in some, though not all, of the cards—many are still ordinary printed cardboard) to special warning alerts, frequent stolen-card bulletins, and periodically revised "blacklists" of stolen or no-pay cards, mailed to all member establishments. The very size of these lists is often defeating. To help overcome this, many of the companies now offer a reward to any clerk or cashier who repossesses a stolen or expired card. The current reward for a BankAmericard, for example, is $25. Increasing the vigilance of clerks handling the cards has helped to reduce the length of time stolen cards remain in circulation.

Then, too, although the cardholder may believe he holds the key to unlimited buying power (the companies prefer to have him feel this way), even credit-card magic now has its limits. Joseph Miraglia's spree during Carte Blanche's first year in operation couldn't be repeated today with any of the major cards. When charges exceed a certain defined debt limit (varying with the cardholder and based on his income and credit history), the companies give special attention to the account. Repossession teams are flown around the country to pick up invalid cards. Obituary columns are checked against membership lists to make sure no one inherits a credit card. There is also a limit on the amount that can be charged without authorization, and, in the case of one member of the Big Three, this was recently reduced from $500 to $100. Since this is usually done discreetly, the cardholder may be unaware that it is done, but when a cardholder presents a card as payment for goods and services exceeding $100, the member establishment must make a long-distance collect call to the credit-card company to obtain authorization for the charge. An around-the-clock staff is on duty for such calls.

There is a still more basic way to reduce credit-card fraud, and that is to make it harder to obtain a card—in short, stricter credit requirements. In January 1965, *Newsweek* reported that six of the major oil companies had signed up with New York's Hooper-Holmes Bureau for their new computer system, which matches new applications against recorded credit risks. The oil companies, oldest in the credit-card field, are also the most cautious in issuing credit. Many of the other credit-card companies (including a number of the bank-card plans) feel that the need to meet competition outweighs the risk. So long as they feel this way, and so long as the cards retain their magic buying power, both amateur and professional magicians will continue their credit-card tricks.

CHAPTER 13

THE PYRAMIDERS AND

THE CORPORATE ASSASSINS

> We are living in an era of the most
> spectacular merchandising and
> commercial swindles of all times.
>
> Nathaniel E. Kossack,
> Chief of the U.S. Justice
> Department's Fraud Division

IN MARCH 1960, several months after Joseph Miraglia's magic had lost its power, a pretty ex-model we'll call Sally Clark appeared in federal bankruptcy court in San Jose, California.

Miss Clark and Mr. Miraglia didn't know each other, but both were products of the American credit explosion. Miss Clark didn't have a credit card, but then, she hadn't needed one. Over a ten-year period, using at least 17 different aliases and 511 different charge accounts, she had managed to run up a grand total of $86,249 in unpaid bills. There was a significant difference between the operations of the clerk from Queens and the former model from San Jose: he had committed a crime, or rather a whole series of crimes: she hadn't.

Miss Clark is just one of a large number of enterprising Americans who have discovered the other side of the credit coin. A sampling of their discoveries will be related in this chapter. They range from charge-account swindlery and other credit chicanery to murder. The murder not of men but of businesses and corporations, often accomplished with total legality.

Playing the Floor Limit

There is a truly remarkable fact of merchandising life, unpublicized by merchants themselves but no longer a trade secret, inasmuch as thousands of swindlers have discovered and made the most of it in recent years. Very simply put, it is this:

In many large stores, including nearly all department stores, you do not need a charge account to charge.

Most stores which do a large daily volume of cash and credit business find it nearly impossible to check each charge immediately to ascertain whether the customer actually has an account. To do this on every charge transaction would take longer than most customers are willing to wait, or would require a huge credit staff. As alternative, these stores have adopted what is known as a *floor limit*. That is the amount below which an item or items may be carried out without immediate processing of the charge or verification of the account.

Some stores do check every charge. Others have floor limits, but only in certain departments or at certain seasons, such as Christmas. Some restrict this practice just to the floor, to carry-out transactions; many, however, have the same amount for floor, mail, and telephone sales. The amount varies from store to store—it may be as low as $5 or, as in the case of at least one specialty shop with branches in most major American cities, as high as $200. The average is probably $50.

This means exactly what the reader thinks it means. A man or woman may scout a store, through simple observation of the clerks and customers and charge amounts estimating fairly easily the floor limit, then, returning at a busy time, load up, charging items—always under the limit—in several different departments, signing bogus names and addresses to the charge slips and walking out unquestioned, arms piled high with packages. One woman took thirteen Chicago stores for $4000 in floor-limit charges in just two days.

This swindle is not only ridiculously simple, it is very difficult to stop. Even if the charge is sent to the credit department before the customer has left the store with the merchandise, very rarely will the store detective be alerted. Most charges by people without accounts are the result of honest error; for example, a husband thinking his wife has an account in that store when it is actually the store down the street. Or there is the possibility that the error is the store's, that the customer has an account but that his ledger card has been misfiled or pulled out for billing. Rather than embarrass the customer, the store will often simply mail out a charge application with the bill. There is still another reason for inaction: stores want new accounts and may figure that, even if the customer hasn't an account, he *should* have one.

It is not even necessary for the swindler to enter the store to effect this con. He may be several thousand miles away. Using this knowledge and the U.S. mails, a machinist's mate stationed at Norfolk, Virginia, managed to collect some $14,000 on an investment of less than $10. He began by purchasing 200 postcards (then still a penny) and an assortment of quality magazines, including the *New Yorker, Mademoiselle,* and *McCall's* for a total expenditure of less than $5. Scanning the magazines, he picked out the ads of the "better" stores—establishments such as Dunhill's, Gump's, Tiffany's, Neiman-Marcus, City of Paris, Saks Fifth Avenue—and sent off one or more cards to each, ordering items which he could use or resell easily, no single order exceeding $100.

He had accounts at none of these stores.

With his 200 cards he failed more times than he succeeded, but his success was sufficient: at least 66 stores sent him some $6000 in merchandise.*

Thus far he had committed no crime. He ordered the merchandise under his own name. There was no indication that he did not intend to pay for it. Under the postal-fraud statutes, intent is extremely important: to make a case, the POD must prove conclusively that a scheme is contrived with "deliberate intent to defraud." When dunned to pay for his bills, the sailor put through a petition for bankruptcy, which was granted.

With his slate wiped clean, he bought another batch of postcards, 300 this time, and sent out more orders, many to the same stores that were his debtors in the bankruptcy case, this time collecting $8000 in goods from at least 72 different firms. Again he successfully pleaded bankruptcy.

With his third batch of cards he was apprehended for mail fraud, tried, and convicted.

This was not an isolated case: about half of the mail-fraud cases

---

* Remarked the credit manager of one of the stores which did not send the merchandise, "He would have fared much better had he spent a few more dollars and used personalized stationery."

reported each month by the POD are of individuals obtaining merchandise without intent to pay. As in this instance, sometimes the real name is used, blurring the distinction between the poor credit risk and the outright fraud; quite often one or more fictitious names are used together with a post-office box or specially rented mail drop. In Louisville, Kentucky, a man using more than 50 assumed names obtained at least $4500 worth of radio and TV parts; a Wilkes-Barre, Pennsylvania, man, his wife, and his brother took 46 firms for at least $2600; three San Jose, California, sisters took some 50 firms for at least $5000; while a whole family in New York City collected at least $25,000 in merchandise over a ten-year period. The qualifying phrase "at least" is used advisedly: according to Chief Postal Inspector H. B. Montague, in such cases only a fraction of the stores bother to report their losses.

There are numerous variations on the theme. A man in Waterloo, Iowa, figured a way to obtain discounts on purchases whether or not the firms wanted to give them: he ordered large quantities of electronic equipment, paying with money orders about one-third short of the full amount, knowing that most of the stores would be tolerant of the "mistake" and send the goods, together with a bill for the amount still due. Other mail-order swindlers will order merchandise from a store, charging it to an account they don't have, then return the goods, using still another name, for a cash refund. Quite often they get it.

Mail-order catalogue houses, with their policy of "easy credit," anticipate a high regular loss to mail fraud and set their prices accordingly. But by percentage of fraudulent orders, their loss is nowhere nearly so great as that suffered by the book and record clubs. Most of these clubs offer one or more free books or records on joining on condition that the member buy a specified number of monthly selections, usually four to six, each year. Nearly all of these clubs advertise extensively, often on magazine inserts with prepaid postcard order forms that save the swindler even the cost of postage. Nearly all operate on the Silence=Consent plan, automatically mailing the monthly selection unless the member sends in a card asking specifically that it not be sent. And nearly all bill the customer after the selection is mailed.

Via this plan a Savannah, Georgia, man obtained 600 records, which he resold for $1 each; estimated loss to the record clubs, $8000. Two teenage boys in the Bronx collected $10,000 worth of literature and music. Dozens of similar cases are reported each month, the average totaling about $1000.

As with any fairly mechanical procedure, there is always the risk of perpetual motion. Either that, or some of the clubs are more devoted to sales than business, the desire to sell surpassing the desire to receive payment. A book club and two record clubs continued sending their monthly selections to one member long after he had been jailed on mail-fraud charges arising in part from their complaints.

Pyramiding

Although the pyramider has been around longer than the credit-card con man, he too has been affected by the credit malaise of the fifties and sixties. Pyramiding (also known as the *rush act,* the *one shot,* the *fast shot, hit-and-run,* and the *load up*) is now easier to play than ever before. So easy, in fact, that it, too, touches on the wondrous.

There was a time, only a few years ago, when a customer applying for a charge account had to wait two or three weeks for credit approval. No more. To keep up with the competition, many stores allow the charge-account applicant immediate credit up to a certain amount. The amount varies, but it is generally as high or higher than the floor limit. Often the store will tell the prospective customer the exact amount ("As a customer service, Mr. Walker, you may charge up to $500 while awaiting approval of your account"), but even when he isn't told, approximation is fairly easy. For the pyramider this provides a perfect setup: he applies for charge accounts in a number of different stores using out-of-town references; he may begin charging that very day, or he may wait a day or two, long enough to divert suspicion but not long enough for his references to be checked. When he starts he works fast, going from store to store, loading up on resalable merchandise.

To indicate just how vulnerable merchants are to this fraud, it is necessary to look behind the scenes, to see what happens when a person applies for a charge account. Credit practices differ from store to store, but the following is widespread enough to fit most.

The applicant must fill out an application. Most (though not all) stores require some identification. Usually a single piece of ID, such as a driver's license or, better still, a credit card, will suffice.

The swindler must now pass the scrutiny of the store's credit department. To separate the fraudulent from the fair, credit managers rely on past experience, little telltale signs, and what some call the "eyeball test." "Every credit man relies on the 'eyeball test' to a certain degree," explained the credit manager of one of the more renowned specialty stores on the West Coast. "It's difficult to explain how it works: when something is wrong, you more or less 'feel' it. It is, I suppose, a combination of on-the-spot evaluation and sixth sense. There are no sure rules: the relaxed customer, for example, is not necessarily the safe customer. Many people with excellent credit are nervous when opening a new account."

Once this hurdle is passed, the essential information is sent to the local credit bureau for checking. Some 3200 of these bureaus, their combined territories covering literally every part of the United States, belong to one trade association, the Associated Credit Bureaus of America.

It has been said that, if your name isn't in the files of one or more of these bureaus, it doesn't mean you don't rate—it means you're either under twenty-one or dead. There is still another exception: the man who doesn't exist.

It has also been said that, if the files of all these member bureaus were combined, they would contain more information on more people than the files of both the CID and the FBI. But they aren't combined. Contrary to the impression given by several recent writers, there is no central repository of credit information, no mammoth computer which holds the past, present, and probable future credit histories of the American people.* Credit information is valuable, and the bureaus buy it from one another. Association members have several ways of doing this. If the information is needed immediately (if, say, a man is considering buying an automobile, or a woman a fur coat, and the dealer or merchant wants the information as fast as possible to avoid losing the sale to a competitor), the local credit bureau may either telephone, wire, or use the Telex to contact the applicable bureau. But most often, as in the case of opening a regular charge account, the "coupon system" is used. Member bureaus purchase books of coupons from the Association. When out-of-town information is required on a person, a coupon is

---

* Only a few of the individual bureaus are computerized. The task of transferring hundreds of thousands of detailed credit histories onto IBM-type cards has proved so expensive that, to date, only the largest metropolitan bureaus have attempted it.

filled in and *mailed* to the Association, which in turn *remails* it to the appropriate bureau. This bureau in turn *mails* back its reply. Under the very best conditions, this requires several days, and the pyramider, utilizing weekends and holidays and especially busy seasons, makes sure that the best conditions don't prevail. The time gap works just as well for the retail swindler as for the swindling retailer.

There are safeguards. If a credit bureau receives three or more credit inquiries regarding the same person in less than sixty days, the file is tagged for observation. But even then there is rarely immediate action unless other suspicious factors are present, since many people moving to new communities open several new accounts shortly after arrival in order to establish their credit. The credit bureau does send out cards notifying the inquiring stores of the number of new accounts, and a good store credit manager regards these cautions seriously. But chances are, if the swindler uses a bogus name, out-of-town references, and moves fast, nothing will stop him. If he uses *different* bogus names and references, his chances of escaping detection increase along with his take.

Occasionally a gypster will use a legitimate name and address and references—only without the real person's knowledge. Or he may play the game of *doubles*.

On an individual scale this works as follows: John W. Fortesque is an honest customer and he's in the men's department of a large department store, buying a suit. "F-O-R-T-E-S-Q-U-E," he spells it out for the clerk, "John Q.," adding his address. The swindler, who has been browsing nearby, waits to see that the transaction is completed satisfactorily, then goes to other departments of the store, where he runs up charges on Mr. Fortesque's account.

This can be played on a larger scale.

William Redding, a Burlington, Vermont, storekeeper, learned of an interesting similarity. There was a soft-drink bottling firm in Amsterdam, New York, called William D. Redding, Inc. The more the Vermont Redding thought about the New York Redding, the more interesting the coincidence became, especially when he learned the firm had an exceptional Dun and Bradstreet credit rating, which he hadn't. During a four-month period, the Vermont Redding placed orders for some $6400 in merchandise by convincing wholesalers that his store was a subsidiary of the New York firm. Caught by the POD, he was found guilty on six counts of mail fraud and eight counts of fraud by wire and conspiracy, and given three years in prison on one count and five-year suspended sentences on each of the thirteen other counts.

Decidedly professional was a forty-three-year-old Baltimore man who turned a Park Avenue telephone-answering service into a head-quarters for fraud. As he explained to the young lady who ran the answering service, his was a large company and he was constantly receiving telephone calls from stores wanting to verify the employ-ment of his personnel. To eliminate this bother, he would furnish her with a list of his employees, and his employees would be given the number of the answering service to use on their credit applica-tions. When anyone called to ask about someone on the list, she was to verify the person's employment, as well as his excellent credit rating. What he didn't tell her was that each of the employees bore an amazing resemblance to his employer. By the time the young lady's naïveté wore thin (it did seem odd that the company em-ployed only men) and she voiced her suspicions to the police, the swindler had taken numerous concerns for some $50,000 in mer-chandise.

In most of the foregoing cases, the frauds could have been stopped by a reasonably selective credit policy, a careful credit manager, and an alert local credit bureau. The last two ingredients are often pres-ent; the first is becoming increasingly rare. Until it returns, if it ever does, the equation *Loose credit=Vulnerability* will apply.

The Busy Bankrupts

There is an easier, and far safer, way to play the credit game. It requires no artifice. You simply open as many accounts and charge as much merchandise as you can (resalable merchandise preferred), and when you finally reach the point where your credit is cut off, you declare bankruptcy. This can be done in each of the fifty states: it is least desirable to try it in Maine, which still has debtor's-prison laws, and most advantageous in California, as the aforementioned ex-model discovered. One tabloid writer dubbed Miss Clark "The Queen of Credit" when it was revealed that she had stuck 64 cloth-ing and furniture stores, 30 florists, 32 doctors, 6 dentists, and a legion of other merchants for $86,249 in unpaid bills on 511 dif-ferent charge accounts. All this while working intermittently as a $60-a-week medical secretary.

In recent years, personal bankruptcy filings have increased at a fantastic rate. From 1958 to 1962, they jumped from 63,617 to 132,135, a gain of almost 110 percent. There can be no doubt that most of these were all too legitimate, a direct product of modern debt merchandising. But some were legal fraud. Crime *does* pay, so long as the law doesn't call it crime.

When an individual decides to file for bankruptcy, he can choose one of two ways. He can file under Chapter XIII of the Federal Bankruptcy Law under what is known as the "wage-earner" plan, whereby he agrees to repay his creditors in installments over a certain period of time. Or he can file a straight voluntary bankruptcy, whereby he agrees to let his attachable assets be sold off for the benefit of his creditors. Straight bankruptcy filings outnumber wage-earner petitions by seven to one.

California leads all other states in bankruptcy filings. It is also the most liberal in what it allows the bankrupt to retain. In the Golden State a bankrupt may keep: all necessary household furniture and fixtures, including one television set; one shotgun; $1000 in savings and loan deposits; three cows and suckling calves or four sows and suckling pigs; and all his life insurance, so long as the premiums do not exceed $500 a year. This isn't all: there is the matter of real estate. If the bankrupt's equity in his home is under $12,500 and if he has filed a declaration of homestead, he can keep the house, no matter what it is actually worth. If his equity is larger or if he hasn't filed such a declaration, he still gets the first $12,500 on the forced sale to use in buying another home.

There is a once-affluent businessman now residing in fashionable Bel Air who, by combining two strategic mortgages with a homestead exemption, has managed to retain intact his not unostentatious mansion. He has for company no cows and suckling calves or sows and suckling pigs, but he doesn't seem to mind, preferring instead his extensive collection of Rembrandts, paintings being exempt from seizure as necessary household furnishings.

The Corporate Assassins

A new breed of murder specialist has appeared on the American scene during the past decade. According to Nathaniel E. Kossack, chief of the Justice Department's fraud division, there has been a tremendous increase in the number of planned, criminally fraudulent bankruptcies. Between 200 and 300 of the nation's 16,000 annual commercial and industrial bankruptcies are known to be fraudulent, with a cost to American consumers and taxpayers of between $50 and $75 million.[1]

The game is not new, but the techniques are. Back in the twenties and thirties, the great financial swindler Serge Rubinstein once explained his own *m.o.* in two short sentences: "I figure out how much a company is worth dead—not living. I'm most interested in finding out if the liquidation price of the company's assets is more than the price of the stock." Today, according to Kossack, it is not the cash but the credit that is all-important. A syndicate, or group of four or five persons, often with underworld backgrounds, will find a small merchandising concern which is sound and has a good credit history, although it may currently bear heavy liabilities, permitting them to buy it cheaply.

There is a known period of time after the sale of a business before the new owners can be evaluated by Dun and Bradstreet. Working during this interim, the swindlers make a large cash deposit in a nearby bank to establish a good local credit rating. Then they order huge quantities of merchandise for which they make almost immediate cash payment, further boosting their credit rating.

The merchandise is then moved into quick-sale outlets and sold for as much as 25 percent below cost.

The next month an even greater quantity is ordered, and still more the third month—but payment is delayed until finally the firm is forced into bankruptcy.

By this time the goods are gone and the money dispersed in such a manner that it is impossible to recover.

As this chapter was being written, the U.S. Senate investigations subcommittee announced that it was investigating a group of "fast-buck artists" who, through a series of manipulated loans and *a total cash investment of less than $65,000,* allegedly purchased control of *eight* Colorado banks, whose total assets were in the hundreds of millions. Though stopped by the Colorado Banking Department shortly after accomplishing this spectacular feat, the men, it is alleged, had already netted $420,000 through forged notes, fictitious-name loans, and similar chicanery, bringing one of the banks to the point of insolvency. The days of Rubinstein may be gone, but apparently they aren't forgotten.

The Advance-fee Swindle

What with shoplifting, thieving employees, merchandising swindles, stock shrinkage, and similar trials and tribulations, it isn't too surprising that some merchants reach the point where they want nothing more than to sell their businesses and seek less fraud-prone surroundings. Those who do so may find there is a new swindle specially designed and waiting for them: the advance-fee racket.

Working under the cover of impressive firm names and using persuasive "buyers," the advance-fee operators seek out small businesses that are in trouble, offering to sell them for their owners at prices far above their actual worth, in return for an *advance* fee of 3 to 5 percent of the anticipated net. All the victim actually obtains for his money is a promise and perhaps a small listing in a mailing piece that real-estate firms throw away without even opening. Since this swindle first appeared in the 1950s, annual losses have run at a fairly steady $50 million, despite numerous arrests and convictions. When the BBB, POD, FTC, and other law-enforcement groups began focusing the public spotlight on the racket, one of the biggest operators in the field put out a special pamphlet entitled *How To Sell Your Business and Beat the Con Men*, which his salesmen distributed to potential marks. Its disarming effectiveness would have made even the Yellow Kid jealous.

CHAPTER 14

MAN VS. THE MACHINE

OR

HOW TO BEAT

THE BELL SYSTEM

> Nothing says you like your voice.
>
> Bell System
> advertisement

As EVERY Sunday-school student knows, there is one infallible test of honesty: "If you found a dime in the slot of a pay phone, and knew no one was watching, what would you do?"

The moral is inescapable: If you wouldn't steal from A.T.&T., you wouldn't steal from anyone.

The number and variety of telephone swindles in use today might be attributed to such early religious training, were there not far better reasons, first and foremost that it's remarkably easy to cheat the phone company, whether of a dime, the cost of a long-distance call, or the proceeds of a pay-phone collection box. At present there are more than eighty million telephones in the United States. Each is capable of defrauding its parent company. Of these, more than one million are coin-operated, their coin boxes holding in excess of $485 million in revenues. The majority of these phones are accessible, and vulnerable, to the public twenty-four hours a day. Moreover, telephone fraud offers its perpetrators a better-than-average chance of anonymity, a not unpopular justification ("They're a monopoly, they can afford it"), and that rare but very real satisfaction of proving that man is still the master of his own creation, the machine.

The most amazing thing about phone fraud is not that there is so much of it but that, as compared to fraud losses in most other businesses, its yield has been kept so low.

The Vanishing Slug and Other Coin Tricks

In 1889, thirteen years after Alexander Graham Bell's invention of the telephone, the first successful public coin-operated telephone was installed in Hartford, Connecticut, on the ground floor of the Old Hartford Bank, Main Street and Central Row. The occasion was momentous, and that first day only specially invited dignitaries, prominent citizens, local, state, and federal officials were allowed to test the innovation. There is a legend in the Bell System that when the coin box was opened that night the coins were outnumbered by the slugs.

Apocryphal or true, the swindle potentials of the telephone did not long go unrealized. Those early slugs have proven especially durable, in 1963 accounting for a loss of about a half-million dollars to A.T.&T. The problem of accurately measuring fraud has been mentioned; here, one would imagine, exact statistics would be available—so many slugs were used as substitutes for so much money. This would be true if someone hadn't invented the "bobbing" and "vanishing" slugs.

The most common slug, in use for more years than the Bell System would like to remember, was simply lead melted and molded into the form of a nickel. Until well into the 1930s, these could be bought in most cigar stores and pool rooms, 100 for a dollar. Laws making their use illegal did little to decrease their currency, nor were company engineers successful in their attempts to design a mechanism which would reject slugs automatically. Devices which "felt" the coin's features or measured its weight proved unworkable because of the wear of ordinary usage. Not until the passage of laws prohibiting their possession did the slug trade diminish. For a time cheap rings, bent to coin size, were in brief vogue, followed by foreign coins the same size as the nickel, dime, or quarter.* Altered

---

* In the 1950s the appearance of the German *pfennig*, then worth about ten to a cent and exactly the same size as the New York subway token, necessitated a change in all Manhattan's subway-turnstile mechanisms.

coins—pennies reduced to dime size by acid, nickels smashed into quarter shape with a hammer—were also major problems until the passage of strong laws prohibiting the mutiliation of currency. As recently as 1963, however, Secret Service agents broke up an acid-dime counterfeiting ring on the campus of Oregon State College. Those who question the practical value of a college education should have some of their doubts assuaged by chapter's end: in recent years, many of the more novel telephone frauds have first appeared at America's respectable academies of learning, together with some of the oldest tricks newly resurrected—proof, depending on one's point of view, of the dangerous liberalism or creeping conservatism of the modern college student.

Not long ago, telephone-company investigators and local police raided a "vanishing slug" factory located in a Columbia University dormitory. This was one of the more conservative frauds. Though both the date of origin and inventor go unrecorded, the vanishing slug was in widespread use early in this century, in cold-water tenements with coin-operated hot-water heaters. No special skill was required in the manufacturing, and the equipment itself was simple and inexpensive: a piece of wax, paraffin, or chewing gum, plus a few drops of water. The wax was pressed around a quarter to make a mold; the mold was filled with water and placed in the icebox to freeze. The resultant product worked just as well as a quarter slug, but had the added advantage of disappearing almost immediately after use. The Columbia students were easily trapped shortly after moisture was found in the phone coin box, as only one room on that dormitory floor had a refrigerator. Too, the students, with less common sense than the tenement housewives, had made clay molds.

The Mechanics of Telephone Swindlery

Modern Americans are much too wise and all-knowing to fall for one hoax perpetrated on early telephone subscribers. A wag posing as a telephone-company maintenance man would call dozens of people, warning that at two that afternoon the company was going to blow the dust out of the phone lines. To prevent a bad mess, the company advised putting sheets or pillowcases over the instrument. It is said that sometimes the linen remained there for days, the householders carefully keeping their distance even when the telephone rang. We know better today, of course. Still, ninety years after its invention, the working principles of the telephone remain at least a partial mystery to most adults. As a test you might consider the following: when you make a long-distance call from a pay phone, does the operator count the money you deposit or is there a coin-counting mechanism built into the phone box? The former, of course, is correct: the operator counts the money, by listening to the sounds the coins make when they strike the bell mechanism inside the box. The sounds are so familiar we tend to forget them. This is the difference between the accustomed American and the successful swindler: the latter can't afford indifference. Habit patterns are almost invariably his downfall, while lack of observation and curiosity would deprive him of two essential tools of his trade. One reason frauds such as the pyramiding of "floor limit" charges mentioned in Chapter 13 remain relatively low in frequency is because most people are unaware of them. Yet anyone with several charge accounts has probably charged and taken items out of a store after merely signing his or her name, seeing but not observing the fraud potentials. Since the 1890s, the telephone swindler has had his own ironic interpretation of the words "bell system."

Coin bobbing was one of the earliest of such frauds. By drilling a hole through a nickel and attaching a piece of string, or by soldering a thin wire to the edge of the coin, the phone cheat could make his call and have his coin too. This was easily worked, since the bell was located high up in the box or housing, close to the coin slot. Engineers in the Bell Telephone Laboratories succeeded in thwarting this practice by lowering the bell and narrowing the slots. The single multicoin slot, now coming into use, makes return of the coin impossible because of the circuitous route it follows.

In the fall of 1963, the manager of a Mount Vernon, Illinois, laundromat found his coin-changing machine rifled of about $150, though he had the only key and there was no evidence of forced entry. Not until the box was disassembled did the police find a telltale clue, a tiny fiber of cotton thread. The thief had simply drilled a hole in a 50¢ piece, attached a string, and bobbed the coin in and out until the box exhausted its change. Yet coin bobbing is as old as the vending-machine business—so old in fact that some vending-machine manufacturers eliminated the turning-mechanism which formerly cut the wire or string (or jammed the machine), assuming, erroneously, the trick to be forgotten and the safeguard no longer necessary.

At least a dozen different swindles capitalizing on the bell system came into use. It remained for one imaginative swindler to devise a method which didn't use coins at all, except for the dime needed to get the dial tone, which is automatically returned on long-distance calls. Using a portable recorder he taped the bell sounds, then, when making a call, would play them back for the operator's benefit. As a result, the bell sounds in the newest pay phones are heard only by the operator.

The following, slightly more complicated scheme was widely used during the latter half of the 1930s.

On the face of each pay-station telephone-box housing was stamped the name of the telephone company. In California, for example, the lettering read *Pacific States Pay Station.* Inside the housing, directly behind the last two words, and exactly between the two *a*'s, was a lever which controlled the registering of the coins as they passed into the coin box. The swindler would pry up the upper housing just enough to insert a thin piece of cardboard about one-half inch in width. He then placed his long-distance call. Each time he dropped a coin through the return slot, he pushed the cardboard against the lever. The bell would ring, and the coin would pass on out through the return slot. The company first attempted to forestall this by covering the lever mechanism with cardboard, but later had to resort to a metal cover.

Swindlers then approached from a new direction. They found that while a special, not easily duplicated key was needed to open the coin-box lock, the lock on the upper housing was easily picked. Once open, a piece of black thread was tied to the lever and carried over to the receiver hook. The call was made, only this time a tug on the thread accomplished what the piece of cardboard had done previously.

Another mechanical swindle, requiring far less preparation and equipment, was effective until well into the 1950s. With a pocket knife, a little paint was scraped off the outside of the telephone-box housing; a common straight pin was then stuck far enough into the phone's outgoing line to make contact with the copper wires. By applying the head of the pin to the scraped area, the coin-box mechanism could be short-circuited.

Such frauds have kept Bell Telephone Laboratories designers busy. No sooner does a new model appear with built-in safeguards circumventing one or more current frauds than one or more unforeseen frauds make their appearance, as when a five-year-old of extraordinary lung power was caught emptying a box by putting his mouth over the coin return slot and sucking the coins out.

Many of the mechanical tricks in present use are directed at cheating telephone users rather than the company. One is the "stuffed box." A swindler will stuff a wad of paper as far up the coin return slot as his finger will reach. Anyone attempting to use the phone after this will discover he can get neither a dial tone nor his dime back. Later the swindler will return, remove the paper with a hooked wire, and collect the accumulated coins. Often such swindlers work in pairs, with regular routes or territories, one stuffing or removing while the other serves as lookout. A well-located booth may yield three or four dollars a day, while the pair may service two- or three-dozen booths. Two similar tricks are now having a special vogue in New York City, where teenage gangs have been coin collecting in train, bus, and airline terminals to such an extent that getting a dial tone is a decided gamble.

The simplest technique is to jam a straight pin into the phone just above the receiver hook. The caller lifts the receiver and deposits his dime but, since the receiver does not make connection, fails to get a dial tone. Nor is the coin returned, not until the young swindlers return for their pins.

The other method is only a little more complicated. Over the years telephone-company engineers have put more and more of the phone wiring inside the housing. On all but the newest-model pay phones, however, underneath the "writing desk" (that narrow panel where one hypothetically has room to consult the directory or jot down numbers or notes) there are several wires leading into an auxiliary box. When these wires are disconnected, by yanking, the phone is made inoperative. As before, the caller loses a dime. The youths return, retouch the wires, lift the receiver, drop it, and pocket the proceeds. The problem has become so extensive, despite numerous arrests, that one radio commentator has recommended that New Yorkers wanting to make a call from a pay station first bang the front of the box sharply to make sure the phone isn't loose, put in one nickel, and, if no click is heard, forego putting in the second 5¢ piece. Accepting the half-swindle as one of the economic facts of life requires a certain degree of sophistication.

Lock-picking is another of the arts of telephone fraud. Losses by this method have been greatly reduced by a double-box, double-lock arrangement, with the actual coin box now placed well behind the outer housing.

These tricks are subtle compared to those which account for A.T.&T.'s second largest loss.* During 1963, the company lost approximately $1.6 million in cash to coin-box looters; in damaged equipment the cost ran to $2.4 million. A common technique was ripping the box from the wall with a chain attached to a car bumper and smashing it open with a sledge hammer.

In January 1964, the New York *Journal American* ran an article entitled "An Addict Makes a Call on a Phone Booth."[1] A young narcotics addict, caught (and photographed) while looting a coin box, observed that most Manhattan phones could be tapped for about $40. "That's eight $5 bags of horse, two days of fixes depending on your habit. It's a fad, you know. Word goes out that the phones are good in a certain place and you can work them for a couple of weeks . . ." In the same article the reporter, after a block-by-block survey of East Harlem, found that of every ten pay phones only one was in working condition. The New York *Times*, in July of the same year, reported the results of its own survey of Manhattan sidewalk and subway pay phones, finding that nearly half—46 out of 100—were out of commission at least once during the month due to larceny or vandalism.[2] Surprisingly, one New York Bell official reports that, to date, there has never been a coin-box looted in the Bowery.

Compared with other businesses, theft and fraud losses for the entire Bell System are remarkably low, less than $10 million in 1963 against a profit of $1.5 billion. Though the 1963 figures for coin-box theft represented a 4 percent increase over 1962, the rise was attributed to the installation of New York's new so-called "tamperproof" parking meters, there being a clear ratio between phone coin-box and parking-meter thefts: when one goes up, the other goes down. Losses to slugs have been steadily decreasing year by year, as have losses to most other types of *measurable* fraud (about $270,000 in 1963). The revamping of all Bell System pay stations,

---

* The largest known loss sustained by the Bell System is not from fraud, coin-box looting, or equipment destruction, but theft of phones for resale. No accurate figures are available, but it is known that the amount exceeds the $4 million loss to coin-box theft and equipment destruction. In a single recent case, two men were arrested in a New Jersey motel; in their possession were keys to every Bell System equipment supply room in Brooklyn and Queens. The company is most reluctant to discuss this particular case, noting only that the keys were copies. One highly placed Bell official admits privately that the loss in this instance may exceed $6 million.

now already in progress, is expected to reduce coin-theft losses drastically, though it is presumed that thieves and swindlers will, as usual, be up to the challenge. The new booths are open-faced and remain lighted around the clock; eventually each will be equipped with a silent alarm system which, when tampering occurs, will result in immediate police notification. There is a new, supposedly more secure system of coin-box locks; armored cords are being used to deter theft of headsets; while the use of special backboards, security studs, and through-bolt devices will, it is believed, render strong-arm methods more difficult. Another deterrent, particularly of frauds, is the inauguration of Centralized Ticket Investigation, a system at present still in limited use, whereby eventually the mechanics of all long-distance calls will be recorded electronically, providing a method of accurately billing individual calls as well as enabling investigators to spot pattern irregularities not otherwise observable.

In each of the foregoing crimes, the swindler has left certain clues, if not to his identity at least evidence that a fraudulent act has occurred: a smashed pay phone; a slug; a coin box short of its usual amount. There are other telephone frauds only partly reflected in the statistics, since there is no way to estimate the extent of their use. Requiring no tampering with the equipment, workable from any type phone, they leave few if any clues indicating a fraud has been committed.

Codes

These are as varied as the imaginations of the people who use them. There is at present no way to estimate their number or frequency of use or the amount in long-distance charges they subtract from telephone-company revenues.

A New York advertising man who lives in Connecticut wants to let his wife know which train to meet. Sometime between three and three-fifteen each afternoon he calls home. His wife counts the number of times the phone rings, consults her marked Hartford-New Haven schedule, and is waiting when the train pulls in. This, the ring code, is assumed to be the most popular code now in use. Barring the tipoff of a spiteful "friend," it is presently undetectable (though, with Centralized Ticket Investigation, the regularity might betray the pattern). It does have decided drawbacks. The saving is small and the inconvenience large—one member of the family having to be home at the time of the call—and it makes no allowance for the human element: the absent-minded husband who forgets to call, the neighbor who unknowingly calls at the usual time and rings a half-dozen times before hanging up; the day the husband and the neighbor and the butcher call one after the other . . . But it is widely used, and the fact that it is indicates something about our parsimony or our standards of morality or both.

Also common is the college-student gambit. Suzie Smith is away at college. Too busy to write, she wants to talk to her parents without having to pay for the call. To do this, she places a long-distance person-to-person call to herself at her home phone number. The conversation may go something like this:

Mrs. Smith: Hello.
Suzie: Operator, would you please tell me when my three minutes are up?
Operator: Yes . . . I have a long-distance call for Susan Smith.
Mrs. Smith: She's not here. This is her mother. Can I take the message?
Operator: Will you speak to anyone else at this number?
Suzie: No, I want to speak to her personally.
Operator: When do you expect her back?
Mrs. Smith: Late.
Suzie: Very late?
Mrs. Smith: Yes.
Operator: Do you wish to leave your number or will you call back?
Suzie: I'm going out. I'll have to call back.

Seemingly an ordinary dialogue, but in a few well-chosen words Suzie has managed to tell her mother that she is well and happy but too busy to write (by just making the call); that her schoolwork is going well (by placing the call to Susan rather than Suzie Smith); that she needs more money (the reference to the time); that she will be coming home over the weekend (personally). Mrs. Smith in turn has asked if she will be home Friday night (late=Friday); Suzie has said no, she won't be there until Saturday (very late= Saturday). She has also told her mother that she has a date (I'm going out . . .).

Any departure from routine, extra dialogue, or a tone of amateur conspiracy may indicate to the operator that a code is being used, and she can cut off one party while talking to the other. The simpler the code the less easily detected.

Suzie and her hometown boy friend also have a code, which enables one or the other to save the difference between station-to-station and person-to-person rates. He places a call to Miss Suzette Smith. Suzie's roommates have been alerted. If Suzie is out, they say just that. If she is there, or answers the phone herself, the reply is "She's gone to the movies." The boy friend then cancels the call and calls back station-to-station.

A traveling salesman, who called home each night to let his wife know his whereabouts, arrived in Detroit. He placed his person-to-person call to Mr. Homer V. Hickle. His wife answered and informed the operator that Mr. Hickle was out for the evening. The cuteness of the code, in this instance, led to the salesman's apprehension and conviction.

The use of a long firm name—such as Smith, Smith, Jones and Smyth—offers the possibility of a long message, even longer if it is made to seem that one firm is calling another.

In 1962, a number of motel operators in Utah were apprehended for using still another code. Each of the motels, located in various parts of the state, had one unlisted number on its switchboard, known only to the other motel managers. When making reservations they would use this number, the number of rings indicating the type of accommodations desired, the switchboard operator answering only if there was such a vacancy.

False Charges

This fraud leaves a trail of evidence; sometimes, however, the trail leads nowhere.

You place a long-distance call by direct dialing. The operator comes in to ask "Your number, please?" You tell her and the call goes through.

Probably everyone has wondered what would happen if he gave the operator a number other than his own. Anyone who has received a telephone bill with a charge for a call he didn't make knows what happens. Though spokesmen for A.T.&T. minimize the extent of this problem, it is one reason why long-distance calls are now itemized on all telephone bills.

Obviously the operator doesn't know your number. Otherwise she

wouldn't have to ask. The question is: Can she tell if you are lying?
The answer: Sometimes.

Exactly what does she know? Before you've said a word (or a
number, if you have all-digit dialing), the operator already knows
(from the circuit over which your call has passed) your area code
and the first three digits of your telephone number (the old exchange number, MUrray Hill 3, for example, or a continent's width
away, KLondike 8). The last four numbers she doesn't know. But she
does know one thing the caller presumably doesn't, that in those
last four digits (0000 to 9999) scattered blocks of numbers, different in each city, have been assigned to pay-station phones. This
prevents the charging of a long-distance call to a pay station; it also
puts a partial check on the manufacturing of random numbers. At
present a number can be fabricated safely only by a change in either
or both of the last two digits.*

Once such a call goes through, the charges are billed to the fraudulent number. If the user of the number examines his bill closely and
complains that he never made such a call, the company will call the
dialed number, noting that on such-and-such a date a long-distance
call was received from said city at said exchange and asking for the
name and number of the party who placed the call.

Usually, if no prearrangement has been made, the correct number
will be supplied. If the person replies, as some do, "I don't know
who that was, that was a wrong number," the party is in trouble,
since the length of the call testifies otherwise. In such instances the
number may be watched for reoccurrences, or the call may be billed
directly to that number. In any case, the complicity of the second
party increases the criminal charge, if the initiating party is caught,
from simple fraud to the far-more-serious conspiracy to defraud.

This takes care of the amateurs. The professional phone cheat,
aware of the loopholes in the system, is more selective, restricting
his calls to hotels and businesses, usually safe, for rarely do their
switchboard operators keep records of incoming calls.

A reverse switch on this trick is sometimes effective. On some
pretext the swindler visits the offices of several companies, noting
the busiest and most understaffed switchboard. When he wishes to
make a long-distance call he then calls that company and asks the
operator for an outside line; if she is particularly harassed, she may

* Although the odds against such a happening are phenomenal, some years ago a
West Coast long-distance operator was momentarily nonplussed on hearing a
caller recite her own home phone number.

plug him into one automatically. He then makes his long-distance call, charging it to the company's number.

Most party-givers know too well still another telephone fraud— that of the guest who assumes that, in addition to drinks and canapes, long-distance calls are on the house. As a result, many people have locks on their phones which secure the dial wheel, preventing its use. The knowing swindler isn't inconvenienced. He is aware that the dial itself is only a circuit breaker, that by pushing the button under the receiver the same number of times as the place of each digit on the dial, he can accomplish the same thing. Ten pushes gives him the long-distance operator.

The presumptuous guest will probably always remain a problem, but most other false-charge frauds are now on their way out, as eventually all origin numbers will be recorded electronically. This system is already in effect in some areas.

The Telephone Credit Card

Of all the credit cards, now in the hundreds, that issued by the Bell System would appear to be the most vulnerable. It is the one card which is never shown, its user never seen. To charge a call, the cardholder has only to give the operator the number on his card.

To fabricate this number is very simple.

The 1965 card instructed the customer: "Say to the operator THIS IS A CREDIT CARD CALL. CARD NUMBER . . . ," followed by the number.

The number consisted of: the first three digits of the cardholder's telephone number (the exchange in numerical form); a dash; the last four digits of his telephone number; another dash; and a four- or five-digit suffix. The suffix consisted of: a letter representing the current year (for 1965 this was K), followed by a three- or four-digit number. This last number is related to the area code and is the same on all cards in that area.

To learn the letter for the current year and the area number, the swindler must have a legitimate credit card. This is easily obtained. The telephone company will issue a card to anyone requesting one, so long as he has a telephone and has paid his bills regularly.

To manufacture a fictitious number, the swindler then need only consult the telephone book, pick out any legitimate number, and add on the letter and the area number.

"The practices for the use of credit cards have been so arranged that a minimum amount of information is required, thus making their use as convenient as possible," observed Donald F. MacEachern, Chief Accountant for A.T.&T., in a recent issue of *Bell Telephone Magazine*. "This convenience stimulates usage and we want to keep it that way . . ."[3] It also simplifies fraud, but apparently the company believes convenience and usage outweigh the risk.

Yet, despite its simplicity, of all the major credit cards, that of the Bell System has the lowest annual loss. For 1963 the total loss was so low—less than a quarter of a million—that both American Express and Diners' Club consulted Bell to determine how losses were kept down. The answer was simple but probably not very helpful. Unlike the other credit cards, which can be used to pay for meals, lodging, gifts, round-the-world flights, the Bell System card is for a single, relatively low-priced service—a long-distance telephone call. It differs too in that there is no possibility of kickback fraud. And its fraudulent use has all the built-in liabilities of the other false-charge swindles—two parties are involved in every call, one usually known to the company, while the blocks of pay-station numbers and other devices serve as additional partial safety checks. The telephone credit card is beatable—but only penny-ante swindlers consider it worth the risk and effort.

The Black and Blue Boxes

Of all the telephone frauds, this accounts for the lowest known losses. Its known incidence rate is probably lower than that of *any* telephone fraud—to date, only twenty-one cases having been discovered.

A.T.&T. officials draw little consolation from these facts. It isn't the "known" which worries them but the "unknown." For most of these twenty-one cases came to light either by tipoff or accident. There is at present no way to detect this fraud when it is in operation, and it leaves no clues. It may be worked on any private telephone in the United States. And even when detected, there is no basis for even a guess as to the money it subtracts from Bell System revenues. Of all the telephone frauds, this has the highest future swindle potential. It might be circumvented—but at present only by revamping the electronic dialing machinery of the entire Bell System. To give an indication of how seriously it is taken by A.T.&T., all recent cases involving it have been heard in chambers, closed to the public and the press.

Late on the night of March 25, 1961, New Rochelle, New York, police, acting on a tipoff, simultaneously raided three houses suspected of being the nucleus of a large bookmaking ring. As usual in such raids, they were accompanied by telephone-company investigators. What was found surprised everyone. Police were amazed at the size of the operation: betting slips and layoff records indicated a $30-thousand-a-day or $10-million-a-year business. The telephone men were less amazed than disturbed at what they discovered: attached to each of the more than thirty-five telephones was a small box, no larger than a brick, containing tubes, wires, printed circuits, and various other electronic components.

Both the number and the subtlety of these particular devices worried the investigators. When the first of these devices had appeared some dozen years earlier, Bell scientists had nicknamed it the "black box." This model was the simplest and most ingenious yet to appear. Attached to the wires of a telephone, the box put out an electronic signal which interfered with the Bell System's long-distance timing mechanism, blocking any record of incoming dialed telephone calls. A bettor could call in from any pay station in the country, and at the conclusion of the call the device would signal the pay station that the call was incomplete, not only erasing any record of the call but returning the caller's money. It was, from the bookies' point of view, a perfect invention.

It took telephone investigators less than a week to trace the components of the device back to their inventor-manufacturer in Florida, a former lineman for Southern Bell who, using his living room as his workshop, was able to turn out ten boxes a day, for which bookies were paying $1500 apiece. A.T.&T. investigators considered themselves phenomenally lucky: to date, only 100 of the devices had been sold, most of which they were able to track down. Convicted on a misdemeanor charge of violating a state law prohibiting the attachment of unauthorized equipment to a telephone, the inventor was also later enjoined from further manufacture of the devices or distribution of his plans.

The black box continues to make periodic reappearances (in 1963, seventy were found in an abandoned station wagon in Mamaroneck, New York). No one knows how many are currently in use. A Bell official states, wistfully, "We'd like to think there are very few."

One evening in February 1964, three Cornell University engineering students were entertaining some forty of their fraternity brothers with a demonstration of a remarkable device they had invented—when they were rudely interrupted by a police raiding party, who arrested the three young electronic geniuses and seized their device. This was the so-called "blue box." While not novel, Dayton Garlick, chief security officer of the New York Telephone Company, pronounced it "quite an ingenious device." Used when making outgoing calls, the twelve-tube contrivance fed electronic impulses into the mouthpiece of the telephone so that the call bypassed the telephone company's monitoring equipment. Long-distance calls in any number could be made without charge or record. Since 1960, the blue box has made four appearances, all on college campuses: at Stanford, Rose Polytechnic Institute, the University of Denver, and Cornell.

Despite the potential threat of these and other devices, telephone swindlery is one of the few types of fraud which has not increased in recent years. One reason has been cited—the low cost of the swindled commodity, the telephone call. There are other reasons.

Until a few years ago the communications industry was faced with a legal void. In general, theft of communications services, of whatever kind, was not a crime. Bringing the problem before legislative groups, A.T.&T.'s attorneys succeeded in having laws passed which made such thefts criminal acts in all the states in which the company operates.

Since 1960, all types of theft and fraud have been handled by a single security unit within the Bell System, the unit's duties being threefold: prevention, detection, and prosecution. Though the total investigative staff numbers under 400, their effectiveness in the last category betters even that of the U.S. Postal Service: in 1963, of approximately 2500 arrests, all but 300 resulted in convictions.

But perhaps the greatest deterrent is the fact that people are dependent on telephones. All states now have regulations allowing the company to refuse service to anyone caught ducking charges for calls.

The Electronic Con Man

Every coin-operated device—Nevada slots, Coke machines, public lockers, automats, jukeboxes, subway turnstiles, pinball machines—

has gone through its own swindle evolution. In our increasingly automated, computerized age there seems no reason to suppose that
such fraud will decrease. Recently it was revealed that some 200
people on the New York City payroll were promoted to higher status
than they merited through manipulation of an IBM machine. Already in some fields, such as banking, there are machines investigating other machines. One needn't wait until 1984 to see an electronic
detective chasing an electronic con man: that day is already here.
Still, despite all the publicity given "tamperproof" parking meters
and similar devices, it is decidedly risky to discount the human
element.

In mid-1964, as a service to its guests, San Francisco's famed
St. Francis Hotel placed an electronic dollar-bill changer in its lobby.
San Francisco *Chronicle* columnist Herb Caen remarked on the innovation in his column, wondering how the machine knew the difference between a dollar bill and an ordinary piece of paper.

Within a few days he had an answer. An anonymous reader wrote
in, "It doesn't." Enclosing a fake dollar bill from Woolworth's, plainly
marked "Play Money," the reader advised, "Don't get carried away.
That machine can be fooled every time."

Slipping into the lobby of the St. Francis as surreptitiously as a
well-known columnist can, Caen approached the machine and
slipped in the bogus bill.

"I don't mind telling you I expected it to light up, read Tilt! blow
horns, bells, and whistles and cry Thief!" Caen later wrote in his
column. "But nothing happened. Except that a dollar in change
immediately appeared in the tray below."

Only then noticing a small sign on the machine, which said that
the U.S. Government would fine anyone $1000 for using phony
money, Caen confessed and presented his loot to the credit manager
of the St. Francis, who accepted it in horrified disbelief.

A call to the man who distributed the electronic marvel, however,
brought complete unconcern. "We have the most trouble with guys
who make Xerox or Thermofax copies of real dollar bills," the man
told Caen. "But that $1000 fine scares most people off. And every
piece of fake money is turned over to the police for fingerprints.

"We've had tricks played on us from here to San Jose," the distributor admitted, "but it's still a dandy little machine."[4]

CHAPTER 15

INSURANCE FRAUD:

THEY CAN AFFORD IT —

BUT CAN YOU?

> Human nature constitutes part of
> the evidence in every law suit.
>
> Green vs. Harris, 11 R.I.5

T HE California Highway Patrol car maneuvered out of the traffic on busy Nimitz Freeway south of Oakland, California, and parked on the shoulder of the road. Its driver looked at his watch, sat back, and lit a cigarette. The patrolman, forty-four, a veteran with thirteen years on the Oakland police force and nine years on the patrol, was habitually punctual. This time he was decidedly early. He had arrived at the scene of the accident even before the cars which were supposed to crash.

On a highway outside Fredericktown, Missouri, a Pontiac sped around a big semitrailer, then suddenly slammed on its brakes. The cab of the trailer smashed into the rear of the car, flipping it into a ditch. When police arrived they found the car's occupants—a young man, his wife, and their nephew—partly paralyzed and in excruciating pain. Or so it seemed. It was an act, perfected during the course of twenty-three similar accidents in nine other states.

The woman, pinched for shoplifting in the East Coast department store, sobbed uncontrollably, refusing to answer questions. Her answers weren't actually required; it was an ironclad case, the store detective having seen her slip the angora sweater into her shopping bag. She was offered the usual out—if she signed a paper admitting her theft, and promised never to come back to the store, she would be released. She refused. The manager called the police. Fingerprinted, photographed, and booked for petty theft, the woman was allowed one telephone call. She called her attorney. On his arrival she produced, in front of witnesses, a sales receipt for the sweater, bought and paid for two days earlier.

The woman won her suit for false arrest, collecting $9000 from the store—or, rather, the store's insurance company—in an out-of-court settlement.

The Missouri trio collected only jail sentences for their carefully staged accident, though they had collected some $20,000 in bogus claims on the twenty-three preceding it.

On the strength of the patrolman's fake accident report, the "victims" of the Nimitz Freeway "accident" received $10,000 in insurance payments. Twenty-one people were eventually arrested in the California ring and accused of filing fraudulent claims on spurious automobile accidents. The officer pleaded guilty to his part in this and a similar accident, was ordered to make restitution (his cut was only $600), and sentenced to one year in jail.

The name of the game is False Claim, alias Beat the Insurance Company. Rich men exaggerate minor dents into expensive collisions; poor men learn the ins and outs of collecting unemployment insurance while still working; beggermen file umpteen nuisance suits cheaper to settle than fight; doctors pad injury claims, overtreat patients, and legitimize the fraudulent; some lawyers still ambulance-chase; merchants conspire to collect on their own burglary insurance; fire chiefs certify arson as spontaneous combustion. Thieves all, but only the professionals think of insurance fraud as a crime; the amateurs, and they are in the majority, rationalize:

"I've been paying insurance for fourteen years and have never had an accident. I think I deserve something from the company for being such a good risk."

"Everyone does it. The companies know this and expect it and set aside so much money for it. That's why the rates are so high. They secretly laugh at anyone who doesn't take his share."

"I lose a month's work. There's $500 right there. And another $1000 in hospital and doctor bills. Let's say I'm honest and put in a claim for $1500. What happens? They automatically assume I'm lying, hire their own doctor to say so, and cut the amount in half. So, instead, we sue them for $250,000. And the company settles out of court for $15,000. A third goes to my lawyer, two-thirds to me. So what if I do come out ahead? If the insurance company had been honest in the first place they could have settled for $1500. Instead they tried to cheat me and have to pay $15,000 for their distrust."

It can be put even more simply—"They can afford it." *They* is the corporate impersonal. And much insurance fraud is wholly impersonal. A son, opening the door of the car for his mother, accidentally knocked her down. She sued him for $15,000. There was nothing personal in it. She wasn't really suing *him*—she was suing his insurance company.

In the wee small hours of the morning, two Chicago streetcars collided. Morning newspapers had time for only a brief mention of the accident before going to press. By noon, forty-five people had filed claims against the Chicago Transit Authority for damages sustained in the collision, unaware, since the newspapers had failed to mention it, that the two streetcars were empty except for their crews. About the same time in Boston, newspapers reported a streetcar-truck collision. This time 240 people filed claims. At least 172 lied. The total capacity of the streetcar, including standees, was 68. There was nothing personal in it. They were suing the city.

Quite often, as we'll see, this impersonality borders on the inhumane.

Every game has two sides, and this one is certainly no exception. Policy writers are often specialists in wordsmithing, denying in small print what is almost promised in large.* Adjusters sometimes go to amazing lengths to persuade semiconscious accident victims to agree to immediate cash settlements (guiding the hand with the pen, for example, common enough to be nicknamed the "ether settlement"), or imply that there is something vaguely unethical about hiring an attorney when, after all, "We're hired to help you—settling claims is our job." Doctors take the chair of the local medical society as a steppingstone to the chair on the witness stand and the very lucra-

---

* Several years ago some plaster used in a new building began to shrink and crack. The builder held the manufacturer of the plaster liable; the manufacturer, with product-liability insurance, passed the bill on to his insurance company, which refused to pay until ordered by the court to do so. Commenting on this decision in an insurance trade publication, an officer of one of the largest insurance companies in the United States said: "We believe that this kind of occurrence is an ordinary business risk which a manufacturer ought to absorb but the job of finding policy language to exclude that which we really want to exclude is a tough one. Any of you could earn the undying gratitude of the industry by suggesting simple language that would accomplish the purpose."

tive business of being an expert witness for the insurance companies. The companies themselves deny claims that they know are legitimate, afraid that by establishing precedent they will encourage others; they cancel policies by categories, treating individuals as types or actuary-table statistics rather than as separate people, each with his own history that makes him a good or bad risk; they delay payments unnecessarily (but profitably, since they have the use of the money in the meantime); they foster the impression that huge jury verdicts are commonplace and the cause of high insurance rates when they are rare and have little actual effect on rates (91 percent are under $3000, only 3 percent over $10,000, only one in 2500 claims results in a jury verdict of more than $3000); and they often imply fraud where none exists, making the legitimate claimant appear dishonest, his attorney doubly so.

Several years ago, at the instigation of the companies themselves, a nationwide poll was conducted into the public's attitude toward claims handling. Its conclusions: 90 percent of the claimants who had dealt with their own companies felt they were treated fairly; 76 percent of those who had dealt with other companies felt the same way; but among the public at large, only a little over half felt that the insurance companies settled fairly and promptly. Personally they were usually fair; generally they were open to suspicion.

The law recognizes the situation and its probable effect on juries. In all but two states, lawyers are forbidden to mention before juries that insurance exists; even accidental disclosure is grounds for a mistrial. The companies recognize the situation too, settling some 90 percent of their cases out-of-court, in compromise settlements, sometimes even when they suspect the claim to be fraudulent. It costs an insurance company about $1000 to defend a simple damage suit in court. If they can settle for less they usually will. Even if the amount is more, they may settle rather than run the risk of being hit with a still larger jury verdict.* It is hard to imagine a situation more ready-made for fraud.

In recent years a number of the major insurance companies have attempted to eradicate public suspicion by projecting a new image.

* But they rarely hurry to do so. There is another form of "time gap" here. By forcing the claimant to start legal proceedings, with the attendant delay of months to *years* before being heard on crowded courtroom calendars, then settling just before or during the trial, the companies may keep the claimant—nearly always in need of the money—on the financial defensive, vulnerable to a low compromise settlement.

In printed advertisements and TV commercials, the insurance agent is portrayed as a close friend of the family, in attendance at parties, social gatherings, and such memorable moments as graduations and weddings (all of which he, albeit modestly, helped make possible, as his clients never fail to bring out). Instantly present with help when needed, he never questions a policy claim. He is always an "agent," "your service man," a "counselor," a "friend," never a "salesman" whose business it is to "sell insurance." Just what effect this has had on public attitudes is problematical: the companies themselves say insurance fraud has increased at a fantastic rate during the past decade.

The suspicion is decidedly mutual. N. Morgan Woods, who heads the American Insurance Association's Claims Bureau, an investigative agency representing more than 200 stock and mutual underwriting firms, has as his job the detection of insurance fraud. Woods believes, without qualification, that three out of four automobile-liability claims are to some degree fraudulent. He says, "Based on twenty years of observation and experience in insurance investigations, I would estimate that about 75 percent of the automobile and general liability claims are tainted with some aspect of fraud."[1] Others in the business set the figure at as high as 90 percent.

Since much insurance fraud presumably goes undetected or unchallenged, it is impossible to estimate the size of the annual bite. According to Robert Chapman, manager of the Chicago office of the Claims Bureau, known spurious auto claims alone have risen at the rate of 10 percent every year since 1952. Woods believes that the loss in this area alone accounts for between $350 and $420 million annually. Some project the amount, on all types of insurance fraud, to about $1 billion per year. Before dismissing this, and its not necessarily opposite view—that the companies have been known to cheat too—as equally exaggerated, it might do to look at a few of the ways the game is played, remembering that with insurance fraud it's not how you play the game but how much you win that counts.

Auto Accidents: The Most Intimate of Embraces

The *blowup* is probably the most common form of insurance fraud. The accident is legitimate, but the extent of the damage is blown up, or magnified.

Take the case of Mr. John Q., a hypothetical case, though only in that its particulars could fit any of a number of Americans who each year become swindlers without really intending it. John Q. is a respected member of the community, a churchgoing family man, civic-minded by virtue of giving one Saturday each month to the Boy Scouts. Mrs. Q., his wife, is a wonderful woman, a perfect helpmate except when it comes to driving, or aiming, the car. Taking his car to a local garage, John Q. asks apprehensively, how much would they charge to uncrumple the fender? The shop mechanic confirms his worst fears; it will cost about $70. John Q. has a $100-deductible policy, and his expression shows it, and the mechanic is an expert at recognizing this particular expression. "You know," the mechanic says, "you've got some bumps along the side, and your grill could use straightening. It seems a shame for you to pay for all this yourself." He pauses; John Q. nods sadly. "Tell you what," the mechanic goes on. "You look like an all-right guy. I'll take care of this for you. We'll work it out so your insurance takes care of everything. You need a paint job anyway; I'll toss that in, too. After all, it won't cost you anything."

With this pleasant thought firmly implanted in his mind, and with profuse thanks, John Q. leaves, promising to return the following day to fill in the claim. The mechanic puts his assistants to work while he roots around in his desk for some estimate forms. Most insurance companies require competing repair estimates from three different garages, the lowest bidder getting the job. Most garages (and *most* is used advisedly) keep on hand not only their own printed forms, but those of cooperative competitors. Insurance companies know this; proving it is another matter.

If John Q. misses any sleep that night, it is probably due to indigestion rather than to conscience pangs. After all, his worst offense is exaggeration.

When he returns to the shop the next day the mechanic informs him casually, "You know, you'll have to report this to the police as a wreck." When John Q. looks startled and says "But it wasn't a wreck!" the mechanic points to a just-barely-recognizable object on the other side of the shop: it's his car, but now one whole side is bashed in. The claim, he now learns, is for $912.12. He hadn't intended anything like this! All he had in mind was a little "padding." A second look at his car, and he decides it's too late now to do anything except go along with it. He files the claim. The company sends out an adjuster, who inspects the damage and makes his report. And the company pays the full amount.

If John Q. is typical, along about now it may occur to him that what once seemed a disturbing incident has become something of a windfall. Even if this weren't his idea, he'll probably make a good bit of money on it, at least a couple of hundred dollars. Chances are, he's wrong, and all he'll get is the mysterious restoration of his car to its previous condition and just what repairs he was promised. Some garage operators will, if pushed, give their conniving customers a token payment, but rarely. Chances are, too, John Q. will later discover, that not all of the padding went into the claim. The paint may be inferior, the repairs shoddy, "dum-dum," a cheap puttylike substance used to cover up rather than repair the damage. He may even come to suspect, much later, that some of the parts which were previously good are now not so good, that his tires, for example, have suddenly taken on new mileage. And there is—as both he and the mechanic realize—not a thing he can do about it. He has committed fraud, and mostly for someone else's benefit.

Just how many garage and body shops are playing this game today is impossible to estimate. Most "puffed," or "padded," claims aren't this large; some are larger. The Claims Bureau asserts that repair bills covered by insurance contain an *average* overcharge of $60. This is known, in insurance jargon, as "water"; old Uncle Daniel Drew should have patented his process. The garages are not without a defense: many claim that the amounts allowed by the insurance companies for repairs do not accurately take into account the age and condition of the automobile, the difficulty of obtaining parts, the cost of labor, etc. And it follows that sometimes it is the customer who suggests or demands. "What else can we do? This is a highly competitive business," one garage owner told the author, in what by now must seem one of the oldest and most popular of refrains.

Not too long ago, Claims Bureau investigators were tipped off to a large-scale operation in upper New York State. The garage worked only on Buicks, Oldsmobiles, and Cadillacs—automobiles on which fairly high claims could be made. Claims agents soon discovered that the garage was a well-organized headquarters for fraud. Autos brought in for minor repairs became total wrecks overnight. A man and a woman who had never seen each other, who had in common only the fact that both had brought their automobiles into the same garage for slight repairs, suddenly found that, on paper at least, they had engaged in that most intimate of embraces, the head-on collision. The shop specialty was "instant wrecks," often involving as many as five cars.

To prove this was another matter. Woods and his men knew that when a car was brought in, and the owner proved obliging, the car would be almost entirely disassembled, the good parts hidden and replaced with damaged parts, but they were unable to find the source of the parts.

"Finally," relates Woods, "we discovered *hundreds* of smashed fenders, radiators, wheels, rear doors, anything you could name, up on a roof—all catalogued by car, year, model, and color."

An insurance-company claims adjuster, a lawyer, a secretary, and the vice-president of a bank were among the thirty-four convicted.

During the past decade similar operations have been uncovered in just about every major city in the United States. Many were organized rings, specializing in *staged accidents,* their takes varying from several thousand dollars to more than $1 million. When the staged accident is played in its simplest form, *rubbing,* two junk-heap cars are repaired just enough to run, heavily insured (often through the connivance of an insurance agent or bank official), then sideswiped on a deserted road, after which substantial claims are filed. More complicated forms of the game include multicar wrecks, special financing arrangements, and multipolicy claims. One eight-state ring, based in Panama City, Florida, collected more than $200,000 in insurance settlements on 105 staged wrecks.

Paper accidents are also popular and often the hardest to disprove. The Claims Bureau has about fifty full-time investigators on its staff, most of them ex-FBI men. But their job differs from other types of law enforcement in one particular. As Woods explains it, "Usually when an FBI agent or a police officer goes out on an investigation an act has been committed, and it is his job to affirmatively establish the identity of the person who committed the crime. Our investigators, on the other hand, are often confronted with proving the negative, that something did not happen—often a difficult thing to do."

Lack of police cooperation in some areas makes the job even more difficult, according to Woods. Since insurance frauds are usually a nonviolent type of crime, and since most police departments and district attorneys are preoccupied with handling violent crimes, they have little or no time to pursue the fake claimant, leaving this to the Claims Bureau and the investigators for the individual companies. "Besides," Woods adds, "too often these agencies do not take a serious view of the theft of money from an insurance company."

Nor do the courts. I-men, in this case working closely with members of New York District Attorney Frank Hogan's office, spent seven years breaking up one large New York gang estimated to have netted as much as $1 million in fake claims. The investigation alone lasted from February 1952 to May 1955; the trials stretched out until September 1959. Fifty-four men and women were finally indicted, from various walks of life. Of these, four had their indictments dismissed, one man died awaiting trial, one stood trial and was given a suspended sentence, while the other forty-eight pleaded guilty and were given suspended sentences also.

Still another problem in obtaining convictions is the "respectability" of many of the participants. In one recent case involving a paper accident, two policemen, two doctors, an insurance-company adjuster, the vice-president of a bank, and a lawyer all swore to particulars of an accident which each knew had never happened.

To counter such fraud, several years ago a number of insurance companies insisted that owners of damaged cars use garages specified by the companies. This led to different abuses, as some of the garages were so anxious to remain on the preferred list they went out of their way to favor the companies. In 1963, after many complaints of shoddy workmanship, the Justice Department obtained consent decrees from three insurance trade associations which agreed, on behalf of their member companies, to discontinue this practice.

Break My Arms and Legs

Because the grass *is* greener on the other side of the fence, many insurance cheats don't limit themselves to simple property-damage claims, not when the personal-injury field seems so ripe and easily harvested.

The blowup, the staged accident, and the paper accident can all be played in injury as well as noninjury cases, the difference being that in the former the possibilities and take are far less limited. As also, it would appear, are the extremes to which some will go in their attempts to defraud the companies.

One recent June, a young Southern California aircraft-plant worker we'll call Richard Allen approached one of his coworkers, here called James Elliott, with a macabre scheme.

The plan went as follows. Elliott would sideswipe Allen's car and knock it over a cliff in Los Angeles' Exposition Park. Elliott, Allen, and Allen's wife would then climb down to the scene of the wreck, where Elliott would take a brick and break Allen's arms, legs, and a couple of fingers and ribs, after giving him a shot of morphine to help ease the pain. To make sure there would be ample blood, just before placing him in the wreck Elliott would smash Allen's nose. Mrs. Allen agreed to go along with the plan only to the extent of being drugged unconscious and placed in the car; she drew the line at broken bones. She would pretend back injuries and whiplash. The Allens would then sue Elliott and split the settlement from his insurance company. Elliott agreed.

Deciding that it might be better to inflict the injuries before the smash-up, then carry the pair down to the wreck, the conspirators decided more help was needed and solicited still another man. Though horrified, he pretended to agree, then contacted the Los Angeles Police. They didn't believe him. He next tried the Los Angeles Sheriff's office. They didn't believe him either, but, per routine, informed the Claims Bureau. Whatever doubts they may have harbored vanished after they succeeded in recording the conspirators' conversations. In one, Allen, asked whether there was any chance they might be caught, replied, "Hell, no. No one would ever believe I was crazy enough to have my bones fractured to set up a phony accident."

Since no overt act had been committed, the sheriff's deputies and claims investigators had no choice but to let the accident proceed as planned. One night in mid-June the conspirators met at a prearranged spot in the park. Through binoculars their every move was watched. Just as Allen's bones were to be smashed, a Los Angeles Police patrol car happened on the scene. Believing they had discovered a narcotics ring, the patrolmen were about to arrest the four when alerted to the stake-out on their car radio. Allen, however, decided to postpone the accident; the watchers, deciding they had seen enough to prove their case, made their arrests. In January 1959, the conspirators pleaded guilty to charges of attempting to violate the state insurance code and were given jail sentences. A check of Allen's past revealed that he had made at least thirty-four previous claims for injuries and/or damages, all of which had been paid.

Extreme as this case may have been, it is bettered by that of one Missouri ring. Operating—literally—with the help of a doctor, the group specialized in amputating arms. Few professional defrauders will go this far, but there are numerous cases in Claims Bureau files of people who have been willing at least to gamble on receiving this much injury or worse. Among them are the *rear-enders* such as the husband, wife, and nephew whose successful career ended outside Fredericktown, Missouri.

Rear-enders specialize in pulling in front of cars and slamming on their brakes. Often innocent drivers are used as the second parties. The results are sometimes fatal, though rarely to the rear-enders, practiced in the art of withstanding expected shock.

Preparations for such accidents are sometimes extensive. Members of a Birmingham, Alabama, gang would scrape their arms and legs raw with bricks to simulate abrasions, cut their gums in order to spit blood, and eat cakes of laundry soap to induce fever and nausea.

The Fall of the Floppers

Floppers often resort to such artifice. A flopper is an intentionally accident-prone individual who has a habit of walking into slow-moving automobiles, slipping on lettuce in supermarkets, sliding off counter stools, falling on newly waxed floors and icy walks, tripping on worn upholstery, getting caught in bus doors, pinched by escalator treads, and similar mishaps.

Most of us try to avoid situations which could result in accidents; the flopper seeks them out and makes them happen, then lets out a hue and cry to attract witnesses from blocks around, while he (or she) displays near-instantaneous and usually horrifying symptoms.

Undisputed Queen of the Floppers was a woman whom insurance investigators dubbed Rimrock Annie. Unlike others of her kind, who carried around such incriminating evidence as razor blades and cheese graters to use "in case of accident," Annie improvised with what she had. Her specialty was head injuries. Biting her lips would produce blood, which she would then put in her ears. She had a tricky way of shaking her head that made it look as if the blood were spurting out. A dilated left pupil, actually the result of a childhood mastoid operation, fooled more than a few doctors into thinking she had suffered a concussion, as did her practiced double vision. Altogether she collected on some fifty claims, for amounts that ranged up to $3500, before being trapped by a paper doll. To pass the time in the numerous hospitals she frequented she made paper cut-outs. One Denver insurance-company adjuster found these so amusing that he mentioned them to a Claims Bureau friend.

Natural endowments help in medical fakery. Claims Bureau files contain numerous cases of people with the ability to disjoint their limbs and hips at will. One of the most successful practitioners of this type of foolery was a man who suffered from a rare ailment known as "glove aphasia"; he had no feeling in his left hand. Able to withstand the pins and needles of inquisitive doctors, he successfully collected for partial paralysis dozens of times.

Whole families play, too. In a short period, one man submitted twenty-eight personal injury claims; his wife, fifteen; their twelve-year-old son and his five-year-old sister, three apiece. They were second-rate, however, as compared to one St. Louis family. The husband, wife, and their six clumsy—but full-grown—children stumbled their way into $10,000 in personal-injury settlements (specializing in quantity, their claims ranged from $8.35 to $300) before all eight were sentenced to jail en masse.

Flopping is one of the few forms of insurance fraud which has decreased in recent years. Its high point came during World War II when a number of floppers assumed professorial status and conducted classes in symptom faking for draft dodgers. Though their numbers are fewer, some of their tricks remain in vogue. Every day some restaurant owner quickly and quietly pays off one or more customers complaining of ptomaine poisoning. He may even suspect that the symptoms—pain, nausea, and a sharp rise in temperature— are in part pretended, in part due to applying lye soap under the arms, where it reacts directly on the blood vessels—but probably considers an out-of-pocket settlement of $25 to $50 preferable to the risk of ruinous publicity. There is a relatively simple way some restaurant owners use to detect such fraud, and that is to offer the alleged victim $101—in most states this odd figure means the difference between a misdemeanor and a felony, a few weeks in jail or several years in prison. The ptomaine faker is usually a petty chiseler, unwilling to assume the risks of the big time. One well-known Hollywood restaurateur, now retired, estimated that during his long career he was approached on the ptomaine ruse at least 500 times. Each time he referred the sufferers to his insurance company. Only two accepted the invitation, and both claims were quickly disproven. His guiding rule was simple: "If they won't try for the big insurance money, they haven't a case."

A kindred fraud is the *foreign substances racket*.

A middle-aged, well-dressed man took a big bite into his hamburger, screamed loudly with pain, and with bloody fingers extracted a tack from his mouth. It was quite a show, for the $5 or $10 he usually collected, and he kept it up for some ten years, carefully avoiding the insurance companies and apprehension, until failing memory (or perhaps the quality of the hamburgers) made him visit one spot twice.

A middle-aged, well-dressed woman entered a Times Square cafeteria and ordered breakfast, consisting of fruit juice, oatmeal, coffee, and toast. She didn't scream, but merely moaned loudly and brought her hand to her mouth in horror. There was a stone in her oatmeal, and it had broken off her front tooth! The manager was quick to assure her that the cafeteria had insurance for foreign-substance claims and referred her to his insurance company. On learning that the woman was in New York City for a single day and had to catch an afternoon train, the insurance adjuster obligingly sent her to a dentist, who determined that a porcelain crown for her tooth would cost about $100. The adjuster made an immediate cash settlement. So, it appeared, did a number of other adjusters, during the next five days, and for the same tooth. She was never caught.

Hotels are just as vulnerable as restaurants, especially to negligence suits. A man checks into a hotel, goes to his room, and starts to take a refreshing shower. Moments later he's screaming into the telephone: "The shower suddenly turned scalding hot! I've been badly burned—for God's sake, hurry and send a doctor!" His fiery red skin (the result of overexposure to a sunlamp) may be proof enough for a quick settlement.

If the insurance company isn't consulted, that is. With the investigative procedures employed by the companies in their settlement of claims, many of these deceptions would be quickly exposed. They work sometimes, however, because the restaurateur or hotelman, fearing a large claim sure to affect his insurance rates or coverage, "plays safe" and pays out of his own pocket.

Health Insurance Fraud

Children playing "Doctor" rarely want to take the part of the patient. This isn't true of some adults. A South Carolina couple were recently convicted of turning a net profit of $13,562.71 on their various accidents and illnesses, using the multiple-policy dodge. When the wife came down with acute gastritis in 1960, her medical expenses were $287.71; she collected $2562.47 on thirteen separate policies. A $470 fall in the bathtub netted $3261. As the Post Office Department put it, "Unfortunately, the concern displayed by the couple in providing for such emergencies in advance was not accompanied by equal concern for the legal niceties. In applications for insurance with at least twenty companies, they omitted the answers to some highly germane questions—omissions which constituted mail fraud." Entering pleas of guilty, he received a three-year suspended sentence, hers was for two. Each was fined $1000.

In Newark, New Jersey, a union member pleaded guilty to submitting fraudulent claims against the Welfare Fund of Teamster Local 478. Obtaining billheads of dentists, he had submitted 117 false claims for dental work for various members, collecting some $8000 from the Welfare Fund, splitting the proceeds with the members. He was placed on five years' probation and fined $750.

Or consider the case of the nonexistent sick employees of the company which wasn't there. According to New York District Attorney Frank S. Hogan, in 1959 a Hillsdale, New Jersey, man invented a firm known as the Coffee-ette Company. A claims approver for a life insurance company, the man is alleged to have taken out a group-insurance plan for the company's fourteen nonexistent employees, opened bank accounts for each, and filed sick claims of from $20 to $712, for a total of $66,465 in the ensuing five years.

False Arrest

Although the fake false-arrest suit is usually thought of in terms of a retail swindle, insurance companies usually bear the financial burden.

On a Friday afternoon, a prosperous-looking individual enters the showroom of a new-car dealer in a Connecticut community and asks to see the newest-model Super Torque Zip. The salesman doesn't even have to exert himself for this sale, for after only a brief inspection the man says "I'll take it." Pulling out his checkbook, he asks the amount. Following a short but futile argument in which the salesman attempts to convince him of the merits of buying on time, the man writes out a check for the amount, $6000. His identification is excellent—his wallet bulges with credit cards. Though the bank is closed, the dealer is able to reach the local retail-credit office, which asserts that the man has a fine, if somewhat new, credit history. The dealer accepts the check. The man drives off.

A couple of hours later he pulls up in front of a Zip agency in New York City. He just bought this car, he explains, but he's just learned that his business will require him to be out of the country for at least two years. Will the dealer give him $4000 in cash for it?

Suspicious, the New York dealer places a call to the Connecticut dealer, who, marveling no longer at the easy sale, screams, "Hold that man! He's trying to swindle us with a bum check!"

The man is arrested and held over the weekend. Bright and early Monday morning the check is presented at the bank and, to the horror of both dealers, is cashed. The man now has perfect grounds for two false-arrest suits, one which he'll file in New York City, the other in Connecticut. If either dealer has called him a "thief" or "swindler" in the presence of witnesses, he can throw in a few counts of slander also.

The jewelry switch, mentioned in Chapter 9, and the shoplifting arrest, mentioned at the start of this chapter, are two more variations. Contrary to the fears of many retailers, however, the fake false-arrest suit is relatively uncommon.* The threatening noises are often made, and sometimes a merchant can be panicked into an on-the-spot settlement, but quite often it doesn't go beyond the stage of threats.

Why would a swindler who has succeeded in establishing grounds for a false-arrest suit fail to file one?

For the same reason that much insurance fraud eventually results in apprehension and conviction: the Index.

The Index is a master filing system kept by the Claims Bureau. Every insurance claim, no matter how small, is filed and cross-filed in the Index (at present it contains in excess of twenty million cases). The cross-filing includes separate entries for the type of injury or suit, the manner in which it was sustained, the claimant's legal name (filed phonetically), each known alias, the claimant's physical description, etc.

The very ease with which much insurance fraud is perpetrable makes it self-defeating. When a person stumbles onto a good thing, he finds it accompanied by two strong temptations: (1) to tell others how easy it was, and (2) to do it again. Many Claims Bureau

---

* It can be assumed that legitimate false-arrest suits will increase significantly, however, if more stores employ the "bounty" system for apprehending shoplifters mentioned in Chapter 9.

cases (like many Internal Revenue cases) are solved by tip-offs from informants. Even more are betrayed by the Index, for most insurance gypsters are recidivists, or repeaters. Most successful insurance fraud is penny-ante, in the realm of small uncontested claims. Few, if any, of the "whopping" jury settlements one occasionally reads about are touched with fraud. The fantastically detailed techniques employed by the insurance companies in investigating claims which threaten to be sizable keep most insurance cheaters in the low-income bracket. To make real money from an insurance company, the crook has to be a repeater. And the repeater leaves a trail, a pattern in the Index. Appropriately, insurance fraud is a risky occupation.

We come now, for nearly the last time, to that familiar question—Who pays?

The legitimate claimant pays, in reputation. The blanket charge of fraud that some in the insurance business are so prone to throw out covers both the cheater and the far more common claimant who has a wholly meritorious claim.

Another who similarly pays is the claimant's attorney, alias the "ambulance chaser"—or so much insurance company literature would have us identify him, describing a situation once common but today decidedly less so, due in part to the threat of disbarment that accompanies such activities, but also to the efforts of these attorneys, through the American Trial Lawyers Association, to enforce ethical standards in their own ranks. Since both the companies and the attorneys have their own strong feelings on the subject,* it is interesting to see what an impartial but knowledgeable outsider has to say. Observes criminologist Mabel A. Elliott in *Crime in Modern Society:*

"Certain rackets operate almost wholly within the law. 'Ambulance chasing' is one of the most widely publicized. Unfortunately all the angles of this racket have never been disclosed . . . The unethical ambulance chasing on the part of the insurance agents representing those responsible for accidents has seldom been effectively

---

* For the insurance-company viewpoint, see "Why Your Car Insurance Costs So Much," Richard Dunlop, *Traffic Safety*, October 1958; "Damage Suits: A Primrose Path to Immorality," Morton M. Hunt, *Harper's*, March 1957; and "When the Lawyer Gets the Spoils," Murray Teigh Bloom, *Reader's Digest*, March 1960.

For the claimant's attorney's side of the story, see *Ready for the Plaintiff*, Melvin M. Belli, Bobbs-Merrill Co., 1956, reprinted by Popular Library, 1965.

aired. The number of insurance adjusters who call on victims of accidents while the latter are (1) at the scene of the accident or (2) still in a dazed condition at the hospital or elsewhere must total many times the number of lawyers who are anxious to help the victims bring suit. In fact it is a common practice for an insurance company adjuster to take advantage of the weakened or dazed condition of the victim and induce him to sign a release absolving the insurance agency from any further responsibility . . .

"Unquestionably certain ambulance chasers have been in league with persons involved in fraudulent accidents, and with persons who claim to be seriously injured when at worst they have suffered minor injuries. But it seems equally patent that the powerful influence of the insurance companies has created a one-sided picture of the ambulance chaser with an idea of reducing the number of legitimate claims. By vilifying thus the members of the legal profession who defend victims of accidents, the companies cause laws, juries, and public opinion to tend to put legitimate and illegal (or unethical) claims in the same category."[2]

And, of course, if you have insurance, you pay too, in dollars and cents.

Each year, American insurance companies collect some $9 billion for the insurance they write. Where does this go? In a simplified breakdown, using the figures the companies themselves have released through the Insurance Information Institute, for every $100 in premiums collected, $65.50 is allotted for the payment of claims, $29.50 for insurance-company operating costs, and $5 for unexpected contingencies and profit to the company. The average profit margin is said to be about 1 percent.*

That money allotted for the payment of claims goes into a special pool. Today, for every $100 paid into this reservoir, the insurance companies are paying out $116.70. According to the Insurance Information Institute, between 1953 and 1963 the companies have lost $850 million in bodily-injury policies alone, going into the red every year except two.

Hold your sympathy for a minute. What happens when a company pays out more than has been allotted for claims? It raises the

---

* The breakdown is much debated. The insurance companies say of each premium dollar, about 35¢ goes for operating expenses and profits, 65¢ for claims; independent surveys say 52¢ goes for operating expenses and profits, 48¢ for claims.

premium rates the following year. Between 1953 and 1963 the average rate for motor-vehicle liability rose 57 percent. Yet each year during the same period most insurance companies made a sizable margin of profit. Just because a company loses money, it doesn't necessarily follow that it can't make money too. For example, State Farm Mutual Insurance Company reported that record premiums had failed to offset its losses during the first half of 1964, resulting in a net loss of $7,239,822. The world's largest auto insurer also reported, however, that investment income of $14,573,352 provided a cushion that produced profit, after dividends to policyholders and some other miscellaneous items, of $3,025,939. This compared with an over-all profit of $3,483,016 in the first half of 1963, when the company lost $5,777,153.[3]

The old saw "They can afford it" is all too true, for *they* don't pay for it; the cost is passed on to the policyholder. And since it is the policyholder who pays, the companies have little, if any, incentive to keep the rates down. The insurance salesmen, working on commission, actually stand to gain by the higher rate.

Lest there be any doubt on this point, listen to the following:

William Davis, of the National Automobile Theft Bureau: "Whenever a person defrauds an insurance company, he imposes a direct tax on the reputable buyer of insurance. The dishonest claimant who gets paid is largely responsible for boosting insurance rates."[4]

N. Morgan Woods, of the Claims Bureau: "Insurance companies only operate with the premium paid by the public and those premiums must increase in cases where this sort of fraud [padded claims and fake accidents and injuries] exists."[5]

E. A. Cowie, vice-president in charge of the claims department of the Hartford Accident and Indemnity Company, on products-liability actions: "Just as in the case of automobile insurance, it is the public which ultimately pays the bill, for manufacturers must pass along the costs of products liability coverage to the consumer just as they do their other costs of doing business."[6]

Fraud, of course, is responsible for only a portion of what we pay in insurance rates. Automobile liability rates have also risen because there are more automobiles and more legitimate accidents and because the costs of repairs and parts have increased. (Detroit's "stylish" designs have helped make the modern American car exceedingly repair-prone.) Bodily injury rates reflect the increase in accidents, as well as the rising cost of medical care. And products-liability rates have increased in part because manufacturers are being found more liable. As legislative and judicial thinking move toward greater protection for the consumer, the manufacturer assumes a greater responsibility for defects or negligence involved in the manufacture and use of his products. Although the consumer doesn't pay directly for such protection, he pays for it nonetheless. When a drug company (to use a nonhypothetical example) is found guilty of manufacturing and marketing a dangerous or unsafe product resulting in death or injuries to those using it and is sued, successfully, for millions of dollars in claims, the insurance company covering that manufacturer has to pass on the tab in increased rates to other manufacturers covered by its policies, who in turn have to increase the cost of their products to cover the new rates. In brief, "no man is an island"; you may be paying more for your washing machine, stove, refrigerator, or TV set because a child died of improperly prepared polio vaccine.

No one knows how much of the premium dollar goes for fraud, how much for legitimate claims. A spokesman for one of the largest insurance companies in the United States has stated that, if all insurance fraud could be eliminated, insurance rates in many areas could be cut 20 percent or more. No one seriously suggests, however, that this will ever happen. And there are many who feel that in the present climate of mutual distrust there is not even much likelihood of fraud being greatly reduced.

The horizon is so unbright that the writer of an article which appeared in a national magazine not long ago, after surveying the insurance-fraud scene concluded: "In the meantime, the suit-happy spree goes on, helping some, hurting others and gradually strangling in its own sinews the elements of justice. The only choice is to be a winner, to take part in what one insurance man has called 'an open-sesame greater than any jackpot ever conceived in the gambling halls of Las Vegas!'"[7]

Who pays? You do. The insurance companies can afford it—but can you?

V

THE VULNERABLE VILLAINS

It is a double pleasure to deceive
the deceiver.

La Fontaine
Fables

CHAPTER 16

HOW TO BE A WINNER

SOME OF THE TIME

> The generality of men are natu-
> rally apt to be swayed by fear
> rather than by reverence, and to
> refrain from evil rather because of
> the punishment that it brings, than
> because of its own foulness.
>
> Aristotle
> *Nicomachean Ethics*

SEVERAL years ago a longtime subscriber to *Consumer Reports* wrote the editors of that magazine explaining why he had failed to renew his subscription. He liked the magazine, he said, and felt the job it was doing was extremely important. But he had reached the point where he was tired of thinking of himself as a "consumer," eternally besieged and beset.

By now, most, if not all, readers are equally tired of hearing themselves referred to as "vulnerable Americans." This chapter is designed to supply some—very little, but some—respite, by indicating what has been, is being, and might be done to dissipate at least a portion of the climate of fraud overlying so much of the American scene.

In facing the fraud problem realistically, one must begin by accepting certain premises:

(1) "Fraud is like prostitution," Irving M. Pollack, assistant general counsel of the Securities and Exchange Commission once remarked. "It will be with us forever." Fraud is a condition of our

society. No matter how comprehensive the laws, how excellent their enforcement, some will fall victim to the most patently phony schemes, even more to sophisticated trickery.

(2) Crime in the United States is changing, qualitatively as well as quantitatively. James V. Bennett, who headed the Federal Prison System from 1937 to 1965, stated on his retirement: "The masked bank robber with a gun in each hand is not so great a social menace as the honest-looking teller who quietly pockets a few dollars that are not his . . . White collar crime composes the vast bulk of our crime problem. Its large mass lies unseen and iceberg-like below the lesser bulk of such visible crimes as auto theft, bank robbery, burglary and the like."[1]

(3) The situation will probably grow worse rather than better, for as our economy expands, so will the opportunities for fraud and other white-collar crimes.

(4) The means for combating the problem have not kept pace with the means for spreading it. Our "legislative Galahads" are all too often forced to use the sword, the shield, and the crossbow to counter the nuclear weapons of modern swindlery.

(5) The most successful con men have donned the garb of businessmen; some successful businessmen have taken up the tricks of the con man. As both gravitate toward the realm of permissible legality, where the measurement is not "Is it ethical?" but "Is it legal?" the distinction between the two, if indeed there is one, grows exceedingly dim.

(6) Some of the oldest maxims are no longer true: today it is possible to cheat nearly all of the people nearly all of the time without ever appealing to their larcenous side.

(7) Strong and determined action must be taken to give the individual American even minimal protection.

Having accepted these rather unpleasant truths, it is possible to consider some ways of lessening our vulnerability.

Some Stopgap Measures

In this age of instant mass communications, the deceptive ad and the wholly fraudulent promotion can reach millions in moments, but months or years may pass before either may be stopped. If the individual is to have even a semblance of protection against fraud, some means must be found to close this gap.

The time gap: The FDA has injunctive power and often uses it; it can seize a dangerous product and remove it from the market. Similarly, the SEC can remove from trading a fraudulent stock issue. The FTC also has injunctive power, but only over advertising injurious to health. At present there is no way for the FTC to call an immediate halt to an illegal promotion which drains the public pocketbook. Suggestions that the FTC be given broader injunctive powers have resulted in strong business pressure on Congress, effectively killing such plans.

In March 1962, President Kennedy, in his consumer message to Congress, proposed an alternate solution—that the FTC be given the power to issue temporary injunctions or cease-and-desist orders when prompt action is necessary to protect the public, these orders to remain in effect until the FTC has completed its formal proceedings. FTC Chairman Dixon has requested such authority from Congress, but to date with no effect. Had such powers been available, five or more years could have been chopped off the Holland Furnace Company case.

The legal gap: The wide distance between modern frauds and antiquated legislation has been mentioned repeatedly. This in-between territory has become a con man's land not unlike the old Oklahoma Strip, where crooks can operate without censure. The trouble is, during the '80s and '90s one could avoid the Oklahoma Strip; today this palimpsest overlies much of the United States, and the individual can neither avoid nor escape it. As Consumer Counsel Nelson has put it, "More money is being taken from people today with a pen than with a gun, and the pen makes it legal."

The spotty protective coverage of the various state laws—here inadequate, there nonexistent—make all the more apparent the need for federal legislation in many areas. The prospect of such legislation is less than promising.

The authority gap: In theory, when an illegal scheme appears which falls within the jurisdiction of more than one federal body, the agency that can halt the illegal act more promptly or the one enforcing the law with the stiffer penalty takes over. For example, recent cases passed from the FTC (which has no criminal powers) to the POD and Justice Department (which do) include interstate land sales, bogus-liquidation schemes, aluminum-siding frauds, and various referral gyps.

In theory this appears to be an excellent way to halt fraud without increasing the size or power of the federal government. In practice, however, it often falls short of the mark. Cooperation between various federal agencies is sometimes nonexistent. Not only are agencies often exceedingly jealous of their authority, resulting in a duplication of effort, but disagreement over who should handle some of the more difficult problems may leave them unhandled. Not infrequently one agency will be totally unaware of what another is doing.

In the spring of 1965, a bipartisan group of nineteen senators, headed by Senators Jacob Javits (New York) and Maurine Neuberger (Oregon), introduced a resolution in the U.S. Senate to establish a Select Committee on Consumers. The function of this committee would be to study the economic problems of consumers, determine the effectiveness of federal agencies in dealing with them, and recommend legislation for solving them.

Among the suggestions to come out of the hearings of the Subcommittee on Fraud and Misrepresentations Affecting the Elderly, headed by Senator Harrison A. Williams (New Jersey), was one urging the establishment of a special Citizens' Advisory Committee to evaluate the efforts of the FTC to determine whether its legal weapons are effective enough to combat today's increasingly professional gypsters.*

A study of the various federal agencies, conducted not in criticism but in an attempt to make them more effective and to better their liaison, seems essential.

The authority gap is even wider between the federal and state governments. Often this is not so much a lack of cooperation as a lack of even simple communication. In 1965, FTC Chairman Dixon asked Congress for funds to establish an Office of Federal-State Cooperation, as a means of stepping up enforcement of antitrust, antideception, and consumer-protection laws. By hiring one lawyer, at $20,000 a year, and utilizing present FTC employees, Dixon believes American consumers could be saved millions annually in losses to fraudulent schemes. Each year, the FTC gets some 7000 letters from irate victims of consumer frauds, many concerning local rackets beyond the reach of federal laws. Working in close coopera-

---

* The subcommittee also suggested the establishment of an "FBI of medical fraud." Known as the Bureau on Medical Quackery, it would assess the total problem of health rackets in the U.S. today; serve as a clearinghouse for cases of fraud and deception; assist local governments and other agencies in combating these problems; and make recommendations for additional federal legislation if and when deemed necessary.

tion with the attorney generals of the fifty states, this "clearinghouse for fraud" would enable the FTC to tip off a state about rackets within its own borders or, in turn, alert the FTC to widespread abuses which might best be handled on the federal level. Senator Williams has called the proposal "one of the most far-reaching suggestions yet made for the greater protection of consumers"; yet to most Americans Dixon's suggestion must come as a surprise, since we take for granted that such cooperation and interchange already exist. They don't.

A similar approach was recently inaugurated on a statewide level by California's Attorney General Thomas C. Lynch. Lynch's office will act as a sort of "DEW Line," or distant-early-warning system for fraud, alerting law-enforcement agencies in the various cities and counties to any large-scale movement of swindlers. First tried on one of the most difficult subjects, the roving gangs of aluminum-siding gypsters who are often out of state months before the finance companies start pressing their victims for payment, early alerts triggered by first complaints resulted in 103 criminal cases in seven counties.

Some of the most promising developments have taken place at the state level. The several state consumer counsels have already been mentioned. One particularly auspicious new start is the inauguration of some dozen state bureaus of consumer frauds. The first of these, the New York Consumer Frauds and Protection Bureau, was established in 1957.

There are limits as to what the federal regulatory agencies can do. On receiving an individual complaint, they can only investigate and, if action is warranted and in the public interest, act to stop the seller from making future misrepresentations. They can't arbitrate personal claims. They can't get the victim his money back.

The state bureaus, working out of the offices of the state attorney generals, often can. In 1963 the New York Bureau processed some 9200 complaints and succeeded in getting some $1,200,000 in cash and services refunded in actions involving referral schemes, dishonest repairmen, bait advertising, door-to-door sales, contract fraud, and similar crimes. "We can help about 90 percent of the time," observed New York Bureau Chief Barnett Levy. "In the other 10 percent, the firm involved may have gone bankrupt, or the claim may be unreasonable. When we feel that a consumer's claim is unjustified, we tell him so. We won't knuckle under to a firm, but neither will we browbeat it."[2]

These bureaus can be demonstrative or tough. During 1963 the New York Bureau set up codes of ethics for food-freezer and food-plan organizations, encyclopedia distributors, and health and dance studios. It was also instrumental in having legislation passed which hits hard at wordsmithing, by broadening the definition of false advertising to make the practice of making material omissions a crime. It also used, sparingly but with great effectiveness, its strongest fist: it dissolved several corporations for persistent violations and fraud.

At present there are consumer-fraud bureaus in Alaska, California, Connecticut, Illinois, Kansas, Massachusetts, Michigan, Minnesota, Missouri, New Jersey, New York, Ohio, and Washington. Each has had marked success in different areas. The Illinois Bureau, for example, has been spectacularly successful in halting frauds in appliance and automotive repairs.

California has also taken recent action against a similar breed of racketeers, but through a separate state bureau. In 1963 the California legislature set up, on a trial basis, a State Electronic Repair Bureau, with its specific task the countering of TV repair fraud. In recent years "setnapers" have become a major problem in the Golden State. Unscrupulous repair firms will examine a TV set, give a low estimate for repairs, then bill the set owner for 300 percent and more in excess of actual work done. If the owner is unable to pay immediately, the company will take over the set on a mechanic's lien and "sell" it to a subsidiary, which will rent it out for from $16 to $23 monthly. Within two months after the bureau came into existence, it received over 6000 complaints involving more than 500 establishments: the first 20 investigated, in the Los Angeles area, revealed only one operating honestly.

To catch these swindlers, agents posed as ordinary customers with TV trouble. A rigged set would be used, with a loose wire or defective tube, but with all the parts secretly marked with chemicals visible only under a special light. When the set was returned, often with a "new" picture tube which was actually the old tube with the back repainted, arrests would be made.

TV and radio repairmen in California must now register with the Bureau (the $35 annual licensing fee goes to finance regulation of the industry); they must submit written estimates of repair work and obtain written permission before making additional unforeseen repairs; and any defective parts which are replaced must be returned to the customer. Ethical dealers, attempting to clear their

ranks of these gypsters, were active in supporting the creation of
the Bureau, which has recently been moved from trial to permanent
status. Such support wasn't forthcoming in another area. An attempt
to set up a similar bureau to oversee automotive repairs was strongly
opposed by auto dealers, oil companies, and certain large chain
stores which sell auto parts and repair services. The bill was killed
in committee.

A Maryland congressman, Charles Mathias, Jr., recently advanced
an interesting suggestion for eradicating automotive-repair fraud.
Have the auto and gas industries set up automotive diagnostic centers, staffed by expert mechanics, to tell a car owner disinterestedly
what repairs his car needs and how much the work ought to cost.
Given written explicit information on the work needed, the owner
could then go to any repairman he chose, have the work done, and
return to the diagnostic center for a checkup to make sure it was
done properly.

Whether the auto and gas industries, with so great an interest in
repairs, parts, and planned obsolescence, could do this disinterestedly seems doubtful. It seems even more doubtful that they would
let federal or state agencies bring the plan into being.

The gap between state and municipal fraud enforcement is long-
standing and often acute. With the exception of regular bunco
games, the old reliables of swindlery, local police departments are
rarely trained or equipped to handle most modern fraud. As Sutherland observes in *Principles of Criminology,* "Gross forms of fraud are
easily detected by the regular police but no expert investigators are
provided to deal with the subtler forms of fraud which flourish in
many areas of business and the professions."[3] A strong local BBB
may help to close this gap, but much too often the consumer is
almost wholly dependent on state and federal enforcement, while
businesses, to combat their own fraud problems, have to rely more
and more heavily on special police, detective services, and their own
security forces.

The Biggest Problem

The greatest problem facing regulatory and law-enforcement
agencies is that they must deal with a *fait accompli.* They can only
stop an illegal promotion once it is in effect, often after much of
the harm has been done. This is particularly true in regard to fraud-

ulent advertising, with its potentials for Instant Deception. Rather than ever chasing the tails of these comet schemes, preventive measures, before-the-fact techniques, are needed to stop the deception or fraud before it starts.

There are several possibilities.

The concept that the burden of proof is on the accuser is basic to our legal system. But today an undue burden of proof is on the regulators. Instead of the government having to prove that the claims are lies, the advertiser might be required to prove they are true before making them in the mass media.

This is not as revolutionary as it sounds. Federal laws require premarket testing of most drugs for purity and safety. We are in as much need of honesty and reliability. The New Industry Guidance Program of the FTC works on a similar principle. A businessman may inform the FTC of a course of action he proposes to follow and request an opinion as to its legality. To date, the number who have utilized this service has been discouragingly low—199 in 1964, its second full year in operation.

Such a system would, of course, mean more governmental regulation, either by the FTC or by a separate federal agency, and it would be a form of censorship.

There is an alternative.

A deceptive TV commercial or a fraudulent advertising campaign can be halted at any one of a number of points before it comes in contact with the public. It can be vetoed by the executives of the advertising agency where it was conceived, by the sponsor whose product it represents, by the broadcasting systems over which it is to be aired. It can be discouraged by the trade associations to which the advertising agency and the sponsor usually belong. This is self-regulation, so highly advocated by those in business, so appealing in principle, but, one must admit with sadness, so infrequently practiced.* Almost every major business, industry group, and trade association in the United States has a beautifully worded Code of Business Ethics which, if observed, would go far toward eradicating the fraudulent schemes of all but the fly-by-night operators. But all too often they hang there, on waiting-room and office walls, a deco-

---

* For some significant failures in business self-regulation, see *The Real Voice*, Richard Harris, Macmillan, 1964, and *All Honorable Men: Corruption and Compromise in American Life*, Walter Goodman, Little, Brown and Company, 1963.

rative touch that neither covers nor counters actual business practices.*

The inability of business to regulate itself inevitably leads to
greater governmental regulation. It takes no prophet to predict that
—barring some unforeseen and long-overdue housecleaning—eventually there will be a Federal Bureau of Advertising.

Fixing the Blame

In most detective stories the villain gets caught. In real life this is
also true, but only of some villains. Most bad-check passers, thieving
employees, insurance cheats, and others of their bent are eventually
apprehended and brought to some form of reckoning. There are
clear statutes covering most of their offenses. They operate under
the threat of prison.

No such fears need disturb the dreams of the corporate swindler
of the public, for he holds a privileged position in our society. He
can commit fraud with near-impunity. His reckoning may come
eventually, but he can be sure that it will be token, well worth the
risk, and that in all probability he won't be involved personally.

Much fraud investigation stops far short of the actual villains. It
may be a company away—hitting the aluminum-siding gypster but
leaving untouched the banks and finance companies which, all too
often knowingly, make his swindles possible. Often it is closer—
citing a company but not those who operate it.

"The corporation is a legal entity," a well-known Chicago industrialist told a Los Angeles business group recently. "It is not in fact a
person. It is a property right. It is not a human right. It has no
conscience . . ."[4]

It is also frequently a shield. America suffers not only from a
split-level morality but a split-level guilt. Very rarely is an attempt
made to fix the blame on those on whom it actually belongs.

In 1960–61 twenty-nine American corporations were found guilty
of conspiring to rig bids and fix prices in the electrical industry,
frauds which cost other businesses and the American public billions
of dollars. In February 1961, in an unusual, much-publicized action,
seven executives of such firms as General Electric and Westinghouse
were given jail terms of thirty days for their part in this scandal. It

* See Appendix A.

would appear that, for a change, some attempt had been made actually to fix the blame.

A glimpse at the backgrounds and positions of these men dispels such illusion. They were "middle executives," Walter Goodman notes in his study *All Honorable Men.* "Not high enough in the organization to profess innocence, yet too high to practice it," these were men who "must continually interpret management policy, make the daily decisions and do, or order others to do, the sometimes dirty work of the marketplace . . ."[5]

The American public was asked to believe that these middle executives, solely on their own initiative and without the knowledge and consent of their superiors, decided to conspire with their supposed competitors to rig government bids, allocate markets, and set industrywide prices, actions that greatly affected the future of each of their companies. Federal District Judge J. Cullen Ganey, who tried the case, was not so credulous. "One would be naive indeed," he said, "to believe that these actions were unknown to those responsible for the conduct of the corporations."[6]

A similar suspension of common sense is required to accept the final verdict on the quiz-show scandals of the late fifties. In the Congressional hearings, the public confessions and apologetics that followed the revelations that Twenty-One, The $64,000 Question, and similar game shows were rigged, the participants having been given the questions and answers in advance, the American public was asked to believe that only a few minions of the producers, not the producers themselves, or the advertising agencies, or the sponsors, or the networks, knew or even suspected what *Variety* had matter-of-factly mentioned as early as 1957.

Occasionally the blame is fixed. The Holland Furnace Company case is one example, the finding of criminal fraud against the advertising agency which handled the Regimen promotion another, and the conviction of Anthony "Tony" De Angelis still another. But these are exceptions. In general, although those who carry out the illegal acts are sometimes found responsible, the men who initiate them are rarely even mentioned by name. If corporate fraud is to be even slightly discouraged, some effort must be made whenever possible to fix and personalize the guilt for illegal acts, even if it eventually rests on respected presidents of corporations or entire boards of directors. Company policy is made by men, not staff memos.

The very nature of the swindler presents another problem. He is quite often a charming fellow. His imaginative tricks may even awaken a begrudging admiration, from a safe distance. It has been said that time is kinder to him than to any man: today's con man becomes tomorrow's rogue and the future's lovable rascal. Even judges aren't entirely immune to this charm. As Judge David Sparrow wrote in *The Great Swindlers*, "I find myself in agreement with the late Mr. Justice Hawkins who, though he was so severe with murderers, had a sneaking regard for rogues. They are, often, such attractive, pleasing creatures, such good company, and, more often than not, they are the creatures of circumstance."[7]

In sentencing Anthony De Angelis to ten years in prison for masterminding the biggest swindle in U.S. financial history—the $150 million salad-oil fraud of 1963*—Federal Judge Reynier J. Wortendyke, Jr., felt called upon to remark to the former hog-butcher-risen-to-commodities-titan, "although you have caused terrific loss of money to many of your fellow Americans" (a substantial Wall Street brokerage firm and seventeen lesser companies folded as a result of De Angelis' activities, while American Express survived with some $100 million in claims against it), ". . . you, yourself, Mr. De Angelis, have exemplified what can be achieved with only limited backing, without influence, by courage and wisdom . . ."[8]

The Fraud Tax

In theory, the fine is supposed to serve a dual purpose, acting as both a penalty and a deterrent.

Today, when levied against corporate villains, it often isn't even equivalent to the costs of the investigation and prosecution. It has become little more than a light tax—sometimes collectable, mostly avoidable—for the privilege of committing fraud.

When one company swindles another in an antitrust action, there is a provision in the law which enables the victimized company to sue the defrauder for triple damages.

The consumer, the ultimate victim of such frauds, has no such redress. It is not only difficult for him to get a portion of his money back in most swindles, and impossible for him to get any of it back in others, but, as a result of a recent Treasury Department ruling,

* For the De Angelis story, see Pulitzer Prize-winner Norman C. Miller's *The Great Salad Oil Swindle*, Coward-McCann, 1965.

he must now pick up a sizable portion of the tab for corporate wrongdoing.

Because of their convictions for conspiring to fix prices in the electrical industry, General Electric, Westinghouse, and their co-conspirators became liable to triple-damage claims by those electrical companies defrauded by their actions. To date, these claims have amounted to about $400 million.

In August 1964, the Internal Revenue Service, in one of the most controversial decisions in its history, ruled that the triple damages, attorney's fees, and miscellaneous other legal costs incurred by the twenty-nine electrical manufacturers could be deducted from their net income as *"ordinary and necessary business expenses."*

Does this mean what it appears to mean?

It does.

It means "the loss of millions of tax dollars to the government," according to Senator Philip A. Hart, chairman of the Senate Judiciary Antitrust and Monopoly Subcommittee, and Representative Emanuel Celler, chairman of the House Judiciary Committee, who issued a joint statement protesting the decision.

It also means, they stated, that in the future "The ruling is likely to hamper effective antitrust enforcement both by mitigating the penalties which Congress has prescribed and by its tacit assumption that a hard-core criminal price-fixing conspiracy is 'ordinary and necessary business.' "[9]

"You and I are taxpayers," observed *The New Republic's* TRB; "we didn't engage in the price conspiracy. In fact it was directed against us; and yet you and I as taxpayers are called upon to foot the cost of the damages, because the supposed penalty goes to reduce taxes which the defendants would otherwise bear."[10]

To date, the ruling still stands. And the estimated $250 million it is likely to cost the American public in the case of the electrical manufacturers is only the beginning, for there have been recent price-fixing cases involving triple damages in the drug, steel, baking, linoleum, and carpeting industries.

Ideally, if corporate fraud is to be discouraged, fines must be raised to the point where they again function as both penalty and deterrent. Ideally, there should be some way that money misappropriated from the public could be reappropriated for the public. A man cheated of $200 on the purchase of a new car, due to price-fixing which raised the cost of the car's steel and electrical components, probably wouldn't consider it worth the time or expense to sue for redress, even if he could. But if he could collect triple damages, it might be worth the effort to file a taxpayer's suit. No consumer is likely to file a suit because he was cheated of a nickel's worth of breakfast food in a short-weighted cereal package, or a dime because the odometer on the taxi in which he rode over-registered. But by levying a fine commensurate to the amount collectively defrauded, a portion of which could be used to regulate such illegal activities, the consumer would at least have the satisfaction of knowing he had helped to defraud the defrauder.

The Gentlemen's Agreements

It is easy to criticize the consent order, the affidavit of discontinuance, the fraud order on the grounds that they are neither penalties for nor deterrents to fraud, that they even constitute a separate set of standards for business. This is true, but much more important, they are among the few ways currently available for stopping deception and fraud relatively quickly.

Ideally, there should be a limit as to the number of such orders a company could collect over a given period of time before some stronger penalty is imposed (a year's ban on advertising, for example).

The Vulnerable Villains

To combat the fly-by-night operators, the individual consumer is largely dependent on statutory and regulatory enforcement, and, as noted, the enforcers are largely unable to extend more than partial protection against such operators.

Against the established company which reverts to fraud the individual does have a few weapons. For these villains are vulnerable also. They have their Achilles' heel. They are exceedingly self-conscious about their public images.

It is more than a little ironic that nearly every large company has a special department, or utilizes the services of a firm of public-relations consultants, to project their friendly, human qualities, while when cited in a fraud case they suddenly become impersonal, "soulless," a legal abstraction.

There are several ways the individual consumer can take advantage of this seeming soft spot. One is to practice *Turnabout*. Rather than playing the games of wordsmithing, pricemanship, and false percentages, where the odds are rigged in favor of the house, the individual makes up his own game, with his own rules, its purpose to spotlight such deceptive artifices.

Two basic variations follow, either or both of which can be modified to fit the occasion.

The first might be called *Detection*. On discovering a deception or fraud, one brings it to the attention of the appropriate agency. As examples, a merchant's bait ad for a sewing machine can be clipped from the newspaper and mailed to the local BBB, the deceptive ad for a nationally advertised product sent to the FTC, a suspicious mail-order charity solicitation remailed (together with the original envelope) to the POD, etc. If one is actually a victim of the fraud, a letter, with all pertinent details, should be included.

The second form of the game, *Boycott*, calls for observation, determination, and occasionally sacrifice, but it has its own particular satisfactions. One can start by keeping lists of misrepresented products, learning the names of their manufacturers, and then boycotting all the products of those companies. Avoiding whenever possible those stores which most blatantly indulge in fictitious pricing, customer baiting, and similar artifices is another variation.

Merely boycotting products is ineffectual, however, unless one also lets the company know the game is being played. This means writing to the company, informing them that you have stopped buying their products and why. It is important that the letter be legible, brief, and that it be directed to the point where it will have the greatest impact. The president of the company which manufactures the product is usually the best target. To obtain his name and address, one need only consult *Thomas' Register of Manufacturers*, an up-to-date copy of which should be available in the reference section of most public libraries.

The tone may vary, depending upon the seriousness of the offense. For example:

Dear Mr. Smith:

Last week I purchased a No. 2-size can of your Brand X peaches for 26¢. The label has a picture showing three peach halves in a dish and has a legend reading "Serves 4." On opening the can I discovered five peach halves. I would be interested in hearing your explanation for this discrepancy.

Postponing further purchase of Specific Foods, Inc., products until receipt of your reply, I remain,

Sincerely,
Mary Jones

If the offense is light, as in the case of simple wordsmithing, a less somber tone might be used. Whatever the approach (the serious one is usually best), it is important that the letter be signed and bear a return address. An anonymous letter will, quite rightly, be ignored. A signed letter may be ignored, too, or draw a form reply, but the differing responses are what make the game interesting. A letter to a manufacturer complaining that his large tube of toothpaste was more expensive per ounce than his smaller size brought one player a seven-page, single-spaced reply, ending with an admission that he was right. (The tube sizes were readjusted shortly afterward; perhaps others were playing the game too.) A letter from a young housewife to the manufacturer of a dishwashing product complaining that his "new improved" product did not do what it was said to do on TV brought a refund, a case of the product, and a request that she give it a longer test. (It still didn't do the job promised, but it won a devoted customer, despite its shortcomings.)

How effective are such letters? One can rarely be sure. The ancient "bug letter" story comes all too readily to mind. For those who don't recall it, it went somewhat as follows:

A passenger on one of the major railroads discovered bedbugs in his berth. On arriving home he wrote a heated letter to the main office of the railroad, and in a very short while received a lengthy reply. His letter had come as a great shock to the company, the letter explained. This was the first such complaint in more than thirty years. Immediately upon receiving it, the Pullman car in which he had been a passenger was pulled from service and thoroughly fumigated, while the three employees responsible for checking to see that such things never happened had been given suspensions.

It was a long, persuasive letter conveying the feeling that somebody did indeed care. Or would have, rather, had the typist not inadvertently included a brief interoffice memo which read:

Send this man the bug letter.

The story is dated. It may be that today, when the corporate image is all-important, a letter of complaint will work wonders. Vance Packard feels this is true:

"A lone consumer may feel helpless in facing up to a giant corporation with plants in 123 cities," he writes in *The Waste Makers*. "Actually, this lone consumer should know that this monolith tends to over-react to criticism of its products. One strong letter, addressed to its president, can create concern in the executive suite (even though the president himself is probably spared from seeing the letter). Two letters of protest will create panic. Three letters of protest will create pandemonium."[11]

If only for their cathartic effect, such letters seem worth the effort. That they do sometimes accomplish more is a bonus.

But this is largely a negative approach. The game can, and should, be played positively too. In scanning the supermarket shelves or in watching TV or in reading newspapers or magazines, one occasionally finds companies which go out of their way to advertise or label their wares honestly. In California, for example, home of legally shortweight bread, last year Safeway Stores, on their own initiative and not because they were required by law to do so, stopped stocking the 15-oz. "pound" loaf and now offer full 1- and 1½-lb. loaves at no increase in cost. It is equally important that such acts be commented upon. A thank-you note may be even more effective than a complaint, for it reaches an already receptive audience. If aware that its efforts are noticed and appreciated, a company is far more likely to initiate follow-ups in the future.

A Consumer's Grift Sense

Deception and fraud aren't games, of course. But if one views the situation in total seriousness, he is apt to conclude that it is hopeless. Approaching it with a sense of some of its patent absurdities at least makes it bearable.

The letter and the boycott are limited weapons. And eventually one tires of using them. Fraud is a part of our society, but it is only a part, and one would rather spend his time and energy on more pleasant pursuits. Yet if one goes even for a few rounds and then gives up the ring, he will at least have accomplished something in the way of self-education, by developing an awareness of deceptive artifices.

There is no wholly effective defense against fraud. There is no such thing as an invulnerable American. But vulnerability has its degrees, and the least vulnerable American is one who develops a healthy skepticism, what might be called a consumer's grift sense.

"It may be," Mrs. Esther Peterson, President Johnson's Advisor on Consumer Affairs, remarked in one of her speeches, "that we are raising a generation of Americans who are developing defenses against advertising and may become immune to it."[12] It may be, but in the meantime we can only try to acquire such an immunity, meeting fraud, which is basically a violation of trust, by withholding our own trust, at least until there is evidence that it is warranted and won't be abused.

So in the end we return to the one maxim which hasn't changed with time—*Caveat Emptor,* Let the Buyer Beware.

A detective once asked Count Victor Lustig to what he attributed his phenomenal success. Lustig, a con man of the old school, who sold money machines, cheated at cards on oceanic liners, and at his peak twice sold the Eiffel Tower to wealthy junk dealers for scrap iron, is said to have replied, "These were confident people. Where could things be better for a confidence man."

APPENDIX A

In 1964, the Advertising Federation of America, the Advertising Association of the West, and the Association of Better Business Bureaus drew up and adopted a code of business ethics to govern the activities of their members.

It seems fitting that if the public is to judge advertising, it should do so by advertising's own professed standards, and so this code is reprinted here in its entirety.

THE ADVERTISING CODE OF AMERICAN BUSINESS

We hold that advertising has a responsibility to inform and serve the American public and to further the economic life of this nation. Believing this, the following principles are hereby affirmed.

1. *Truth*
   Advertising shall tell the truth, be free of the capacity to mislead or deceive, and shall reveal material facts, the concealment of which might mislead the public.

2. *Responsibility*
   Advertising agencies and advertisers shall be able and willing to provide satisfactory proof of claims made. Advertising media shall require such proof when claims are considered questionable.

3. *Taste and Decency*
   Advertising shall be free of statements, illustrations or implications which are offensive to good taste or public decency.

4. *Disparagement*
   Advertising shall offer merchandise or service on its merits and refrain from attacking competitors or disparaging their products, services or methods of doing business.

5. *Bait Advertising*
   Advertising shall be bona fide and the merchandise or service offered shall be readily available for purchase at the advertised price.

6. *Guarantees and Warranties*

Advertising of guarantees and warranties shall be explicit. Advertising of any guarantee or warranty shall clearly and conspicuously disclose its nature and extent, the manner in which the guarantor or warrantor will perform and the identity of the guarantor or warrantor.

7. *Price Claims*

Advertising shall avoid price or savings claims which are unsupported by facts or which do not offer bona fide bargains or savings.

8. *Unprovable Claims*

Advertising shall avoid the use of exaggerated or unprovable claims.

9. *Testimonials*

Advertising containing testimonials shall be limited to those of competent witnesses who are reflecting a real and honest choice.

SOURCES

Preface: THE FRAUDULENT CLIMATE

1. Edwin H. Sutherland, *Principles of Criminology* (N.Y.: J. B. Lippincott Co., 1947), p. 21.
2. Saul Bellow, "A Talk with the Yellow Kid," *The Reporter,* September 6, 1956.
3. *Newsweek,* April 1, 1957.

Chapter 1: WORDSMITHING: THE ART OF ARTIFICE

All references to FTC cases in this and succeeding chapters are from *The Federal Trade Commission News Summary,* 1958–66, or other official FTC records or publications.
1. New York *Times,* July 6, 1964.
2. Daniel J. Campion, with Myron M. Stearns, *Crooks Are Human Too* (Englewood Cliffs, N.J.: Prentice-Hall, 1957), p. 18.

Chapter 2: THINGS ARE SELDOM WHAT THEY SEEM

1. *Advertising Age,* December 21, 1959.
2. New York *Times,* December 11, 1964.
3. Denver *Post,* April 12, 1964.
4. Ruth and Edward Brecher, "How To Avoid Being Cheated by the Pound or Gallon," *Redbook,* August 1960.
5. *Nation-wide Survey of Weights-and-Measures Law Enforcement,* sponsored by the Consumers Union and the Council of Consumer Education, and conducted by Professor Leland J. Gordon of the Weights and Measures Research Center, Denison University, 1960.
6. Reported in *Consumer Reports,* November 1964.
7. *Consumer Reports,* December 1964 (Buying Guide Issue), p. 146.
8. Mrs. Helen Nelson, *Packages and Prices* (Sacramento, Calif.: Office of the Consumer Counsel, State Capitol), 1962.
9. From an address before the 27th Annual Conference of the California

Association of Weights and Measures Officials, Santa Rosa, Calif., September 25, 1963.

10. André Fontaine, "Trading Stamps—Who Gets What?" *Reader's Digest*, June 1963.

11. *Consumer Reports*, May 1963.

12. San Francisco *Examiner*, October 11, 1964.

Chapter 3: THE MARK IN THE MARKETPLACE

1. Joseph Weil, as told to W. T. Brannon, *Yellow Kid Weil: The Autobiography of America's Master Swindler* (Chicago: Ziff Davis Publishing Co., 1948), pp. 32–33, 119.

2. James Ridgeway, "The Great Odometer Mystery," *The New Republic*, January 23, 1965.

For the story of Louis Enricht the author is largely indebted to Harold Mehling's most entertaining tome, *The Scandalous Scamps* (N.Y.: Holt, Rinehart & Winston, Inc., 1959).

Chapter 4: STORMING THE CASTLE

1. Ralph Lee Smith, *The Bargain Hucksters* (N.Y.: Thomas Y. Crowell Co., 1962), p. 22.

2. San Francisco *Examiner*, March 24, 1964.

3. San Francisco *Chronicle*, April 23, 1964.

4. As quoted in *Consumer Reports*, February 1965.

5. As introduced in testimony by the General Counsel of the FTC in the Holland Furnace Company criminal contempt proceedings.

6. *Your Home, Paradise for Gyps* (Cleveland: Cleveland Better Business Bureau, 1954).

7. A. M. Watkins, "It's Time To Slam the Door on Home Improvement Swindlers," *The American Home*, May 1963.

8. Pierre Berton, *The Big Sell* (N.Y.: Alfred A. Knopf, Inc., 1963), p. 231.

Chapter 5: THE INVISIBLE CON MAN

Most of the references to POD cases in this and succeeding chapters are from the Post Office Department's publications on mail fraud, particularly the monthly *Enforcement Action* for the years 1963–66.

1. As quoted in Sylvia Porter's syndicated column "Your Money's Worth," San Francisco *Chronicle*, December 14, 1964.

2. Berton, *op. cit.*, p. 54.

Chapter 6: THE FALL OF THE CASTLE

1. Truth in Lending Bill speech of the Honorable Paul H. Douglas of Illinois in the Senate of the United States, *Congressional Record,* February 7, 1963.
2. *Ibid.*
3. From Senator Douglas' introduction to *Buy Now, Pay Later,* pp. xv–xvii.
4. F. Thomas Juster and Robert P. Shay, *Consumer Sensitivity to Finance Rates: An Empirical and Analytical Investigation* (Washington, D.C.: National Bureau of Economic Research, 1964). A summary appears in *Consumer Reports,* October 1964.
5. Irwin Ross, "When You Borrow, When You Buy—Watch Those Interest Rates!" *Reader's Digest,* November 1963.
6. Mrs. Helen Nelson, "Consumer Credit—Uses and Abuses," *The Credit Union Magazine,* December 1963.
7. Richard A. Phelon, "The Scandal in Personal Bankruptcy," *Dun's Review,* March 1963.
8. San Francisco *Chronicle,* November 6, 1964.
9. San Francisco *Chronicle,* December 4, 1964.

Chapter 7: CAMELOT REVISITED

1. Paul Friggens, "Beware the Ranchero Racketeer," *Reader's Digest,* January 1963.

Chapter 8: FOOL MEDICINE

Food and Drug Administration publications provided much of the source material for this chapter. Among these, the FDA's monthly bulletin *Enforcement and Compliance* for the years 1962–66 was a primary source.
1. *FDA's Campaign Against Nutritional Quackery Progress Report* (Washington, D.C.: U.S. Department of Health, Education and Welfare, Food and Drug Administration, October 1963), pp. 7–8.
2. In an address to the 2nd Regional Conference on Health Quackery, Atlanta, Ga., March 13, 1964.
3. San Francisco *Chronicle,* May 8, 1965.
4. Ralph Lee Smith, *The Health Hucksters* (N.Y.: Thomas Y. Crowell, 1961), p. 207.
5. J. Campbell Bruce, "Quacks and the Elderly—A Mounting Menace," San Francisco *Chronicle,* January 14, 1964.
6. *Ibid.*

Chapter 9: TURNABOUT

1. Alan Hynd, *The Giant Killers* (N.Y.: Robert M. McBride, 1945), p. 284.
2. As quoted by Sylvia Porter in her column "Shoppers with Sticky Fingers," San Francisco *Chronicle*, February 5, 1965. Two other columns by Miss Porter also yielded source material for this chapter: "The Season for Shoplifting," December 23, 1964, and "All-Out War on Grocery Thieves," February 8, 1965.
3. *Crime in the United States: Uniform Crime Reports*, issued by John Edgar Hoover, Director, Federal Bureau of Investigation (Washington, D.C.: U.S. Department of Justice, 1963).
4. As quoted in "Shoplifting—Newest Crime Wave," Don Wharton, *Family Weekly*, March 17, 1963.
5. Porter, *op. cit.*
6. Norman Jaspan with Hillel Black, *Thief in the White Collar* (Philadelphia: J. B. Lippincott Co., 1960), p. 38.
7. Interview.
8. Porter, *op. cit.*

Chapter 10: EVERYBODY'S DOING IT

1. Lee Berton, "Robbing the Boss," *Wall Street Journal*, August 20, 1964.
2. Gloria Steinem, "A Bunny's Tale," *Show*, May and June 1963.
3. Mary Owen Cameron, *The Booster and the Snitch* (Glencoe, Ill.: Free Press, 1964), p. 11.
4. Jaspan, *op. cit.*, p. 109.
5. New York *Times*, November 13, 1964.
6. Jaspan, *op. cit.*, p. 26–27.
7. *Crime Loss Prevention* (Chicago: Continental Casualty Company, 1947).
8. Donald R. Cressey, *Other People's Money: A Study in the Social Psychology of Embezzlement* (Glencoe, Ill.: Free Press, 1953), p. 30.
9. Myron Brenton, *The Privacy Invaders* (N.Y.: Coward-McCann, Inc., 1964), p. 60.
10. Jaspan, *op. cit.*, p. 236.
11. Cameron, *op. cit.*, p. 171–72.

Chapter 11: PAPERHANGING MADE EASY

1. Cressey, *op. cit.*, p. 82–83.

Chapter 12: CREDIT CARD SWINDLERY: A NEW AND MAGICAL WORLD

1. Joseph R. Miraglia, "My $10,000 Credit Card Binge," *Life,* October 26, 1959.
2. Hillel Black, *Buy Now, Pay Later* (N.Y.: William Morrow and Company, 1961), p. 12.
3. *Ibid.,* p. 22.
4. *Time,* February 9, 1962.
5. Evan McLeod Wylie, "Hold Onto That Card," *Today's Living,* New York *Herald Tribune,* March 12, 1961.
6. From an article by staff writer Zeke Scher, Denver *Post,* February 14, 1964.

Chapter 13: THE PYRAMIDERS AND THE CORPORATE ASSASSINS

1. New York *Times,* May 20, 1964.
For the "no asset" bankruptcy story the author is indebted to Richard A. Phelon, *op. cit.*

Chapter 14: MAN VS. THE MACHINE OR HOW TO BEAT THE BELL SYSTEM

1. New York *Journal American,* January 25, 1964.
2. New York *Times,* July 9, 1964.
3. *Bell Telephone Magazine,* Summer 1964.
4. San Francisco *Chronicle,* July 20, 1964.

Chapter 15: INSURANCE FRAUD: THEY CAN AFFORD IT—BUT CAN YOU?

1. Except where otherwise noted, Mr. Woods' remarks are from statements supplied by the Claims Bureau.
2. Mabel A. Elliott, *Crime in Modern Society* (N.Y.: Harper and Brothers, 1952), pp. 152–53.
3. San Francisco *Chronicle,* August 6, 1964.
4. As quoted in "Phony Accidents Are Costing You," Charles and Bonnie Remsberg, *Family Weekly,* May 13, 1962.
5. N. Morgan Woods, "Fraudulent Automobile Insurance Claims," *Police,* September–October 1961.
6. E. A. Cowie, "Res Ipsa Loquitur in Products Liability Actions: Insurance Company Viewpoint," *Insurance Counsel Journal,* October 1962.

7. William Barry Furlong, "The 'Damage Demons' of Chicago," *Coronet*, October 1959.

Chapter 16: HOW TO BE A WINNER SOME OF THE TIME

1. San Francisco *Examiner*, July 11, 1965.
2. Arlene and Howard Eisenberg, "You *Can* Get Your Money Back," *Reader's Digest*, February 1964.
3. Sutherland, *op. cit.*, p. 16.
4. As quoted in *Consumer Reports*, April 1964.
5. Walter Goodman, *All Honorable Men: Corruption and Compromise in American Life* (Boston: Little, Brown and Company, 1963), p. 24.
6. John G. Fuller, *The Gentlemen Conspirators* (N.Y.: Grove Press, Inc., 1962), p. 16.
7. Judge Gerald Sparrow, *The Great Swindlers* (London: John Long, 1959), p. 9.
8. *Newsweek*, July 7, 1965; *The New Republic*, July 24, 1965.
9. San Francisco *Chronicle*, August 2, 1964.
10. *The New Republic*, January 2, 1965.
11. Vance Packard, *The Waste Makers* (N.Y.: David McKay Company, Inc., 1960), p. 253.
12. San Francisco *Chronicle*, November 12, 1964.